OLD-TIME
TOOLS AND TOYS OF
NEEDLEWORK

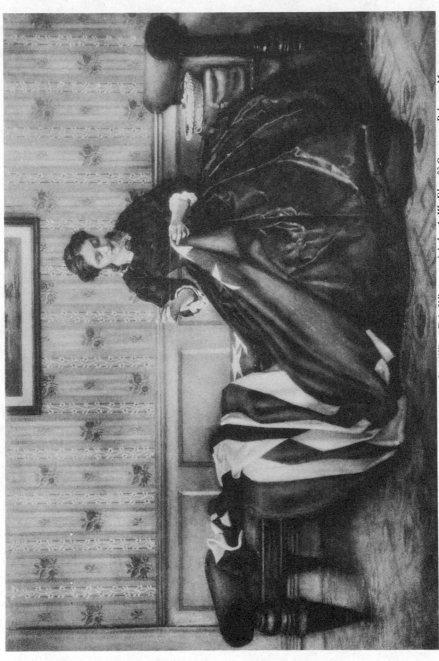

Courtesy of Dr. Frederick Whiting, after the painting by William Fair Kline; copyright by A.W. Elson & Company, Belmont, Mass.

HER TRIBUTE

OLD-TIME
TOOLS AND TOYS OF
NEEDLEWORK

BY

GERTRUDE WHITING

Honorary Fellow of the Metropolitan Museum of Art. Fellow of
the Institute Professional Neuchâtelois de Dentelles. Founder
of the Needle and Bobbin Club and Bulletin. Founder
of The Spinster, Hollins College, Virginia. Author
of A Lace Guide for Makers and Collectors.
Lace Worker to India.

DOVER PUBLICATIONS, INC.
NEW YORK

This Dover edition, first published in 1971, is an unabridged and unaltered republication of the work originally published by Columbia University Press, New York, in 1928 under the title *Tools and Toys of Stitchery*.

International Standard Book Number: 0-486-22517-8
Library of Congress Catalog Card Number: 77-154866

Manufactured in the United States of America
Dover Publications, Inc.
180 Varick Street
New York, N. Y. 10014

WITH ADMIRATION FOR THE EXQUISITENESS OF HER
POSSESSIONS, SO REFLECTING THE CHARM AND RE-
FINEMENT OF THEIR COLLECTOR; AND WITH WARM-
EST THANKS FOR THE GRACIOUS PERMISSION MOST
GENEROUSLY GRANTED TO REPRODUCE SOME OF THESE
PRECIOUS PIECES, REGARDLESS OF THE RISK AND
DISTURBANCE INVOLVED; I DEDICATE THESE PAGES
ON "IMPLEMENTS OF LOVING LABOR"

TO

MRS. DE WITT CLINTON COHEN

ACKNOWLEDGMENT

Parts of four of the following chapters appeared in the finely illustrated magazine *Antiques* — Notes on Scissors in July, 1923; Hast Thou Ne'er a Thimble in May, 1924; On Needle-Books and Needle-Cases in December, 1925; and an article on pincushions in the autumn of 1926.

I here thank the publishers of *Antiques,* and also the directors of the Needle and Bobbin Club for their great courtesy in permitting me to use again a number of valuable illustrations from their publications.

GERTRUDE WHITING.

Photographs by Frederick Bradley, A. Tennyson Beals, the author, and others.

CONTENTS

LIST OF ILLUSTRATIONS

ix

PREAMBLE

'Scissors and spice and everything nice' suggests the snappy, spicy and altogether delightful tales, together with the weird witch stories, delicious gossip, serious history, and tokens of inventive skill that time has gathered round femininity's quaint collection of delicate stitchery tools. Here you have not only sharp-edged "snaps" or scissors and perfumed pomanders, but pointed stilettos and sweet-scented beeswax; biting, burnishing emery; Valentine bobbins and gossipy beetles; rare needle-cases; jeweled winders — fitting gifts all, if certain superstitions be duly observed!

Would you read an older list of feminine foibles and fine workbox and toilet fitments? Here follows one from *Rhodon and Iris*, dated 1631; though woman's "implements of loving labour" reach much further back than that — back, back, indeed, to remote antiquity:

"Chains, coronets, pendans, bracelets and earrings,
   Pins, girdles, spangles, embroideries and rings;
   Shadoes, rebaltoes, ribbands, ruffs, cuffs, falls,
   Scarfes, feathers, fans, maskes, muffs, laces, cauls;
   Thin tiffanies, cobweb lawn, and fardingals,
   Sweet fals, vayles, wimples, glasses, crisping pins;
   Pots of ointments, combes, with poking-sticks and bodkins,
   Coyfes, gorgets, fringes, rowles, fillets and hair-laces;
   Silks, damasks, velvet, tinsels, cloth of gold,
   Of tissues with colours of a hundred fold."

Now readers who have seen my *Lace Guide for Makers and Collectors* know that it belongs to the tabulated didactic realm, dissecting and cataloguing as does the botanist his flower when he demonstrates its calyx and pistil, its stamens and the veins that flush its petals. But the following pages hope merely to lilt along as the spirit moves, not dissecting and picking apart, not telling of the grammar and syntax of sewing and spinning — wherein is no tingling joy — but of what might be called the gear, harness, furniture, lumber, appurtenances, paraphernalia, accoutrements, appliances, accessories, doodads thereof; forgetting rules and directions, sizes and prices, but escaping rather from the world actual into the beautiful world fanciful, indulging again in the peaceful, homely enjoyment of those artistic little instruments which thrill alike the embroiderer and the lace-lover!

Reading of the old-time tools makes one long to create a perfect workbox, exquisite within and without, equipped with choice imple-

Metropolitan Museum of Art

MAN SEWING, FROM SKETCH BOOK OF RIZA ABBAS,
EARLY SEVENTEENTH CENTURY. PERSIAN.

ments drawn from the varied countries that have contributed charming or clever inventions to woman's indispensable *housewife*. It is indeed a worth-while undertaking so to equip oneself that one may be lured on to the daily task, and that one's stitchery, simple or elaborate, may be wrought midst the charm of far-flung suggestions, ranging up and down the whole wide world. If the modest little maid of Victorian times looked forward to a day when she, with so little a spur as put-up hair, would sew with zest, think of what we might accomplish! —

"When I'm a grown-up woman,
With my hair up on my head
I'll sit and sew till very late
And never go to bed!"

Well, for some of us who cannot sew, or for the many who may happily form a future set of fine worktable fittings, there is much material for immediate quest and for the collector's anticipatory day-dream. We can read about these instruments and mentally picture and determine the sort we will try to secure, relishing in advance the feel of their worn and polished forms, admiring the grace of their lines, their fine chasing, their tapering sharpness.

A dainty sewing tool collection of markedly feminine charm holds value, not only as a spur to be up and about one's daily stint; as an aid to imagination in the planning and execution of one's finer work on tambour or loom or pillow; not only to the youthful stitcher about to enter a new field of grown-up endeavor; as a quaint object of quest for the discriminating collector; but also in an artistic and in a commercial way. One of the world's leading museums and a potential museum are both hoping that a truly good collection of this sort may come into their hands.

But some other aspects of these diminutive utensils strike deeper chords of response — the vast, trackless antiquity of woman's uncounted, unsigned, ever renewed little efforts in stitchery and her development of technique, tools and materials, beginning perhaps with the piercing of fig leaves and the braiding of their stems. Yet the early part of the Old Testament alludes to clothing — what a gap, though, between Eve's work and Jacob's making for Joseph a coat of many colors! What patient persistence with tentative tools, what innumerable trials of new ideas, with failures and little discoveries ending in much-merited success, and still later in instruments of rare and minute perfection! Think of the perseverance of it — to-day's new-made garment, torn to-morrow; mended; yet soon worn out, only to be replaced by another — "woman's work is never done." And of the modesty of it — who discovered sewing, who invented embroidery, tapestry, lace? How many pieces of signed embroidery have you seen — are not some of them as fine as any other great work of art? Have you ever seen a piece of signed lace, though it may have been a masterpiece requiring the skilled manipulation of hundreds of the very daintiest of tools? Fitting gifts indeed are these, soul gifts, soul treasures:

> " No sacreder thing may one beloved
> E'er bestow upon another
> Than an implement of loving labour.
> I say me that womankind
> Hath weaved her hope upon the thread
> Of her weavin', aye, and hath shuttled since time.
> Aye, methinks that Heaven's gateway
> Must be webbed by the holy threads
> Plied by woman's hands.
> A fitting gift, Beloved,
> For he who would find his heart,
> Must labour."
>
>   — Patience Worth.

SWEET-SCENTED BEESWAX

"A letter! hum! a suspicious circumstance, to be sure! What, and the seal a true-lover's knot, now, ha? or an heart transfixed with darts; or possibly the wax bore the industrious impression of a thimble."
— *The Jealous Wife:* George Colman, born 1732.

WHY does the word *beeswax* carry a pleasant, if somewhat vague, impression? Is it the balance of syllables, the alliteration of the "s" and "x," or a thought of sweet-smelling wax and incredibly wonderful little bees? Perhaps the following quotation from Dallas Lore Sharp will in part answer our question by putting into words for us what we now dumbly feel:

"I have carried bees through the apple-blossom season without a break, and into the thick of the wild-raspberry flowering near the middle of June. Since early spring the colonies have been rapidly gathering strength and momentum until now from some of the hives a mighty host of reapers are in the field, and singing as they toil. The vale, the hillside, the overshadowing pines, and my own soul are overflowing with the humming harvest song. No other sound in nature is like the sound of work, the only song that all the aërials of earth and ether are tuned to — the little wire in my neighbor's kitchen, the line between the planet's poles, and those mighty cables of space that catch the turning of the spheres and the winging of the bees, broadcasting the universal song of doing from star to star. . . . I am content to listen in. My own hands have wrought here. I have entered into this labor. I am conductor for this symphony of bees. They are in tune with me. Or is it that I am in tune with them, and in tune with the universe?"

Now, "*Beeswax* when pure," we are told, "though usually pale yellow in color, is sometimes nearly white, the difference being due to the pollen consumed by the bees. For instance, when bees are collecting pollen and honey from heather, the pollen being white, the wax is also white; whereas, when collecting from sainfoin, the pollen being orange-colored, the wax also partakes of this color."

5

To this I add a short detached quotation that leads towards a stitcher's special interest in wax, following it with the derivation of the word "wax":

"There are quite a number of ornamental devices for holding *beeswax*, some with silver ends, one with mother-of-pearl outside." — *The Cult of the Needle*, by Flora Klickmann.

Beeswax, we are told, was spelled *wex* in Middle English, *weax* in Anglo-Saxon, *Wachs* in German, *vax* in Swedish and Icelandic, *vox* in Danish, *vosku* in Bulgarian, *vosk* in Bohemian, *wosk* in Polish, *viaszk* in Hungarian, *waszkas* in Lithuanian — truly a most consistent word, an article that one could intelligibly inquire for anywhere! Apparently we are not the only folk who fancy and retain that waxen sound.

A quaint old English allusion that I found to wax is by Chaucer, referring to its use by draftsmen in the manner that etchers would use it: "Tho tok I and *wexede* my label in maner of a peyre tables to resceyve distynctly the prikkes of my compas."

And, in modern English, Holmes also refers to wax in describing one of his characters: "He held a long string in one hand, which he drew through the other hand incessantly as he spoke, just as a shoemaker performs the motion of *waxing* his thread."

This 'waxing one's thread' leads straight to our special interests — the use of wax in sewing and in fancywork, in bead-stringing, and in drafting patterns for embroidery, together with the tools adapted to these graceful and gracious toils. In this connection, I wonder whether your workbag boasts a miniature wax beehive, ribbed round and round from its broad base to its curved conical apex? Or an egg of wax in an oval wooden darning-ball that unscrews midway to give access to the wax within? Or maybe a thick brown wax leaf or flower, or a little fluted cake that looks just as though it might be maple sugar all ready to *wax down* on freshly fallen snow? For: "*Sewing-wax* (*beeswax*) is usually made up into small, round cakes, about one and a half inches in diameter. It gives stiffness and smoothness to sewing-thread."

"*Waxed-end*, in shoemaking, a thread the end of which has been stiffened by the use of shoemakers' wax, so as to pass easily through the holes made by the awl; also, a waxed thread terminating in a bristle,

THE TINGLING AND HIVING OF BEES, AS ENGRAVED UPON THE GREAT NORMANSELL SILVER LOVING CUP, "THE GIFT OF RICHARD NORMANNSELL, GENT., TENANT TO YE COMPANIE OF WAX CHANDLERS" — A CUP CHASED OVER ITS WHOLE SURFACE WITH SUBJECTS RELATING TO THE PRODUCTION AND MANUFACTURE OF WAX.

for the same purpose.   Also reduced to *wax-end.*"   [And very appropriate for bead-stringing. G. W.] — *Century Dictionary.*

About shoemakers' heel-ball, the two following quotations somewhat differ:

" A thick, resinous substance, consisting of pitch, rosin and tallow, used by shoemakers for rubbing their thread."

To produce " shoemakers' superfine heel-ball: melt together *beeswax,* two pounds; suet, three ounces; stir in ivory black, four ounces; powdered rock candy, two ounces.   Mix, and when partly cold, pour into tin or leaden molds.   These balls are used not merely by shoemakers, but for copying inscriptions, raised patterns, et cetera, by rubbing the ball on paper laid over the article to be copied."

Indeed, this is a splendid way of quickly but surely tracing beautiful scroll designs found in low relief on old marbles, and of taking *rubbings* from other old treasures whose patterns would form excellent models for quilters, embroiderers and lace-makers.

In the Paradise of China — Hangchow — I strolled into a fascinating rocky garden whose walls were harmoniously enriched with chiseled ideographic writings.   These were the reproductions of valuable old seals gathered together into this treasure spot by those able to appreciate the beauty of the tracery and the desirability of preserving rare documents — the members of the Chinese Seal Society.   Pinnacled upon a ledge of rock stood the society's tea house, where carefully rubbed reproductions of such work throughout that land can be examined and purchased.   Of course, visitors are regaled with a tiny cup of jasmine tea!

Perhaps present readers — since they are probably of the fairer gender — might be entertained to learn how steadily they patronize the bee, so I append a cold-cream recipe:

Oil of almond, five pounds; white wax, one pound; spermaceti, one-half pound.   Melt by gentle heat, then stir in one pound (sixteen ounces) of rose-water and six drops of attar of roses.

For cleaning, too, readers may be glad to know that wax — which is composed of carbon, hydrogen and oxygen — is soluble in ether, chloroform, benzol, turpentine and boiling alcohol, but not in cold alcohol.

Naturally, housekeepers are familiar with the laundress's use of wax wrapped in cheesecloth and attached to a little wooden handle, the whole resembling the old-time sugar sucker or baby's pacifier; the waxer being used to prevent flatirons and clothes from clinging too ardently together, just as a good dancer, though he may wish to cling to his partner, prefers to glide lightly over a highly waxed floor. Laundresses, in lieu of waxers, occasionally use candle butts. In either case, however, if the wax be animal, how delicious it smells as it touches the hot iron!

BATIK WORKERS IN DJOKJAKARTA, JAVA. ONE GIRL IS BLOWING ON HER TINY POINTED TUBE TO COOL THE MOLTEN WAX; ANOTHER IS HEATING A TUBEFUL; WHILE THE OLDER WOMAN IS DRAWING IN WAXEN LINES WITH HERS.

Not long ago in Southern India, a lad fell from his cart upon its revolving wheel, severely cutting his scalp. The boy's parents filled the gash with ground-up peppers and beeswax. Strangely enough his head became badly inflamed and one eye closed, so the youth was taken to a hospital, where he is now slowly recovering!

In Cambodia the natives, after their habitual chew of tooth-staining betel nut, soften the lips by the application of beeswax, plain or perfumed with saffron, cocoanut oil, musk, sandal, amber, jasmine, champac or frangipani. This practice extends apparently far back into antiquity.

Wax is used, as many know, in the making of *batik*. When in Java, I saw old, old hags and beautiful, soft, satin-skinned maidens working side by side upon the raised floors of their open-front, matting-walled houses. Out in front grew the tree cotton, while within was the cool shade cast by the two-peaked straw roofs. Each woman had her tiny pitcher-beaked wax-pot set on a charcoal brazier. She poured the languid melted fluid from the pot's wee nose along an imagined line of her cotton — or rarely, silk — cloth. When all the front was covered, the designer-worker reproduced the waxen pattern on the back to act as a complete resist, so that the pattern, when plunged in a color vat, would be proof against absorbing dye. Thus only the unwaxed portions take the color. Three such waxings and dippings are required for most batiks — pronounced in Java *bat'iks,* with the accent, as in so many short Eastern words, upon the first syllable.

At the Indian border of Afghanistan, I watched a small brown boy sitting cross-legged and spreading soft wax, without any drawn lines to guide him, in a pretty pattern upon a purple cloth. This he then dusted with gleaming gold powder, which still adheres. He arched his neck over the work, then held if off for inspection, enjoying it, I be-lieve, as a chef enjoys decorating with a tube of waxen frosting the top of a birthday cake, though the lad's ambition doubtless dreamed far beyond, to a day when waxing designs would lead to weaving or embroidering the more precious stuffs he watched brought in by the camel caravans that weekly passed his door.

Another use of wax, American as well as foreign, many of us re-member, some of us indulged in — the melting and molding of tinted waxes into flower forms, the warming of multicolored waxen sheets to shape them into autumn leaves. There were fascinating little pots and pans for all of this, as well as miniature copper cutters, like cooky-cutters. The sheets of shaded wax were about three inches wide by five long, laid between sheets of tissue paper to prevent sticking. Of course, there were plain rose, plain green and other simple-hued sheets, as well as the speckled, the streaked, and the shaded ones for fall leaves.

In ancient times, the Egyptians deposited wax figurines in notable graves.

The early Greeks and Italians kept bees, drying the wax by moon-light to whiten it. They had waxen dolls, and tablets of wax to inscribe. The tablets could be smoothed and used again.

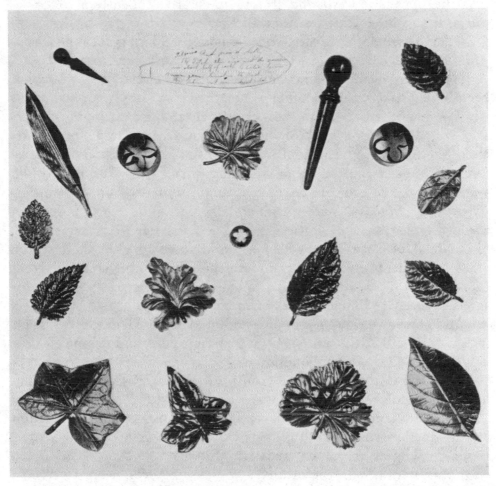

From the author's collection

BEAUTIFULLY MADE, LITTLE OLD COPPER CUTTERS AND MOLDS; A SHARP AND A DULL ROSEWOOD STICK FOR IMPRESSING THE WAX INTO THESE MOLDS; AND A PAPER PATTERN, FOR CUTTING OUT AND SHAPING WAX LEAVES AND PETALS.

Pausanias tells us that one of the oldest temples dedicated to Apollo was raised by bees from wax.

"It will be seen that beekeeping must have been carried on exten-sively, as honey was the only sweetening substance; but by the intro-duction of sugar, beekeeping was decreased and the production of wax was reduced to a minimum. Besides the Reformation, which reduced the Church demand for tapers, powerful competitors appeared in commerce, and wax obtained from various plants and minerals, such as stearine, paraffin, ceresin and others, which are frequently used for the purpose of adulterating beeswax, further lowered its price."

" At the present time the Greek Orthodox Church makes the largest use of wax, for this and oil are the only illuminating agents used."

But all this while, diametrically across the globe, bee-culture has been little pushed, though among the Himalayas stray, gaping, open-windowed houses of several crude, uneven stories, with prayer flags and holy yak tails flying from the four corners of the flat roofs, are endowed and set aside as homes for the hill bees. Recesses with perforated, wooden-paneled doors are made in the walls, and a guardian or *zamindar* protects the darting, buzzing inmates from marauding hornets, caterpillars, martens, and that great wild lover of sweets — the bear. Incidentally, seriously stung bears have sometimes been found dead, because their swollen eyes and noses were unable to search out food. The beeswax of Assam and the Khasia hills is usually sold in rolls cast in bamboo molds, much as Chinese wax candles, for safety's sake, are shipped in hollow bamboo stalks.

And now in view of the recent regrettable fire at Madame Tussaud's in London, and of the amusingly interesting facts and personages involved, I bring you a final quotation:

" No account of the Prince (cousin of Louis XV) de Conti's visit has been handed down, but a few words uttered to Curtius (brother of Madame Tussaud), conveyed beyond all doubt his genuine admiration for the doctor-artist's skill in his new profession as a sculptor in wax (1762). Miniatures in colored wax, modeled in fairly high relief, glazed and framed in the ordinary way as pictures, seem to offer a general idea of the work that emanated from that studio during these momentous years. . . . The pity of the loss is that the work, taken directly from life, afforded a faithful record of important personages. Though the miniatures do not seem to have brought Christopher Curtius very great reputation, yet they were the means of leading him to the modeling of life-size portraits in this same material. . . . Among the many distinguished visitors who honored the studio in 1780 was one designed to exercise a great influence on Madame Tussaud's young life. This was the King's sister, Madame Elizabeth of France. So infatuated did Madame Elizabeth become with this pleasant work of modeling in colored wax, which was soon to become a veritable craze, that she asked Madame Tussaud to instruct her, and for that purpose asked her to live with her at the Palace of Versailles."

An English wag remarks that —

" The stillborn figures of Madame Tussaud,
  With their eyes of glass and their hair of flax,
They only stare whatever you ax,
  For their ears, you know, are nothing but wax."

Those, however, who are deft with their needle and thread know that the bit of brown beeswax in their workbag is not to be scoffed at!

WINDERS, REELS, TURNS OR SWIFTS

" Handy woodmen seek the forest,
Fell the trees which crowd its borders,
Mills the turning
Do with swiftness,
Into spools is turned the forest."
— Louise J. Kirkwood.

SO many sorts of turns and swifts originated a long, long while ago that it is difficult to describe them in any accurate chronological order! Do you suppose that the different Asiatic winders were invented and in common use before Europe had turned to civilized arts? We all know that the Romans found the Gauls and Helvetians — with the exception perhaps of their Druid priests and priestesses — wearing skins and furs for clothing; but the Romans were more advanced, and before them the Greeks. However, the countries to the eastward had more luxuries, I believe, than the early Grecians, so I shall tell first of some winders and customs attached to them that I have observed in the Far East.

The Pink City of Jaipur! Pink house walls above, flaunting cerise scarfs and scarlet saris below; while hither and yon are strips of bright turban cloth stretched and drying or waving and drying in the brilliant sun. And still above fly the countless kites of the big and little boys. For be it known that men fly kites in India! Upon every side in Jaipur one may see the wound reels of cherry or white twine — these four-cornered, bamboo reels are long, and fat with string — prepared for the kite-flyers. Upon every street, and in the country upon roadside rocks, can boys be seen gluing colored paper stabilizing tails to their pet toys. Lacking glue, they break a certain sort of twig and smear its sap upon the paper. When these objects are flown, two competing flyers try to entangle each other's cords, each jerking, in an effort to break his adversary's line. Thus are purses wagered and won.

Well, together with twine and plain cloth dyeing, does Jaipur knot-tie-dye, spin gold thread, and weave rugs. When we were there, her

LA DEVIDEUSE OR LA PELOTONNEUSE, SOLD AT THE DUC DE MORNY SALE FOR $18,300.
BY JEAN BAPTISTE GREUZE, BORN AT TOURNUS, FRANCE, AUGUST 21, 1725; DIED AT PARIS,
MARCH 21, 1805. THERE IS ALSO AN ENGRAVING AFTER THIS PAINTING, BY LAURENT CARS.

men were also embroidering, in the palace, two royal trousseaux! Before the workers, on long, low tables, were thin paper traced patterns, gold thread, and small metallic green beetle wings. I tried to wheedle away a tracing, but failed; for were not these designs for the exclusive use of the thirteen-year-old prince's future brides — his aunt of twenty-six and his niece, whom he was to marry in a fortnight? His milk-white steed, in training for the event, was ridden through the streets

From the author's collection *Photo by the author*

Left: A TIME-WORN, YET HANDSOME, JAIPORE REEL FOR THE DRAWING OUT OR THINNING OF GOLD WIRE AND THREAD. IN THE CENTRE TOP IS A BRIGHT RED ENAMELED BUTTON — REALLY, THE TOP OF THE PEG ROUND WHICH THE DRUMHEAD REVOLVES. THE MEANS OF REVOLUTION — A SMALL BOY WITH A SHARP SPIKE OR STRONG SKEWER — HAS LEFT HIDEOUS WORMY-LOOKING TRACES UPON THE TOP OF THE REEL. TOWARD ITS FORE RIM CAN BE CAUGHT A SUGGESTION OF ITS SMOOTH, YELLOW PAINT FINISH. THE LOWER FLANGE IS RED.

Right: KOREAN THREAD HOLDER OF MADREPERL SET IN BLACK LAC.

of freshly whitewashed houses, beneath careening kites and the ever-growing number of festive banners; his massive silver anklets and "hocklets," scarlet embroidered straps, fancy cords and floating tassels, arresting attention on every side. We patted him; he was as sleek and soft as silken velvet.

Along these same streets flashed swift-turning, rainbow-colored wheels. What could they be? We entered a characteristic open-front shop, filled with long, low stools or tables, at each of which was fitted one of the whizzing wheels. They were painted in concentric circles with hard-finish yellow, green or magenta paint, an agate or coarse jade or enamel button in the centre. One reel of each pair was deftly turned by either a small boy or a bearded man, who stuck relentlessly into its polished top for handle a sharp steel stick, thus wearing count-

less wormy-looking hoary holes. All wheels were wound with gold
and silver embroidery wire, which each pair reeled from one to the
other, pulling, thinning the cord to a desired size. A diamond disc —
imported from Europe [1] — stood in a vise upon each tabourette, re-
fining the metal thread as it passed dizzily through from "windee"

Courtesy of R. J. Raber

A TYPICALLY BEJEWELED DRAVIDIAN WOMAN,
WINDING A BOBBIN UPON A CRUDE WOODEN SLAT-
WHEELED WINDER.

HANKS OF JAPANESE SILK AND A WINDER.

to winder. Such a "swift," at least, I did, after haggling, manage to
secure.

Again, an Indian winder; but for a different purpose. In a back
section of Delhi sat men in their open-front shops along an alley street
full of stale spilth. Though the sunlight entered scantily, the street was
bright, rendered colorful by the workers dotted hither and yon, with
powder-filled dye-pots by their sides — blues, reds, oranges. Into the
jar would plunge a man's hand; then, with a palm full of powder, he
would wind through it, spreading widely and evenly, on the slightest
of wooden winders, his hank of raw white thread. Later the spindles

---

[1] These discs, costing eighteen rupees (six dollars) each — a high figure for an Asiatic workman to meet — are imported through France from England.

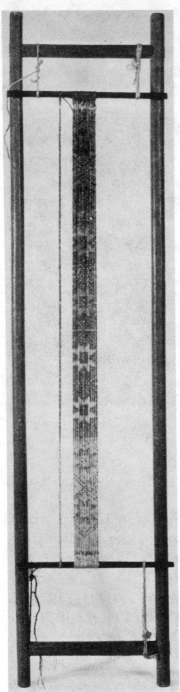

were gathered up for the color-fixing of their powder-dyed contents.

India seems so old as to have been without beginning, and so does distant Cambodia; but in the latter country a certain king's (Houen-t'ien's) jealousy of other men's eyes feasting upon his particularly beautiful queen's (Lieou-ye's) rare graces, led, according to the history of the T'si, to his inaugurating the custom of clothes for women; thereby stimulating the introduction or invention of weaving and setting for us an approximate date — some time not far previous to the third century — in connection with Cambodian winders. These belong to the realm of warp weaving.[2] They are setting-up frames and in a way measuring frames as well. In Cambodia the winders are used for woof rather than for the more usual warp weaving: it is the woof thread for the shuttle that is measured and stretched skein by skein, or shuttleful by shuttleful, upon the winding frame. While still upon

[2] See warp weaving under "Fast-Flitting Shuttles."

THE CAMBODIAN WINDING FRAME UPON WHICH THE NATIVES FOR CENTURIES HAVE WRAPPED THEIR WEAVING SILK BEFORE DYEING. EACH STRAND — ONE IS PURPOSELY SET APART — FILLS ONE SHUTTLE BOBBIN. TINY STRAW KNOTS NEAR THE BASE SHOW WHERE THIS WHITE SILK IS TIED UP IN A STAR PATTERN TO PREVENT THE TIED SPOTS FROM ABSORBING THE RED DYE INTO WHICH EACH STRAND WILL BE PLUNGED. THE UPPER PART OF THIS MOUNT HAS BEEN DYED AND, THE STRAW BEING REMOVED, SHOWS WHITE STARS AGAINST A RED FIELD. THE THREADS, OF COURSE, ARE ALL CAREFULLY MEASURED BEFORE BEING TIED UP. THE PATTERN THUS IS ALL SET, NOT IN THE LOOM DURING WEAVING, BUT BEFOREHAND! THE STRANDS WHEN READY ARE SLIPPED OFF THE FRAME FOR DIPPING. THEN WHEN DRY, THEY ARE WOUND UPON THE BOBBINS THAT SERVE AS SPOOLS INSIDE THE WEAVING SHUTTLES. [GREATLY REDUCED.]

the frame, the thread or silk is prepared for dyeing. After dyeing, each separate strand or skein or shuttleful is wound upon a bobbin, ready for its insertion into the shuttle each time that it is emptied in the process of weaving. A frame one metre long is used in connection with a loom that is to weave material one metre wide — the length of the frame corresponds to the width of the goods to be made up. This is the winder alluded to in the chapter on shuttles.

Warp weaving is practised in Japan also. The product, called *Oshima Kasuri* or *Hasuri,* is worn by nearly every schoolboy and youth in Japan. It appears as a sombre silk stuff — dark blue or brown — dotted or starred with dull white. If the background be blue, the blue threads will tinge the edges of the white undyed woof threads; if brown, the spot edges will appear a little yellowish. The name of the Oshima winding frame I do not know.

While in Japan, an item of practical everyday western life led me not only into many shops, but also into the discovery of some items of everyday Japanese life:

Armed with a sample spool of sewing-silk and a card thereof — the silken thread wound, as in France, about four successive notches cut into a card, capable of being cut and sold in quarters or halves, as a card of buttons — so armed, I started out confidently to buy a spool of orchid-colored silk. Though I could not speak Japanese, I thought the two different examples of what I sought would suggest to the shop-keeper sewing-silk upon whatever form of spool might be current in the country. In the first store entered, the clerk prided himself upon his English and so quickly caught up my word spool that I did not show my sample. He honorably regretted, however, that unworthy shop no have; and instructed my jinricksha runner where to go. The 'ricksha boy toted me to a shop full of knives, forks and *spoons*. After that I insistently thrust forward my *spool*. At the third place the shopkeeper, his wife, his son, in turn examined in silent amazement my proffered card and spool, shaking their heads in negation. But they made a suggestion to the runner. We thereupon trotted to a large department store. The boy led me in to have a pair of cotton slipovers, gathered upon an elastic, placed over my street-soiled shoes before venturing into the clean Japanese interior. At each floor I was pointed upstairs, until upon the top story lay revealed a counter full of embroidery silks. There was floss; there was heavily twisted rope silk; no sewing-silk. I fared forth to another dry-goods store. Then to a wholesale silk merchant's, where I knew fair English was spoken. The kindly almond-eyed merchant carried on a long conversation with my boy, and we started another quest for that simple spool of silk. At last I learned from observation that not even skeins, but only small hanks of silk, are to be had in a thoroughly Japanese city. So, though I needed but little, and find small quantities more desirable when traveling, I succumbed to the inevitable, but clung to an idea of finding a fitting shade. That too had to be abandoned. Still wondering what fastidious folk do about stitching their fine kimonos, I bought a hank of vivid violet silk, fine however.

Have you seen scrubbing-drying boards about the streets of Japan? They hold the explanation. A valuable kimono is never plunged recklessly into a tub. No, fine garments are only basted together with black or white cotton, to be pulled out for laundry purposes, leaving two flat front, two back, and two straight sleeve pieces, that are laid upon a board, scrubbed, and left — as a traveler leaves handkerchiefs upon a mirror — to dry. Ironing perhaps would too greatly flatten the texture of crinkly crêpe, and sharp heat weakens silk. Besides, the board accomplishes two tasks in one. By the way, Japanese inner kimonos are of cotton woven in large, clean factories; for silk, they say, is often a cottage product — thus, less sanitary. To see what delectable garment a Japanese may have on, peek at the revealing slits of his or her falling sleeve.

On my shopping jaunt, I saw upon a Japanese tailor's sewing-machine a bamboo reel of four uprights some three or four inches apart, the thread — white cotton — wound thereon.

The word "winder" is self-explanatory. Pretty parlor winders are often termed "turns" or "swifts." You are all familiar with the reel on a fishing rod? But in sewing circles a reel is a roller of wood turning in a frame for winding thread; also a workbag appliance — frequently of mother-of-pearl or silver [3] — on which to wind silk; and in addition the circular wooden or flat pasteboard article on which sewing-cotton is sold when not made up in balls. In Ireland reels

[3] Some of the paper-thin chased little mother-of-pearl fish that folks so use are really counters for a Chinese game.

CAREFULLY WASHING, DRYING AND PRESSING GOOD STRIPS OF
JAPANESE DRESS MATERIAL.

STRETCHING AND RICE STARCHING A STRIP OF JAPANESE SILK.

are called "spools," and in the north of England they are commonly designated "bobbins."

We see listed in the inventory of Queen Clemence of Hungary an ivory winder of careful execution, now in the museum at Hal, Belgium. This wheel is similar to the delicate ivory one illustrated in the chapter on awls. And later, in 1638, the catalogue of the Vente Lemérotel Saint-Malo speaks of "*un petit dévidouer de boys pour la somme de XV sols*" (a little wooden swift for the sum of fifteen sols). An item

KINDLY OLD JAPANESE WOMAN FILLING A FOUR-SIDED SPINDLE.

of 1746 — "*un dévidoir à trois pieds, dont les batons se plient*" (a three-footed turn, with folding sticks), and a "*petit dévidoir à mettre sur table*" (a little turn to place on the table), sound very modern, for this is the type most frequently found even to-day. It resembles the demountable Swiss specimen. *La Mère Laborieuse*, by Chardin, shows the sort usually seen in the eighteenth century. Some were in precious metals. In an address of Sieur Mercier, master turner, there arises the question of "*dévidoirs à soleil et à tambourg*" (sun swifts and tambour turns) — which I regret being unable to explain.

In Auvergne there were winders of a different sort upon which — as upon cards — to wind the finished lace, as ribbons are wrapped around heavy cardboards. But the French eighteenth century boards were of wood, primitively whittled or finely carved, and perhaps occasionally painted. Seventeen of these are shown in the Trocadéro. They are labeled *plioirs*.

Poor prisoners in Sweden, striving to keep their hands busy and their minds occupied, resorted to the device of carving castaway soup bones. Surely these must have been the trusties, the honor-roll prison-

 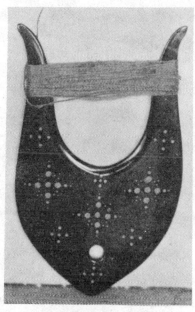

From the author's collection   *From the collection of Mrs. De Witt Clinton Cohen, New York*

Left: A QUAINT OLD AMERICAN SPOOL-HOLDER OF INLAID MAHOGANY, WITH A WORK-DRAWER BELOW AND A CUSHION ABOVE. THE LITTLE ROUND KNOBS ARE HANDLES BY WHICH TO PULL OUT STIFF WIRES THAT RUN THROUGH THE SPOOLS AND SLIP INTO STEADYING SOCKETS BENEATH. [MUCH REDUCED.]

Right: OLD HARP-SHAPED FRENCH TORTOISE-SHELL THREAD WINDER WITH GILDED DOTS.

ers, to have been allowed the free use of sharp instruments! The elaborate William and Mary bone cotton winder is of this type, of which a similar specimen is pictured in connection with lobster claws and agates. In the latter example the two men's heads unscrew and reveal their slim bodies as needlecases, while the woman is merely an ornament. At the top are tiny pincushions.

Winders or swifts of narwhal were carved and sometimes stained in patriotic blue and red by American whalers while cruising for a catch. This was certainly a good way to keep out of mischief and to employ the otherwise waste material that came their way. The narwhal is indeed a unicorn, and his beautifully fluted, spirally twisted

Courtesy of Madame de Ferro

COLLAPSIBLE SWISS *DÉVIDOIR* AND *BOBINOIR* FOR WINDING SKEIN OF LINEN DIRECTLY ON TO
BOBBINS: A TYPE OF WINDER USUAL ALSO IN ENGLAND AND GERMANY.

tusk furnishes splendid ivory. Pliable splats were also made of this and tied into graceful unembellished winders, just as flexible bands of tortoise shell were in earlier days.

Mrs. Burrage of Maine owns the handsomest spool-rack I have happened upon. It is some ten or twelve inches tall, of silver, with wrought platforms to uphold the layers of spools, and bird finials perched at the tips of the silver rods, to screw down and hold them in place.

Gift of Mr. Ayné Rambert to the Musée Ethnographique du Trocadéro, Paris

Courtesy of the Musée du Trocadéro, Paris

TWO NON-SYMMETRICALLY DECORATED LACE BOARDS FROM AUVERGNE. THESE ARE CALLED *PLIOIRS À DENTELLE*; LITERALLY, FOLDERS. [QUARTER SIZE.]

Courtesy of the Musée du Trocadéro, Paris

Winder from Puy de Dôme, France

TWO EIGHTEENTH-CENTURY CARVED LACE WINDERS — ONE WITH A STUDDED EFFECT, THE OTHER APPEARING TO BE PAINTED AS WELL AS CHISELED. [QUARTER SIZE.]

Courtesy of the Musée du Trocadéro, Paris

TWO OLD PIERCED WOODEN LACE HOLDERS OR WINDERS FROM LE PUY, AUVERGNE. [QUARTER SIZE.]

An amusing primitive bobbin winder consists of a plain lidless wooden box containing a flat upright notched stick, roughly, deeply cut. With the box on one's knees, the notch away from one, a lace bobbin laid in the indentation, and a ring buttoned or fastened to one's waist or belt, one needs only to place a continuous string or thong through the ring and around the bobbin to set the latter in motion by the rapid pulling of the little cable. Of course, the thread for the bobbin should be reposing opposite it on a reel or turn, attached presumably to a table, the turn or swift holding upon its outstretched arms the necessary skein.

Various terms exist for similar processes and are a bit confusing: thread is conducted from a *windle* to a quill or bobbin, while a *yarn-spooler* also is an appliance for filling *spools* or bobbins. A *yarn-winder* is synonymous, the dictionary says, with a *yarn-spooler* or *yarn-reel:* but it states that a *yarn-reel* winds the yarn *from* the cop, coppin or bobbin. Then there is a spun-yarn *winch,* which is a small *winch* with a flywheel, used on ships for making up spun yarn. Reeling yarn means to make it into skeins by winding it round the appliance used in manufactories for the purpose, or thence on spools.

When thread is cut from a spool the end that comes off first, not the newly broken one, should be threaded into the needle if kinking is to be avoided; and when one's thread knots, it should be given an occasional leftward twist.

In using the Austrian bobbin, one screws the top-like leaden weight [4] into the small hole at the base of the bobbin handle. After removing the barrel-like wooden thread cover from the spindle of the stick, and attaching the thread to the lower end of the spindle or shaft near the handle, one begins winding the linen. The thread can be passed between the fingers of the left hand to regulate the tension. The base or tip of the leaden winder or top should be placed firmly upon the lap unimpeded by folds of the skirt. The upper part of the bobbin should be supported against the inside of the four extended fingers of the left hand. Then the bobbin should be given a twist and rapidly twirled by taking its tip between the thumb and forefinger of the right hand and pushing the stick away with the thumb, turning it in the direction in which one would wind a clock. The

---

[4] See whorls, under " The Song of the Spinning-Wheel."

Courtesy of the Musée du Trocadéro, Paris

BROAD LACE HOLDER DATED 1773, FROM AUVERGNE.
[MUCH REDUCED.]

Courtesy of the Musée du Trocadéro, Paris

NARROW WOODEN LACE HOLDER, EIGHTEENTH CENTURY,
AUVERGNE. [MUCH REDUCED.]

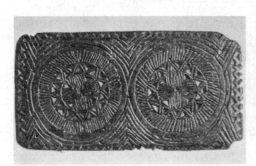 

Courtesy of the Musée du Trocadéro, Paris   *Courtesy of the Musée du Trocadéro, Paris*

Left: A WELL-WORN WOODEN LACE WINDER. [QUARTER SIZE.]

Right: THE SPIRAL CARVING ON THIS OLD FRENCH WINDER SOMEHOW SUGGESTS THE FAVORITE PORCU-
PINE DEVICE OF LOUIS XII. [QUARTER SIZE.]

rotary motion rolls the thread about the bobbin in the same way that peasants wind their thread, when spinning, upon a spindle whorl. As the thread accumulates, it should be spread over the spindle from the bottom upwards toward the tip, but ought not to be allowed to pass more than half-way up the shank, as the barrel-shaped protector slides, when the bobbin is in use, downwards against the handle, leaving the upper end of the spindle exposed. After looping the thread so that it cannot unwind, one slips the wooden cap over it to protect it, leaving the end of the thread sticking out beyond it ready for use. The weight is then unscrewed and removed from the bottom of the bobbin.

A usual method of threading lace bobbins is by using a small hand-cranked table wheel, set on a wooden plinth or platform, the whole resembling a small spinning-wheel to be turned like a hand sewing-machine. A bobbin set in clamps a few inches from the wheel, but on the same base, is rapidly turned when the wheel is cranked, by a cord that passes around both wheel and bobbin-end, or a drumhead that may be supporting and clamping the bobbin at one end. The thread is paid out from a reel placed near the bobbin. Not long ago one Sladen, of Bristol, England, advertised a patent winder adapted to " any sized bobbin."

A very modern American appliance is a steel bobbin holder destined to clamp to the small upper or turn wheel of a sewing-machine, to be set in motion by treading the machine as usual — or by electricity!

"A skein winder, though convenient, can, however, be dispensed with, as a skein of thread can be held around the left hand and wound on a spool or bit of cardboard in the right hand, by just placing one end of the skein over the left thumb, bringing the skein across the inside of the hand and around, across the back; again over the palm and around the back a second time; then across the inside of the fingers a third time, laying the other end of the skein around the little finger. The fingers and thumb should then be stretched apart to keep the thread from slipping off. Care should be taken not to twist one strand of the skein over the other, but to keep the two sides parallel.

" A bobbin winder, too, is an unnecessary article, especially for a lace-maker to store or carry about with her, as the bobbins can be easily and quickly wound by tying a heavy white thread, preferably a

A FINE GOTHIC PIERCED LACE BOARD OR WINDER FROM AUVERGNE AND A LESS ARTISTIC BUT VERY HUMANLY IMPERFECT ONE OF THE SAME CHARMING PERIOD. [QUARTER SIZE.]

CARVED BONE COTTON WINDER, $6\frac{1}{2}$ INCHES HIGH AND $3\frac{1}{2}$ WIDE BY $2\frac{1}{4}$ THICK, OF THE TIME OF WILLIAM AND MARY.

By kind permission of the Whaling Museum, New Bedford

AMERICAN SCRIMSHAW NARWHAL SWIFT, MADE ON SHIPBOARD BY EARLY WHALERS AND
DECORATED IN DARK BLUE AND VERMILION. [GREATLY REDUCED.]

tightly twisted or glazed one, single or doubled, to a long pin, and sticking the pin firmly into one's pillow or the upholstered arm of a convenient chair. The point of the pin in this case should be slanted towards one to anchor the work, as in hemming. The heavy white thread referred to in a previous sentence is called a cable. A cable should be, roughly speaking, about eighteen inches long, but many workers prefer a very much shorter one. The loose lower part, not necessarily the very end, of the cable is customarily twisted twice around

From Beer, Devonshire

OLD ENGLISH BOBBIN WINDER. [MUCH REDUCED.]

the forefinger of the left hand, coming up in front of it, and held firmly against it by the thumb. To secure the lace thread to the bobbin, an end should be placed towards the right across the handle flange at the lower end of the spindle and held there for a moment by the right forefinger. Then winding the thread twice down behind the back and up around the front of the spindle, one turns the thread end back towards the left across these two twists, using the left thumb and forefinger, replacing the right-hand finger to secure the reversed end, while one continues to wind three or four rounds of thread on top of it. The worker can then begin using the cable, in the meantime replacing the first right-hand finger by the second if necessary. The lace spool or thread holder is laid in one's lap or somewhere else just below the left hand, and the lace thread comes up to the bobbin on which it is to be wound, behind the little and fore fingers, in front of the two centre ones of the left hand. This permits of an adjustable tension. The bobbin is held horizontally in the right hand with its head towards the left, the handle sloped slightly to the right to make

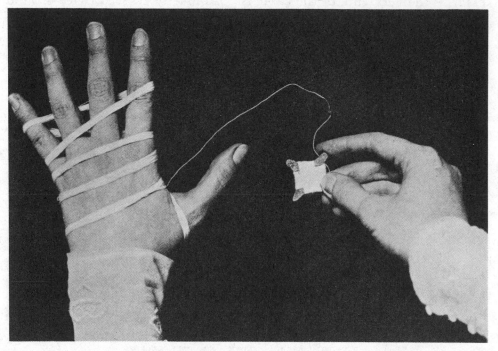

Taken from A Lace Guide for Makers and Collectors, by Gertrude Whiting, copyright by E. P. Dutton & Co., New York

A DEMONSTRATION OF UNWINDING A SKEIN OF THREAD FROM THE HAND ON TO A LITTLE WOODEN WINDER.

the thread wind nearer the handle end than the cable end of the spindle. The thread groove around the head of the bobbin or upper end of its spindle just next to the spreading head flange is laid in front of and against the cable. The lower end of the cable is then brought up in front over the bobbin, and down behind it, making one loop around — without a knot. The bobbin should slip or slide up and down in this loop, so the loop ought not to be kept too tight or the bobbin cannot move. If, however, the cable is too loose, the bobbin will slip out. Practically the whole trick lies in this tension, but that this is easily and quickly mastered is shown by the fact that some little four-year-old meningitis patients learned it without difficulty. The cable must be around the stick only, not in with the thread, or the bobbin cannot turn. The two first fingers of the right hand are placed above and down behind the bobbin to the left of its handle-flange; the other two right-hand fingers are similarly placed,

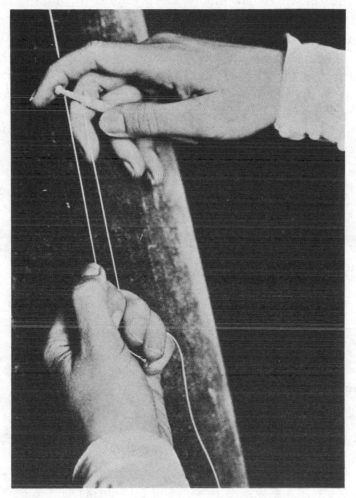

Taken from A Lace Guide for Makers and Collectors, by Gertrude Whiting, copyright by E. P. Dutton & Co., New York

SHOWING HOW TO LOOP A BOBBIN HEAD INTO A CABLE AND HOW TO HOLD AND GUIDE THE BOBBIN LIGHTLY UP AND DOWN AS IT SLIPS AND TURNS IN THE SIMPLE SEMI-TAUT LOOP.

but to the right of the flange; the forefinger to the left of the cable, the other three to the right, one over the thread or spindle part, two over the handle. This keeps the bobbin properly centred, and these fingers are used to push or slide the bobbin down the cable, allowing the stick to roll. The thumb of the right hand is placed below the bobbin to the right of the cable and handle-flange, in what is the slender part of most bobbin handles, thus leaving a clear view of whether the thread is winding smoothly, and pushing the stick up-wards on the return movement without the bobbin's rolling. To pre-vent its rolling, the thumb, of course, grips it more tightly for the moment. Once this simple trick is mastered, it seems very easy and is great fun; in fact, one feels as though one were playing a game rather than really working." (Quoted from *A Lace Guide for Makers and Collectors,* published by E. P. Dutton & Company.)

This chapter seems a little like the sophistry that tries to prove that you are on the other side of the street, or that three cats are really less than one cat; for having described the uses, beauties and joys of winders, I have proceeded to tell you how to do without these swiftly turning, singing instruments. So let me suggest that you harmonize these two opposites by buying a beautiful reel to use at home, but economize space by learning to manipulate skein and thread unaided when you travel.

WINDERS, REELS, TURNS OR SWIFTS

" *Speak her fair and canny, or we will have a raveled hasp on the yarn windles.*"
— *The Pirate:* Sir Walter Scott.

" *Everywhere the blind see through their fingers. She could embroider. . . She could card silks accurately, and even pick up with the needle's eye the fine end in the broken cocoon, and wind it off and reel it with a hand that never wavered or mismoved.*"

— *The Feast of Lanterns:* Louise Jordan Miln.

" *What wonderful threads of gold they make also! They put a piece of gold through a cast with a variety of holes, pulling it through each in turn, and finally when it grows longer and longer, and passes the last hole, they sing, cozening it —*
' *Thin as a woman's hair,*
And glowing as a fawn clad with the setting sun.' "

— *My Brother's Face:* Dhan Gopal Mukerji.

SCISSORS TO GRIND, SCISSORS TO GRIND!

" What are little boys made of?
Scissors [1] and snails ·
And puppy dogs' tails,
And that's what little boys are made of."
                                        — Mother Goose.

SCISSORS and shears denote something very snappy that I fear I am scarcely keen enough to measure up to, though like the stubborn chatterbox who always contradicted her husband and was bound to have the last word, even though it cost her life, I could continue to shout, " It's scissors, it's scissors! " At the prime minister's handsome, historic country house — " Chequers," in England — hangs a Hawtrey family painting, dated 1740. The rich, polished walls of the room are diapered with carved haw trees set between the initials " W " and " H." Now, the painting, by C. Philips, depicts an ancestral grandmother, Mrs. Revett, being ducked for obstinacy by her insensate husband — he pointing one finger downward upon her head to keep her from bobbing up, and to indicate the single blade of a knife; she holding a pair of opened fingers above the water to denote the double blades of a pair of scissors. The legend beneath the picture relates that when she had almost drowned, he gloated, " Now will you say it was a knife? " — " Scissors," said she, then sank. Twice she rose to the surface, both times repeating, " Scissors! "

The old forms — cysowres, sisoures, cisors, cissers, sizars — show that our present term is of French origin, from the former *cisoires* — shears — modified to *ciseaux;* singular, *ciseau* or *cisel,* a chisel, derived from the Latin *caedere,* to cut; *cisorium,* a cutting instrument; or *scindere,* to cleave. The Latin *scissor* was a carver or a gladiator.

The use of scissors by the Aryans several centuries before Christ is implied by a passage in Wilson's *Rig Veda.* This leads us to realize

---

[1] Some versions say *snaps* (metal-workers' shears) and some *snips* (glass-blowers' nippers) for *scissors.*

that the double cutting instrument is in fact much older than European history indicates.

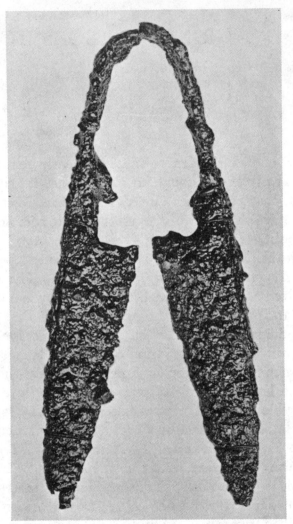

Courtesy of the Hispanic Society of America

OLD RUSTED METAL HORSE-CLIPPERS FOUND AT LA CAÑADA HONDA, SPAIN.

[SLIGHTLY REDUCED.]

Shells and sharp-edged stones were probably the first implements used for this purpose. But in Roman days came iron, bronze and steel shears of a single piece of bent metal sharpened at the ends.

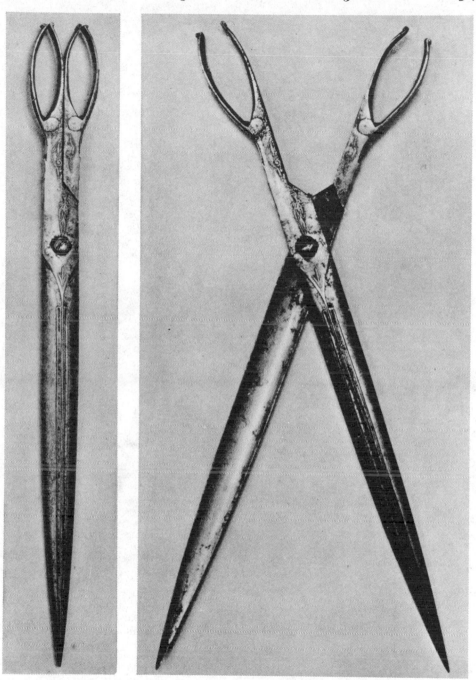

From the collection of Mrs. De Witt Clinton Cohen, New York

SIXTEENTH-CENTURY HAND-WROUGHT TURKISH STEEL SCISSORS INLAID WITH GOLD AND HAVING
DELIGHTFUL SPRING HANDLES THAT CLING TO THE FINGERS AND GIVE ONE A FIRM GRIP.

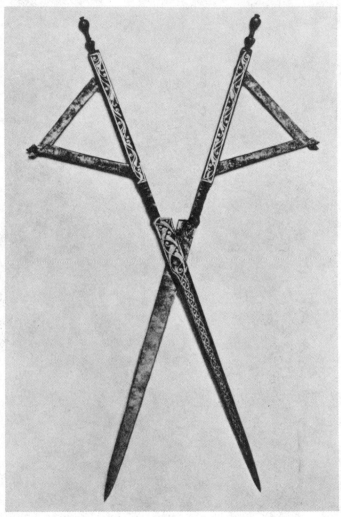

From the collection of Mrs. De Witt Clinton Cohen, New York

VERY OLD PERSIAN STEEL SCISSORS INLAID WITH GOLD, HAVING
FASCINATING COLLAPSIBLE TRIANGULAR HANDLES.

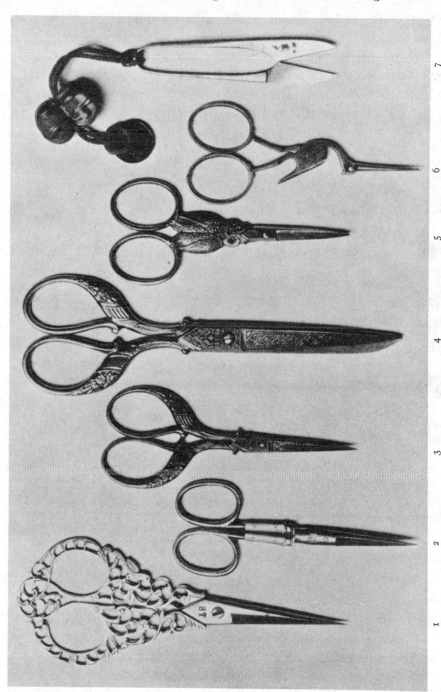

1. MODERN ITALIAN STEEL SCISSORS. *Courtesy of Mrs. Henry E. Coe.* 2. MODERN GERMAN EMBROIDERY SCISSORS WITH IVORY INSETS. *Courtesy of Mrs. William Adams McFadden.* 3 AND 4. LARGE AND SMALL MODERN SPANISH SCISSORS OF TOLEDO STEEL WITH GOLD HANDLES AND DESIGN IN RELIEF. *Courtesy of Mrs. William Adams McFadden.* 5. MODERN STEEL SCISSORS WITH DESIGN OF GOLDEN OWL HAVING EMERALD GLASS EYES. *From the author's collection.* 6. MODERN BLACKENED STEEL EMBROIDERY SCISSORS WITH GOLDEN STORK. *Courtesy of Brooklyn Museum.* 7. MODERN STEEL JAPANESE SCISSORS, SIGNED ON THE BLADE. TO THE HANDLE IS ATTACHED A DOUBLE EMERY AND A GOOD-LUCK COIN, AND THE FOLLOWING VERSE ACCOMPANIES THEM:

"IN FAR ²APAN THESE SCISSORS WERE BORN,
AND THE TASSELL WITH EMERY, JOIN IN THE SONG
OF TRYING TO HELP YOU MAKE HAPPY THE DAY
AND DRIVE DULL CARE AND WORRY AWAY."

In Pompeii occurs a decoration of cupids cutting flowers, and there is, at the Museum of Sens, a Roman painting of a man cutting cloth. A Greek earthenware group portrays a barber cutting the hair of an old man. These single-strip shears continued up to medieval times. In the Cathedral of Chartres is treasured an instrument of torture, an object resembling scissors, but probably used for tongue-slitting.

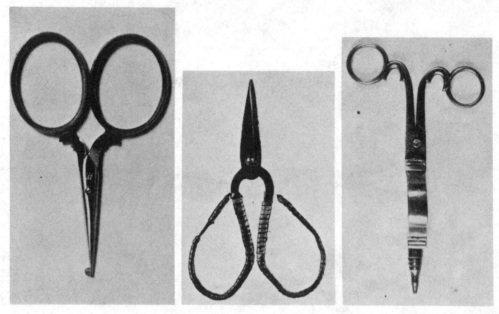

The three are from the author's collection

Left: EMBROIDERY SCISSORS WITH TINY FLANGE OR KNOB AT THE TIP OF THE UNDER BLADE, TO PREVENT ITS DIGGING INTO THE MATERIAL WHEN BEING SLIPPED BETWEEN TWO LAYERS OF STUFF, AS WHEN DETACHING THE EXTRA OR WASTE MUSLIN FROM THE EMBROIDERED NET OF CARRICKMA-CROSS LACE. [ACTUAL SIZE.]   *Centre:* STRAW-BOUND CHINESE EMBROIDERY SCISSORS USED BY PUPILS IN THE SICCAWEI CONVENT, SHANGHAI.   *Right:* A PAIR OF CROOKED OLD HISTORIC BELGIAN LACE-MAKER'S CANDLE SNUFFERS.   [GREATLY REDUCED.]

The early, bent scissor form is known in French as the *ciseaux de force*.

The modern implement, as we know it, appeared in the sixteenth century and is attributed to the Venetians, though some crossed blades belonging to the fourteenth century have been found. The Persians originated the bird-form scissor with the elongated beak serving as a blade. The Dutch lay claim to having honored their picturesque

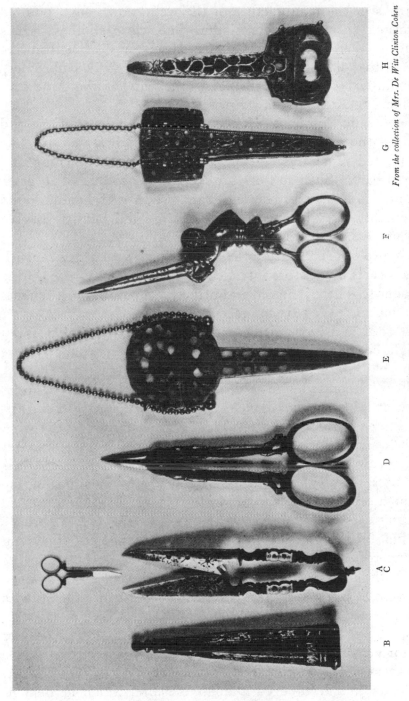

From the collection of Mrs. De Witt Clinton Cohen

A: ABOVE, VERY VERY TINY STEEL SCISSORS, POSSIBLY INTENDED FOR A WATCH CHARM AS OCCASIONALLY SEEN IN NORTHERN INDIA, OR PERHAPS MADE AS A PLAYTHING. B AND C: RARE FRENCH STEEL SHEATH WITH FINELY PIERCED *CISEAUX DE FOCRE.* D: FRENCH STEEL *JAMBES DE PRINCESSE,* SHOWING FRENCH LOUIS HEELS. E: VALUABLE FRENCH STEEL SCISSOR SHEATH. F: GROTESQUE OLD GOLD SCISSORS DEPICTING A BECAPED SPANISH CAVALIER WITH SWORD. G: A FINE SILVER CASE DECORATED WITH VARIED, TRANSLUCENT, SOFTLY COLORED FRENCH ENAMELS. H: A VERY OLD PIERCED STEEL FRENCH SCISSORS SHEATH.

national storks in the manufacture of the well-known slim, pointed "stork" scissor, so excellent for ripping fine, close stitches! This may be true, for there is another bird-shaped scissor — of pelican-like appearance — that may be the Persian tool. The stork embroidery snips here illustrated were given me by the wife of the American Consul-General to Amsterdam.

The Renaissance brought wick cutters or candle snuffers and coal scissors — those fascinating extension, twisted brass affairs, like magnified jointed sugar tongs — narrow grill works of opening and folding metal bars. Such scissors are called *lazy tongs*. The brass lampwick snuffers here pictured are old and crude, with handles quite unlike in length. They belonged to the Pierre Mali family, Belgian Consuls-General to New York for four generations.

The idea also of ornamenting the instruments with a device, such as entwined hearts on scissors intended as wedding gifts, rose during the Renaissance. There is an old seal depicting a pair of open scissors bearing the motto, "We part to meet again."

Tortoise-shell and ivory girdle cases were introduced that small scissors might be conveniently carried about. Some instruments were inlaid with gold and gems. The damascened variety from Toledo, Spain, is always decorated with golden arabesques. Little boys, under the supervision of experienced men, chase the Toledo instruments, laying the golden wire into the resulting slots, hammering the wire, plunging the scissors, for tempering, into great wooden tubs of water in front of them; then busily hammering and pounding upon their drawn-up knees, for all the world like cobblers. All this in dim, big buildings, high ceiled — I think one, in fact, is an old church, turned over to secular uses. The proud workman plunges a dagger perhaps through a big, bronzy English copper laid on a plank, to show you that the tempered steel can easily pass through both without turning an edge! Or the man brings forth a tight gray coil of cleanest steel, and taking its tip, unrolls it, displaying the supplest of sword blades that, when released, promptly coils again. This is one of the factory's tests, a spectacular *tour de force*. Toledo embroidery scissors are tested for perfection of clean-cutting edge by clipping wet tissue paper with them. This, of course, they must not tear or fail to sever. You recall Saladin's keen-edged Damascus sabre, which he demonstrated to Richard Coeur de Lion? After the latter had hewn some heavy article with his two-edged sword, cleaving it in twain, Saladin tossed a gossamer tissue into the air and, after a wave of his scimitar, handed two neatly cut pieces of scarf to the English king.

Folding pocket scissors also were invented during the Renaissance. France, in the eighteenth century, had a fad for the so-called *jambes de princesse* — princess's legs with fancy boot-tops and high heels! These legs were the scissor handles.

Nowadays we have graduated sets of three or four pairs of different-size scissors in one leather case: but now, as formerly, since sharp edges might cut friendship, one is supposed to accompany the gift of a knife or a pair of scissors with a penny to avert ill luck. In mythological days, it was not only Friendship, but Life itself that might be severed, for though one of the Fates spun the Thread of Life, another — Atropos — cut it off. The painting of the three Fates or Parcæ which has been attributed to Michelangelo distinctly shows the one-piece bent shears of earlier days. K'iung Siao, Pi Siao and Yiin Siao are three Chinese nature goddesses dwelling on Three Fairies' Island — San sien tao. The third one has a pair of two-dragon magic scissors that cut men or even gods in twain and that hold the essence of earth, moon, sun and heaven.

Then there comes a spring or summer morning when even the most reluctant bud has burst into bloom and from above one's head coquettishly coaxes one to pick it. Then one sallies forth with a quaint little shallow picking basket and the rose scissors and makes an end of flirtation. And it is such fun — since the scissors hold the rose after it is cut and its thorns can't prick! These nippers have curved blades like manicure scissors.

Besides, there are other fancy varieties: curved manicure scissors, some with a file on each blade; grape scissors with a groove on one blade into which the other fits; and adjustable buttonhole scissors with sharp points a half-inch long and then a non-cutting gap along the blades, and with a screw to determine whether the whole half-inch or only a little of it may shut down and cut.

At present, one might remark that the finest scissors are hand-forged of the very best steel only, this being necessary to insure a keen cutting edge, hardness and uniformity, so that a high, smooth polish may be given the metal, together with tenacity to withstand the heat incident to forging, and later to hold their correct and exact form after the blades are tempered and chilled.

Sometimes only the cutting edges are of steel, welded to iron shanks and bows, or handles; but these must be burnished, for irregularity of surface interferes with polishing. These are called *shot* scissors. Tailors' shears sometimes have brass or bronze bows riveted or dovetailed to steel blades.

First a strip of metal the length of the whole tool is cut and one end curved into the shape of the finger hold or bow. The opposite end is then hammered into a blade. This is done by eye guidance, and is called *forging*. The two halves of the scissors are then *fitted* — that is, filed to match precisely and drilled in the centre of their shanks, preparatory to being screwed together.

Next they are passed through the process of *grinding*. Following this they are bound together with wire after one heating and cooling, and reheated to a brownish yellow or purple color, which indicates the proper temperature for their tempering and second sudden cooling. *Polishing* ensues. Great care is required in order to obtain a proper cutting adjustment, so the surfaces of the blades are slightly bossed and each has a small triangular prominence to make the blades cant more and more towards each other as they close.

Not long ago a pair of clever scissors was invented in France. The product sounds like a "stunt," and is probably more useful than ornamental. For this all-round pair eighteen different uses are claimed! The flat side of the under blade has a straight edge marked off as a ruler and measure. Toward the bow end, near the joint, when the blades are open, appears a tiny crotch which catches and cuts wire. Next to it a larger circular one clips cigars. A screw between the handles adjusts a buttonholer, which, in addition, is toothed so that it can hold and sever a small tube. One edge of the upper blade serves as a nail file. The square flattened end or butt of the upper blade forms a screwdriver, which can also be used to pry up a box lid. A tiny notch near the bevel of the under blade enables one to withdraw cartridges from firearms. A spread portion (like the plate or die of a seal ring), flattened out upon the outer rim of one handle-bow, may be used as a tack hammer. The lower blade has, at its centre, a projecting cylindrical pivot, but this is ellipsoidal to the upper blade. The latter has an elliptic opening for the pivot to slip into, becoming cylindrical, so that the blade can rotate on the pivot. With this little arrangement (similar to some of the removable handles on convertible Sheffield vegetable dishes, whose covers may be turned and used for additional bases) one may disjoint the scissors at will. When apart, one blade may be used as a penknife to sharpen pencils, or for other purposes. The base of one bow contains a tiny revolving steel wheel for cutting glass. Glass may also be cracked or split apart by means of a small notch next the wheel. The other handle extremity has a diminutive toothed wheel (like a pastry jagger) for marking paper or perforating dress patterns. The tip of one blade can be used as an ink scratcher or eraser. The last or eighteenth use of this omnipotent scissor — as a stereoscope — seems rather doubtful!

A different useful device that sounds like a stunt, but truly is easy and really a lace-making time-saver, is the Devon-

From the collection of Mrs. De Witt Clinton Cohen, New York

OLD MOTHER-OF-PEARL SCISSORS AND SHEATH WITH GOLD SIDES AND EDGES. [ACTUAL SIZE.] MOTHER-OF-PEARL SCISSORS WITH GILT FINISHING ARE DAINTY AND, IN SIMPLE DESIGNS, NOT RARE; BUT THE PAIR HERE ILLUSTRATED WITH ELABORATE DESIGN AND SHEATH TOO IN THE PEARL SHELL ARE HARDER TO FIND AND MORE TO BE PRIZED. SUCH DAINTY IMPLEMENTS ARE NATURALLY MORE APT TO BE MADE UP INTO SMALL SCISSORS; WHILE HANDSOME SHEARS ARE WROUGHT RATHER IN STEEL OR BRONZE, SOMETIMES IN SILVER. SHELL-HANDLED SCISSORS SHOULD, OF COURSE, BE TREATED AS THEY DESERVE, AND PROTECTED FROM FALLS OR BLOWS, FOR ONE MOMENT'S CARELESSNESS MAY MAR THE PRODUCT OF DAYS OF SKILLED AND PATIENT TOIL.

shire trick of *bowing-up*. May I quote from Miss A. Penderel Moody's account of the method? — " Cutting off in Couples. — Twist the threads from a pair of bobbins in a single loop round the closed blades of a pair of rather blunt scissors. With the points of the scissors catch and hold the double threads so firmly as to draw the loop over the points without cutting the thread until it has passed over. The couples are then ready knotted together for further use."

One New York collection shows some shagreen and galuchat scissor cases, as well as others of gold-tooled dull red leather, with leather-covered scissor handles to match. In the same collection are mother-of-pearl sheaths with black enamel designs and gold edges. There are finely wrought all-gold French *étuis*, with figures of Columbine and graceful scallop shells. Another enameled sheath is of a peculiarly intense light blue enamel, dotted with white enamel flowerets. It is a Louis XIII piece. Other enameled cases are English Battersea work in pink and green, with flowers. One shows a wee church and steeple. The Dutch favored silver sheaths, engraved to match the scissors themselves. Upon an eighteenth century French steel scissor case belonging to Mrs. De Witt Clinton Cohen is the following device:

> " *L'amour nous unie.*
> *Plutôt mourir que de changer.*
> *Si la foi manque, adieu l'amour.*
> *Je périrai plutôt.*"
>
> (Love unites us.
> Rather die than change.
> If faith lack, farewell love.
> I had sooner perish.)

So much for older cases. Newer ones come across the sea from China : satin cases embroidered with ideographs meaning long life, bats denoting happiness, quaint pointed peaches symbolizing longevity, and little grotesque creatures — the dog of Fo, et cetera. These two-sided sheaths are bound together by a tiny row of triangles made up of two or three stitches each, known as *dogtooth* edging.

Utilitarian cases come of the familiar Shaker type of bronzed kid, bound with brown silk binding-tape; also of ordinary leather, bound by a tin edging, hairpin shaped. For a steady sewer, a fountain-pen or pencil sheath of common, stitched leather, with a safety-pin behind to attach the case to one's waist or skirt, makes a very handy scissor-holder. Seamstresses frequently tie the two opposite ends of a long ribbon to the two scissor handles, and putting the doubled ribbon round

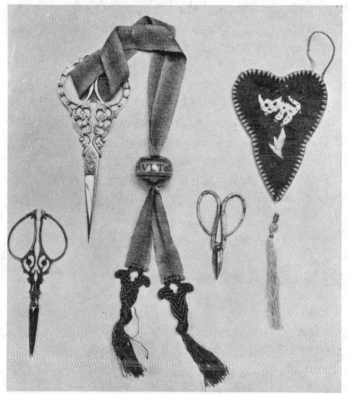

From the collection of Mrs. De Witt Clinton Cohen, New York

1. TYPICALLY DESIGNED OLD STEEL DIJON SCISSORS. [HALF SIZE.]
2. ITALIAN STEEL SCISSORS WITH OLD MAJOLICA RONDELLE OR BEAD — INSCRIBED *AD MULTOS ANNOS*, OR LONG LIFE — FORMERLY GIVEN BY VILLAGE LADS TO THEIR FAVORITES TO USE AS TIPS ON THEIR SPINDLES. [HALF SIZE.]
3. SMALL CHINESE STEEL SCISSORS AND EMBROIDERED SILK CASE WITH TASSEL. [HALF SIZE.]

their waists, slip the scissors through the noose. Thus the blades cannot dangle dangerously open, and the scissors are at hand.

The romantic appeal of the scissor grinder is indicated in the following lines, entitled the *Lay of the Scissor-Grinder,* by Augusta de Bubuna:

" Out in the summer sunshine fair,
   The scissor-grinder with silvery hair
   Goes on his way, the hand-bell rings
   As he trudges along, and softly sings
   While he stops to sharpen the cold dull steel
   On the roughened stone of the whirling wheel,
   And the people who loiter along their way
   Smile at the scissor-grinder's lay.
   ' Oh life,' he sings, ' is a tangled thread,
   It's being born, and it's lying dead;
   It's loving much, and it's being wed;
   Then it's smiling — or shedding tears instead;
   And there's knots, and there's twisted, crooked ends
   In the work Dame Nature to some of us sends,
   And we ofttimes wish for sharp scissors to clip
   The uneven edges of our workmanship;

" ' But the world it goes round, and round, and round;
     And it's morning and noon, and then follows the night;
   And the earth's but a wheel in immeasurable space,
     Revolving through darkness and blinding light,
   And it's down and up, and up and down,
     And it's sunshine and shadow, all through and through,
   And the wheel ne'er stops turning, but ever rolls on
     With a rhythm exquisitely, perfectly true;
   But the power that guides and directs and attends
     This wonderful wheel in our human life,
   With its tangled threads and twisted ends,
     Its pleasures and joys, its war and strife,
   Ah, that is the hand that sharpens to smite,
     Only when *needed* it so must be.
   For us it is meet but to see the *Right*
     In all that is ordered by such decree! '
   And the old man ceases his work and song.
     ' His task is done,' then the people say:
   ' Oh wise are the words, and true and strong,
     Of the scissor-grinder, old and gray! ' "

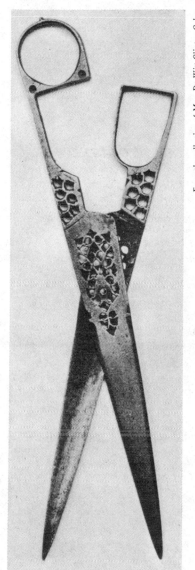

OLD PERFORATED TURKISH STEEL SCISSORS WITH UNIQUE HANDLES OF UNEVEN LENGTH. [SLIGHTLY REDUCED.]

From the collection of Mrs. De Witt Clinton Cohen

From the collection of Mrs. De Witt Clinton Cohen

EIGHTEENTH-CENTURY FRENCH HAND-WROUGHT STEEL SCISSORS WITH INLAID GOLD HANDLES, BELOW WHICH A SERIES OF APERTURES SUGGEST A FLEUR-DE-LIS. THE CENTRE OF THE SCISSORS AND THE RIDGE OF THE BLADES ARE INLAID WITH SILVER WIRE, AND THE INSIDES OF THE BLADES ARE SLIGHTLY HOLLOWED. [SLIGHTLY REDUCED.]

SCISSORS TO GRIND, SCISSORS TO GRIND!

" Without rasour or sisoures."
                                        —*House of Fame:* Geoffrey Chaucer.

*" Wanting the Scissors, with these hands I'll tear
(If that obstructs my Flight) this load of Hair."*
                                        —*Henry and Emma:* Matthew Prior.

*" Knives to grind, good masters,
   Sweet mistresses, scissors to grind."*

*" We lawyers, like shears so keen,
   Ne'er cut ourselves, but what's between."*

*" An old river lay like a broad band of silver . . .   And the great pink-throated
cranes that came and mounted on the mossed pebbles at its bend seemed not to cut
with the sharp scissors of their slender pointed beaks the imperturbable smoothness
of its glass."*
                                        —*The Feast of Lanterns:* Louise Jordan Miln.

WORKBASKETS, WORKBAGS, WORKBOXES AND TABLES

" I have a little workbox that Grannie gave to me.
It's pink and blue with ribbons, and lots inside to see.
' For my busy little seamstress,' said Grannie, low and sweet.
' And my Dear, 't will please me if you keep it nice and neat.' "

— Louise J. Kirkwood.

THIS title presents perhaps a prosaic picture: but think of the multitudinous bag forms — practical, quaint or clever; of the dignified boxes dug from ruins and installed in museums for our delectation and copying; of eastern boxes, lacquered, carved, inlaid; of primitive baskets from the far North, the heart of torrid Africa, or our own cunning craft designers; of sweet, simple colonial sewing tables, dainty intriguing ones from pre-Revolutionary France, and imperial princesses' sewing tables from Napoleonic days! Is there indeed no lure, no flavor in this worthy quartette?

Most baskets, old or new, can be utilized as one or another sort of sewing basket; barring, of course, the extremes of age, immensity, microscopic tininess and peculiarity of shape. Therefore it adds to one's interest, I think, to know a little of basketry and of its antiquity and to have some notion or hint of the provenance of one's workbasket and the meaning of its design.

In basketry we begin with nature itself — mostly even with that very early phase of nature that delighted in swamps and marshes — for the materials that enter into basketry are reeds and osiers, rushes and grasses, generally swamp grasses. And long ago among many, perhaps all, primitive folk, were these materials twisted, twined and intertwined to form cording, carrying bottoms, and mats. Carrying bottoms make acceptable worktrays or wide-mouthed baskets, as the case may be. Hottentots are skilful weavers of plant roots, while the yellow race is clever in split bamboo basketry. A few of the Hottentot

51

baskets have been brought home by travelers, and many Asiatic baskets are obtainable in modern American shops.

But our own Redskins have never been excelled in the art of forming baskets, coarse and fine, solid enough to hold water, or shallow with decorative interstices, for gaming — these too making good trays for spools, scissors, et cetera. Our fifty- or sixty-odd different North American tribes, not to mention those to the great southward, have used many varying materials, according to locality and desired effect. Dye formulas were passed from mother to daughter, who plucked, carried, scraped and steamed various bulbs and barks, or dried stems and crushed and pulverized flowers for their coloring matter. So the red woman's labor has entertained, perhaps inspired, as well as assisted the white woman in her tasks. Amerind designs are endlessly interesting. A square-stepped zigzag may mean the valley, then the plain and the mountain; upon one step may appear a whirling tornado in the form of a hollow spinning top; men will stand elsewhere, and deer too perhaps. In one tribe a circle will always be a male emblem, and lines or bands a feminine sign. Therefore it is of interest to learn the tribal origin of one's basket in order to trace its symbolism. A little wriggly line sometimes indicates a snake; a long upturned V, a horse. Certain Indians make birch baskets completely covered with bold plain embroidery of ivory-like porcupine quills that shade slightly toward their base. These dainty white specimens are appropriate if a small sewing kit be needed upon a dressing table. Brown birch-bark baskets are also embroidered — generally, though, with stained quills. Besides the fascinating and endless tribal baskets, done with care and dyed with vegetable colors — rare pieces well worth owning — there are many temporary modern pieces, made without regard to old symbolic pattern, and dyed with aniline colors that fade and run. County fairs are full of libels upon the art of fine basketry. This art is capable, though, of immense development.

Without studying long enough to become professional — sure of hand and eye — one can nevertheless make oneself a simple basket. Even the blind, though far away from training centres, have this opportunity, for there is a book on the subject embossed in Braille and written by Mary White Talbot.

The Mexican *petaca* and the similar telescoping flat straw envelopes of Hawaii are very useful as little traveling housewives. Large covered baskets are splendid for the household mending that must be done gradually through the week, while the old double melon-shaped splint basket of Virginia is easy to take out into the woods or into a canoe with one's knitting and perhaps a few goodies.

The Japanese do not use wrist bags, but *furoshiki,* on which they spend much artistic skill. A *furoshiki* is just a great firm but supple silk handkerchief, carried in the bosom of one's kimono until needed, then brought out and tied around one's goods, opposite corner to opposite corner, as a peddler ties his pack or a tramp does up his few belongings in a bandana. Now, in olden time such a practice somewhere in the world gave rise to the invention of the more orderly tied-up bag.

There seems some indication too that the sack or silk pouch to contain the back hair gave rise to our bag, which serves so many uses, among them that of the sewing sack.

Now, though I do not know what the Igorrotes call them, I know that besides a handsomely woven G-string, a hill man of the Philippines wears a horizontally striped white and black bag with very long cotton fringe and a heavily coiled brass wire handle. This he slips under the side of his sash string, thereby not only suspending the bag to free his hands, but also drawing it up high so that nothing is apt to spill out. The heavy handle counterweights it. To match this handle, a real brave wears from calf to ankle a concave tapering coil of even heavier brass wire; while his women folk sport similar *bracelets* from elbow to wrist. The bags, however, are useful to us as well as to the tribesmen, and are being extensively copied in colors and more practical proportions by Bishop Brent's Easter School at Baguio — even the town name seems appropriate to our interests!

Handsomely embroidered — old and copied — Greek cuffs are being stitched up nowadays into alluring bags for us practical moderns.

All sorts of beautiful bags are being embroidered in Italy by the Industrie Femminile, the Aemilia Ars, the San Georgio and other splendid societies for the promotion and preservation of fine stitchery.

Amusing little white kid circular-bottomed pouches, red underneath, with brass cut-outs, similar to stencils, of dairy processions laid over the red leather, can be picked up around Appenzell, Switzerland.

Such bags are intended to hold the cowherd's tobacco, but may be otherwise used by iconoclastic Americans.

Our Cree Indians are making some gored and several-sided suede bags, edged and tasseled with distinctive beads, usually white on gray or black leather, that are most acceptable for various dressy purposes. These bags are somewhat melon-shaped and are sold at "Harvey's"

From the author's collection

HENNA RED, SAGE GREEN AND BLACK LACQUERED BETEL-NUT BOX AND TRAYS FROM THE IRRAWADDY RIVER VILLAGE OF MYITCHIE IN BURMA. THE CYLINDRICAL SET IS BUILT UP OF SPIRALLY WOUND HORSE-HAIR HELD IN PLACE BY STRONG GUMS UNDER THE INTRIGUING COAT OF LACQUER. THE BOX, NATURALLY, IS SOMEWHAT PLIABLE, THOUGH SEVERE PRESSURE WOULD CRACK THE SURFACE. THE TWO SHALLOW TRAYS REST ONE ABOVE THE OTHER IN THE BASE, EACH COMPARTMENT INTENDED TO CARRY A SEPARATE INGRE-DIENT — LEAF, NUT, LIME — OF THE OMNIPRESENT EASTERN "CHEWING GUM"; WHILE THE FEATHER-WEIGHT LID, WHICH CAN BE BLOWN OR LIFTED OFF BY A STRONG EXPIRATION FROM BELOW, FITS DOWN OVER THE WHOLE. THIS SET WOULD MAKE AN ENTERTAINING COMPARTMENT WORKBOX.

along the Santa Fe railroad. Of course there are many other sorts of Indian beaded pouches.

Burma weaves an effective typical square bag with shoulder straps. Many travelers purchase these.

All of these sacks, large or small, square or curved, are practical for either extensive household sewing or portable embroidery suitable to take along when going on a visit.

Bags with large circular bases are handier — because one's spools, thimble, scissors, lie spread out in sight upon a floor — than bags sewed up without a bottom, causing one to fumble about in the dark or dump out the bag's roly-poly contents.

Sacks with various inside pockets are temper saving. Moreover, there is a clever over-arm bag that *is* in a way pockets. To make it, take a long, broad ribbon — a rich or pretty one, of course — say, two feet long. Turn in each end one inch, one to the right, one to the left, and place the turn-ins face to face. Then gather them together and secure the thread. That is the over-arm strip, or handle. Of a plain colored ribbon, narrower and harmonizing with the main piece, make two equal-sized, but smaller bags to serve as pockets, with draw strings to tie up their separate contents. At the base of your over-arm sling, measuring carefully, set in the pockets. One pocket's edges will be whipped along one edge of the sling, with the pocket opening facing, of course, upward toward the gathered handle ruff. The other pocket should be overcast to the opposite edge of the big ribbon. Between the little sacks now appears a bigger pouch, an excellent nest for a ball of yarn or gaping socks.

Two convenient little sewers' sacks to take when going away from home are the open-ended one of attractive ribbon with a whalebone in each hem to hold the bag's mouth flat and closed, but to allow of slipping therein cut-off bits of thread and other scraps; and the small rubber envelope in which to keep a moist wrung-out washcloth for wiping one's fingers.

Boxes are so many, so various — stunning and strong, miraculously inlaid and carved, handsomely tooled and lacquered — that I know not where to begin my description of them; so I shall just start at the apparent commencement by explaining that Latin had a word *buxus*, meaning boxwood or anything made of boxwood. *Buxus* in Old High German became *buhsa* and in German *Büchse*. In Anglo-Saxon it was *box*. In very early days it applied — boxwood indeed has a small trunk or stem; so nothing of size can be made from it — only to small receptacles.

If boxes were only lidless trays, we could satisfy our general passion for collecting them *ad libitum* by piling them in nests. Do men, I wonder, have the same instinct for hoarding bottles and boxes? Of course we know that many of them longed for a row of quaint and grotesque rum bottles!

You have probably seen in Sorrento heavenly blue boxes inlaid with minutest blue and white mosaic? Mr. L. Ettlinger has a remarkable set of Sorrento fan and jewel boxes inlaid in well-toned colors

From the author's collection   *From the author's collection*

Left: THREE-PIECE BROWN CHINESE BASKET WITH BROWN SILK TASSELS, AMBER BEADS AND OLD "CASH" COINS, ALL TOPPED BY A LUCKY IVORY ELEPHANT. THIS DIVIDED ARRANGEMENT FORMS EXCELLENT COMPARTMENTS FOR SEWING MATERIALS. [GREATLY REDUCED.]

Right: SMALL PORTABLE TRASH BAG OF FANCY RIBBON, FOR THREAD ENDS AND SNIPS OF CLOTH THAT NEED TO BE NEATLY DISPOSED OF WHILE ONE MAY BE DOING FANCYWORK IN A FRIEND'S DRAWING-ROOM, AT AN AFTERNOON TEA, A CLUB MEETING, ET CETERA. THIS BAG HAS WHALEBONE RUN INTO ITS TWO TOP HEMS, THE TWO BONES BEING EASILY PUSHED APART WITH ONE HAND, YET HAVING A TENDENCY TO SNAP TOGETHER AND KEEP ANYTHING FROM SPILLING OUT.

upon black. There is, however, very little black, for this set of the Empress Eugenie's is full of boxes and drawers and gaming boards and mirror frames and pigeonholes, intricately fitted together so that one front presents a desk; the other, a toilet or boudoir table; all exquisitely inlaid above, below, in front and at the back.

I have my grandmother's old buhl box of inlaid brass and tortoise-shell. Another she used is made from the handsome bird's-eye of a chestnut brown knot of wood, inlaid with mother-of-pearl. These boxes have lost their contents.

The Chinese offer us a host of beautiful boxes in which to treasure our sewing utensils — long, low red cases covered with a network of lucky gold gammadions or swastikas; and another kind that, like the early, original box, tends to be small. For a fabulous sum, however, one may purchase such a piece of chest dimension. But the circular and gracefully rounded medium-sized cinnabar lacquer box is the most appealing for fine embroidery in the making. The boxes themselves are covered with deep-cut patterns of gorgeous flowers — all Chinese red or henna on a ground of the same. Such a piece of the prized type takes forty years to make! The box itself is built up of layer after layer of pure lacquer similar in composition to shellac, upon a thin, solid base. Each coat of lacquer slowly dries and is covered by another, till sufficient firmness and thickness has been obtained to chisel it in deep relief. Black-and-gold lacquer, all-gold lacquer and egg-shell lacquer boxes are also obtainable from China and Japan.

The Chinese cover chests, tiny and great, with skin, generally scraped pigskin, quaintly painted. These chests have ponderous brass locks of the amusing, horizontally barred, Chinese padlock type. When big, such chests — some quilted inside, some of planed camphor wood — are excellent for storing embroideries and lace.

In stunning old Forde Abbey, England, I saw a room with great, graduated, intricately cut-out, highly polished brass chests; lined, I think, with wood. Great-grandfather, grandfather, father, son and grandson chests were each and all exactly alike, except in size.

The Spanish *vargueno*, with its myriad carved, or ivory and ebony inlaid, small drawers, all behind safe cupboard doors, is a handsome and excellent piece of furniture for the careful keeping of lace and embroidery. These Spanish desks are very elegant.

One of the department-store imported traveling jewel cases of fine crushed leather, fitted with adjustable trays and carrying handle, makes also a most convenient and encouraging workbox; for it cheerfully displays its ample base and extends on either side its four trays, two by two, at the opposite edge of the box, like some trunks that boast self-lifting trays, each elevated above and beyond its neighbor.

Tables long ago were mere slabs of stone, bowls upon tripods, and "bords" upon trestles: but tables as we know them, and particularly sewing tables, are rather recent. May I quote from among the first notes I have found concerning ladies' worktables?

Mr. Luke Vincent Lockwood, writing of the Heppelwhite and Sheraton period, says: "Delicate little sewing tables are to be seen in both these fashions, the tops of which are sometimes arranged to lift, disclosing a [flat] cabinet with compartments designed to fit sewing utensils of all kinds. Another familiar arrangement has a drawer with the compartments, and just beneath, a frame to which is attached a silk or velvet bag; the frame pulls out like a drawer, and the bag is thus held open, making a very convenient repository for needlework of all kinds."

Mrs. Frances Clary Morse tells us of a Sheraton table she had that was circular, with little bronze feet. Such tables had three drawers, the two upper ones opening with a spring and revolving upon a pivot. In these little drawers, Mrs. Morse continues, may still sometimes be seen the beads from the time — about 1800 — when it was fashionable for young ladies to make bead bags. The table top has an opening in the centre — similar to the traveling jewel box with its spread-out trays — which originally had a wooden cover, and the space below was intended to hold one's sewing. At the rear of the top are two short, turned posts supporting a little shelf meant to hold a candlestick or the silver sewing-bird that was used by needlewomen of those days.

"Another style of worktable shows a curious octagon-shaped stand, with the sides of the octagon-shaped interior divided into little boxes for sewing materials. The middle compartment extends down into the eight-sided pillar. The workboxes are covered by the top of the table, which lifts upon hinges."

Mrs. Giles Whiting has a handsome Empire sewing table with a central leg, bearing out somewhat the appearance of clustered Roman fasces in an effect of brass rods. The corners of the square polished wooden base terminate in handsomely wrought brass lions' feet. The table top too is square, with brass rim finishes. The lid is lined with a mirror; while inside are compartments for many fine sewing tools, as well as some wee gilt-finished glasses or "thimbles," to bear stimulus to weary workers. This table is a legacy from the octogenarian daughter of the lord keeper of London's tower.

Triple-topped Queen Anne tables are useful for sewing that involves the use of many different stuffs or implements, for three separate shelves are thus at hand. And the pie-crust table too appeals, since spools or bobbins cannot roll off to the floor.

Rolling suggests two other items — churns and lapboards. The former are old-fashioned too, but are nowadays being converted, in Connecticut, into three-legged worktables. This conversion requires, of course, the tub or horizontal barrel-shaped churn, not the upright kind. Upon removing the painted wooden lid, one discovers a gay silk lining tacked in place, and a variety of handy pockets. As to the lapboard, we all know the stationary sort; but separate, fitted sticks stuck firmly to a muslin back and capable of rolling up for transportation are also obtainable.

I did not mention Martha Washington saddlebag worktables, for everyone knows them, and the market is flooded with such popular modern pieces — very useful indeed; nor the high-legged, ponderous marble-topped table, still extant, but too tall and too slippery for a sewer.

Has the working quartette not proved true to its title — very workaday indeed, yet capable, as promised, of interest and variety to anyone wishing to go on a treasure hunt for fine equipment? This is a favorite pastime of visitors to Paris, who are wont to seek out the *monts de piété* in a search for rare *bibelots*. But one need not indeed confine her search to Paris!

WORKBASKETS, WORKBAGS, WORKBOXES AND TABLES

> "*Yet since his neighbors give, the churl unlocks,*
> *Damning the poor, his triple-bolted box.*"
> —J. Warton.

> "*Was not the basket even of Helen of Troy tipped with gold?*"

> "*Down went the blue-frilled workbasket, dispersing on the floor reels, thimble, muslin.*"
> —*Felix Holt:* George Eliot.

"*Think how nice it would be, when Mother is busy with her sewing and mending, to sit beside her on a little low chair and help her with that big sewing basket overflowing with work!*"

—*Illustrated Sewing Primer:* Louise J. Kirkwood.

"*A girl bends over her sewing. How small she is, a mere child! Yet it is not for the making of doll clothes that she toils hour after hour. She is preparing for marriage, this tiny maid, who must stand on tiptoe to lift the lid of her great oaken dowry chest.*

"*She is sewing a shirt. It is an old tradition that for a wedding to be happy the bride must make her husband's bridal shirt with her own hands. She wonders what manner of man will wear the garment. Will he be gentle, bold, a laughing youth or a crabbed old man? It is not for her to choose.*

"*It is for her only to sew, to spin, to dye, to weave, to fill the chest.*

"*Who is this girl? Is her name Helga, Deirdre or Guinevere? Gretchen, Yvonne, Nausicaa? In what country does she sew and spin? In ancient Ireland or Scandinavia? Homer's Greece? Germany or France of the Middle Ages? The England of Queen Elizabeth?*

"*She is of all countries: the child-woman who fashions articles of use and beauty for her bridal chest.*

"*The girl of our time, too, dreams of nest-building. And as the father of the old-time maiden threw about his child the protection of a marriage dower, so the father of our century prepares his daughter for her wedding day by gifts of gold and silver, of linen and lace. It is a pretty and convenient observance of an old tradition to accumulate these treasures in a hope-chest.*

"*See, then, the chest which a wife of to-day has brought to her modern apartment. It speaks of strange, dark times when women were chattels. But its owner is no chattel. Her husband is of her own choosing. He is not a master, but a friend. Her marriage is a partnership of equals.*"

— "*Hope-Chests*": *The Girl Scouts Report, 1925.*

"*And bags by the way, are so useful! I have one full of left-over linens; another, of skeins of silk; a third, of extra utensils; a fourth, of common sewing things; and so on; not to mention a fancy workbag to take about with me; a street bag for small purchases; a coin or a treasure bag; a picnic bag; a hat bag and suitcases!*"

RARE VERY EARLY STONE NEEDLE
PUSHER FROM EGYPT.

THIMBLE, THIMBLE, WHO HAS THE THIMBLE?

" Come hider to me, sone, and look whedir
In this purs ther be any croyse or crouche,
Sauf nedel and threde and themel *of lether."*

— Thomas Occleve.

THIS chapter opens with the picture of a needle pusher; my own first sewing lessons opened a similar chapter, for I refused to be encumbered with what seemed to me a clumsy addition to nature. So I pushed the needle till I wore, at first a sore little hole, then a callous spot on the tip of my finger. My wish to be able to have dolls' clothes, which a wise aunt forbade unless I made them, kept me from ceasing to stitch, while pride kept me from accepting the aid I had scorned. Till a few years ago a queer little discolored hollow was still visible upon my finger. Did our ancestral seamstresses all bear such trade-marks till they too learned properly to protect themselves?

Probably the earliest form of finger protection was a shield of bone or wood bound on the finger. Open-ended bronze thimbles have been found among the ruins of Herculaneum, and two ancient bronze

61

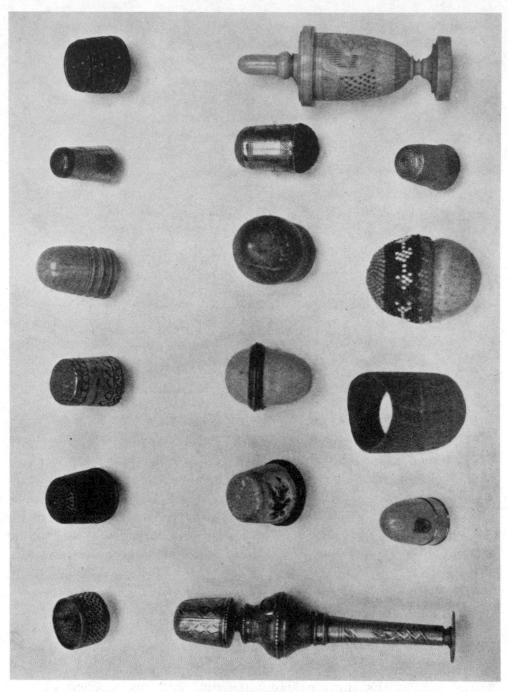

(See following page for titles.)

thimbles with tips are to be found in the Genevieve collection. These may be some two thousand years old. Great Britain boasts the two Briton words *Byswain,* meaning finger-guard, and *Gwniadur,* or sewing-steel, which would rather indicate that the early natives of the British Isles used at least a primitive thimble in sewing their probably pretty tough skin garments. Bright golden bronze and brass thimbles are said to have been dug up in 1856 with some Roman remains off Dowgate on the Thames. One was an open ring with the usual tiny indentations; the others, with caps, were much more acutely conical than any thimble since medieval times. The tips were smooth, but the sides were finely pitted; the bases, however, were finished off with plain bands.

In spite of discoveries and proofs of early metallic "thimmels" or "thimbils," the Middle Ages still found Central Europe using leather "thummels," called in the fourteenth century "themels." Such leathern specimens, sewed up one side, and with a stitched-on cap, are still occasionally to be found in the South of Ireland.

VARIOUS FORMS OF THIMBLES

Top Row, Left to Right

a. CHINESE SILVER SEWING BAND OR OPEN THIMBLE.

b. OLD RUSSIAN BRASS THIMBLE, PIERCED AT APEX. FREQUENTLY TRADED WITH THE HINDUS AND ARABS, WHO MADE THE THIMBLES INTO BELLS AND SEWED THEM TO THE EDGES OF THEIR CHAMOIS BURNOUSES.

c. MODERN NAVAJO INDIAN SILVER THIMBLE.

d. OLD FRENCH IVORY THIMBLE.

e. OLD ENGLISH SLIM SILVER THIMBLE WITH IRON TOP OR CAP, THE WHOLE BELONGING IN THE PINK BATTERSEA BOX SHOWN AT *i.*

f. RUSSIAN IRON BAND WITHOUT CAP.

Middle Row, Left to Right

g. OLD ENGLISH SILVER POMANDER OR POWDER-SHAKER, USED TO KEEP THE HANDS DRY WHILE SEWING. THE BASE IS AN ENGRAVED SEAL; THE TOP IS CAPPED WITH A THIMBLE. INSIDE ARE A SILK-WINDER AND A NEEDLE-CASE.

h. OLD PINK BATTERSEA THIMBLE WITH FLORAL DESIGN.

i. OLD ENGLISH PINK BATTERSEA THIMBLE-CASE.

j. BRONZE THIMBLE OF 300 B.C., EXCAVATED IN SYRIA.

k. OLD ENGLISH PEWTER THIMBLE CONTAINING A BLUE VELVET EMERY, CAPPED WITH A REAL ACORN TOP.

l. OLD DELICATELY CARVED URN-SHAPED FRENCH IVORY *NÉCESSITÉ* FOR THIMBLE AND SCISSORS.

Bottom Row, Left to Right

m. OLD FRENCH MOTHER-OF-PEARL THIMBLE WITH PANSY AND BANDS OF GOLD.

n. OLD ALASKAN CARVED THIMBLE USED ON THUMB. BONE, WITH MARROW REMOVED.

o. OLD IVORY CASE WITH TOP OF TINY PINK AND GREEN BEADS, CONTAINING IVORY THIMBLE.

p. THIN OLD GOLD FRENCH THIMBLE.

Like the earliest of finger guards, sailors' thummels were worn on the thumb, as the particular spelling of their variety of thimble indicates, and were, and still are, rings — generally of bone — rather than domes, with small disc-like expansions or plates, similar to those on seal rings, in which occur small depressions or crisscross scratches to catch and steady the needle. Modern marine thummels, now known as " sailors' palms," resemble leather bracelets. The metal thimble itself is a flat disc, sharply, coarsely cross-barred or pitted, and about the size of a five-cent piece. A rim of worn, discolored leather, formed

A   B   C   D

A: SILVER THIMBLE INLAID WITH CORAL. *Owned by Miss Florence Loder, New York City.* B: MODERN GOLD THIMBLE FROM PARIS, WITH SQUARE INDENTATIONS AND A BORDER SHOWING MAIDENS SPINNING AND SEWING. DESIGNED BY VERNON AND EXECUTED BY THE MAISON J. DUVAL IN 1900 AS PRESIDENT KRUGER'S WEDDING GIFT TO QUEEN WILHELMINA. *From the author's collection.* C: MODERN SILVER GILT THIMBLE. *From the author's collection.* D: WORLD WAR SILVER LIBERTY-BELL THIMBLE, INSCRIBED "PROCLAIM LIBERTY IN THE LAND TO THE INHABITANTS * * * * * BY ORDER OF THE ASSEMBLY OF PENNSYLVANIA IN PHILADELPHIA 1752." *From the author's collection.*

like the wrist-holder for a watch, surrounds the old salt's thimble, holding it over the palm of his thumb. The leather palm is steadied by two openings — one large, for the hand; the other smaller and more circular, for only the thumb; with a thimble pad placed just below the dividing bridge.

The claim that Holland invented the thimble seems a bit absurd, but I submit one or two statements on the subject.

N. Hudson Moore, in *The Lace Book*, 1904, says: "To the Dutch is given the credit of inventing many things. They claim the invention of the thimble." A similar statement has been made by Haydn in his *Dictionary of Dates*, 1855: "The art of making them was brought to England by John Lofting, a mechanic from Holland, who set up a workshop in Islington, near London, and practised the manufacture of them in various metals, with profit and success, about 1695."

These dates, you naturally notice, are rather modern, after what we have just read. What really is meant, perhaps, is that the Dutch invented some special thimble-making device; but the statements concerning it are too broad and inaccurate.

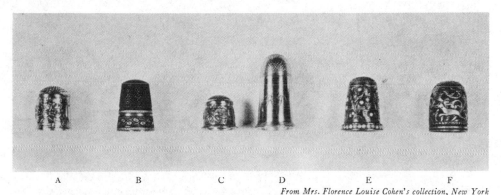

A   B   C   D   E   F

From Mrs. Florence Louise Cohen's collection, New York

A: AN ELABORATE STEEL AND RED GOLD DESIGN ON A PALE YELLOW GOLD THIMBLE. B: A TOLEDO THIMBLE OF OXIDIZED STEEL AND GOLD. C AND D: A DIMINUTIVE AND AN EXTRA TALL GOLD THIMBLE WITH INITIALS. E: A SCROLLED RUSSIAN SILVER THIMBLE PROFUSELY SET WITH POLISHED TURQUOISES. F: A VERY VALUABLE OLD STEEL THIMBLE.

Two other brass examples found along the Thames River, at London Bridge, in 1846, show, one, a band with an eleven-pointed star; the other, a motto — "God save the Qvene." And Don Saltero's Coffee House at Chelsea had a thimble, marked "I wis it better," from the ruins of Stocks Market. Curt phrases such as these were popular in England during the reign of Good Queen Bess.

In the seventeenth century a coppery brass mixture was created, called "Prince Rupert's metal." This also was used in thimble-making.

Fine French steel thimbles, with all-over vine or scroll patterns and pitted backgrounds, are quite valuable. Rarer, though, are French iron thimbles. The pretty thimbles in shagreen, especially in galuchat boxes, are presumably French. The cases sometimes are more attractive, however, than their contents.

Thimbles of boxwood have been made in Germany. Venice manufactured them out of glass!

Russian thimbles are apt to be rich in metal. They have, by peoples of adjoining territories, been put to other than their original uses, for in Asia they are found, adapted, by piercing, to purposes of decoration. The egg-shaped gold thimble-case shown in the picture is quite deeply and exotically chased and cut.

Not only are Russian thimbles sewn like little dangling metal bells

From the collection of Mrs. De Witt
Clinton Cohen, New York

A GOLD THIMBLE IN
FINE RARE OLD SOFT DEEP
GREEN SKIN CASE.

From the collection of Mrs. De Witt Clinton Cohen, New York

1. HANDSOME OLD RUSSIAN GOLD EGG, RICHLY CHASED WITH BIRDS
AND FLOWERS. INTENDED TO HOLD A THIMBLE, NEEDLES AND PINS.
2 AND 3. OLD YELLOWED BONE THIMBLE CASES.

upon the borders of some Siberian and Mongolian garments, but so are white, pink and blue celluloid thimbles used to advantage by our Indians for sartorial purposes. An acquaintance remarked that upon walking through the American Museum of Natural History something caught her eye as both familiar and strange. She noted an Indian garment, with slashed fringing I believe, but for a few moments failed to analyze the puzzling familiarity as a systematic and graduated ornamentation of colored thimbles skilfully blended with native decoration!

I dreamed, one night, of an imaginary Russian thimble-case, dome-shaped like the bulbous top of a Russian church tower. Its plump little round base was of polished gray steel, while the curved narrowing peak was of separated bars of gold, diminishing in breadth till they joined at the tip. The base of each bar was welded to the steel in a triangular point, like French godets let into a dress skirt, one bar base just adjoining the next. Along the edge of each gold band ran two tiny lines of fine chasing, while between the bars one caught glimpses of the precious thimble housed within.

In 1701 Marguerite Leconte, who married Bayley Pell, brought with her from France to New Rochelle a plain but dainty gold thimble with continuous dimpled tip and sides, the indentations running right down to the bottom of the thimble. It is now the treasured possession of Marguerite Leconte's great-great-granddaughter, Miss Mary M. Campbell, of Orange, New Jersey.

Then was introduced the rim finish at the base of the thimble; and the more modern silver implement, often decorated, as in Elizabeth's day, with posies and verses, came into full swing.

Finger shields, too, were invented. A finger shield, to quote the description in the *Dictionary of Needlework*, is:

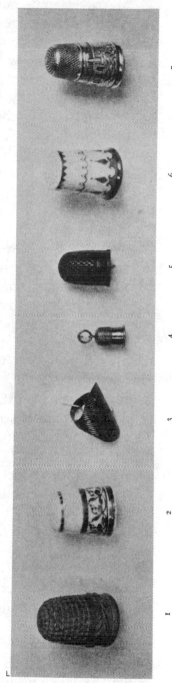

1. CLUMSY MELLOW OLD BONE THIMBLE. *From the collection of Mrs. De Witt Clinton Cohen.*

2. ENGLISH CHINA THIMBLE WITH GREEN SCROLLS AND PINK BERRIES, THE INDENTATIONS BEING ALL GLAZED OVER. *From the collection of Mrs. De Witt Clinton Cohen.*

3. OLD SILVER CHILD'S, OR LITTLE FINGER, SHIELD FROM NEVIS, BRITISH WEST INDIES. *From the collection of Miss Isabel S. Huggins, New York.*

4. PETER PAN, IT MAY BE RECALLED, GAVE A THIMBLE AS A KISS TO LITTLE WENTY. THIS MINIATURE GOLD KISS WAS ORDERED AND GIVEN BY MISS MAUDE ADAMS, WHO SO SUCCESSFULLY IMPERSONATED PETER PAN, TO ONE OF HER FRIENDS. *From the collection of Mrs. De Witt Clinton Cohen, New York.*

5. A SMALL BLACKENED THIMBLE THAT SURVIVED THE BOSTON FIRE OF 1878. *From the collection of Mrs. De Witt Clinton Cohen.*

6. A ROYAL WORCESTER CHINA THIMBLE WITH DESIGN IN VIOLET AND GOLD, PITTED AT TOP ONLY. *Property of Miss Mary L. Van Lennep, New York.*

7. NARROW UPRIGHT SILVER THIMBLE, DEPICTING THE THAMES AND LONDON BRIDGE. *From the collection of Mrs. De Witt Clinton Cohen.*

"A silver appliance made to fit the first finger of the left hand, on which materials are laid and held by the thumb in plain sewing. It resembles a ring, one side being an inch wide, and the other quite as narrow as an ordinary finger ring. It is employed to protect the finger from the needle when much hard sewing has to be done, or the finger has been accidentally hurt."

The western thimble of to-day should be worn on the long finger of the right hand. It ought to fit, as someone said, as firmly and comfortably as the "Tam cap on your head."

Thimbles are now made in five successive operations to facilitate the stretching of the pressed steel or other metal, which must be of even thickness. Of course we are all familiar with the ordinary pink, white, and baby blue celluloid thimble of the present-day five-and-ten-cent store! The lava souvenir thimbles from volcanic countries are brittle and not very practical, although the word *lava,* of course, gives an impression of strength.

Not only Russian thimbles have been put to other than stitchery purposes — the *Century Dictionary* tells us that "Years ago there was one variety [of thimble] which little boys and girls knew as 'dame's thimell.' It was in constant use in the making of 'thimell-pie' or 'thimmy-pie,' the dame of the little schools then common in all villages using her thimble — a great iron one — upon the children's heads when punishment was necessary (giving a sharp tap or blow). This was called 'thimell-pie making,' and the operation was much dreaded."

Along with thimell-pie went, I regret to say, a punishment that "cut off its own nose," as it were: little stitchers who lagged had their thumbs slammed in the table drawer — as though black and blue or swollen thumbs would render backward hands more nimble!

When the day of pantalettes was on the wane, a Scotch maiden asked, since the other girls had quit wearing their pantalettes, that she might leave off hers. Her mother's shocked reply was an emphatic "No!" So missie ran downstairs; but before going out she rolled up the pantalettes. Mother, however, happened to be looking out of the window. Sharp raps of her thimble on the windowpane recalled the lass who had dared to uncover her calves! Another cannonade from the thimble turned her hesitating steps, and she knew that not only humble pie, but also mother's own thimell-pie, awaited her.

Prohibition may render "only a thimbleful" an expression somewhat of the past, though peg- or pony-sized silver thimbles are still to be had at the silversmith's.

And now one has, unfortunately, to add the description of a sleight-of-hand trick — thimblerigging — not always employed in the useful, innocent way one has come to think that a thimble should be. The trick is played with three small thimble-shaped cups and a tiny ball or pea. Hence the "little pea game." The ball or marble is placed on the table and covered with one of the cups. The prestidigitator

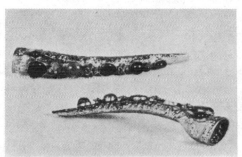 

Lent by Mrs. James P. Sneddon   *From the author's collection*

Left: CHINESE FINGER-NAIL GUARDS OF GOLD, SET WITH CARNELIANS AND KINGFISHER FEATHERS EMBEDDED IN LITTLE QUATREFOIL FORMS OF THE METAL. RECENTLY A CHINESE GRAND OPERA PRIMA DONNA SANG IN HONOLULU AT AN HONORARIUM OF $800 A MONTH. IN ONE OF HER RÔLES SHE WORE TEN FINGER-TIP PROTECTORS. NOW WE ARE TOLD THAT EACH OF TUT-ANKH-AMEN'S TOES AND FINGERS WAS ENCASED IN A GOLDEN SHEAF! [HALF SIZE.]

Right: A SAILOR'S PALM AND AN ADJUSTABLE CHINESE SILVER THIMBLE. [HALF SIZE.]

then starts moving the thimbles about, wagering that no one can tell under which little cover the pea is to be found; and the person who takes up the bet is not often allowed to win.

So having traced the history of thimbles and having described the occidental varieties thereof, together with related western customs, I am going to cross to the eastern continent to tell of two or three personal thimble episodes there.

Quite the reverse of shortened feet, the former owner of my Chinese thimble wore long nails. Short nails in the land of the Celestial are said to indicate manual labor. Thus sewing apparently is not manual.

My tailor too, though " a *work*man to sew clothes," favored long nails!
But a Chinese thimble is compatible with this custom, for it slips down
over the longest finger, to its second joint.   The thimble is topless,
a broad ring or band with a plain end and an unjoined, overlapping,
chiseled, strap-like one that can give to fit a plump wearer or, like a
spring, hold tightly upon a tiny digit.

My little Chinese thimble owner was making "melon seeds," or
tiny frog buttons, of the scraps from her baby's calico jacket, which
they would both fasten and adorn, without hurting the wearer or splitting in the wash.   We should do well to adopt "melon seeds."

I paused at the head of the old stone stairs where she sat, to watch
the sewer of seeds and learn her secret; and, lost in interest, was surprised, upon looking up, to find we were surrounded by onlookers as
eager to inspect the white woman as I was to scan my yellow sister!

Then came bargaining for the thimble — a sixteen to one propo-
sition (I really think there were more than that against me) and each
had a suggestion.   Twenty *cash* equal five cents: multiply that by a
hundred!   My mind was soon thoroughly muddled translating into
units the fractions suggested and demanded by audience and teacher,
but finally the pretty silver thimble was purchased for all of twenty
cents American!

Eleven blue Tam O'Shantered, red pomponned, sashed and goateed
Indian Lascars upon the Irrawaddy River were twisting, plaiting, sewing for the ship.   Two sat rolling hemp into a double-ply cord, thinning
the ends before introducing a new strand.   Two were making sennit
of the cord.   Some with two long, half-inch sticks were knitting this
cord into attractive door-mats.   Others were stitching the braid into
serpentine deck runners.   This required strong, three-sided needles;
pincers for pulling them through especially resistant spots; and to
each sewer, a sailor's thimble sunk into its pigskin bracelet.   After
threading a needle, the sailors untwisted slightly their Manila or other
cording to slip its end back through one or two loops.   This naturally
prevented unthreading.   Should the sailor be sewing sailcloth awn-
ings, as upon our ship, you would see him among a row of other double-
sashed Lascars, all standing and balancing upon planks raised high on
sawhorses, a few pushing their needles with the left hand, others with
the right, cigarette in mouth.   Some, with open jackknives between

their teeth, cobble-stitched or double-buttonholed our overhead canvas. Their thread was waxed and doubled, both to strengthen it and to prevent its slipping out of the needle. I saw a Chinese boatswain carrying to the stitchers the small end of a cow's horn, filled with wax pricked full of extra needles — a rust-preventing needlecase!

Even traveling about the opposite side of the globe, there were tourists mending with our humble (?) department-store self-threading needles. And do you not remember the fad for thimbles — much lauded and hawked at county fairs — with a device for facile threading, a protruding eye-guide at the edge?

From the collection of Mrs. De Witt Clinton Cohen, New York

OLD FRENCH APPLE-SHAPED CASE OF IVORY, CONTAINING
IVORY THIMBLE.

Now follows a globe-trotter's sad "it might have been" had the truth been known in time! It was Christmastide at Calcutta, and the thimble was enameled with translucent *red* flowers at that — real, luscious Indian red posies with some opaque white enameling on a gold ground. But it looked so bright and shiny that I mistook it for a made-in-quantity modern production and scorned the vendor's really not exorbitant price. Only later did I learn that such delicate yet sumptuous inlay is generally found but on the back of conscientiously executed jewelry of an age which took for granted excellent finish on wrong as well as right side!

And now, how many sorts of thimble has this double chapter shown us — leather, bone, ivory, wood, iron, brass, bronze, Prince Rupert's metal, silver, gold, madreperl, china, glass, and enamel work; from countries and cities scattered around the world—Herculaneum, Rome, Venice, Britain, Ireland, the Netherlands, France, Germany, Russia, Alaska, Arizona, together with China, Burma and India! Altogether an imposing array, and all to further stitchery, whether upon stout leather, coarse canvas, or the sheerest of tiffanies! A thimble perhaps for every stuff that is sewed, from East to West. Surely, one has little excuse, in the face of so many cleverly wrought accessories or assistants, to postpone that " stitch in time " !

THIMBLE, THIMBLE, WHO HAS THE THIMBLE?

THE THIMBLE

Allan Ramsay

" In tenui labor: at tenuis non gloria."

— Virg.

" What god shall I invoke to raise my song?
What goddess I of the celestial throng?
Shall bright Apollo lend to me his aid?
Shall chaste Lucina bring my muse to bed?
Oh! rather, greatest beauty of the sky!
I write for Lydia; hear your vot'ry's cry,
You gave your charms to her — What can you then deny?

" All o'er this globe, where Phœbus darts his rays,
What strange variety accosts our eyes!
We see how nations variously incline,
How different studies favour different men;
Some love to chase the fox throughout the day,
Others to dance the winter night away.
Unlike to these, some love the trumpet's sound,
And cries of men, when gasping on the ground;
To some, of fancy warm it gives delight,
Instructed by the muse's verse, to write
Of bards, some generals in fight rehearse,
Others with groves and fountains crowd their verse.
Greater than theirs has fallen to my share —
A theme sublimer far demands my care,
I sing the Thimble — armour of the fair.

"*Hail! Heaven-invented-engine! gift divine!*
You keep the tend'rest fingers free from pain.
Sing, lofty Muse, from whence the Thimble sprung —
The Thimble — safeguard of the fair and young.

"*In ancient times, ere mortals learnt the trade,*
Bright Venus for herself her mantles made.
As busied once, in Cyprian grove she sat,
Her turtles fondly sleeping at her feet,
With hands alone to sew the goddess tried,
Her wand'ring thoughts were otherwise employed;
When, — lo! her needle — strange effect of spite —
Wounded that skin it could not see so bright;
She starts, — she raves, — she trembles with the smart;
The point that pricked her skin, went to her heart.
Sharp pain would not allow her long to stop;
My doves, she cry'd, haste to Olympus' top;
The tim'rous beauty gets into her car,
Her pinioned bearers swiftly cut the air,
As quick as thought, they reach'd the sacred ground,
Where mighty Jove with Juno sat enthron'd.
What ails my child? to her then cried the god;
Why thus in tears? What makes you look so odd?
Would you a favour beg? — A while she stood,
Her ivory finger stain'd with purple blood;
Then thus: — Oh! father of the gods, she prayed,
Grant I may be invulnerable made!
With look sedate, returned the awful sire —
Daughter, you do not know what you desire;
Would you to Pluto's regions run?
Would you be dipt in Styx, like Thetis' son?
Could you unfrighted view Hell's dismal shore?
What shall I say then? — Go, and stitch no more.

"*Ashamed — unsatisfied — away she hies*
To try her fate again, beneath the skies.
Shall I, she said, while goddesses well drest,
Outshine each other at a birth-day feast;
Shall I in simple nakedness be brought,
Or clothed in rags? Intolerable thought!
No, rather may the blood my cheeks forsake,
And a new passage thro' my fingers take!

"*In fertile Sicily, well known to fame,*
A mountain stands, and Ætna is its name. —

Tremendous earthquakes rend the flinty rock,
And vomit forth continual fire and smoke:
Here, Vulcan forges thunderbolts for Jove
Here, frames sharp arrows for the God of Love;
His Cyclops with their hammers strike around,
The hollow caverns echo back the sound.

" *Here, Venus brought her pigeons and her coach,*
The one-eyed workmen ceased at her approach;
When Vulcan thus — My charmer! why so pale?
You seem prepared to tell some dismal tale.
Does fierce Tydides still his rage pursue?
Or has your son his arrows tried on you?
Oh! no. — What makes you bleed then? answer quick. }
Oh no, my lord, my husband! Know, a prick
Of needle's point has made me wond'rous sick. }
Fear not, my spouse! said Vulcan, ne'er again,
Never shall any needle give you pain.
With that the charming goddess he embraced,
Then in a shell of brass her finger cased.
This little engine shall in future days }
Continued he, receive the poet's praise, }
And give a fruitful subject for their lays; }
This shall the lovely Lydia's finger grace —
Lydia — the fairest of the human race!
He spoke — then, with a smile, the Queen of Love
Returned him thanks, and back to Cyprus drove.

" *When Venus, Lydia, with beauty blest,*
She granted her the thimble with the rest;
Yet cannot brass or steel remain for ay,
All earthly things are subject to decay.
Of Babel's tow'r, so lofty and so proud,
No stone remains to tell us where it stood;
The great, the wise, the valiant and the just,
Cæsar and Cato, are returned to dust;
Devouring Time to all destruction brings,
Alike the fate of Thimbles — and of Kings.
Then grieve not, Lydia! cease your anxious care,
Nor murmur lest your favorite Thimble wear.
All other thimbles shall wear out e'er long, }
All other thimbles, be they e'er so strong, }
Whilst yours shall live for ever — in my song." }

ON THE FOREGOING BY ——

"*Fair Lydia's Thimble, Ramsay! to thy name,*
Shall be a passport thro' the gates of Fame."

"*And now for a fling at your thimbles,*
  Your bodkins, rings and whistles,
    In truck for your toys,
    We'll fit you with boys,
  'Tis the doctrine of Hugh's Epistles.

"*To pull down their King,*
  Their plate they would bring,
    And other precious things:
  So that Sedgwick and Peters
  Were no small getters
    By their bodkins, thimbles and rings."
— *Collection of Loyal Songs:* compiled by Thomas Wright.

"*Cushy cow bonny, let down thy milk,*
  And I will give thee a gown of silk;
A gown of silk and a silver tee,[1]
  If thou wilt let down thy milk to me."
— *Mother Goose.*

"*They sought it with thimbles, they sought it with care;*
  They pursued it with forks and hope;
They threatened its life with a railway-share;
  They charmed it with smiles and soap."
— *The Hunting of the Snark:* Lewis Carroll.

"*The nobles being profuse in their contributions of plate for the service of the king (Charles I) at Oxford, while on the parliamentary side, the subscriptions of silver offerings included even such little personal articles as those that suggested the term the Thimble and Bodkin Army.*"
— *A History of Taxation and Taxes in England:* Stephen Dowell.

"*The legend that Minerva herself taught the Greeks the art of embroidery illustrates how deeply the art was understood; and the pretty story told by an old botanist of how the foxglove came by its name and its curious bell-like flowers is worth repeating. In the old Greek days, when gods and goddesses were regarded as having attributes of humanity in addition to those of deities, Juno was one day amusing herself with making tapestry, and, after the manner of the people, put a*

---

[1] *Tee* is a corruption of the archaic or provincial *dee*, a thimble, from the French *dé*.

thimble on her finger.   Jupiter, ' playing the rogue with her,' took her thimble and threw it away, and down it dropped to the earth.   The goddess was very wroth, and in order to pacify her, Jupiter turned the thimble into a flower, which now is known as Digitalis, or finger-stole."

" This little fairy tale can scarcely be taken as proof conclusive of the existence of either needle tapestry or thimble use, but its telling may amuse the reader."

— Chats on Old Lace and Needlework: Emily Leigh Lowes.

INSTRUMENTS OF PRECISION — MEASURES

"Even now a tailor called me to his shop, . . .
And therewithal took measure of my body."
— *Comedy of Errors:* Shakespeare.

ONE hears of a measure of oats and of giving scant measure; well, here is a scant measure of sempstress' measures — tape-measures, yardsticks, lap rules, mesh gauges, et cetera.

Mesur was a former English spelling of *measure;* the Spanish write *mesura;* the Portuguese, *mensure;* the Italians, *misura;* all coming from the Latin *mensura,* a measuring, a thing to measure by.

Gage is often spelled *gauge,* coming from the Middle English *gawgyn,* the French *jauger* and the Latin *gaugiare;* but we have also *jagalium* in Middle Latin. Really the origin of the word, and therefore its first spelling, is uncertain; though the last form just mentioned led to the measure of what can be held or contained — *jalea, jale* (a bowl), gill and gallon — rather than to general measurement, sometimes interior, sometimes exterior.

Dressmakers speak of a "gauged" or puckered skirt, meaning a skirt gathered at regular intervals.

A "gauging" thread is used by weavers to note a stop at some desired point. Such a thread is only temporarily introduced, later to be withdrawn.

Egypt certainly had mesh sticks over which to net the familiar mummy nets, sometimes so richly beaded or hung with little vivid faïence figures. These sticks, also called meshes or gauges, are really spacers — a big open-meshed net is formed or tied together over a broad fat stick, a fine net over a thin small stick that naturally does not spread apart the threads into large loose loops. Gauges are of wood, metal, bone, mother-of-pearl, et cetera.[1] They are numbered as to size in the same way as needles.

[1] The Tinguians use sticks and needles of bamboo and carabao horn.

Peru too may have used mesh gauges, though much old Peruvian net was presumably made, as were the fancier Egyptian nets, by a process age-old in Ruthenia and recently revived in Denmark, Holland, Norway and presumably Sweden. A stick in this instance is used to retain the threads in their respective positions, but not to measure and determine the distance between meshes.

From the collection of Mrs. De Wit Clinton Cohen

From the author's collection

Left: OLD GERMAN CARVED BOXWOOD TAPE-MEASURE, HIGHLY POLISHED, WITH A GROTESQUE PIVOTED HEAD THAT WINDS UP THE MARKED SILK RIBBON.

Centre: A PICTURESQUE OLD TAPE-MEASURE OF DEEPLY AGED BONE ON AN IVORY UPRIGHT.

Right: DYAK MESH STICK USED IN NETTING, FROM *LACIS* BY CARITA.

Gauges, or as the French say, *filières,* are made up in numberless forms for the measurement of knitting-needles. Most forms have a graduated series of numbered holes around the rim of a square or circular steel card. Wire-drawers too find these essential. They can usually be obtained at art needlework shops or at cutlers.

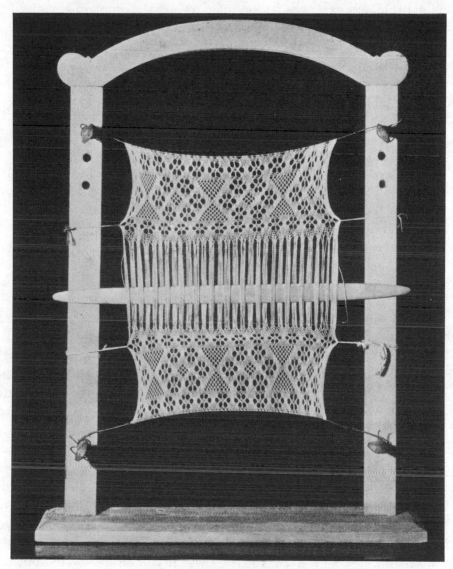

From the author's collection

CALL IT A LOOM, A FRAME, A STRETCHER — WHAT YOU WILL. A GREEK TERM HAS BEEN
APPLIED TO THE RECENTLY DISCOVERED SPINNING-KNEE OF GREECE, SO PERHAPS AN EGYPTIAN
WORD MEANING "STRETCHER-FRAME" SHOULD BE GIVEN TO THIS APPLIANCE. AS SHOWN IN
THE PICTURE, THE WIRES UNDER AND OVER WHICH THE THREAD IS FIRST SET UP CAN BE TIGHT-
ENED BY MEANS OF PEGS. BY MANIPULATING THE THREADS IN THE CENTRE — LIFTING ONE IN
FRONT OF THE OTHER — A DOUBLE STITCH IS PRODUCED, ONE ACCUMULATING ABOVE, A LIKE
ONE AT THE SAME TIME BELOW, IN THIS WAY FORMING WITH ONE SET OF OPERATIONS TWO
IDENTICAL STRIPS OF LACE. [QUARTER SIZE.]

Macramé workers need moreover a metal comb and a yard or metre measure, or better, a stiff ruler.

In Alaska one sees old yellowed bone sticks, straight along one edge, slightly curved along the other, neatly marked or notched for measuring. The incisions have browned with age, and the bone has become delightfully polished from handling.

A nail is a measure employed for fabrics, and describing two and a quarter inches, so that four nails equal a quarter-yard. An inch, we read, is equivalent to three barleycorns or the twelfth of a foot.

From the collection of Mrs. De Witt Clinton Cohen

WALRUS TOOTH WITH CENTRAL EYE, USED AS AN AWL, A NEEDLE OR A BODKIN, AND
MARKED AT REGULAR INTERVALS TO SERVE AS A MEASURE.

Rule of thumb,[2] though not in ells or inches, must, of course, be very old indeed! Nowadays, upon a basis of inches and yards, a lady's shortest thumb joint is supposed to measure an inch, while from the knuckle to the tip of a woman's longest finger is counted an eighth of a yard. My own second finger measures three-eighths of an inch less than that. A finger, for measuring purposes, however, is four and a half inches. A man's foot is considered to be a foot long; a feminine arm's length, a yard; and from milady's nose to her farthest reach, equally a yard. Fingering, however, is a worsted employed for the knitting of stockings. An ell is a forearm long, called in French *l'avant bras;* that is, 74 inches or 1.85 metres. This seems a long forearm! A metre is 39.37 inches long. Now bear with me while I quote to you from the great Larousse: "*Aune* (Latin *ulna, avant-bras*). *Ancienne mesure de longueur* (1 *mètre* 188)." And if you enjoy solving puzzles, please read the contradictions (or so they seem to my poor pate) writ down in my footnote from the *Century Dictionary.*[3]

[2] In speaking of some far eastern workers one feels like saying "rule of eye." These embroiderers are such by inheritance. No improvements are introduced among their tools — they themselves are human machines. Men embroider more than women, and measure space approximately by eye, no two parts of the pattern being filled in just alike.

[3] "Ell. — [ME. *elle, elne.* AS., *eln,* an ell (18, 20½, 24, etc., inches), = D. *el, elle* = OHG. *elina, elna,* MHG. *eline, elne, ellen,* G. *elle* = Icel. *alin* = Sw. *aln* = Dan. *alen* = Goth.

S. F. A. Caulfeild tells us that " the cloth-yard of old English times was of the length of the arrows employed both in battle and for the chase. A statute of Edward VI enacted that the measure of cloth should contain to every yard ' one inch containing the breadth of a man's thumb ' or 37 inches. This ' thumb measure ' still obtains in the trade. Goods for export are measured by the ' short stitch ' or 35 inches, and the thumb — that is, the bare yard; while goods for the home market are measured by the ' long stitch ' — or the yard of 36 inches and the ' thumb ' — that is, what is designated ' good measure.' "

Another natural or anatomical form of measure is that provided by the familiar inch-worm, who inches up and down a limb, accurately measuring his length upon the bough. You remember that in order to annihilate this strange, pestiferous instrument of precision and plant destruction, the United States introduced the English sparrow.

From Renaissance France we have broidered ribbons with lines a certain distance apart — centimetres, et cetera, were not introduced till 1799. Some ribbons, instead of being worked, are only inked. The French word, in fact, for tape-measure, is *mètre en ruban*. The Spanish say *la cinta* (ribbon) *para medir;* and the Germans, *das Bandmass* or *das Rollmetermass*.

We all know the naughty story about the little boy, the roll of tape and the worm; but shall we follow instead the sorted and measured quahaug so much relished by gastronomes? Round about Boston these clams are sorted by the stalwart Cape Cod fishermen into Seeds, Cherrystones, Boston Mediums, Little Necks, et cetera. The industry is so prevalent that village shops in the vicinity carry silver or white

---

aleina (for **alina?*), an ell, whence It. *auna*, F. *aune*, an ell; orig. the forearm (as in As. *eln-boga*, E. elbow), = L. *ulna*, the forearm, the elbow, an ell = Gr. ὠλένη, the forearm: see *elbow, ulna*.] A long measure, chiefly used for cloth. The English ell, not yet obsolete, is a yard and a quarter, or 45 inches. This unit seems to have been imported from France under the Tudors; and a statute of 1409 recognizes no difference between the ell (aune) and the yard (verge). The Scotch ell was 37 Scotch inches, or 37.0958 English inches. The so-called Flemish ell differed in different places, but averaged 27.4 English inches. Other well-ascertained ells were the following: ell of Austria, 30.676 English inches; of Bavaria, 32.702 inches; of Bremen, 22.773 inches; of Cassel, 22.424 inches; of France, 47.245 inches; of Poland, 22.650 inches; of Prussia, 26.259 inches; of Saxony, 22.257 inches; of Sweden, 23.378 inches. The ell of Holland is now the meter."

You note that near the opening of the paragraph an ell measures from 18 to 24, etc., inches. The " etc." waxes and grows strong, till about the centre of the quotation we are informed " The English ell, not yet obsolete, is a yard and a quarter, or 45 inches " !

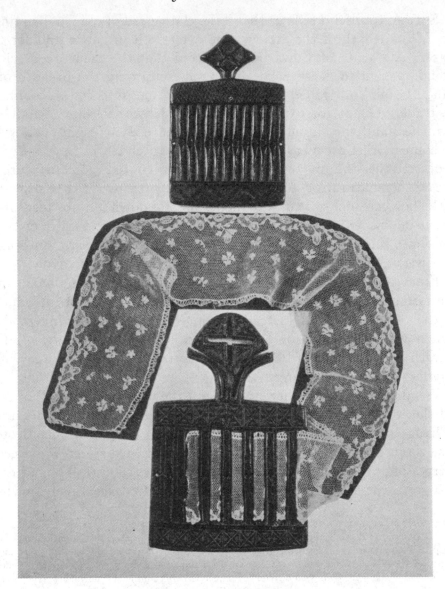

From the collection of Mrs. De Witt Clinton Cohen

TWO RARE FRENCH LACE MEASURES FROM OLD ALENÇON. TWO LARGER BUT SIMILAR
RIBBON MEASURES ARE IN THE TROCADÉRO AT PARIS. THE PAIR HERE PICTURED HAVE
THE POLISH AND PATINA OF AGE, MAKING IT A LITTLE HARD TO SAY WHETHER THEY ARE
OF BOXWOOD OR WALNUT. THE WHITTLING IS UNEVEN AND RUSTIC. IN FACT, WE ARE
TOLD THAT THE MEASURES WERE GENERALLY MADE AND PRESENTED BY VILLAGE SUITORS
TO MAIDENS OF THEIR CHOICE. THE LACE FINISHED DURING THE DAY WAS WOUND UNDER
ONE STICK AND OVER THE NEXT, AND SO FORTH ALTERNATELY. APPARENTLY THE WORKER
WAS PAID FOR EACH STICK'S WORTH OF POINT THAT SHE EXECUTED — A CURIOUS AND
INVOLVED WAY, IT SEEMS TO US, OF MEASURING A SIMPLE LENGTH OF LACE. [SLIGHTLY
REDUCED.]

metal quahaug-shell tape-measure cases, with the usual roll of ribbon within. Perhaps the pretty dancing scallops of the neighborhood also have lent their shell form, so pleasingly fluted, to the local designers and dealers in tape-measures. At least, they have given their shells as covers or sides for velvet-edged pinballs.

A lucky tape-measure can sometimes be had in the form of an Irish pig made in nickel, for the pig in Ireland plays so important a part that it has come to represent good fortune. You doubtless recall the climax of the song of the Irish suitor on his way to Tipperary Town: " 'T was the little pigs that done it, och! the dear little girl!"

A practical modern measure shows inches on one side of the tape, centimetres on the other. There are also tapes in brass and in boxwood cases, as well as in bone or ivory — sometimes prettily carved — and in mother-of-pearl and other shells, all having a pin through the centre on which the tape is wound, and some having tiny projecting handles by means of which the ribbon may be wound up. Flora Klickmann says that in her workbox "Tape measures appear in various forms and unwind themselves either from a barrel, or by turning the tail of a donkey, or from the top of a kind of pepper-box lighthouse. This last is a noble ornament, because, in addition to the tape-measure, it provides a pincushion at its base and a piece of wax halfway up, for waxing your thread."

Architects and scientific men, of course, have to use a tape that does not stretch or shrink, so that large, strong pocket measures with steel tape and a lock catch to hold the metal ribbon unrolled to just a given point can be purchased in draftsmen's shops.

Modern dressmakers often have loose, uncased, double, yellow strips of tape, the first foot of which is stretched over stiff whalebone or steel, to render the measure partly ruler.

Measuring sticks must once have been mere rough notched sticks. Sewers still notch stiff paper or old cards as guides for individual pieces of work. With just one notch or mark to go by, a worker naturally has less chance of making a mistake. Those who do much home dressmaking often have sewing tables with an inlaid dark wood measure. Pliable flat lapboards, mounted on strong muslin and intended for rolling up, to travel or put out of sight, also have inlaid yard rules of contrasting wood.

Wooden instruments with sharp brass edges — good for tearing paper straight; three-sided rules with measures of different degrees and standards upon their sides — these triangular sticks warp less than the others and are made of finer wood; thin flat ivory rulers — excellent as line guides in copying from a book or paper: all these and many others are familiar to us. The writer has a handsomely carved, malachite green, Manchurian hairpin, long and smooth-edged, that, while decorative, serves excellently as a guide for tracing straight lines in preparing patterns, and for following or keeping place when copying manuscript. These hairpins are sometimes sold as paper cutters, and vary in size. The particular pin or ruler just alluded to is a foot long, its face deeply chiseled into the eight Buddhistic altar symbols.

At Old Deerfield, Massachusetts, in the Memorial Hall, is a box containing thin wooden patchwork and quilting guides. They are walnut blocks, fan-shaped — the sides slightly concave; and letter-S shaped, though the " S " curves are not acute, but gradual. No other forms are left in the box; but there is chalk therein with which to trace the outline of the guides upon one's cloth. Celluloid S's, T's and triangles from an art supply shop, might in these prosaic times serve such a purpose.

Sarah M. Lockwood, in *Antiques,* writes:

" Then the quilting begins, those endless, endless stitches! Sometimes in the old days it was given to a woman who made quilting her life's work. She was paid, not for the amount of quilting she got through, but for the amount of thread she used, which may account for some of the amazing work on some of the old quilts. The way to beat that game was to take forty or fifty stitches to the inch! "

In designing sewing models, one has sometimes to enlarge or to reduce a pattern. An accurate guide in doing this is cross-ruled paper. Whatever appears within a given square of one size is copied into the corresponding square of the other size; a pricker being used if possible to mark the square one happens to be at work upon, acting somewhat as a bookmark, to prevent one's losing the place. " Point " paper is used also for the purpose of indicating in its minute squares the coloring to be employed in embroidering pieces of tapestry, cross-stitch, petit-point, et cetera. Such paper is sold also under the French name *quadrille* paper.

Another way of pattern minimizing or magnifying [4] is by using a draftsman's pantagraph — financial magnates use them in order to sign many checks at once. Treasurers' pantagraphs are built to fit the company's great check-book, holding a stylographic pen over each check. As the writer signs his name, ninety-nine other pens follow

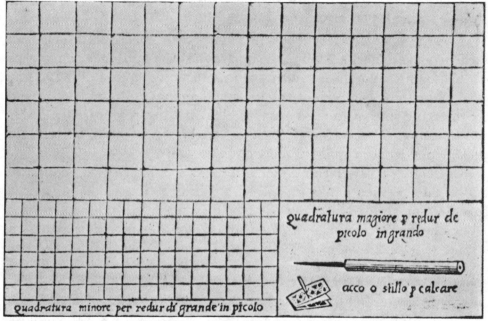

quadratura magiore p redur de picolo ingrando

acco o stillo p calcare

quadratura minore per redur di grande in picolo

From Corona delle nobili et virtuose donne, 1593, by C. Vecellio

BY USING (NOWADAYS) LARGER OR SMALLER QUADRILLE OR CROSS-SECTIONED, CROSS-RULED PAPER, PUTTING INTO THE BIGGER OR SMALLER SQUARE THE SAME DESIGN OR AMOUNT OF DESIGN THAT APPEARS IN THE ORIGINAL SQUARE, LEAVING VACANT THE SQUARES CORRESPONDINGLY EMPTY IN THE COPIED PATTERN, ONE CAN EASILY ENLARGE OR REDUCE ONE'S CARTOON. BY EMPLOYING A PIN OR STILETTO AND MOVING IT FROM SQUARE TO SQUARE, ONE CAN READILY KEEP TRACK OF ONE'S PLACE.

[4] Linen merchants use "pick glasses" for magnifying and counting the number of threads in any given piece of goods. Such glasses frequently fold for pocket use; but they must embody one or another form of accurate counting device — in most cases a half inch, or centimetre, square opening or sight that acts as a platform for the little circular glass. These — square hole and glass — fold open at a proper distance from each other, so that the magnifying adjustment is just right for use.

For picking out fine lace work, the tiny eighth-of-an-inch glass that enlarges thirty diameters, transforming a mere wisp of thread into a seemingly mighty cable, is excellent. The more powerful a magnifying glass may be, the smaller must be its size. Watchmakers' single eyeglasses are useful to some lace-makers.

A minifying glass is helpful to the original embroiderer who wishes to grasp the general effect being produced by her work as she proceeds in its creation. For this purpose it is also well to hold one's work from time to time before a mirror.

his every move. But designers' pantagraphs pivot with a stylus or pin upon the pattern's original lines, a pencil held in the adjusted arm of the drawing device repeating the lines at a given distance.

A different mode of drawing a straight line on one's goods is by pulling out a thread, which sometimes draws automatically after it an attached thread of another color. This, of course, can be done only in straight-ahead, plainly woven stuffs.

Household Equipment tells us that "the time usually spent in measuring and marking fabrics to insure the even cutting of long strips of the material may be saved by the following method: Pull apart the extension dining-table to a distance of half an inch. Place the material on the table so that the line along which it is desired to cut lies over this opening. Secure the cloth with weights and let the left side of the opening act as a guide to the scissors in cutting."

Cotton yarn, after spinning, is reeled off in lengths or hanks of 840 yards; 18 such hanks are called a spindle. The whole is twisted together and secured. Worsted hanks are longer than those of cotton; while the hanks of linen thread contain 300 yards. This equals a cut, 48 cuts making a spindle of 14,400 yards. Nevertheless, the size or number of threads does not alter the lengths put up; rather do the number of skeins in a hank have to accommodate themselves to the situation; so that with finer material there would be a greater number of skeins. The basis of a skein length is usually some predetermined weight.

A yarn-metre, used in spinning, is an attachment to a slubber, fly-frame, spinning-frame, or mule, for measuring the yarns as they are made, we are told. It indicates the amount in hanks and in decimal parts of a hank.

"*Water twist* means a coarse yarn of twenty pounds to the hank, and is used for warping; while *mule twist* is intended as weft thread. *Worsted hank* is a yarn done up in one-half pound skeins, and sold by the single, dozen or one-half dozen pounds." A cotton lea equals one and a half yards.

Clock reels have a wooden box at the centre of the wheel. Inside the box is a simple system of cogwheels that one may set to break one's yarn when a skein or hank thereof has been wound upon the pegs set into the face or side of the wheel rim. Some of the boxes have a dial and hand outside to show how much yarn is in the winding on the wheel. When the hand and its corresponding internal mechanism reach the gauge mark, a springboard slips suddenly off the tip of a cog, giving the wheel a sharp yank, thereby snapping the yarn. These reels are rarely polished, varnished or painted, and are frequently to be found in old American barns or attics. The whole wheel on its post or straddle legs stands about three feet high and sometimes has rather the appearance of a toy windmill.

Fingering — stocking worsted — is sent out from the factories in half-pounds of eight one-ounce skeins, though Mesdames Caulfeild and Saward warn one that the measure is generally scant! In some places the words " hank " or " skein " have varied meanings — the former including two or more skeins, consisting of two or more threads twisted or tied together.

From the Icelandic we have *hangr*, a *hank*, a coil, the coil of a snake, coming from the verb *hang* — as in the sentence, " An old native fisherman, however, brought up a *hank* of very small and uninviting fishes." Middle English used the spelling *hanken*, with the idea of fettering, fastening by means of a cord, forming into *hanks*.

In Old French, skein was spelled *escagne*, then *écagne;* Middle Latin was *scagna;* while the Irish said *sgainne* and the Gaels, *sgeinnidh*, flax or hempen twine, something split off.

Now, what an array of articles and artifices, mostly to measure or draft just two lines — straight or curved — or the distance between some two! Most of the instruments, though of course very precise, sound prosaic enough; so when you outfit your sewing table, do watch and search for something pleasing as well as practical, something to relieve the dreary " matter-of-factness " of this weighty skein of measures!

INSTRUMENTS OF PRECISION — MEASURES

" *Skeyne of threde.*"
—*Filipulum.*

" *With his shears and measure in his hand.*"
— *King John:* William Shakespeare.

"God winds us off the skein, that he may weave us up into the whole piece."

"The curs ran into them as a falcon does into a skein of ducks."
— *Hypatia:* Charles Kingsley.

"Let the yardstick dispute heraldic honors with the sword."
— George William Curtis.

"You condense it with locusts and tape:
Still keeping one principal object in view —
To preserve its symmetrical shape."
— *The Hunting of the Snark:* Lewis Carroll.

"When I can measure, cut and sew,
Won't that be a lot to know?
But I'm only a little girl, you see,
So don't expect too much of me."
— *Illustrated Sewing Primer:* Louise J. Kirkwood.

"Hemming, Mother tells me,
Must be neat and very fine,
The stitches small and even,
All in a nice straight line."
— Louise J. Kirkwood.

"'Judge Not that Ye Be Not Judged.'
"Your spoken word reveals you: the tape measure that you apply to others, will
in turn be used by them to measure you."
— Dr. H. H. Tweedy.

KNITTING-NEEDLES AND CROCHET-HOOKS

" When daylight is flitting,
We take up our knitting."

" Work Tibet, work Annot, work Margerie,
Sew Tibet, knit Annot, spin Margerie,
Let us see who will win the victory."
— *" Work Girls' Song,"* in *Ralph Roister Doister:* Nicholas Udall.

AND how, pray, did knitting originate? Can you not guess? Did you not originate it yourself? " What a silly question," you say, " as though I were as old as the hills!" Now, I am not that old myself, yet I saw knitting originated; in fact I originated it. You are incredulous? Well, it just happened. And so did it probably just happen to someone, or many someones, ages ago.

I was nine years old of a Sunday afternoon, when company called. Under the circumstances I was a bit shown off before being relegated to a rear room. There I discovered my aunt's yarn, and to kill time, twisted it around my fingers — forth and back. With a finger of the other hand I looped one thread under or over another; then adding another line of looping, I noticed that something solid — a stuff — was beginning to develop. Ere long I had a little narrow sheet of worsted work like a doll's coverlet. But I knew not how to stop, how to finish off. In fact, I did not know I was knitting. Thrilled with my miniature comforter, I interrupted the grown-ups, begging that it be tied off.

My discovery, worked with Nature's tools, was commended, and a gentleman of the party rewarded me by driving some pins into one of my aunt's spools, showing me how to furnish myself with a plenty of worsted reins. In this case, four pins took the place of four fingers, though the pins ranged in a circle produced, of course, a continuous circular fabric instead of the flat work fashioned on my hand.

Not knowing the source from which this picture comes, the author regrets that she is unable to give credit to the artist

"WHERE'S THE CAT WHOSE TWISTED CRADLE
ALL THE CHILDREN, YOUNG AND OLD,
HAVE BEEN MAKING — STILL ARE MAKING —
WILL BE MAKING — TURN AND FOLD,
TWIST, AND SLIP, AND TURN, AND DOUBLE,
TILL THE VERY WORLD IS OLD?"
                   —DORA WHEELER.

(*Cnyttan* — the original Anglo-Saxon word — means to weave threads by the hand.)

My aunt still further encouraged me — and thus did a second generation come to break the Sabbath Day — by giving me my mother's quaint little old wooden knitting spool. My mother, surreptitiously rein-making one Sunday morning upon the back stairs, heard Grandfather coming and, in her confusion, swallowed the glass-headed pin with which she was lifting the worsted loops over the wooden pegs of her spool. So in her day, too, pins were used as lifters, as they are

From the author's collection

Left: AN OLD-TIME WOODEN KNITTING SPOOL WITH FOUR PRONGS AT ONE END AND FIVE AT THE OTHER.

Right: A WHITING, PERHAPS, MADE NOT OF WHITE METAL THOUGH, BUT OF SILVER. HE FASTENS TO ONE'S BELT AS A BROOCH, AND CONCEALS, RUNNING ON THE BACK OF HIM FROM HIS NOSE TO HIS SPLIT TAIL, A STRAIGHT TUBE TO ACCOMMODATE ONE'S KNITTING-NEEDLE.

now, instead of a grown-up's longer knitting-needle; but if you will examine the illustration, you will notice that in place of the primitive pins driven into the spool by our guest, or of the double, bent wires of the present day, the older spool has wooden pins. Moreover, one end has four of these; the other, five; so a finer or coarser hollow cord could be looped upon the same implement.

Alluding to the commencement of knitting, or rather to its very early application, I include a Malayan myth: "Mat Noah began: 'Once upon a time, long, long ago, when there were no poisonous snakes and the python was the king of reptiles, there lived a woman called Aunt Eve. One day the python, who was snow-white, met Eve, and she asked the snake to live with her. After much persuasion, the python consented on condition that Eve knit a pattern on his back in order to make him beautiful. Eve began and knit the most beautiful patterns on the snake's back, commencing from his tail.' "

The first knitting guild was founded in Paris [I do not know the date. G. W.] and named after St. Fiacre. He died *circa* 670. The *Century Dictionary* states " that he was a native of Ireland, the country of the Scots." Another authority speaks of him as " the son of a Scotch king." Hence the Scots claim the invention of knitting. Both Italy and Spain practised the art prior to the sixteenth century.

To knit upon the wooden pegs set round the rim of a heavy wooden ring or open rectangle is much the same as to knit a set of child's reins upon a spool. By the way, effective linen cord for adult uses can be just as well produced upon this simple device as can the mere worsted plaything. Double mufflers, bags and other tubular articles can be made on this ring or frame or *rake*. Machine-made stockings, of course, are done upon this principle. By omitting one peg, however, flat lengths of knitting can be produced. Perhaps you have heard of the woman who had knit fifteen socks, but had not yet finished a pair?

Having suggested the possible beginnings of such a thing as knitting, may I outline the odd drift of one of its more developed forms from the destruction of the Spanish Armada to Lady Allardyce's present-day mission in Newfoundland? Some of the historic fleet drifted northward toward Fair Isle,[1] the Hebrides, and the Island of Mull, where the inhabitants seized the defeated's clothing, horizontally striped sometimes with bands of crosses, bands of birds, bands of quaint little women or madonnas. These foreign designs were incorporated into the local knitting. The wool used for the excellent Shetland work comes from the mourat (a brown sheep), the shulah (a gray one), and the less esteemed black and white varieties. Fair Islanders obtain their wool dyes from seaweeds, ragwort and madderwort, which produce delicate pinks, gray-blues and soft browns. But fisherfolk go sailing for new schools of fish, and some sailed to

[1] The ship belonging to the Duke of Medina Sidonia is said to have been wrecked at Fair Isle in the Shetlands. The sailors, according to local tradition, taught the inhabitants to knit, so introducing the art into Scotland and England. But before that date, knitted stockings from Spain had been presented to Edward VI, and some stockings, we read, had been made in England.

Labrador and Newfoundland, bringing to the new northern world some old southern ideas — just as present-day fashion has brought these same quaint Hispanic patterns to the attention of the new generation as Fair Isle, "Wigwam," and "Nonia" knitted sweaters.

A work now seldom seen is the netting, knitting or crocheting of smooth flat gold or silver thread twisted around a core of silk. Such metallic thread is called "passing" and was much used in the Middle Ages.

Have you ever wondered about the needles formerly used to knit wee mittens and socks for dolls? Our grandmothers took such tiny stitches — no wonder they took pride, too, in their work! My grandmother knit for small, twin, china dolls I had, two sets of mittens, with a cord to pass around each dolly's neck, imitating the cord passed behind my own to keep me from losing my mittens. The miniature articles were white, each no larger than a dime, with thumbs the size of glass-headed pins, and a baby blue border at the wrist. It seems to me these must have been knit upon needles the thickness of invisible hairpins. There is a wire knitting-needle known as a knitting-wire.

Knitters' needles come made of steel, bone, wood, imitation amber, pink or blue celluloid, et cetera. Some substances are better suited to one sort of work, others to different varieties. Individuals also have personal preferences, some liking stiff, some limber, instruments. The dilettante may fancy carrying out the color scheme of her work-bag or her frock. Gauges or *filières,* with graduated holes to pass or "thread" (*filer*) the needles through, are common. They make the necessary accuracy easily possible. What sort of product would result were two needles of one size; another for the same piece of goods, larger; and still another, a trifle smaller? Knitting-needles are sometimes known as knitting pins, especially if there be a knob at one end of the needle.

One must not imagine that all knitting-needles are straight, or even should be straight. Does that seem odd? Peasants in mountainous districts, climbing steep hills with loads of faggots, or of heavy wet clothes washed in a stream at the foot of the incline, piled upon their poised heads, cannot well look down as they knit; nor can busy mothers of ten or twelve growing children, and younger women who must play " big sister " and " little mother " and also spin for their own trousseaux, waste time while walking up and down a hill, even when on business bent, or even when on their way to school with a strapful of books. No, they must knit en route. They must not glance down at the work; at least they must not tip their heads — for their bundles would land in the dust or roll down the cliff! So knitting must be held close to bended bodies toiling up the steeps; and little folk, should they stumble, would not so easily be pierced by a bent-back needle. Therefore do these peasants choose curved needles.

Peasant knitting in one section leads gradually to that of another; and if you have observed abroad, you have noticed that European knitters frequently clickety-click away at lightning speed with their hands held close to their belts. Of course, there is a reason — one needle is held in a vise that slips under the apron-string. Flat, curved wooden holders show a worn or whittled slot across the face of the *gaine* (the technical French term) where the apron-string or belt has passed and firmly pressed day after day. Down into this holder runs a small slot. Into the slot in turn is slid the lower end of a knitting-needle. This naturally furnishes the worker with an extra implement or with a support for one of her tools. Some holders or *affiquets* — another French name — have rings near the middle, through which to pass a steadying cord. In the seventeenth and eighteenth centuries there were tooled steel sheaths. Bone or ivory holders must exist, and tin ones could during the World War be had in the United States. These holders are sometimes called sheaths. The lengthened type of knitting-sheath is known as a knitting-stick.

Knitting-needles are " pesky critters " to carry around — they bore through pockets and push through bags, they fall through cracks and catch and bend. They are dangerous too. Our cook, for off moments, kept knitting in her pocket. One morning, Mother was out marketing and the maid thrust her hand into her long pocket to pull out the ever-present knitting. A steel needle ran right through the palm of her hand, and I, having just heard of such a thing as lockjaw, pushed one of my play blocks between her teeth so there would surely be an opening through which to feed her. Then I ruthlessly yanked out the offending needle and handed it over for her to go on knitting, requesting to see what she was making. Since the wound, being small, quickly

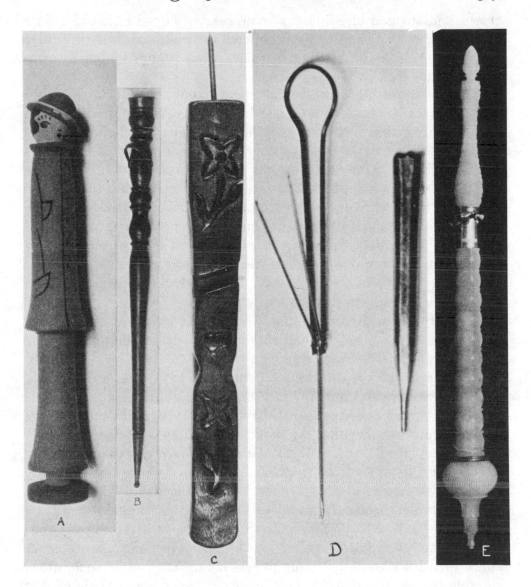

B and C from Mrs. Cohen's collection; A, D and E from the author's collection

A: THE WOODEN SOLDIER, A MODERN AMERICAN KNITTING-NEEDLE CASE. B: AN OLD ITALIAN SILVER-TIPPED, DARKLY STAINED BONE HOLDER, TO FREE ONE HAND WHILE KNITTING. C: AN OLD CARVED WOODEN HOLDER SHOWING THE GROOVE WHERE THE APRON-STRING SHOULD PASS. D: A TRIPLE FOLDING CROCHET-HOOK WITH AN OPEN-ENDED SHEATH THAT ALLOWS JUST THE ONE HOOK WANTED TO PROTRUDE, HOLDING BACK THE OTHER TWO, AND FORMING A COMFORTABLE HANDLE. E: A GRACEFUL, DAZZLING WHITE MOTHER-OF-PEARL CROCHET CASE AND HANDLE WITH GOLD BANDS. THIS PIECE FORMERLY BELONGED TO THE GRAND DUCHESS OF BADEN.

closed and stopped bleeding, I saw no reason why she should abjure knitting; though I thoroughly frightened the poor girl, insisting there was every reason for keeping her jaws wide propped with my uncomfortable block!

Hence I warn all knitters who wish to avoid the block, that they should invest in needle ends, or at least use corks for protectors. I have a pair of tiny Swiss chamois horns — naturally hollow — connected by elastic cord, to slip over the tips of a set of steel needles when not in use. Many amusing devices — especially painted wooden ones, Darby and Joan, et cetera — were made up during the war.

Old cylindrical ivory cases, sometimes tooled leather spectacle cases, all sorts of dainty or stunning old French *étuis,* and carved wood pen cases, are available and practical, as well perhaps as delightful, for housing one's needles when traveling or visiting or when the slippery creatures are not in use. If more than one set be kept in a single case, it is well to tie each lot by itself.

Mrs. Florence L. Cohen has a charming *sablé* knitting-needle tube with a dear little old ivoried screw-cap, from the famous Iklé collection of St. Gall, Switzerland.

Crochet-hooks are crotchety. When one wishes an ample hook, one is apt to have at hand only medium or fine ones. And should one need a very fine hook, it is sure to have a speck too much metal in the neck, or turnover, causing the hook, which may accommodate only the sheerest thread, to create too large a gap when passing through loops. Or the arch of the neck being as slim as possible, one may find too little turned-over wire or steel — so little that it will not hold a thread to pull it through its noose, just dropping the thread instead at a critical and exasperating moment. So examine well the minute construction of your hooks when buying them. Keep their delicate heads stuck into little wads of tissue paper, laying the whole tool into a suitable box or sheath. Medicine-dropper cases are sometimes just right.

Handles also need consideration. Callous spots come from badly adapted handles chafing one's joints. One person prefers a flattened handle; another, a slim cylindrical one of steel; another, a fat bone handle. Crochet-hooks can be had set like buttonhooks into flattened tubular tin handles with wire loop ends, that fold at the handle joint, thus lying back along the shank to guard it and extending beyond the hook's point to protect it. One occasionally sees a gutta-percha handle.

The handsomest crochet-hook I have ever seen is a truly fairy thing of mother-of-pearl bound with gold. The tapering smaller end is spirally carved, with a tip of acorn shape, this whole end unscrewing and displaying a socket into which to set a hook. So this royal tool carries its own protective case. Next comes the shiny shell shank or handle to the hook, and beyond that, growing larger, a bulbous end that reminds me of the dome of a Russian mosque with a fine finial of gold. The dome also unscrews, showing us a hollow handle full of varied steel hooks. This instrument belonged some eighty years ago to one of the Grand Duchesses of Baden — Sophie, I think — and was one piece of a set that included reel, thimble, stiletto and scissors in a very old and handsome box. Its next owner, at a dinner party, gave one piece to each lady present. Thus came this ethereal hook into my hands. It is now in the Brooklyn Museum.

Crochet is a kind of knitting done with a hooked needle.

I have read that in the sixteenth century a hook was necessary for "Nun's Work," for this apparently was the old name for crochet work.[5]

Under "hairpin lace," in one of the last chapters, we find that a mere crochet-hook is needed in the actual making of the lace, though it forms upon a two-pronged fork.

And in reading of fringing-forks under "Some Stray Accessories," we discover that a crochet-hook again is needed to complete the fringer's outfit.

Then the chapter "Hoops, Tambours and Frames" tells us, I believe, that though the lawn or net or other tissues may be stretched in a tambour, the stitch of that name is worked through the stretched goods with a humble steel crochet-hook or tambour-needle, which is usually fitted with a handle of ivory or hard wood. The foundation of all crochet work is the chain or tambour stitch; while the so-called tambour or tamburet stitch "in crochet is a kind of stitch by which a pattern of straight ridges crossing each other at right angles is produced." Tambour lace is made in many sections; but that produced in Limerick, Ireland, has rather taken the name unto itself.

[5] As it was for much other fancywork.

Macramé also calls for a hook, and so do bobbin-lace sewings or *accrochages*. In England, all but beginners accomplish this feat with a needle-pin; but the Continent turns to the finest of fine hooks.

A MODERN ENGLISH NEEDLE PIN, MADE BY FIRMLY EMBEDDING THE EYE END OF AN ORDINARY NUMBER SEVEN NEEDLE INTO A CONVENIENT WOODEN HANDLE. SOME HANDLES ARE ONLY OF ROUGHLY WHITTLED WOOD WITH THE NEEDLE, LAID LIKE A GRAFTED TWIG, IN A GROOVE FILLED WITH CARPENTER'S GLUE AND TIGHTLY BOUND ROUND WITH STOUT THREAD TO KEEP THE NEEDLE FROM SLIPPING EVEN EVER SO SLIGHTLY. THESE NEEDLE PINS ARE USED FOR TAKING SEWINGS — THAT IS, HOOKING UP OR PULLING THREADS THROUGH LOOPS, CALLED *CROCHETAGE* IN FRANCE, WHERE FINE CROCHET-HOOKS ARE USED IN PLACE OF NEEDLE PINS.

Have I made you feel that I have been discussing slippery, treacherous creatures with cat-like claws, ready to pierce and scratch and tear — sleek little polished instruments that need watching and humoring and a place of their own to be kept in? Well, they do. Not only do they catch and mercilessly tear, but they warp and bend and rust. To prevent the warping of a bone needle's disposition, do not treat it too dryly or place it near the riling heat of the register or radiator. But do not, with a steel needle or hook, go so far in the opposite way as to dampen its ardor to the point of developing a rough, biting, rusty, crusty disposition!

AWLS, BODKINS, PRICKERS, PUNCHES AND STILETTOS

" Cloth of bodkin, *or tissue."*
— Ben Jonson.

" That other signet of gold, with my puncheon *of ivory and silver, I give and bequeath unto Robert my secunde son."*
— *Chronicles I:* Fabyan.

WHEN one does eyelet work or darns netting in fancy forms, one must of course be provided with a stiletto of some sort; so why not with a fair or jolly one; and how be properly prepared to select the fairest specimen without knowing somewhat of the history and of the sorts and kinds of these useful little tools? There is the primitive red man's awl that has accomplished such stunning effects, and the Latin's finished instrument destined to help produce the beauties of the Renaissance. Between them lies a wide range of choice for modern selection. Therefore let us touch upon some points in the history and use of these dangerous but indispensable little objects.

Stilettos (of Italian provenance) or *poinçons* (of French provenance) can, as far back as 1380, be found enumerated in inventories as a recognized part of a housewife's outfit. They figure also among office furnishings and traveling equipment, as noted in Charles the Fifth's inventory: " Ungs couteaulx a clou, a porter en boys, c'est assavoir ung grant, ung petit et ung *poinçon*, avec forcettes qui sont d'argent; et est la gayne estoffee d'or, et la chesne a quoy ils pendent, d'argent " (a wooden knife to wear, that is to say, a large and a small one, and an awl, with small silver shears; the case lined with gold, the chain by which they are suspended being of silver).

Stationers, basket-makers, leather workers and bookbinders, of course, must have their awls or punches. The *Mercury* of January, 1679, tells us that an " amant fort passioné pour une belle " offered her " une escritoire dont la serrure, la clef et les plaques de dessus estoient de vermail, aussi bien que le cornet, le poudrier et les manches du canif et du *poinçon*" (a lover, deeply impassioned, offered a beauty of the day a desk of which the lock, the key and the ornamental plates, as well as the inkhorn, the sandbox and the handles of the penknife and the puncheon were of silver-gilt).

A *poinçon*, or piercer, stylus or stiletto,[1] is one of a worktable's

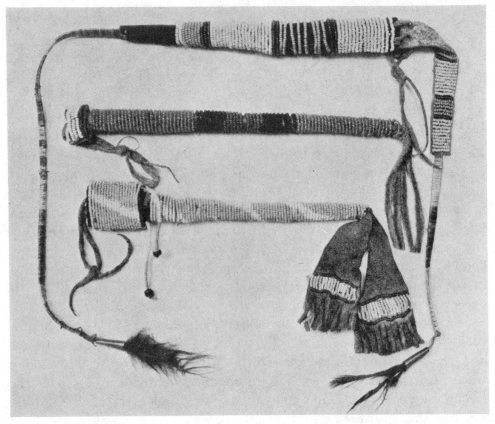

From the collection of Mrs. De Witt Clinton Cohen, New York

AMERICAN INDIAN AWLS ARE USED TO PERFORATE SKINS IN ORDER TO SLIP SINEWS — SOMETIMES STRUNG WITH BEADS — THROUGH THE APERTURES. THE AWL CASES ARE WORN HANGING AT THE BELT.

Top: VIOLET, BLACK AND OLD ROSE BEADS MOUNTED ON CURED WHITE SKIN: LONG CERISE AND WHITE STRAW STREAMER ENDS, TERMINATING IN TIN TIPS AND TUFTS OF CANARY-COLORED FEATHERS. ALASKAN.

Centre: BLACK, GREEN AND SALMON-COLORED BEAD BODY WITH WHITE BEADED CAP. HOPI INDIAN.

Bottom: MOST ATTRACTIVE TURQUOISE AND WHITE BEADED NAVAJO AWL HOLDER, WITH LARGE CRIMSON BEAD TIPS AND TURQUOISE BEADED, SLASHED OR FRINGED TASSEL ENDS!

[1] The word "broach" is sometimes used to signify a bodkin.

useful appliances for making eyelets without cutting the fabric with a blade, thereby rendering it liable to tear. A piercer is used by embroiderers in gold for laying bullion in place, guiding the fine cord around the edges of the work. Eyes for lacings or for shank buttons or for ornamentation are made by piercers or stilettos, while so-called sewing-awls are used for preparing coarser material. Some awls have bent points. Punches are sometimes hollow with a circular cutting edge for felt or leather work. For eyelet embroidery or *broderie*

From the author's collection

Left: OXIDIZED SILVER EMBROIDERY STILETTO IN THE FORM OF A SWORDFISH. [HALF SIZE.]

Right: ADJUSTABLE BRASS ITALIAN PIN OR NEEDLE HOLDER FOR PRICKING BOBBIN LACE PATTERNS. [ACTUAL SIZE.]

anglaise, soft cotton should be run around the outline before piercing a hole; while its waste edges ought not to be cut away till after the work has been washed.

There is a bifurcated tool called a pricker for marking equidistant holes for stitching, and a pricking wheel similar to a pie-cutting wheel, but for indicating the number of stitches to an inch. Saddlers speak too of a " stitch-wheel." The *Dictionary of Needlework* adds: " When tracing designs for embroidery of dark and raised materials, outline the design upon a piece of strong cartridge paper, then prick with a pin, or a No. 6 needle, along every line of the outline, which for the purpose should be laid upon a roll of flannel, or other soft cushion, and make a number of clear round holes, an eighth of an inch or less apart."

An idea prevails that the little old-time cases containing spoon, punch, et cetera, are toilet outfits. On the contrary, these sets were used for drizzling—picking apart valuable gold-thread or gemmed embroideries; the little spoons being used to scoop up seed pearls, et cetera. The delicate, diminutive, ivory, gold and shell wheels one sees, are for enrolling and saving the precious metal thread picked out by the aid of the stiletto and destined for the goldsmith. Some of the reels have a long tongue of gold or bone to slip under one's belt, thus supporting or steadying the wheel upon which one is winding — a charming occupation when accompanied by such exquisite materials and instruments! One old account of *parfilage* tells that "the work is also called ravelings, and consists in unpicking materials into which gold and silver threads or wire have been woven. It was an extremely

From the collection of Mrs. De Witt Clinton Cohen, New York

Left: FRENCH EIGHTEENTH-CENTURY STILETTOS IN THEIR CASES. THE LONGER ONE IS OF STEEL; THE SHORTER — MORE VALUABLE THAN IF OF GOLD — IS OF OLD IRON.

Right: RARE AND EXQUISITE EIGHTEENTH-CENTURY FRENCH IVORY, TORTOISE-SHELL, AMBER AND GOLD WINDING WHEEL, WITH REVERSE COGWHEEL ACTION — AS THE HANDLE IS TURNED IN ONE DIRECTION, THE THREAD-HOLDER REVOLVES IN THE OPPOSITE ONE. THE GOLD IS BEAUTIFULLY CHASED WITH BIRDS AND HEADS. THE CHARMING LITTLE APPARATUS WHEN USED IS STRAPPED UPON A WOODEN BLOCK, THE SHELL TONGUE BEING SLIPPED UNDER THE TIGHT LEATHER BAND. [QUARTER SIZE.]

fashionable employment with ladies in England and France during the latter part of the eighteenth century, and was pursued to such an extent in the court of Marie Antoinette as to have led to many comments upon it by writers of that period. The original object of the work was to obtain from old and tarnished articles the valuable threads woven into them, and to sell such threads to the goldbeaters; but when the ladies who worked at it had used up all the old materials they could obtain, they did not scruple to demand from their gentlemen

TWO EIGHTEENTH-CENTURY FRENCH CHÂTELAINE *BOBINETTES* OR THREAD HOLDERS, THE RECTANGULAR ONE OF CUT STEEL, THE OTHER OF SILVER, FOR FANCYWORK OR DRIZZLING.

friends the sword-knots, gold braids, gold laces and bands that were often worn as part of the fashionable dress of the day; and it was said that a courtier who had a reputation to maintain for gallantry and courtesy was likely to go to an assembly fully dressed and to return from it as if he had fallen among thieves and had by them been deprived of all his braveries. The work is now obsolete."

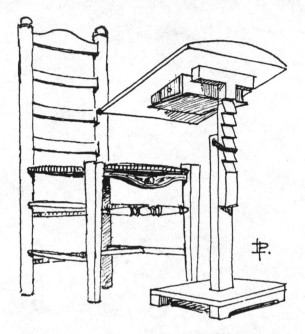

SQUARE STATIONARY PILLOW FASTENED TO A NOTCHED RACK.

Alas! now in our twentieth century the quaint custom of drizzling has disappeared; but the punching of pretty bobbin-lace *prickings* can still be seen in parts of Europe. In Cantu, near Milan, for instance, many women can be found with enormous pillows before them — pillows that curve only from right to left, but not from top to bottom, and rest one end upon the worker's knees, the other upon a tall prop — meticulously copying, prick by prick, new working *parchments* from old, pin-torn, worn-out specimens.

Of modern bodkins or tape-needles, the prettiest, perhaps, are the chased and monogrammed sets of various-sized silver ones in velvet-lined leather cases. Since there are also plain ivory or mother-of-pearl bodkins, possibly there are some gilt-inlaid mother-of-pearl ones, similar to fine French fan sticks.

A Victorian variety of work, we read, "is formed over bodkins and is suitable for quilts and *couvrepieds*, but not for flat articles, since when finished it has the appearance of raised stars or wheels formed into round or diamond-shaped patterns. Commence by taking three equal-sized large steel bodkins, tying them firmly together in the middle and spreading them out to form six spokes, with the three eyes following one another in succession. With the wool or soft thread that tied them together, proceed to weave from one to the next, looping around each bodkin."

Now, having outlined the times and uses of these tiny tools, perhaps we may feel spurred to attempt the making of some dainty eyelet-work collars like those our grandparents wore — yes, for even our grandfathers, when infants, wore darling little long dresses dotted with diminutive eyelets, dresses with ruffles, and collars and caps sometimes to match. Or we may feel stimulated to undertake the embroidery of some delicate narrow edgings of run net, with dainty open centres to the flowerets or stars sprinkled thereon. These embroider quickly and are so acceptable to those we especially love, or for christening or for bridal clothes.

AWLS, BODKINS, PRICKERS, PUNCHES AND STILETTOS

"Life goes all to ravels and tatters."
— Thomas Carlyle.

"There are quaint long needlecases; some are carved; one very uncommon one is of bone, covered with a fine network of beads; these hold silver bodkins beautifully engraved."
— *The Cult of the Needle:* Flora Klickmann.

SHARPS, BLUNTS AND BETWEENS

"The Needle and Thimble
Are Industry's Symbol."

NEEDLES — indeed, what a slim subject to discuss! And yet I warrant there may be some very pointed tales in the world whose turning-points hang upon the mere balance of a needle — episodes in the South Seas, perhaps, commands given or stilled in the face of threatened typhoon; yes, and nearer home, in our own secure drawing-rooms, pointed tales, piercing gossip, or the subtler sort that insinuates itself, prick after prick, until a reputation is slowly bled to death. Slight though a needle may be, introduce it carelessly into a delicate machine and it may shatter the mechanism. Think of the intricacies of a great ship and the trustful souls aboard: but what might become of them should a little needle in a crucial moment lose its head and suddenly point contrariwise?

Needle lore carries us around the world. Some say the Romans gave us needles, some say China. We have been brought up to honor the Chinese with the invention of the compass; though lately I have been told that they are not its inventors! Who knows? If we try to trace the story of needles, however, we may find many facts that we can credit with reliability, and many yarns to delight our idle fancy.

The invention of the needle is ascribed to the goddess Bellona. But two centuries before her era, while the Roman was still wrapping himself in a cumbersome toga, the natives of India were wearing tailored and sewed garments. Even in the *Rig Veda*[1] occurs the passage, "May she sew the work with a needle that is not capable of being cut or broken . . . of which the stitches will endure."

The very earliest needles were not pierced, but were solid and employed like awls or stilettos for punching holes into skins, through

[1] The Vedic word *s'uchi* is identical with that now used to indicate a needle. — "Clothes, and the like, wrought with a needle, last a long time." Wilson's Sañhita of the *Rig Veda*, II, p. 288; IV, p. 60.

which the sinews used as threads were then passed. Some needles were made from the hollow flange of the front limbs of the pteropus bat; some were of fishbone; others were furnished by the vegetable kingdom, which offers so many stout, sharp thorns. In tropical Africa to-day the long splinter midrib of the palm is employed, with one end sharpened to a point and the threading end beaten or reduced to a fibre, to be twisted with an end of the thong or cord that it is, bodkin-like, to draw after it. Bone needles also are still used among primitive peoples, such as the inhabitants of some of the Pacific Islands.

Curved stone splinters pierced at one end have come to light. Needles with eyes, belonging to the Stone and Bronze Ages, have been

From the collection of Mrs. De Witt Clinton Cohen, New York

Top: EGYPTIAN BRONZE NEEDLE, 5500–3500 B.C.
Bottom: EGYPTIAN WOODEN NEEDLE OR BODKIN, 5500–3500 B.C.

found among the ruins of the Lake Dwellings in Switzerland. There are also early bronze needles formed of wire-like strands fused together at all but one point, which serves as an eye. The Babylonians, Phrygians and Egyptians must, judging by the testimony of their work and their civilizations, have had well-developed needles. Ordinary needles and also those intended for surgical purposes have been discovered in Pompeii.

The Chinese, however, are supposed to have been the originators of steel needles, which may have been brought to Europe by the Moors.

A quotation gives us some clue to the situation in England: " Rough as needles were in the days of Editha — wife of Edward the Confessor — she was pronounced by her historian to be ' perfectly mistress of the needle.' "[2] These tiny implements were enjoying estab-

---

[2] We read that " The four sisters of Athelstan, daughters of Edward the Elder, and Edgitha the queen of Edward the Confessor, were particularly famed [for their skill in needlework and

lished usage in Nuremberg as early as 1370. It is said that the trousseau of Bianca Maria Sforza — fiancée of Maximilian I in 1495 — contained a number of "needles with apple-heads" and other needles. This quotation seems questionable, for needles with heads would scarcely perform a needle's accustomed service. Needles, however, are not known to have been introduced into England until the time of Queen Elizabeth in 1560. A quotation tells us that " in the reign of Mary I of England steel wire needles were first made, and then by a Spanish negro, who kept his secret during his lifetime; they were afterwards made in the reign of Elizabeth by one Elias Krause, a German. The great secret was lost after his death, and recovered again about a hundred years later. In the year 1656 Cromwell incorporated the Company of Needlemakers." Long Crendon in Buckinghamshire is the town where Christopher Greening originally started the English manufacture of needles in 1650. The trade, however, migrated to Redditch in Worcestershire, where some twenty thousand families are now supported by this work, to which they are very steady, faithful adherents. The women, though, prove better adapted not only to the handling of the finished needle but also to its production. The first eye-drilling machine was invented in 1826. The wiredrawing is done in Sheffield. Among Redditch needles should be mentioned the former sablé (grain of sand) bead needles, Nos. 14 and 16, a scant inch long, silver-eyed and of cast steel, for mounting those finest of old beads that may never be reproduced, since the Germans in the World War destroyed the manufacturing machinery near Venice. The needles were made by R. Hemming and Sons and are marked " Royal Improved, Warranted not to cut in the Eye, Forge Needle Mills." These needles are of particular interest because the passing of any instrument through the minute *sablé* bead holes has been a moot point. Some packages of the small Redditch needles bear

---

the invention of *opus Anglicanum* — a stitch in embroidery]. After them came Matilda [well-known in connection with the Bayeux Tapestry]."

Mr. Tien Lai Huang claims that the goddess of the silk industry — Lui-tsu of Si-ling — wife of the Yellow Emperor, Huang Ti (2692–2592 B.C.) — is thought to have invented embroidery. The Chinese ideograph therefor — ssŭ — indicates "fine work by women " and " silk " combined. Silk thread, the magazine *Asia* states, was first used for lute strings during the reign of Fo-hi (4473–4358 B.C.) and that silk rearing was the exclusive prerogative of the imperial family from 4357 to 2693. Then it was popularized. Many flowers and three thousand pairs of mandarin ducks were embroidered in silk and gems by a Tang princess.

a tiny picture of Queen Victoria's head in her girlhood. A quaint, paper-lace bedecked box full of these needle papers, together with the beads, has recently fallen into my hands. The outside box contains several lesser glass-topped ones — the glass secured by paper-lace bindings holding the lids in place. And all of the little compartments are planned just to fit the whole.

England in modern times has been manufacturing most of the hand-sewing needles used by the world, though the United States of America is said to have been producing most of the sewing-machine needles — in 1900 making 1,120,532 gross, valued at $1,027,949, not including crochet, knitting, darning, tapestry, chenille, rug, White-chapel, hand-sewing or special trade needles. At one time Aix-la-Chapelle weekly turned out 50,000,000 needles. Needles are gener-ally sold in papers of twenty-five, fifty or one hundred.

In the making of needles, wire is selected, measured, evenly coiled, cut into eight-foot lengths by dividing the coil — each half of which makes one hundred little pieces — and cut into double needle lengths. These are, of course, slightly curved from the preceding coiling, so they are softened by firing and pressed out straight. A century and a half ago the needle wire was made more tractable by greasing it with " hog's lard," and the needles were rendered less brittle by baking and roasting them. Thousands were laid in heaps on buckram with powder of emery and oil, to be polished. Long rolls, squeezed tight at the ends and fastened, sausage-like, with cord, were made of the buckram. Laborers then pushed several rows to and fro on a board for a day and a half or two days. The needles were cleansed in warm soapy water and dried in parcels of bran.

Both ends of the double lengths are pointed, and formerly a good workman pointed some one hundred thousand needles a day by simul-taneously rubbing them by hand over a grindstone; but in spite of his wearing a muffler, he was bound to inhale many fine particles of stone and steel. The modern factory is equipped with a tube into which the injurious dust is steadily sucked away to safety. And a rubber wheel fitted into a fixed hollow stone pushes the needles in quantity over the grinding surface, emitting brilliant showers of sparks.

At first the mechanics had to flatten the surface of the wire where the eye was to be drilled, as the tiny thing was otherwise prone to slip or jump away or to let the drill merely turn it over, sliding down its slippery side and making no impression. One adroit workman can stamp by hand from twenty-seven to twenty-eight hundred needles a day — so quickly indeed that, watching him, it seems as though he were constantly preparing the same identical one for its eye punch. His die flattens and indents both sides of the wire simultaneously. Then women, using a screw press or automatic machine, *eye* the needles, making two holes almost side by side near the centre of the uncut wire, where the indentations have been made. The machine must be very exact in measuring the depressions or a wrong angle will spoil the product. Expert hand *eyers* can punch twenty to twenty-five thousand wires daily!

While held in rows, the needles are next bent forward and backward between the eyes until the wires crack asunder into two separate entities. Whereupon the heads are filed smooth, and the needles are strung or hung upon tiny oscillating wire rods passed through the eyes to burnish the latter.

Then the slippery little creatures are polished with emery, burnished and tempered, being hardened by immersion in cold oil while they are red-hot. In all they are scoured about three times, and the final polishing is accomplished with crocus and alcohol.

Defectives are next picked out and *heading* done. The needles at this stage lie every which way, like spillikins; so they must be placed in rows. A workwoman wraps her right forefinger in a bit of rag and lightly presses a handful of needles against her left palm. The points all stick into the cloth and so can be drawn aside " forward face." Another step is to sort the sizes by laying these little soldiers already " at attention " upon a plank narrower than the shortest of them. The " reviewing officer " with one stroke of the side or edge of her hand raises the whole row, at the same time pressing gently back the manikins and giving them a light shake. This causes the shorter ones to fall back, while the others stick to the upraised, rag-wrapped, commanding hand.

Such a milling requires nine days in all; but after our Civil War, needles here in America began to be made entirely — that is, completely finished — by machine. A skilled man could point twenty-five thousand in ten hours; a machine does the work better, and with one man to guide it, turns out three hundred thousand!

There are " ground downs," formerly ground instead of cut shorter than the ordinary sewing needle or " sharp." " Betweens " also are shorter than " sharps," but not as short as " blunts." These have stouter points than " sharps " and are good for beginners to sew with, and necessary when stitching denim, coutille, kid, et cetera, both on account of strong tips and less inclination to bending.

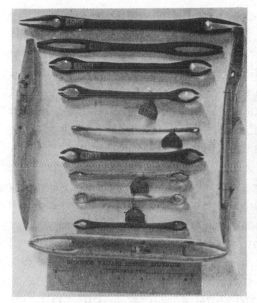

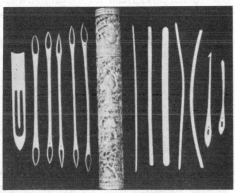

Lent by Miss Lillian Redfield Loder

Courtesy of Bernice Pauahi Bishop Museum

Left: EARLY PACIFIC ISLAND NETTING NEEDLES OF WOOD AND BONE. (SEE *LEAD CUSHIONS* IN THE CHAPTER ON "KEEN-EDGED EMERY," AND UNDER "PILLOWS AND HORSES, MAIDS OR LADIES.") [HALF SIZE.]

Right: A DELIGHTFUL OLD CHINESE IVORY CASE, CARVED TO ORDER WITH QUAINT CELESTIAL FIGURES AND A FAMILY MONOGRAM. THE CASE CONTAINS A COMPLETE SET OF GRADUATED NETTING STICKS AND NEEDLES, TOGETHER WITH A LITTLE HOOK AND SPATULA FOR GUIDING AND CATCHING THE JOINING THREADS. (SEE *STIRRUPS* IN THE CHAPTER ON "A FEW FINAL SUGGESTIONS AND SOME STRAY SEWING ACCESSORIES.") [HALF SIZE.]

For punched work a three-sided Rhodes needle with thread tied into its eye, is correct. For netting one uses a two-ended forked needle of steel, ivory or wood. Thread is wound figure-eight fashion from one split end to the other, lengthwise along the shank of the needle. The thread is passed through an eye near one end. These needles come in many sizes.[3] Needles for use in the tropics come in gold and silver, while gold-eyed ones are always considered superior and are warranted not to cut the thread. Besides knitting- and darning-needles, there are also stocking-machine needles, which are especially delicate — being only one-hundredth of an inch thick in certain parts; leather workers' needles — frequently hook-ended without holes; and many other special trade needles. Altogether there are in existence at least two hundred and fifty varieties of needles, including peruke-makers', tapestry, et cetera.

A needle-threader is a thing not a few of us come to. Generally it is made of bone, sometimes of ivory, to aid dim eyes. I give the dictionary definition since I do not happen to have handled these first

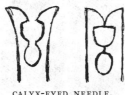

CALYX-EYED NEEDLE,
OPEN — AND CLOSED.
[MUCH MAGNIFIED.]

aids: " Needle-threader. — A small appliance made for the use of persons of imperfect sight. It is usually made of ivory. The top portion above the handle is flat, on which a small metal plate is fixed, through which a hole is pierced; a corresponding hole being in the ivory, of larger size, the needle is passed through it, the eye fitting exactly over that in the plate, so that the thread passes through the three holes at once. Other kinds may be had."

In making fine bead bags, a number sixteen needle is necessary; and our grandmothers' purses were not knit or crocheted, but made wrong side out on hollow, melon-shaped wooden molds. Starting at the apex, one buttonholed downwards, just a bead at a time, with one loop behind each bead. Thus the reverse of old bags shows a point-lace stitch, forming a real " cloth of beads," all the stitchery hidden, not appearing between the beads unless these be separated.

A still finer — almost invisible — yet threadable needle is to be found in the pearl marts of India, perhaps also in the hands of all professional threaders and stringers. With an incredible quantity of bunches of creamy-lustre pearls, large and minute, hanging about him and lying in cases, with associates lying or sitting about and

[3] Among the Tinguians of northwestern Luzon all net work is done by the man who, for this purpose, employs a needle of water buffalo horn. One end of the needle is deeply notched, the other pointed. Along the centre of the needle, parallel to its sides, is a long tongue. Thread is wound from tongue to notch. Spreaders — mesh sticks — may be of horn or bamboo. The operator usually squats on the ground with the net hung above him.

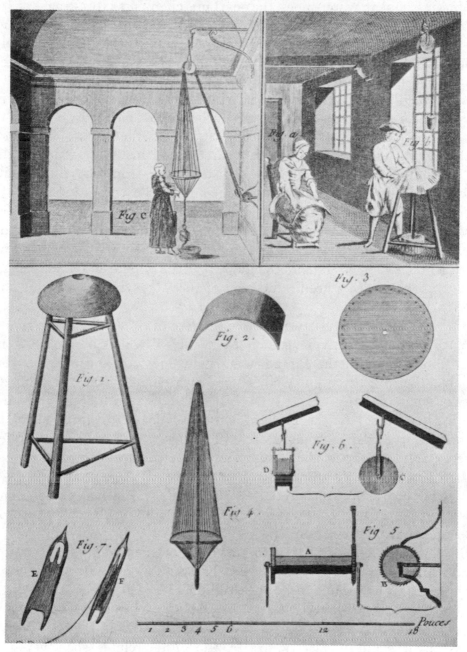

From the ENCYCLOPÉDIE MÉTHODIQUE, M DCC LXXXVI, chez Pankoucke or chez Plomteux à Liège.

PASSEMENTERIE AND PLAITED CORDING.   ENGRAVED UNDER THE DIRECTION OF BENARD, PROBABLY BY ANTONIO BARATTI.

smoking hookah water-pipes, the pearl merchant sits cross-legged, with a low table before him, counting and stringing upon his long pliant wisp of a needle. Such needles are of brass, three inches long, minutely hooked about the silken thread — really, I presume, a home-made article of finest wire.

A needle in Hawaii is called *kui,* and the natives use it deftly in the careful making up of expensive feather *leis* or garlands.

The " Old Lady of Threadneedle Street " is the Bank of England.

Among amusing Old English thread and needle oddities is the " custom of Queen's College, Oxford, dating from the time of its founder, who bequeathed a certain sum to the corporation with a direction that from its income there should annually be purchased for each scholar and presented to him a needle and thread. And now on New Year's there gather in the ancient hall such of the fellows and students as happen to be in lodgings, and the Bursar gravely presents each of them with a needle and a bit of thread, saying, ' Take this and be thrifty.' "

" In China, August twentieth is the fête of the Milky Way, representing the Heavenly River, on each side of which is a star — the Cowboy Star and the Pining Maid, who meet once a year on this date. During the night Chinese girls watch and listen, striving to hear what the stars may say; but before dawn both stars and girls must separate. In the morning the latter leave bowls of water in their courtyards, each maid dropping a needle into the liquid-filled receptacle. If the needles remain upon the surface, the girls can tell their fortunes from the shadows reflected."

Starting in Massachusetts with a child's threatened punishment, we thread our way to the episode of a wise old Guru's pointed lesson in the heart of ancient Asia:

" A darning-needle! O, Mummy! I haven't told a fib. He won't sew up my lips, will he, really? But I haven't said anything naughty! O, Mummy! " Thus runs the frightened recollection of the little New England girl for whom mouth-washing with soap and lip-sewing by our beautiful dragon flies were threatened terrors.

In a Tibetan monastery, so a frontier nurse relates, she saw a god, quite a new one; in fact, only just made — a graceful, willowy Kwan-yin, I imagine from the nurse's use of the feminine gender. The goddess "had been made on the spot, not brought there," the lama priest calmly said, and had taken three months to make. "In front of this idol were offerings, which are never removed — and never (perish the thought!) stolen, however poor the passer-by may be; for the offerings are 'devoted.' They are given by great sinners needing particular help," we are told. "Cowrie shells are given by poor women, darning-needles by men, and many of both articles lay at her feet." Does this imply that men are particularly given to fibbing, or that their clothes need mending and they feel a wave of humiliation when appearing in tatters before a goddess? At any rate, their offerings hint of pricking consciences. Before the statue lay "three or four gold bracelets, large solid gold ones — given by women. 'It is not that the women are the greater sinners,' the lama volunteered, 'but that they are always more repentant!'" But a lama himself may be among the offerings. "After the body of one is burnt, that which is left (the mineral part of the bone) is taken and pulverized, then mixed with damp clay, molded into the shape of a little sand pie, and dried. All Buddhists here are burned," continues the brave nurse, "but only lamas are potted," when their ashes may be offered as a memorial!

An Indian monk — Kumarajiva — had, it is written, an accurate knowledge of Sanskrit and of Chinese, of the Lotus of the Good Law and of the Discipline of the Ten Chants. So the king conferred upon him a title.

One day our monk dreamed of wandering in a pretty park and of being approached by a pair of playful children, a little girl and boy affectionately either holding hands or disporting themselves about the monk. He reported the dream to his ruler, who, being a precursor of Freud, interpreted the vision as a hint of the friar's natural aspirations. "How can a man," said the potentate, "as highly gifted as you be willing or permitted to remain without posterity?" Whereupon two gracious wives were dispatched to Kumarajiva, while in due time ten concubines were added.

So the erstwhile celibate remained at home, turning his back upon the monastery. This, not unnaturally, caused insubordination among Kumarajiva's confrères, who also loved the comforts and honors of a home. But such destruction of discipline was dangerous to the established order of things and must be opposed. Yet how? Well, in gratitude to his majesty, our hero decided to perform a miracle that would deter the brethren from their threatened lapses. So he placed upon a plate a handful of sharp and deadly needles. "Now," said he, "let him among you who would marry, first follow my example," whereupon he swallowed the needles "wholly": but no man else ventured to undergo the ordeal.

Then from *The Sisters of the Spinning Wheel*, by Puran Singh, we learn that "The very rich Duni Chand asked the Guru Nanak to his house and treated him with much affection. Nanak noticed that the house was stuck over with flags, and when he inquired what they might mean he was told that each flag stood for a lakh of rupees that the master had gained. Nanak then politely handed Duni a needle and bade him keep it until he asked for it in the next world. The foolish Duni took the needle to his wife and told her to put it by. 'How can a needle enter the next world?' said she. 'Go and return it to the Guru.' Duni Chand carried his wife's message to the Guru, who said, 'If such a small and light thing as a needle cannot go to the next world, how can thy wealth reach there?' Duni Chand fell at his feet and prayed to know how his wealth might accompany him. Nanak answered, 'Give some of it in God's name, feed the poor, and that portion shall accompany thee.'"

We Westerners ourselves have been told that "It is easier for a camel to go through the eye of a needle, than for a rich man to enter into the kingdom of God." From this suggestion perhaps arises the idea of sloughing off sin through a second birth, as is or was done, for example, at Ripon Cathedral by the passing of a sinner through St. Wilfred's needle! What more can we say? What higher, holier aspiration or function could a needle have than to be the means of purifying, perhaps of saving, a Christian soul? All its millions of daily practical, pragmatic uses surely shrink before this ideal transcendental service to mankind!

SHARPS, BLUNTS AND BETWEENS

" *With her neeld* [*needle*] *composes Nature's own shape of bud, bird, branch or berry.*"

>—*Pericles:* William Shakespeare.

" *It is as scandalous for a woman not to know how to use her needle as for a man not to know how to use his sword.*"

>— Lady Mary Wortley Montagu

" *She was excellent with her needle.*"

>— Epitaph in Westminster Abbey Cloister.

" *Women, with tongues*
Like polar needles, ever on the jar."

>— *Daily Trials:* Oliver Wendell Holmes.

" *Needles and pins, needles and pins,*
When a man marries his trouble begins."

>— *Mother Goose.*

OLD MOTHER TWITCHETT
[*A NEEDLE AND THREAD*]

" *Old Mother Twitchett had but one eye,*
And a long tail which she let fly;
And every time she went over a gap,
She left a bit of her tail in a trap."

>— *Mother Goose.*

" *To look for a needle in a bottle of hay* [*haystack*]."

" *Take your needle, my child, and work at your pattern; it will come out a rose by and by. Life is like that — one stitch at a time taken patiently and the pattern will come out all right like the embroidery.*" — Oliver Wendell Holmes.

" *A magnet hung in a hardware shop,*
And all around was a loving crop
Of Scissors and Needles, Nails and Knives
Offering love for all their lives;
But for Iron the Magnet felt no whim,
Though he charmed Iron, it charmed not him,
From Needles and Nails and Knives he'd turn,
For he'd set his love on a Silver Churn.

"*His most æsthetic,*
Very magnetic
Fancy took this turn—
'*If I can wheedle*
A knife or a needle,
Why not a silver churn?'

"*And Iron and Steel expressed surprise,*
The Needles opened their well-drilled eyes,
The Penknives felt shut up, no doubt,
The Scissors declared themselves 'cut out.'
The Kettles they boiled with rage, 'tis said,
While every Nail went off of its head,
And hither and thither began to roam,
Till a Hammer came up — and drove them home."

— *Patience:* W. S. Gilbert.

"*Mr. Sanderson laughs at the tale of the elephant that soused the tailor who pricked him with his needle, on the ground that being himself fond of water, he cannot infer that man dislikes it.*"

"*Neatly, lightly, swiftly sew,*
Clicking softly as you go.
Shining Needle, none shall be
Ever better friends than we."

— *Illustrated Sewing Primer:* Louise J. Kirkwood.

"*All kinds of sewing we must do,*
And keep our garments tidy too,
Our needles straight, and sharp, and bright,
And cotton clean, and fresh, and white."

— Louise J. Kirkwood.

"*And I, like Grandpa, sitting by,*
Could kisses coy from soft lips wheedle.
A gracious sovereign she, and I
A willing captive to her needle."

— From the poem *Grandma's Sampler:* Alice I. Eaton.

"*In fact, most of us are familiar with needlepoint to-day because fortunately there has come another revival of it and much of it is being done. Ten or even five years ago, to find a woman who knew what petit point was would have been like looking — well, for a needle in a haystack. To-day every second woman you meet is busy with it.*"

— *Antiques:* Sarah M. Lockwood.

KEEN-EDGED EMERY

"Emery-bags also prevail, one taking the form of a charming Dutch woman in a full green silk skirt. This is well over seventy years old."
— *The Cult of the Needle:* Flora Klickmann.

DO you happen to live in a soft coal district? If so, your mother or your local dry-cleaning establishment has probably pointed out to you that the minute edges of coal cinders are very sharp and should be removed from your fabrics before being ground into them as unwelcome cutting agents. Though we do not want such sharp, biting stuff to sink into our textiles, we nevertheless seek something of the sort for the burnishing of our needles when we set out to sew upon these same fabrics. The time-honored burnishers of steel instruments, in machine shops and in the home, are sand and emery.

The word *emery* — have you ever considered it? — is a rather pretty addition to our language; for the word *emery* originated in Greece and is related to a verb meaning to wipe or rub. The old French form was *emeril,* merging into *émeril* and *émeri.* Spaniards and Portuguese say *esmeril;* and Italians, *smeriglio;* while in Germany we have *Schmergel,* later *Schmirgel,* now *Smirgel.*

When I was in Hawaii, after seeing the olivines, pumice and black lava spit up by the volcano I spent a day driving across the big island to the black sand beach — another local freak of nature. Each grain of sand is shiny black, and one seems indeed to be padding along upon a perfect mine of emery, ready-ground by the action of the sea. Whether the sand be really black corundum, I do not know; I fear it is only pulverized lava — that is, pumice — and that the illusion of loose, shifting black emery powder is indeed only an illusion. Lava is generally composed of silica and obsidian; emery, of alumina with traces of metallic oxides, magnetite or hematite, combined with mica, quartz, or tourmaline, even with precious sapphire.

Moreover, most emery is shipped to us from Cape Emeri on the island of Naxos, in Greece, and from Asia Minor. Incidentally, Pliny called the mineral *naxium*. It was discovered in limestone beds in Turkey by J. Lawrence Smith in 1847, when he was there examining Ottoman mineral resources. It is found indeed throughout this general region — near Ephesus, and in mines lying among the hills near Smyrna. Emery has also been found in Saxony, Tuscany, Guernsey; and — in 1864, by H. S. Lucas — at Chester, Massachusetts; in Peekskill, New York — in igneous rock from which it separated and crystallized during the process of the rock's cooling; also in Georgia and in North Carolina. It is in the two latter spots that emery exists in connection with precious sapphire.

The mineral — which under a magnifying glass seems composed of minute bluish crystals — is found in the form of boulders, and is imported in lumps that on account of their extreme hardness — which exceeds that of all substances except the diamond — have to be reduced by machines in stamping mills. In the East now, and perhaps long ago — for there are indications of the use of emery in the making of prehistoric stone implements — fire-setting is the means used for breaking up the boulders. Blasting and diamond drills are employed in Massachusetts. The powder so produced is sifted and sorted. The finest is called *flour of emery*. Mixed with water or oil, or sized and coated on cloth or paper, it is rendered ready for general polishing purposes. Emery stone is a mixture of clay and emery pressed in molds and fired like earthenware. In this way it is formed into polishing wheels. Sometimes, however, the pulverized stone is mixed with soluble glass, or shellac, and allowed to set. Glass stoppers, optical instruments, plate glass and stones are polished through the use of these varied emery products.

But enough real emery seems not to exist for to-day's requirements; so corundum itself — pure or synthetic — and ground-up garnets have in some cases superseded emery powder.

For needlework, however, the corundum is crammed into closely compressed cushions, usually small, but of course heavy in proportion to their size. Needles are thrust into them a half-dozen successive times to polish off irregularities, such as rust or dirt; or at the seashore, are kept in larger emery cushions to prevent their growing damp and rusty. Your workbox probably contains a yellow-specked, red silk strawberry with a little silver top, red cord and silken tassel; or a painted, brown silk darky's head with a twist of bandana about it; or a Shaker-made, highly stuffed, triangular cushion, with two of its ends drawn together to form a handle — a shape suggestive of a heart. Well, as you know, these little sewing articles are stuffed with emery, pure or mixed. Perhaps — if you be a netter — you have also a larger, heavier cushion so stuffed, to use as a weight upon which to pin and secure the far end of your netting — or hemming. So-called *lead cushions* can be found under "Pillows and Horses," while *stirrups* are among "Stray Sewing Accessories."

For children's sewing-bags, these aids to clean slippery needles are essential, for little folks' hands have a way of growing soiled and sticky. The more amusing an emery you can invent for them — a miniature sand bunny, giving a new interest to an old seashore friend; or any other diminutive pet of theirs — the better. And why not ferret out, perhaps strengthen and re-cover, some curious or beautiful old French or Greek device to enhance one's worktable collection?

KEEN-EDGED EMERY

"*Dear Love, thou art the fine resilient steel*
Wrought from the ruder iron of my days;
Thou'rt mine, yet not mine; when the armorer lays
The meliorate metal 'gainst his emery wheel
And gives the burnished sword his final seal,
No impress of the dull mine's rugged maze
The weapon's splendors, glittering with rays
Of running light and pliant power, reveal:
Yet that Toledo blade, whate'er its fame,
Must keep below the radiance of its sheen
Some semplance of the shape it did resign,
Some vestige of the source from whence it came;
So, Darling, come what may our ways between,
Thy life must ever bear its trace of mine!"

— *Distaff and Spindle:* Mary Ashley Townsend.

ON NEEDLE-BOOKS AND NEEDLE-CASES

" Des cure-oreilles! des passe-lacets
De jolis étuis, Mesdames!
Achetez-moi quelque chose, s'il vous plaît,
Des brosses à dents,
Des cure-oreilles
Et des cure-dents."
— Peddler's song.

PINCUSHIONS, papers of needles, small handy boxes, trays, strips of cloth, folded tissue paper, even the corners of dressmakers' mouths, have so often taken the place of bona fide needle-cases, that there is not a great deal to tell of this pretty subject — I must let the illustrations speak for themselves!

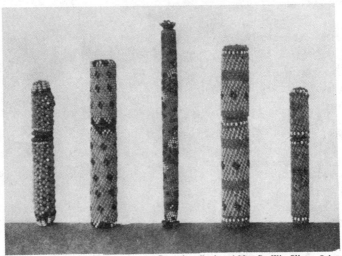

From the collection of Mrs. De Witt Clinton Cohen

FIVE MULTICOLORED FRENCH BEAD NEEDLE-CASES, WITH STEEL, BONE OR WHALEBONE LININGS OR INNER CASES. [HALF SIZE.]

So-called needle-cases or sheaths date from the days of migrating lords and kings who led in battle. The cases held more appliances than needles, and had to be strong, practical, portable. But though

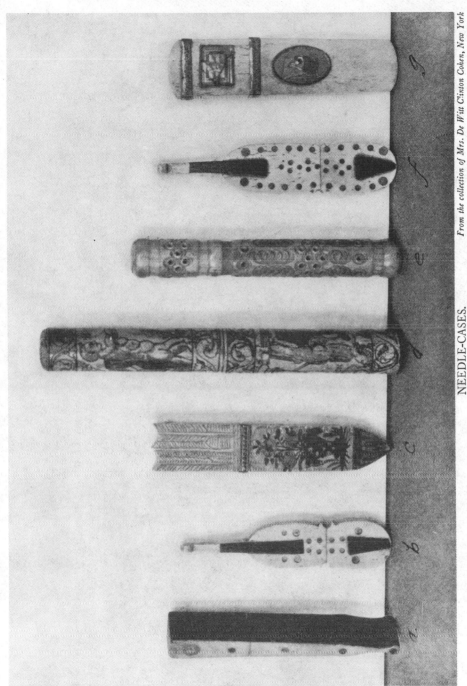

NEEDLE-CASES. *From the collection of Mrs. De Witt Clinton Cohen, New York*

a. OLD IVORY AND WOOD NEEDLE-CASE IN THE FORM OF A CLOSED FAN: ENGLISH. *b* and *f.* OLD IVORY GUITAR-SHAPED NEEDLE-CASES STUDDED WITH STEEL: ITALIAN. *c.* IVORY NEEDLE-CASE IN THE FORM OF A QUIVER OF ARROWS, WITH A BASKET OF FLOWERS PAINTED ON IT IN BRIGHT COLORS: OLD FRENCH. *d.* FINE OLD ETCHED IVORY NEEDLE-CASE: ITALIAN. *e.* OLD PIERCED IVORY NEEDLE-CASE: ITALIAN. *g.* A CHARMING OLD IVORY NEEDLE-CASE WITH GOLD INSCRIPTION PLATE AT TOP, GOLD BANDS, AND A MINIATURE UNDER GLASS: FRENCH.

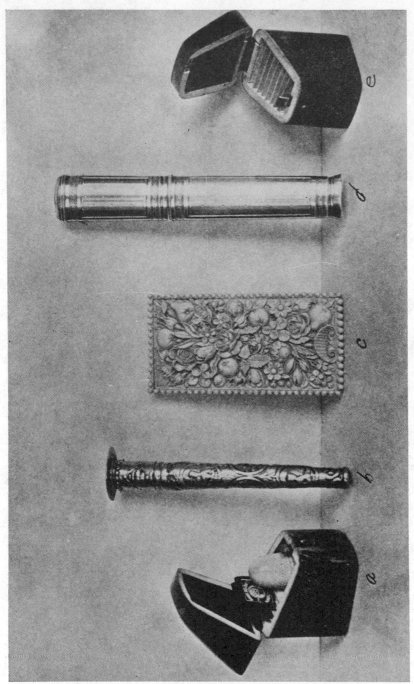

a. OLD ENGLISH TORTOISE-SHELL NEEDLE-BOX.   *From the collection of Mrs. De Witt Clinton Cohen.   b.* OLD SILVER NEEDLE-CASE WITH SEAL BASE. *Belonging to Mrs. Giles Whiting.   c.* OLD CARVED FRENCH IVORY BOX.   *From the collection of Mrs. De Witt Clinton Cohen.   d.* OLD FRENCH SILVER NEEDLE-CASE WITH SEAL BASE.   *From the collection of Mrs. De Witt Clinton Cohen.   e.* OLD TORTOISE-SHELL NEEDLE-BOX.   *Belonging to Miss Isabel S. Huggins.*

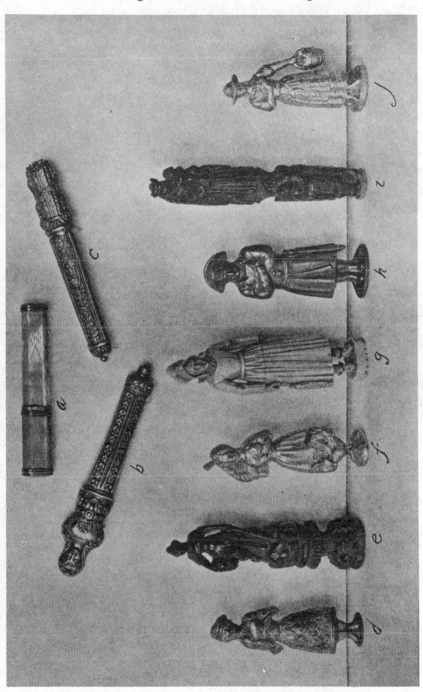

From the collection of Mrs. De Witt Clinton Cohen, New York

a. MOTHER-OF-PEARL NEEDLE-CASE WITH GOLD BANDS: FRENCH. *b.* ITALIAN SILVER NEEDLE-CASE SURMOUNTED BY THE BUST OF A QUEENLY LADY. *c.* SILVER-GILT QUIVER OF ARROWS: FRENCH. *d.* SMALL SILVER NEEDLE-CASE, REPRESENTING A SOMEWHAT ORIENTAL LADY: ENGLISH. *e.* OLD ITALIAN BOXWOOD CASE, DEPICTING SALOME WITH A HEAVY SWORD AND THE HEAD OF ST. JOHN. *f.* ANOTHER LITTLE SILVER HOLDER, REPRESENTING AN ORIENTAL LADY: ENGLISH. *g.* OLD IVORY NEEDLE-CASE IN THE FORM OF A FISHWOMAN WEARING A PEASANT BONNET AND CARRYING A FISH: NORMAN. *h.* SILVER NEEDLE-CASE, REPRESENTING NAPOLEON I. *i.* OLD ITALIAN BOXWOOD NEEDLE-CASE — THE LOWER PART, SHOWING TWO ANGELS UPHOLDING A CHALICE CUP; THE UPPER PART, A MADONNA AND CHILD. *j.* SMALL ENGLISH SILVER CASE IN THE FORM OF A VILLAGE MAIDEN, WITH A CROSS AT HER THROAT AND A FLOWERED APRON, CARRYING A BASKET FULL OF FRUITS AND FLOWERS.

compact and plain without, often of waxed leather covered with woven or braided straw, the inside of a case might be remarkably decorated. Some done in wood were stuck with nail heads; others were of silver, gold, ivory, delicately chased and scrolled; some, inlaid with fine wire or gems. We read of a woolen needle-case of 1391, with layers of silk and tiny stones from the Indies. We read too of a princess's leather

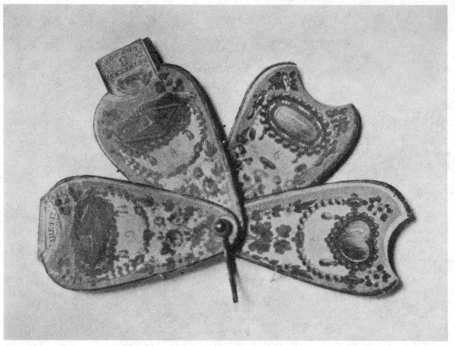

From the collection of Mrs. De Witt Clinton Cohen, New York

OLD FRENCH FAN-SHAPED PRINTED PAPER NEEDLE-CASE BOUGHT IN LYONS.

sheath containing a crystal spoon with folding handle and a spoon of red, sun-baked, boiled carnelian; the whole to enclose *les ustensiles de couture* (sewing utensils).

The inventory of Margaret of Austria, 1524, mentions a small needle-case covered with green velour, in which were tweezers, little scissors, a stiletto, and ten other little instruments with handles of tortoise-shell, mother-of-pearl, and "the rest gilded."

Needles, too, were then of shell, enamel work, or aromatic wood. Shagreen sheaths appeared, for the noted Galuchat had perfected

For descriptions, see foot of page 128.

his method of impressing sharks and other fishy creatures into the service of mankind, and of pressing their skins into finest leather to delight the dilettante.

An inventory of the jewels and stones of the cabinet of the King of Navarre, 1538, tells of a jasper casket in which were three needle-

From the collection of Mrs. De Witt Clinton Cohen, New York

A PINCUSHION, NEEDLE- AND THIMBLE-CASE MADE FROM SCRAPS OF SILK GOWNS WORN BY MARTHA WASHINGTON WHILE MISTRESS OF THE WHITE HOUSE. [GREATLY REDUCED.]

cases embellished with rubies. He secured his precious stones and other jewelry in ten great coffers: these chests he piously called Job, Aaron, Moses, Jacob, Esau, Abraham, David, Solomon, Lazarus and John. In each chest were some of the good Navarre's little handy household *aiguilliers,* consistently labelled with scraps of sentences

---

NEEDLE-CASES

a. TITIAN RED NEEDLE-CASE OF GLASS: EMPIRE.

b. OLD FRENCH CARVED MOTHER-OF-PEARL NEEDLE-HOLDER, TIPPED WITH GOLD AND DECORATED WITH A DAINTY GOLD PANSY.

c. A SOFT SAGE GREEN AND CREAM COLORED STRAW CASE, BEARING THE INITIALS *VDM II* (VIVA D. MARIA II) IN GREEN, AND *VDP IV* (VIVA D. PEDRO IV) IN YELLOW. WHEN DON JOHN VI, KING OF PORTUGAL, DIED, HIS SON DON PEDRO IV SUCCEEDED TO THE THRONE; BUT THEN, BEING HIMSELF THE EMPEROR OF BRAZIL, HE ABDICATED THE THRONE OF PORTUGAL IN FAVOR OF HIS NIECE, D. MARIA II. HIS BROTHER, D. MIGUEL I, MARRIED D. MARIA II, BUT DID NOT COMPLY WITH THE CONSTITUTIONAL RULES ESTABLISHED IN THE COUNTRY. A CIVIL REVOLUTION STARTED. D. PEDRO IV CAME TO PORTUGAL TO AID THE NIECE. THE REVOLUTION ENDED BY EXILING D. MIGUEL. THE PARTY OF D. MARIA WERE LIBERALS AND THE OTHER PARTY ABSOLUTISTS.

d. OLD ITALIAN WALNUT NEEDLE-CASE WITH THIMBLE-HOLDER TOP AND PLACE INSIDE FOR LITTLE SPOOLS AS WELL AS NEEDLES.

e. YELLOW AND HENNA STRAW-WORK NEEDLE-CASE: ITALIAN.

f. OPAQUE WHITE GLASS CASE WITH GOLD TIPPING AND A PAINTED PINK ROSE: SWISS.

g. NEEDLE-CASE FROM SCOTLAND, WITH PLAID SURFACE.

from the sacred creed, each in its correct place and order: *I believe, In God, The Father, All Powerful, Creator, Of Heaven,* and the like.

From this date on, in France, the term needle-holder, *aiguillier, aiguière,* became more strictly feminine and modern in meaning; while sheath or case, *étui,* was thereafter used to designate the more sartorial sort of housewife with all its tiny appointments.

Later, in 1664 and 1692, when needle-cases were of gold, they were taxed as pieces of jewelry, as were our eyeglass clips during the

TWO OLD STEEL NEEDLE-CASES COLLECTED BY BARON HENRI LE SECQ DES TOURNELLES. THEY ARE AMONG HIS SEVEN THOUSAND PIECES OF RARE OLD STEEL IN THE CHURCH OF ST. LAURENT, ROUEN.

World War (though steel spectacle frames were not so considered); while leather sheaths or cases, containing scissors and combs, in the sixteen hundreds were counted as drygoods. We are told, too, that Madame de Pompadour's royal housewife cost only some two hundred and eighty-eight pounds!

In a certain Scotch girl's art manual is discussed the subject of properly designing and embroidering needle-books, emphasis being

"xixe siècle (en France),"
by John Grand-Carteret

NEEDLE-CASE

OF THE TIME OF NAPOLEON I.

From the collection of Mrs. De Witt
Clinton Cohen, New York

AN OLD THREE-PANELED, ETCHED
IVORY NEEDLE-BOOK, MOUNTED ON
ASHES OF ROSES TAFFETA, EACH
PANEL OUTLINED OR FRAMED BY A
DAINTILY CARVED BEADING. THE
CLASP IS OF CHASED SILVER.

[REDUCED.]

From the author's collection

INLAID COLORED STRAW NEEDLE-CASE.
MODERN ITALIAN. [ACTUAL SIZE.]

Des cure-oreilles! des passe-lacets!
De jolis étuis, Mesdames!
Achetez-moi quelque chose, s'il vous plaît,
Des brosses à dents,
Des cure-oreilles
Et des cure-dents.
—*Peddler's song.*

placed upon the fundamentals of laying out the pattern along good structural lines. That is, in a fourfold book, the back of each panel or turn-over might be decorated, the actual turning spaces being left

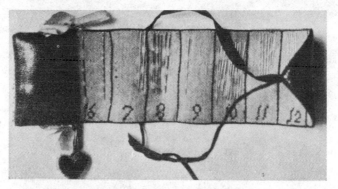

From the collection of Mrs. De Witt Clinton Cohen, New York

ENGLISH BRONZE LEATHER NEEDLE-CASE, LINED WITH FLANNEL. BELOW IS SUSPENDED A TINY HEART-SHAPED PIN-BALL. [HALF SIZE.]

plain to give them a value as hinges; or, vice versa, a band where each fold occurs may be embroidered to mark off the proper spaces inherent in a needle-book, thus suggesting from the outside the various sections and compartments one might expect to discover within. And

From the collection of Mrs. De Witt Clinton Cohen, New York

a. TEN TINY BLACK JAPANNED TUBES FOR HOLDING NEEDLES ACCORDING TO SIZES. THE NICKEL BAR ABOVE THEM HOLDS ON THE LITTLE TUBE CAPS OR SLIPS BACK TO ALLOW ONE TO OPEN THE ENTERTAINING, ORDERLY LITTLE MODERN DEVICE.

b and *c.* DARBY AND JOAN, PAINTED WOODEN NEEDLE-HOLDERS, WHOSE HEADS POP OFF AMUSINGLY: AMERICAN.

d. STREAKED AND GLAZED CORAL LEATHER CASE FOR *a.*

FOUR LITTLE MANIKINS OVER THE SEA,
CLEVER AND HANDY AS EVER CAN BE,
FASHIONED IN FACT BY A PATIENT CHINEE —
TWO NUMBER WIFIE, OR NUMBER THREE-E, —
CAUSE MRS. ONE IS A SELFISH LADEE,
KEEPING THE CASH AND THE MARKET MONEE,
LEAVING THE OTHER TOO LITTLE, YOU SEE.

SO TINY CASES SHE'LL UNDERTAKE
FOR LADIES' NEEDLES TO SELL AND MAKE.
THE NETHER GARMENTS FOR USE'S SAKE
SLIP DOWN A BIT AND THE NEEDLES TAKE
WITHIN THEIR FOLDS, THAT THEY MAY NOT BREAK.
NOR SKIRTS, NOR TROUSERS, THEY DO NOT FAKE:
BUT REALLY NEEDLES THEREIN PARTAKE

OF PRECIOUS CARE AGAINST RUST AND DUST.
TO CLOSE THE CASES AGAIN, ONE MUST
SO PULL THE CORD WITH A GENTLE THRUST —
THE SILKEN STRING ABOUT NECK OR BUST —
THAT ALL SLIPS BACK ABSOLUTELY JUST
WITHIN THE COAT. OR ONE MAY ADJUST
HALF CLOSED, HALF OPEN, AS WISHED, I TRUST.

　　　　　　　　　　　　　— G. WHITING.

then within, just think of the cunningly arranged devices one might run and hem, and pucker and stroke, to stimulate by their fancy the ofttimes lagging impulse to sit down and sew!

In a dream there formed before me a fan-shaped housewife of bronze kid without and embroidered flannel within, each triangular section being a pocket or flap for a different article, scissors being inserted points downward. The little fan was cut on such a decided curve that there was a minimum of base, while the two ends came around like an apple paring and almost met. The case was bound in brown ribbon and was fastened with a dress snap, so that it appeared, when rolled up, like an inverted cone or tiny horn of plenty, showing across the top a succession or coil of promising inner edges.

Homemade needle-cases are frequently whimsy things, constructed like my dream, according to individual fancy; and if a needle-book prove especially apt, or be made, by some dear friend, of cherished scraps, or if it be a bit of one's twenty-first birthday gown, of a lost friend's favorite frock, of Grandmother's rich moire, or of precious little kid bootees, it will be treasured as an album too intimate and rich in memories to cast carelessly aside.

ON NEEDLE–BOOKS AND NEEDLE–CASES

> *" A silver nedyl forth I drowe*
> *Out of an aguyler queynt ynowe,*
> *And gan this nedyl threde anone."*
>   — *The Romaunt of the Rose:* Geoffrey Chaucer.

THE HUMBLE PIN

" See a pin and pick it up,
All the day you'll have good luck;
See a pin and let it lay,
Bad luck you'll have throughout the day."
　　　　　　　　　　　　—Mother Goose.

THOUGH a pin at first thought seems very picayune, how in reality could modern man manage for even a week without such a mite? Imagine an office coat lapel without its handy pin, or picture trying to fashion a gown or even mend without pins! We have used them all our lives and probably never have given their

IVORY GAME-BOARD WITH IVORY PLAYING PIECES IN THE
FORM OF CARVED PINS WITH HEADS OF DOG AND JACKAL.

FROM THE EARL OF CARNARVON'S EXCAVATIONS IN THE ASSASIF,
THEBES　　　　　　　DYN. XII–XVII (ABOUT 2000–1580 B.C.)

Courtesy of the Metropolitan Museum

origin, or their history, or their importance, the skill that has gone into their making, or the great beauty of some of them, even a passing thought.

Still our forefathers must have heeded the matter, for pins could not spring ready-made from the pincushion, and ages must have passed before inventors could even secure the wherewithal with which to fashion a pin.

The original pin may have been split from the shaft of a bird's feather, for the root word — *pinna* from the Latin — means feather. A thorn in Latin is *spina*. Early pins were of thorns, spikes or fish bones. The Egyptians fastened down the eyelids of their dead with small fish bones, and Egyptian peasants of to-day use for general purposes a large thorn from the tree known as *Spina Christi*. There is also a fig tree with sharp, pointed leaves called *Pinus*. The Gypsies employed the new shoots of the blackthorn, boiled in fat to prevent their snapping. Mexico used agave thorns.

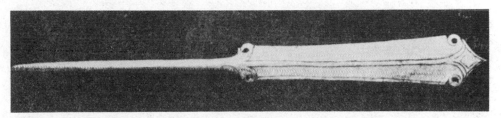

DYAK WEAVING PIN, FROM *LACIS* BY CARITÀ.

Count de Prorok wrote in 1925 from the site of ancient Utica, in Tunis, that "The eternal feminine is no idle phrase. Additional proof of its truth is found in a hairpin industry more than two thousand years ago, which we are now uncovering in our excavations of Utica, the oldest Punic city in North Africa. In one spot we already have discovered more than a hundred hairpins and two dozen buttons, together with many fragments of animal bones, forming the raw material for the manufacture of these articles.

"The buttons, instead of nesevari holes in the centre, have only one through which the cloth of the garment apparently was inserted and caught with a pin instead of being sewed on.

"Women of to-day would hardly recognize the pins with which Utica's smart set arranged their hair in the time of Salammbo. They lack even the hairpin curve, resembling rather a pointed knitting-needle with a head. The straight, single bone, rounded and polished, varies in length from three to eight inches. The heads of many of these pins are beautifully carved, some being sculptured in the form of the human head. Others bear a Punic inscription."

Even in these modern days the women of Spain and Portugal still use pins made from chicken bones!

Bone and bronze pins, all longer than ours, some with ornamental heads, some with double stems, some almost exactly like safety-pins, have been discovered in the Lake Dwellings of Switzerland; and one authority states that as many as ten thousand lacustrine pins have been found. The Egyptians had pins up to seven and eight inches in length, some bearing large, gold heads. Among the Greek remains also, handsome, artistic pins have been found. Some safety-pins or *fibulæ* of Roman origin are preserved in practically all modern museums.

Among the marvelous, awesome ruins and relics of the lost Khmers of Cambodia, only one pin has been found — a bronze hairpin, nicely turned, with an ornamental safety tip. The Khmer sculptures show us that such bar pins were worn purely as a decoration in the pompadour of the young girls; and archæologists, judging from the present Cambodian king's dancing girls, presume that more precious metal hairpins were in use among princesses; for the royal puff and coil pins of to-day have gold-striped irons bars with heads ornamented in colored enamels.

Two parcel-gilt Hungarian *fibulæ* — one filigreed and set with amber, the other of pierced work with studs or knobs, quite

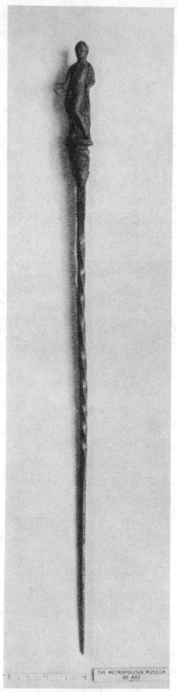

Courtesy of the Metropolitan Museum

LATE ETRUSCAN BRONZE STICK PIN.
[REDUCED.]

a rich pin — both dating from about the fifth century, are in the national museum at Budapest. Replicas of several very early pins are in Room 7, Egyptian Department, and in the basement corridor of Wing H, in the Metropolitan Museum, New York.

We are told that in Wales pins are known as *pindraen*. The material, however, of which they were first made is not indicated.

England had rude skewers of bone or boxwood, followed by others wrought in silver and gold. The pall on the effigy of John Stratford, Archbishop of Canterbury, who died in 1348, is secured with a magnifi-

Courtesy of the Metropolitan Museum, New York

ETRUSCAN FIBULA (SAFETY-PIN) IN GOLD WITH A DECORATION OF ANIMALS: VII CENTURY B. C.
[TWO-THIRDS NATURAL SIZE.]

cent pin. The expression *pin-money* is said to date from the same century, when the ladies, in anticipation of New Year's Day, obtained money from their husbands to buy one or two pins, because on this day the Crown permitted all merchants to handle and sell them. They were scarce and dear and were considered fitting gifts for a suitor to present to the maiden of his choice. Hairpins were called bodkins or hair-needles. Under Edward III there is a charge of twelve thousand pins for the trousseau of his daughter Joanna, engaged to Peter the Cruel. Under Henry IV (1367–1413) the Duchess of Orleans ordered several French pins or *points* from Jehan Breconner, *épinglier* of Paris, and five hundred *de la façon d'Angleterre* — wimples calling for many pins to hold them in place. In 1483, under Richard III, the importation of pins was prohibited; so for a while — until the time of Bluff King Hal — England confined herself to the use of inferior iron wire pins. Then Catherine Howard, Henry's fourth wife, was allowed to

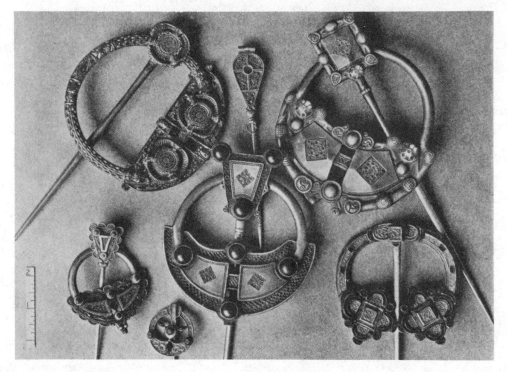

Courtesy of the Metropolitan Museum

THE PIN AT THE UPPER LEFT IS THE "QUEEN'S" BROOCH OF BRONZE-GILT, A TWELFTH CENTURY PIECE, FOUND IN COUNTY CAVAN, IRELAND. — THE SMALL UPPER CENTRE ONE IS CALLED A PIN-BROOCH. — THE LARGE PIECE IN THE UPPER RIGHT-HAND CORNER OF THE CUT IS OF WHITE METAL, INSCRIBED ON THE BACK "A PRAYER FOR O'CHIRMAC," AND FOUND IN COUNTY KILKENNY. THE BROOCH DATES FROM THE ELEVENTH CENTURY. — A HANDSOME LARGE SILVER-GILT BROOCH NOT HERE SHOWN, BUT SIMILAR TO THE PRECEDING PIECE, IS OF THE EIGHTH OR NINTH CENTURY AND IS SET WITH SEVERAL OBLONG AND CIRCULAR PIECES OF AMBER, SET IN PANELS OF INTERLACED RUNIC INSCRIPTIONS. IT IS SCOTCH, FROM HUNTERSTON, AYRSHIRE. — THE BIG LOWER CENTRAL BROOCH OF WHITE METAL, PARCEL-GILT, WAS DIS-COVERED IN TIPPERARY. — THE LOWER RIGHT-HAND BROOCH WITH TWO QUATREFOILS IS OF BRONZE, PARCEL-GILT, AND WAS FOUND AT KILMAINHAM, COUNTY DUBLIN. [GREATLY REDUCED.]

introduce the newer brass wire pins from France. At this time "The widow of John Winchcomb, the famous clothier, is described, after having laid aside her beads, as coming out of the kitchen in a fair, train

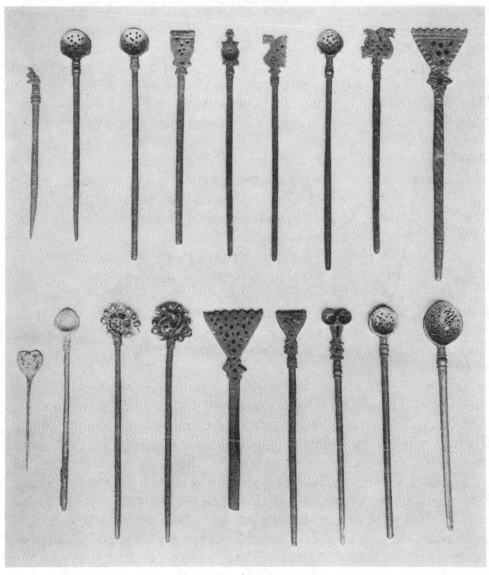

Courtesy of the Metropolitan Museum, New York

WOOD AND BRONZE COPTIC HAIRPINS.

gown stuck full of silver pins, having a white cap upon her head, with cuts of curious needlework under the same, and an apron before her as white as driven snow." In 1543 a statute entitled "An Act for the True Making of Pynnes," was passed, in which it was stipulated that the price should not exceed six shillings eight pence per thousand. The annual amount spent on the importation of pins under Queen Elizabeth was £3297. Around the middle of the sixteenth century blanched wire pins are said to have been passed off for brass ones. Later, in Jacobite and Georgian days, pins had to be very long on account of the heavy wigs.

Meanwhile, over in France, in the fifteenth century, there were two hundred master and six hundred companion pin-makers in the Paris guild. Henry IV of France (1553–1610) renewed their privileges and statutes, so that in twenty years, through growth, the industry had begun to expand to the provinces.

Across the border, a Flamand, writing in 1650, demonstrates the existence of pins in his day and country: "The young girl sits at her work and moves her fingers incessantly, twirling the dancing bobbins with incredible speed. Every moment she sticks innumerable pins to form capricious designs, pricking them in and out, and earning in this child's play as much money as a man can make by the sweat of his brow."

In Cornwall, one was supposed to be able to secure relief from illness by throwing pins into St. Madron's well. Since pins were real treasures in earlier days, this practice takes on the aspect of a sacrifice or votive offering, to propitiate the evil spirits or demons of disease. But a pleasanter custom was celebrated here on May Day, when visiting and village maidens made little good-luck crosses of straws one inch long, each stuck through at the centre with a pin. These light baubles were one by one tossed into the good saint's well, and the bubbles they created were carefully counted, for each bubble represented a year that must elapse before the maid could marry.

In Scotland, people used at night to lay their stockings one upon the other, forming a cross, pinned at the centre. This symbol was hung at the foot of the bed to prevent nightmares.

In England, teachers, to quiet their children and gain attention, were wont to say, "I wish to hear this pin drop." The pupils fell into the trap and unconsciously stopped their whispering to listen, giving the teacher the opening sought.

C. C. Channer and M. E. Roberts tell us that "as the children turn the bobbins over and over, they sing their doggerel verses called *tells*, sticking pins as fast as their little fingers can plant them; at every tenth pin they call out the number, and so the room is full of counting. Now they have taken sides and are going to strive, or race each other, to see which can stick the greater number of pins in a given time. To escape the teacher's cane, they have to put in ten pins a minute, or six hundred an hour; but as the race grows in excitement many of them get between seven and eight hundred, while we grow giddy at the sight, and at the sound of the ceaseless clack, clack of the bobbins. . . . Now and again a child falls short of pins, and goes a-begging. Stopping before a likely giver, it sings, 'Mary Ann [or whatever the name may be], a pin for the poor; give me one and I'll ask you no more.' In this way it generally gathers for itself a nice little store."

When the art of *gri-gri* or voodoo flourished, soft wax was sometimes formed into the shape of the one upon whom it was wished to bring misfortune. The manikin's heart was then transfixed with one or many pins, intended to bring death to the image's prototype. When the wax melted, the death hour was supposed to have struck. Another method of bringing trouble to an enemy was to place four different evil charms — one of them an acorn drilled in two opposite directions, with a pinfeather run through each hole — in the four corners of his or her pillow. But, happily, there were voodoo rites of better omen — strips of bacon pinned or skewered together crosswise over the chimney, warded off witches — so one could protect one's self from the foregoing and other practices of black magic!

There were *prickers*, too; that is, witch-finders, who tested suspected women by sticking them with pins to determine whether they really were witches!

Miss Elizabeth Mattison says that she knows an elderly Scotch lady who, even in these enlightened days, always walks around back of, any stray pin she may chance to spy upon the ground, carefully avoiding stepping past its point, so as to avert the danger pointing her way!

In 1903 it occurred to Henry Ford that the thing to do was to launch a flood of cars " one like the other as pins coming from a pin factory are one like the other." Thinking of the myriad pins in existence, his friend said: "That is all right for pins; but with automobiles, manufacture is more complicated." "The principle is just the same," replied Mr. Ford; " all we need is space."

Adam Smith, in writing *The Wealth of Nations* in 1765, opens by selecting the pin as an example of specialization in economy: " A workman not educated to this business (which the division of labor has rendered a distinct trade), nor acquainted with the use of machinery employed in it (to the invention of which the same division of labor has probably given occasion), could scarce perhaps, with his utmost industry, make one pin a day, and certainly could not make twenty. But in the way in which this business is now carried on, not only the whole work is a peculiar trade, but it is divided into a number of branches, of which the greater part are likewise peculiar trades. One man draws out the wire; another straightens it; a third cuts it; a fourth points it; a fifth grinds it at the top for receiving a head; to make the head requires two or three distinct operations; to put it on is a peculiar business; to whiten the pins is another; it is even a trade by itself to put them into the paper; and the important business of making a pin is, in this manner, divided into about eighteen distinct operations, which, in some manufactories, are all performed by distinct hands, though in others the same man will sometimes perform two or three of them. I have seen a small manufactory of this kind, where ten men only were employed . . . But though they were very poor, and therefore but indifferently accommodated with the necessary machinery, they could, when they exerted themselves, make among them twelve pounds of pins in a day. There are in one pound upwards of four thousand pins of middling size. Those ten persons therefore could make among them upwards of forty-eight thousand pins in a day. Each person therefore making a tenth part of forty-eight thousand pins, might be considered as making forty-eight hundred pins in a day. But if they had all wrought separately and independently, and without any of them having been educated to the peculiar business, they certainly could not each of them have made twenty, perhaps not one pin, in a day — that is, certainly not the

1-240th, perhaps not the 1-4800th part of what they are at present capable of performing, in consequence of their different operations.

Enamel-topped pins were made at Aix-la-Chapelle to use up the shanks of poor needles, but such pins are now manufactured specially and on purpose. A machine can prepare one hundred and fifty thousand shanks a day, and only one man is needed to tend five or six machines. The enamel, or glass, has to be made specially for the purpose, because it must be easily fusible and must also remain viscous sufficiently long for the forming of the head, while it must be bright without the necessity for polishing, and yet not brittle. Two workmen with iron rods, like those of the glass-blower except that they are not hollow, take up on the end of each sufficient glass, which

1   2   3   4   5   6   7   8   9   10
From the collection of Mrs. De Witt Clinton Cohen, New York

VENETIAN GLASS PINS. [SLIGHTLY REDUCED.]

1, 2, 9 AND 10. FOUR BRILLIANTLY COLORED AND METALLICALLY FLECKED FLOWERED STEEL-SHANKED PINS.

3, 4, 7 AND 8. FOUR OPAQUE MILKY GLASS DOVES, ONE ALL WHITE, ONE WITH BABY BLUE, ONE WITH GREEN, AND ONE WITH BLACK WINGS.

5 AND 6. FRENCH POODLES WITH RED GLASS COLLARS: ONE IS CLOUDED WHITE, WITH MENDED PIN; THE OTHER (WITHOUT HIND LEGS) IS OF BLACK GLASS.

is rounded by turning, so as to assume the form of a pear. With their rods they proceed quickly to a drawing-out walk, like a rope-walk, straight, horizontal and about fifty-six yards long. Standing in the middle, the men unite the balls (or pears) of viscous glass and then proceed in opposite directions to the ends of the walk, thus drawing out the glass to the whole length, its thickness varying with the rapidity of the movement between three and seven millimetres (3-16 of an inch), after which the glass rod is cut into lengths and made into bundles.

" The head is formed and fixed at the same operation with great skill by a workwoman seated before a table, on which are mounted a frame, about fifteen centimetres (six inches) high, carrying the glass rod placed horizontally (its end being brought to a convenient distance) ; a gas-burner at about the height of the rod and an air jet for giving a blowpipe flame, all adjustable. The workwoman, who has before her a quantity of steel shanks, takes several in each hand and passes each one in succession, alternately with the right and left, into the heated and viscous portion of the glass rod, withdrawing the shank by a special turning movement so as to take up a little of the glass ; and a turn of the thumb and first finger gives the shank a rotary movement, so that the glass taken up becomes formed into a head which remains attached to the end of the shank, the head cooling while the complete pin falls into a channel. This somewhat complex operation is executed with remarkable address and rapidity, and a skilful worker can head from 25,000 to 30,000 pins daily ! "

— Scientific American.

We are told that the term *bone-lace* comes more probably from fish-bone pins, trimmed to regular lengths, than from sheep's trotters used as bobbins ; for a quantity of trotters on a pillow might prove very clumsy and heavy. The Devonshire lace-makers, living as they do along the coast, and descending mostly from poor fisher families, declare that they could not in those days afford the necessary number of the newly introduced wire pins, but that there were fish bones a-plenty. About the latter part of the sixteenth century, however, the use of pins had become common in England, and it was about this time that pillow lace became popular. An elderly Honiton worker told Mrs. Palliser that she recalled using bone pins in her youth, but that they had been given up on account of their costliness — showing how wire pins had gradually become cheaper. One wonders, however, what fish bone of earlier days could have penetrated the necessarily heavy lace prickings and firmly stuffed pillows without snapping in two. This difficulty may have retarded the development of bobbin-

lace patterns, making it possible to execute only simple designs requiring few pins. The customary plaiting or braiding of the time
seems thus not only the logical undeveloped beginning of bobbin-
work, but the only kind that was mechanically possible. The fact
that these unsupported tresses required pulling into alignment and
so must needs be made of heavy thread, explains also why men in
those days were more frequently given to lace-making than they were
later on. It has also been suggested that many lace designs required
the use of something akin to pins before they were manufactured in
sufficient quantities or were cheap and common enough for peasant
use. May not upholstery nails have been used? In Holland, lace is
sometimes called *Gespelde-werktekant*, or "pin-work lace."

Later, English lace-makers used to put bedstraw seeds, galium,
cleaver, Hariffe or goose-grass seeds boiled in bean-water to soften

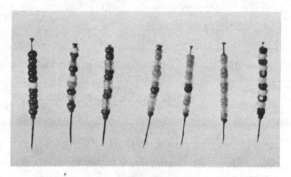

From the collection of Mrs. De Witt Clinton Cohen, New York
SEVEN TINY MULTICOLORED KING PINS, BUGLES OR
LIMICKS: ENGLISH MIDLANDS. [ACTUAL SIZE.]

and color them, on the heads of their larger pins, which they then
called *burheads*. These seeds shrunk and tightened slightly and,
through handling, became hard and polished. The author has also
seen multi-colored sealing-wax headed pins upon some lace-cushions.
It is said that at the *footside* of the lace, the workers were wont to
place yellow wax or green-beaded pins, and at the turn — or *headside*
— red-beaded or red wax-headed ones. In Bedfordshire, a pin headed
with several alternately strung little red or green and white beads,
held in place by the slipped-on wire head from another pin, is spoken
of as a *king-pin*. In Buckinghamshire these are known as *limicks*, and
in South Buckinghamshire as *bugles*. Now that pins no longer are

manufactured with removable heads, the foregoing dainty pillow trimmings are not made. *Strivers*, or specially ornamented timing pins, are sometimes used by lace-makers in the English Midlands.

To-day, in connection with pillow lace, Flora Klickmann writes: "The pins should be very small and slender, with small heads; they should be of sufficient length to hold the lace. Those made for the purpose are sold in packets for a few pence. It is necessary to have a very good supply of them. The pins should be kept clean and free from dust."

Lace-makers' brass pins do not rust even in damp English climate, but they bend; whereas the fine, dressmakers' nickel-plated pins answer lace-making requirements without rusting, gathering verdigris, or bending.

A different type of pin is used occasionally in the making of tatted lace edges, though an ordinary pin is usually employed. I quote from the *Dictionary of Needlework:*

"Pin and Ring. — This instrument is used for two purposes in tatting, one to draw up thread loops so as to connect various parts of the design, and the other to work the purl with. The ring is put around the little finger of the right hand, so that the pin can be used without moving the ring. This instrument is not a necessity to tatting, an ordinary black-headed pin answering as well."

In reality, the French and German knack of wire-drawing was the basis of the modern pin.

Pins at one time were made by filing a wire of the correct size to a point and twisting a finer wire around the opposite end to form a head. These heads, unfortunately, often fell off. Solid heads were first made in 1797 by Timothy Harris of England, who thought of pouring lead and antimony into a mold and letting it solidify. But in 1824 Lemuel Wellman Wright, an American, invented the device of forcing or driving one end of the pin into the mold, where it spread out and formed a head all of one piece with the pin itself. The pins were washed in sour beer or with potash or soda in hot water, tumbled in sawdust and shaken to brighten them, for brass and oxygen form verdigris; then they were boiled for twenty minutes in a solution of tin to coat or plate them. Now they are laid in steam-heated kettles with powdered tin and acid, boiled for some four hours, dried in sawdust, polished in revolving barrels and tossed in trays to remove any dust.

English brass wire pins were first made in 1826. The industry rapidly grew, centring first in London, but thereafter passing to Birmingham.

Later, Samuel Slocum of Connecticut produced a pin-sticking machine, and in 1912 only two children were needed to manage a factory's whole process of planting pins in the papers. Nowadays a single machine turns out a pin from start to finish.

Black pins are japanned by immersion in pans of enamel and dried in a stove or oven.

The *Scientific American* says that " at present the United States, and especially the state of Connecticut, furnishes most of the world's supply of pins; in the year 1900, turning out an average of 113 pins apiece for each American, or 50,167,817 gross, valued at $898,054. But where indeed do all the pins go? More than four million, it is estimated, are daily lost or destroyed! "

Indeed where; and what does one usually do with one's own pins; how many boxes and balls and papers full has each of us bought, received or consumed; into how many channels and uses have they been diverted? How shall we look upon our next new stock of pins; will they have an altered value in our eyes; shall we henceforth handle them with a certain amused respect?

THE HUMBLE PIN

" *There stands the Toilette, Nursery of Charms,*
Completely furnished with bright Beauty's Arms;
The Patch, the Powder-Box, Pulville, Perfumes,
Pins, Paint, and flattering Glass, and Black lead Combs."
The Fan: John Gay.

"*. . . A Tattered apron hides,*
Worn as a cloak, and hardly hides, a gown
More tattered still; and both but ill conceal
A bosom heaved with never-ceasing sighs.
She begs an idle pin of all she meets,
And hoards them in her sleeve; but needful food,
Tho' pressed with hunger oft, or comelier clothes,
Tho' pinched with cold, asks never — Kate is crazed."
— The Sofa: William Cowper.

"My Knot and my Hood,
It sticks in the Mode,
My Kercher in Order it places;
It fixes my Ruffles
And other Pantoffles,
In their Plaits it keeps all my Laces."
—"Miss and Her Pins, Songs for Little Misses,"
from *Puerilia:* John Marchant.

"Pricking her fingers with those cursed pins—
Which surely were invented for our sins—
Making a woman like a porcupine,
Not rashly to be touched."

—*Don Juan:* Lord Byron.

"A pin a day will fetch a groat [fourpence] a year."
—*The Art of Cookery:* King.

"Oh Cousin, let us be content, in work,
To do the thing we can, and not presume
To fret, because it's little. 'Twill employ
Seven men, they say, to make a perfect pin:
Who makes the head, content to miss the point;
Who makes the point, agreed to leave the joint;
And if a man should cry, 'I want a pin,
And I must make it straightway, head and point,'
His wisdom is not worth the pin he wants.
Seven men to a pin—and not a man too much!"
—*Aurora Leigh:* Elizabeth Barrett Browning.

"Then the Snark pronounced sentence, the Judge being quite
Too nervous to utter a word:
When it rose to its feet, there was silence like night,
And the fall of a pin might be heard."
—*The Hunting of the Snark:* Lewis Carroll.

"A lad when at school, one day stole a pin,
And said that no harm was in such a small sin;
He next stole a knife, and said 'twas a trifle;
Next thing he did was pockets to rifle;
Next thing he did was a house to break in;
The next thing—upon a gallows to swing.
So let us avoid all little sinnings,
Since such is the end of petty beginnings."
—*The Ranks in Life, for the Amusement and Instruction of Youth:* J. Drury.
Quoted from *Forgotten Children's Books:* Andrew W. Tuer.

" *A pinhead bigger than the sun!* "

" *A pinhead is bigger than nothing, is it not?   Well, nothing is bigger than the sun.* "

ONLY A PIN

" *Only a pin, as it calmly lay,*
On the carpeted floor, in the light of day,
And shone serene and clear and bright,
Reflecting back the noonday light.

" *Only a boy, but he saw that pin,*
And his face assumed a fiendish grin,
And he slyly stooped, with look intent,
Till he and the pin alike were bent.

" *Only a chair, but upon its seat,*
That well-bent pin found safe retreat.
Nor could the keenest eye discern
That Heavenward its point did turn.

" *Only a man, but he chanced to drop*
Upon that chair, when whizz! bang! pop!
Like the cork from a bottle of champagne
He bounded up from that chair again.

" *Only a yell, but an honest one,*
And it lacked the remotest idea of fun;
And man and boy and pin and chair
In close communion mingled there.

" *Only the pin out of all that four*
Alone no traces of damage bore.
The man was mad and dreadfully sore,
And he lathered that boy behind and before.
The chair lay smashed upon the floor;
Its seat was not hurt, but the boy's was raw. "

Pins has saved thousands of lives by the not swallowin' of 'em. "

—Small boy's composition on pins.

" *And mayhap to find a purchaser for the wool that our kinsman clipped for us but yesterday.   Indeed, his work does not quite please me, and is that of one who is in a way inexperienced, as he anon pinches the sheep with the shears.   But bind the wool in a sheet, Daughter, and pin it with the thorns that you gathered but yesterday in the pasture.* "

—*Chronicles of Kennebunk:* William E. Barry.

WHITE EMBROIDERED LINEN PINCUSHIONS. [REDUCED.] *Left:* LACED TOGETHER AT TOP BY BOBBINET. SIGNED "CAROLINE GRAVES." *Wallace Nutting collection in the Wentworth Gardner House, Portsmouth, New Hampshire. Right:* BEARS PORTUGUESE CROWN SURMOUNTED BY A CROSS. *Collection of Mrs. De Witt Clinton Cohen, New York.*

PINCUSHIONS

" Thou art a Retailer of Phrases, and dost deal in Remnants of Remnants, like a Maker of Pincushions."

— Way of the World: Congreve.

" I will not ride that great Holstein brute, that I must climb up to by a ladder, and then sit like a pincushion *on an elephant."*

—Peveril of the Peak: Walter Scott.

PIMPILOWES, pimpilos, pimplos, pimploes, pinpillows, pinpoppets — well, there's a whole pincushion full to choose from! And were we to reckon up — why, what a collection of pincushions we all have seen in our lives! The men's account would start with the first article to hand — a coat lapel; seamstresses might count the corners of their mouths as the simplest, most natural pin-pockets. However, womenfolk have not stopped here; they have carried their pin-holding devices into the realm of fancy fair.

In 1376 we read in the *Testament of Advice* of La Monteure, Rouen, that she bequeathed to Jehanne du Mesnil her fine sapphire, her paternosters, and her silver *épinguier* (pincase).

The inventory of Marie of Sully, widow of Guy de la Trémoille and of Charles d'Albert, records in 1409 a silver pincase upon which are depicted Saint Peter, Saint Paul, the arms of Pope Urbain, and the Crucifixion.

When pins were scarce, they seem to have been treasured in most carefully closed boxes, as lace-makers' special pins often are to-day.

Pyn-pillows we hear of in the sixteenth century. Perhaps this might be taken to argue that pins were more prevalent at that period than one might think.

The eighteenth century brought the tiny, daintily carved ivory basket, containing a little cushion; and the painted, pale yellow velvet carrot, with a bunch of thin, tissuey, glazed ribbon at the top. Later in the eighteenth century appeared circular knitted cushions.

Formerly the wedding pillow marked with a date was largely in vogue. To the figures were added a monogram or entwined initials, and sometimes a plain heart or a pierced heart. This device was frequently made of neatly arranged new pins, whose shiny heads twinkled and spelled out the legend.

Maternity pillows were also customary. These bore many dear messages of love and cheer.

Then there is the more usual gift pillow, planned perhaps for someone's birthday, and bearing embroidered upon its surface the name and date of the prospective recipient. At one time, many such cushions were ornamented with narrow, shaded ribbon work. Recently so-called *mattress* pillows have been popular. As the name implies, these are miniature tufted mattresses, made generally of Dresden-flowered, white-grounded silk, the color of the blossom being carried out by a flat band of ribbon tied around the mattress once in each direction, with a neat bow at the centre top.

Another very dainty gift cushion or, rather, nest of cushions, consists of several graduated, heart-shaped pillows, the topmost heart being the smallest. Each should represent in pastel tint a color from the rainbow; each should be edged with delicate lace and a bit of ribbon of its own hue with a glint of gold thread in it; and the whole, perhaps scented, packet should be tied together, piled in order, with harmonizing ribbon.

Another type of pincushion is the weighted one, used for holding

From the collection of Mrs. De Witt Clinton Cohen

THREE PINCUSHIONS. [REDUCED.] *Left:* YELLOW AND CREAM SILK, WITH HENNA AND WHITE FLOSS TASSELS. THE DESIGN IS MADE OF PINS ARRANGED TO REPRESENT TWO ROSES OF ENGLAND, A HEART, THE DATE 1764, AND A VASE; THE WHOLE IS SIGNED "S. & B." THE BROCADE IS FROM A DRESS WORN AT THE CORONATION OF GEORGE IV. *Centre:* CREAM GROSGRAIN MOIRE CUSHION FROM FRANCE, EMBROIDERED IN MULTI-COLOR SILKS, CHENILLE, GOLD THREAD, AND PEARLS. *Right:* SEVENTEENTH-CENTURY ITALIAN. COVERED IN SO-CALLED HUNGARIAN EMBROIDERY DONE IN YELLOWS, GREENS, AND ROSE ON A DOUBLE-THREAD SCRIM BACKGROUND. MOST OF THE GROUNDWORK EMBROIDERY, DONE IN BLACK (PRODUCED BY MEANS OF RUST AND TANNIN, WHICH MADE THE SILK BRITTLE), HAS WORN AWAY.

the end of a seam or hem; or used instead of a ribbon stirrup thrown about the foot, or a pin stuck through one's dress at the knee, in order to hold one's hemming or filet netting. Weighted cushions are spoken of more fully in the chapter entitled "Keen-edged Emery," and stirrups are described in the chapter on "A Few Final Suggestions and Some Stray Sewing Accessories." But in connection with hemming, one must mention the most alluring of all these forms, the so-called sewing press — in reality a table vise surmounted by an amusing and very useful clamp in the form of a bird poised with half-spread wings as though about to fly. Not by putting the proverbial pinch of salt on his tail, but by pinching it, one can make this hemming bird open his powerful beak to accept and grip one's sewing. Older birds are of plain bronze; the Victorian and its up-to-date copy are of stamped tin. I should not omit that perched upon the newer birdies' backs are tiny velvet pincushions. Had Switzerland only invented these creatures, we should not have to watch our tongues, for the Swiss probably would have contrived to make humming as well as hemming birds of them.

Many such clamp pincushions exist that are not in bird form. The majority of these are either of polished olive or similarly grained wood; or of the peasant, painted type, in intense gay colors, with little mirrors placed back of the screw vise and beneath the highly stuffed pincushion that is set in the usual little wooden cup.

Mrs. De Witt Clinton Cohen has an unpretentious little old square pincushion with a tiny spiral or coiled wire tacked around the edge — a wire spring, similar to the one depicted among lace pillows, but far smaller. This is intended as a needle holder, each side of the cushion being about a needle's length!

In *Godey's Lady's Book* of 1855, we find the pattern for a harlequin patchwork pinball of velvet, silk or satin "in as many bright and varied colors as possible." Five-sided patches placed angle to angle or tip to tip, then side to side or base to base, and so on around the ball, alternate with bands of four-pointed stars, whose shafts fill the spaces left by the tip-to-tip formation. "When finished, the ball should be stuffed with ends of wool, and the joinings stuck with dummy pins."

We know — in fact, this was only a generation ago — that pins were stored in little metal or wooden cases, called pin-poppets, these

From the collection of Mrs. De Witt Clinton Cohen

HEMMING AND NETTING CLAMPS. [REDUCED.] *Left to right:* 1. ENGLISH IVORY CLAMP WITH SPOOL TOP. 2. ENGLISH BRONZE HEMMING VISE WITH DULL RED VELVET PINCUSHION TOP. 3. DARK BLUE AND WHITE PAINTED SWEDISH CLAMP WITH MIRROR FRONT AND RED VELVET PINCUSHION TOP. 4. ENGLISH IRON SEWING-BIRD. THE MATERIAL WAS SLIPPED INTO THE CREATURE'S BEAK BY DEPRESSING ITS TAIL, WHICH IS BRACED BY A STRONG SPRING. THIS BIRD IS DATED 1740, AND UNLIKE MODERN COPIES, HAS NO PINCUSHION AND IS NOT OF HOLLOW STAMPED METAL. 5. CARVED IVORY CLAMP WITH SOFT GREEN SILK CUSHION TOP. ITALIAN.

in turn being conveniently lodged in the omnipresent pocket of the day.

And of course we all remember the thin, circular, silk-covered pocket pincushion of the late Victorian era; and the flat, wooden-sided one with a velvet band between the covers; generally a souvenir

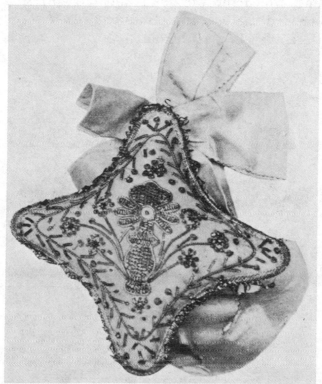

From the collection of Mrs. De Witt Clinton Cohen

SILVER-TINSELED AND RUBY-SPANGLED WHITE SATIN PIN-CUSHION, FORMERLY ATTACHED BY A LONG RIBBON TO A FIGURE OF THE MADONNA. ITALIAN. [REDUCED.]

affair of olive wood and crimson velveteen, with the name of watering-place or resort and the date painted upon one of the covers. Some-times these covers took the form of scallop shells and appealed to the children but quickly came unglued and fell apart.

Then there is the comfortable, fat, smooth satin, heart-shaped cushion of the Shakers — really a stuffed triangle with two corners brought together, forming a loop by which the cushion can be suspended.   Recently a picturesquely bonneted Shaker told me that their particular village pincushions are stuffed with wool to prevent the pins from rusting.   I allude to velvet cushions set into stiff scalloped white bands woven in some Shaker villages.   Poplar wood is finely split and woven with cotton thread to make the stiff cloth of poplar banding, which the workers scallop to correspond with the size of cushion and the width of its tufted velvet sections, binding the cloth with supple silk seam binding.

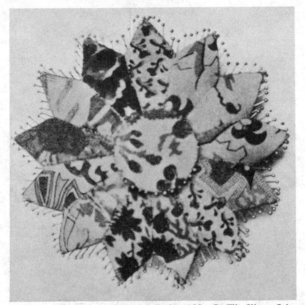

From the collection of Mrs. De Witt Clinton Cohen

FRENCH PARTI-COLORED PINCUSHION.   EIGHTEENTH
CENTURY.   [REDUCED.]

Most of us are also familiar with the red flannel, tomato-shaped cushion.   One of my friends when very young was invited by a boy to the neighborhood fair.   She was too modest to accept anything he offered to buy for her except a red flannel pincushion tomato.   The boy's initials were J.H.D., and out of deference and sentiment the girl felt bound to embroider them upon his gift.   But, somehow, what she managed to embroider — the central letter could not be misapplied — was Ɩ. H. Ꭰ. !

In one large modern household, run with great system, there is a top-floor store and work room, where scraps of different types are kept in great bags hung in a closet. Every year or so all old, flabby pincushions in the house are newly covered and stuffed from this store cupboard. Each bedroom is supplied according to its own color scheme.

The writer knows of a pillow made by a loving mother and stuffed with her little boy's curls, cut off when he outgrew such childish possessions. He was later lost and never found; but when his mother died in her ninetieth year, that pincushion was still upon her worktable.

Pin-poppets and popinjays — I think were I ill that I should enjoy for my gift cushion a jolly sewing-bird, rather than a suggestive mattress pillow, and in his beak my bird might carry the jingle:

> " There's a cheerisome, chirrupy sort of a song
> That's singing and swinging its wee self along,
> And the melody tinkles to this little tune —
> That somebody's going to be well again soon."

Do you think someone could paint one of these birds to resemble the harbinger of spring — the robin redbreast — hanging in his bill another sewing implement, an emery-filled strawberry, that also is suggestive of mild and hopeful spring and early summer days?

But a cushion all made by the fingers of a loving friend — a heart-shaped pillow perhaps, and stuck with a message wished in word or symbol and done in brand-new shiny pins — would touch me too.

THE HIDDEN BALL AND THE SOCK

THY HOSIERY

" The socks I darn for thee, dear Heart,
Mean quite a pile of work to me;
I count them over, every one apart,
Thy hosiery, thy hosiery.

" Each sock a mate, two mates a pair,
To clothe thy feet in storm and cold;
I count each sock unto the end, and find
I've skipped a hole.

" Oh carelessness, this thy reproof,
See how it looms across my sole.
I grind my teeth, and then in very truth
I darn that hole, Sweetheart, I darn that hole! "

I HAVE scant notion why this subject should remind me of Cinderella. Perhaps because at home she drudged and darned, and then came " hidden " from the " ball." Maybe because, like old-time hosen, her slipper was not of glass but of *vair* corrupted into *verre,* the French for glass. Minever (*menu vair*) was used for slippers then, so as well, I suppose, for leggings. Though this is particular history, yet general history freely records the use of short-haired furs and woven, rather than webbed, materials for older hosiery.

Still earlier, of course, legs went bare or were bound. Now, how can I tell of darning-balls when there were no " tock-a-locks " to darn? Obviously I must discourse first upon the rise of hosiery.

In olden days there were chain mail leggings — in French called *chauces de fer,* giving rise to the later terms *chaussures* — and leather or scin (skin) hose — the Anglo-Saxon leather stocking, which reminds one of Cooper's *Last of the Mohicans,* et cetera. Even to-day our kindly Crow Indians still bead-embroider well-cut chamois moccasins that continue upward into puttee-like wrap-arounds.

While old-time rustics went bare-skinned, some humble English classes blanketed their limbs, as Skelton shows us:

> " She hobbles as she goes
> With her blanket hose."

Others rolled their hose horizontally as do our " flappers "; some rolled them on the oblique; while still others elaborately cross-gartered themselves with two spiral puttees wound on in opposite directions, leaving open diamonds between.   Chaucer writes: "The wrapping of their hose, which are departed of two colours — white and red, white and blue, or blue and red — makes the wearer seem as though the fire of Saint Anthony, or other such mischance, had cankered and consumed one-half of their bodies."   These parti-colored, harlequin hose within another hundred years (fifteenth century) became the habit of pages and grooms.

   " Cloath," " taffaty " and velvet hose, laced by means of tabs and *latchets, herlets, auglets, aiglets, aiguillettes* to the breeches, were for only the " high tippy-bobs " — " Hosyn enclosyed of the most costyous cloth of cremsyn."

   Later — 1583 — *The Anatomie of Abuses* tells us:

" Then have they nether stocks or stockings, not of cloth though never so fine, for that is thought too bare, but of Jarnsey, worsted, crewel (mantua hose), silk, thread, and such like, or else at least of the finest yarn that can be got, or so curiously knit with open seams down the leg, with quirkes and clocks about the ankles, and sometimes haply interlaced with gold or silver threads, as is wonderful to behold; and to such impudent insolency and shameful outrage it is now grown that everyone almost, though otherwise very poor, having scarcely forty shillings of wages by the year, will not stick to have two or three pair of these silk nether-stocks, or else of the finest yarn that can be got, though the price of them be a royal, or twenty shillings, or more, as commonly it is; for how can they be less, whenas the very knitting of them is worth a noble or a royal, and some much more?   The time hath been when one might have clothed all his body well from top to toe for less than a pair of these nether-socks will cost."   Of the women — " Yea, they are not ashamed to wear hose of all kinds of changeable colours, as green, red, white, russet, tawny, and else what not."

FIGURINE PINCUSHIONS. [REDUCED.] *Left to right:* 1. SEVENTEENTH-CENTURY FRENCH NUN. 2. WORLD WAR, RED CROSS NUN WEARING CAPE WITH RED CROSS ON LEFT SHOULDER. 3. TARTAR LACE PEDDLER WITH PACK. 4. MODERN BURANO CLAY LACE-MAKER.

"Wear a farm in shoestrings edged with gold,
And spangled garters worth a copyhold;
A hose and doublet which a lordship cost,
A gaudy cloak three mansions' price almost;
A beaver hat and feather for the head,
Prized at the church's tithe."

For in the beginning of the sixteenth century separate hose had been introduced. Long Spanish silk hose were considered a worthy gift for royalty; a "payre" was sent by Sir Thomas Gresham to Edward VI. But these nether garments were still strictly hand-made. The word "stocken" arises from the verb *stucken;* that is, stuck or made with sticking- or knitting-needles. In 1564 came the first worsted hose actually so made in England. Under Henry VII mention is made of a calaber-web hose; but Henry VIII (1509–1547) seems to have been the one to witness the transition from solid hose to web stockings. Howe says that Henry VIII's hose were of cloth (early part of reign, perhaps); but several silk pairs are recorded in his wardrobe:

British Museum, Harl. MSS. — "One pair of short hose of black silk and gold woven together; one pair of hose of purple silk and Venice gold, woven like unto a caul, and lined with blue and silver sarsenet . . . edged with a passemain . . . of purple silk and of gold, wrought at Milan; one pair of hose of white silk and gold knit, bought of Christopher Millener; six pairs of black silk hose, knit." The short hose were, we presume, for the use of the queen; for the article occurs among others appropriated to the women.

But in 1589 one William Lee, Master of Arts and Fellow of Saint John's, Cambridge, invented a stocking frame with hooked spring needles, the kind still in use! Alas, however, tradition states that Lee, in love with a maiden knitting stockings to earn her bread, requited her, because she loved him not, by insidiously seeking to injure, finally hitting upon the idea of a machine to rival and steal away her business. He sent a pair of his own manufacture to Queen Elizabeth, and our schoolbooks say he was rebuffed by the head tirewoman or the lord chamberlain, being told that his gift was of no use, because "a queen has no legs." Yet one authority has it that "Queen Elizabeth's silk woman, Mistress Montague, presented her with a payre of blacke knit silk stockings for a New Year's gift. It appears that these so pleased the queen that she told her silk woman she would henceforth wear no more cloth stockings." Like so many early inventors — or present-day innovators in the East — Lee was driven out for taking away the hand employment of the many: strikes and sabotage are not exactly new! Lee moved to Rouen, where he was well patronized until he was proscribed as a Protestant or until the murder of Henry IV ushered in bad times — accounts differ. Some of Lee's workmen escaped with the machine, planting manufactories at Leicester, Nottingham and Derby. The inventor of the stocking frame, we are told, died broken-hearted! Thus the dictum, "Good parts without the habiliments of gallantry are no more set by in these days than a good leg in a woolen stocking," proved true in the case of William Lee.

In the time of Edward IV, socks of fustian were sometimes worn rolled at the top, as extras over stockings. Upon a rink, one occasionally sees this again to-day, but of course not with socks made of fustian.

Hosiery produced in Thuringia from the fibres of leaf, bark and cone of the *Pinus sylvestris,* or Scotch fir, are famous in Norway and Germany, we hear, against rheumatism. A stockinette cloth of agreeable odor is there woven.

The word *coin* that one sometimes hears in connection with fine hosiery, is a French term for a stocking clock. Right here I might run on into the realm of milady's gossamer lace stockings; but having traced the evolution of hose up to the present day, it is high time I told of their conservative European restoration, their usual darning on the modern darning-ball, and their ultra-modern stoppage.

In French class I remember the teacher's darning, or rather restoring, her stockings while listening to our recitations. She had knit those heavy white cotton stockings — sixteen pairs of them — when a mere girl. At sixty they still stood her in fair stead! For holes were rarely allowed to develop; all weak meshes were replaced before they broke — the proverbial stitch in time. Swiss darning is the method of reproducing stocking-web by means of a darning-needle and a thread of yarn worked double. Such restoration is taught in the schools of Ireland also — I have seen the method chalked out upon the blackboard. And it was taught a century ago in English schools

—for my sewing book of 1823 not only tells how but proves it with four intricately darned samples and a wee actual sock glued upon the page. When I was little and complained of feeling poorly, I was allowed to stay home from school; but in that case I must sit quietly darning my brother's socks. Needless to say, I did not pretend any false ailments!

A friend of mine who, during the World War, acted as farmerette, was told by the farmer's wife to darn her husband's socks. She proceeded to do so in the usually accepted manner of weaving her needleful of thread under and over, but was brusquely stopped and told not to waste time! The wife explained that a thread should be run round the hole in a stocking and pulled or drawn up; then the two opposite edges of the opening should be overcast together in a ridge. And my farmerette remained long enough with that family to know that the farmer must have got round more than once to wearing the ri[d]gid socks.

There is recorded in England's history of tights a complaint about " horrible disordinate scantiness " — a *whole leg of stocking* with too little doublet above. Could those good folks only sit upon Honolulu's sea-wall watching the hourly procession of stockingless and pantless men, maids and grandams returning as though in a cycle to early England's hoseless days, bathing almost " naked and unashamed," what a shock, not too much tights, but too much tightlessness, would deal them!

From Honolulu sailed in early pioneering missionary days the good brig *Morning Star*. Children in the homeland, whence had come these all-enduring missionaries, contributed ten cents a head toward the building of the brig. She was to carry the Gospel to the Micronesian Islands. After ten years the boat was nearly worn out and her name was changed to the *Harriet Newell;* she sailed and never again was heard from. In '66 went forth a second *Morning Star*. She broadsided on a reef. So a third *Morning Star* was launched to Mokil, Ponape, Pingelap, the Mortlock Islands and Ruk. Number three also was reefed. From her worm-eaten wood was made the big bastard darning-ball here shown. The Chief Mate — C. S. Lewis — of the fourth and last *Morning Star* salvaged the block of historic wood and whittled the ball for his wife, Lucy Wetmore.

Do you recall the mysterious deep-sea Tiger Cowrie Shell, split from end to end like a French roll (because it is so covered with brown spotted eyes that it has cracked from the number of evil glances and the venom it has absorbed)? Do you remember its smooth, glossy sides, the pretty, rolled-in, crinkly edge along the crack, its handy, dinner-role shape; and how, having split from the evil concentrated

Courtesy of the Children and Cousins'
Society, Hawaii

Left: AN HISTORIC DARNING BALL SALVAGED FROM THE WRECK OF THE MORNING STAR.

Right: A GRACEFUL GOURD FITTED AS A DARNING BALL.

upon it, it had become a safeguard, a talisman to its owners and was for our grandmothers both the most readily procured and the luckiest of darning-balls? Children of older families with homes near the sea now play with these left-over shells, knowing naught of their picturesque past.

In an old-time New England workbag one might be lucky enough to find a salesman's traveling sample of early Sandwich glass — a rainbow-speckled glass affair intended to show all the colors manufactured by his firm. These sample darning eggs bring fifteen dollars a pair.

A Scotsman respectfully made for his daughter's future employer a pearwood darning mushroom whose handle conveniently holds long needles. An American housewife — the future employer — now treasures it.

We read in the *Dictionary of Needlework* of other " darning-balls, egg-shaped, made of hardwood, ivory, cocoanut shells, and milky glass, employed as a substitute for the hand in the darning of stockings. Instead of inserting the hand into the foot of the stocking and drawing the latter up the arm, one of these balls is dropped into the foot, and the worn part of the web is drawn closely over it; and being firm, smooth and rounded, it forms a better foundation than the hand to work upon. Sometimes these balls are hollow and can be unscrewed in the middle, the darning-cotton being kept inside." And we know the egg-shaped, Japanese puzzle boxes of wood, containing other and still smaller eggs; or similar wooden eggs that separate at the centre and hold an elliptical ball of beeswax. Striped, inlaid wooden eggs one frequently sees in sewers' hands or in the socks they may be busy mending.

Another darning-ball, littler than all these others, also exists. It is the size of a robin's egg and is intended to put into a glove finger. Its fat end fills out thumb tips, and its smaller end — for it is ovoid, not spherical — slips into pink fingertips.

At sixteen I decided to collect a pretty sewing outfit, and at Christmas was encouraged by a sympathetic roommate, who launched me with a silver-handled, ebony darning-ball. Were I at present a boarding-school miss, I wonder would I really darn a hole or ladder, or resort to sewing-machine crisscrossing, or the advertised "new-skins" and gums for stopping runs; not to mention the unsanitary temporary method, applied also to a turned-out hem, which supposedly is then charmed and coerced by this primitive procedure of moistening with saliva to bring about the miraculous acquisition of a new gown?

Verily, whether or not, as Martinus Scriblerus has suggested, a stocking be endued with some degree of consciousness at every particular prick of the darning-needle, still " a stitch in time is worth nine! "

HOOPS, TAMBOURS, RINGS AND FRAMES

" A hoop of gold, a paltry ring
That she did give me."
—*Merchant of Venice:* Shakespeare.

HOOPS and hooples — what very amusing toys we found the latter! Now that we are of a somewhat different age — when did you last see a hoople on a city street? — may we not, nevertheless, enjoy ourselves with such a toy, but a smaller, more comely one? As we have grown up, our hooples have grown down, it seems, into hoops. You might, upon the stuff stretched in your hoop, embroider for some toddler a child chasing his hoople, and so help one advancing from childhood and one advancing toward second childhood to meet in a completed circle.

Little hand hoops are generally of plain wood that one wraps, if necessary, with ribbon to tape or a strip of cotton to lessen the leeway between the inner and the outer hoop, thereby getting a tighter grip upon the material stretched smooth as a drumhead and held firm between the hoops. These are generally circular, sometimes elliptical.

A handsomer variety is the polished wooden tambour, held in a swivel that can be adjusted, and mounted on a leg that is set into a little platform upon which one rests a steadying foot. Tambours, rather than little portable hand hoops, are apt to be used by professional embroiderers and by the peasant groups busy upon their traditional local product — whether the Irish Tambour Lace of Limerick, the Point d'Alençon embroidery of Appenzell in Switzerland, or some other picturesque regional work. I mention Limerick Lace because its chain-stitch variety is distinguished by the name of the implement upon which its net is crocheted — or rather, enchained by means of a crochet hook.

One who thus embroiders is known as a tambour-stitcher; while the thread used is generally tambour cotton. *Passé* from the French *passer* — to traverse — is the same as tambour-work; while " to tambour " is an old verb meaning to decorate with needlework.

Modern hoops come in tin with a spring automatically to adjust the outer hoop against its cork-lined inner mate. The cork, of course, is intended to assist in keeping the goods pinched between the frames from slipping; but alas! this whole invention, though fair-sounding, is in reality rather impotent. A better modern device is the hard black-rubber hoop with an outside screw for tightening the grip.

To embroider filet-net — which is square-meshed — one must stretch it upon a square or oblong frame. Small frames can be bought

Courtesy of the Metropolitan Museum of Art, New York

L'ART DU BRODEUR, BY AUG. DE ST. AUBIN, FOR *DESCRIPTIONS DES ARTS ET MÉTIERS FAITES OU* APPROUVÉES PAR MESSIEURS DE L'ACADÉMIE ROYALE DES SCIENCES. À PARIS, CHEZ DESSAINT ET SAILLANT. M DCC LXI.

ready-made all wound with tape, to which one tacks one's filet. But large frames must be ordered at the hardware shop or of the plumber, to be made of very strong, heavy wire, bent and soldered to the necessary dimensions or even a little larger. Then must one bind one's own frame. The filet should always be stretched, not just fitted in exactly.

Stretching and quilting frames are occasionally termed looms, while looms for the weaving and knitting of stockings and lace are spoken of frequently as frames.

Frames for Mexican drawn-work and for hooked rugs are of wood

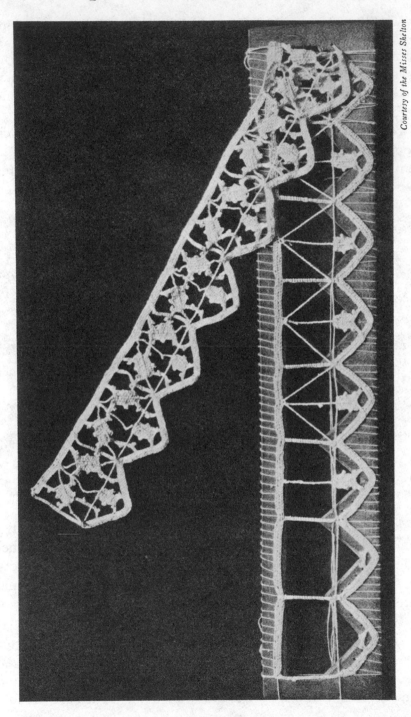

A PUNTO IN ARIA LACE FRAME, USED IN SOME PARTS OF ITALY IN LIEU OF THE MORE CUSTOMARY SHEET OF SPECIAL BLACK PAPER, LAID OVER ONE OR TWO LAYERS OF MUSLIN, TO WHICH POINT LACE OUTLINE THREADS ARE GENERALLY TACKED.

with peg holes — I have seen old window-frames pressed into service for the last-named work. But polished cherry and mahogany frames many feet long, and adjustable in several ways, can be picked up occasionally for drawing-room accomplishments. A fairy godmother once presented me with *nine* handsome old unused frames, each three yards long!

Mesdames Saward and Caulfeild, in their *Dictionary of Needlework*, give the following detailed description of the usual embroidery

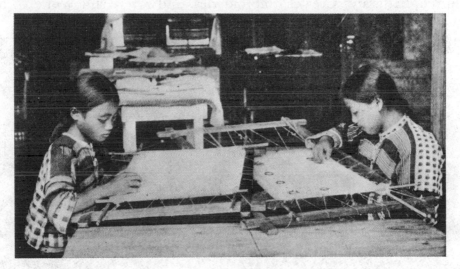

TWO LOVABLE LITTLE IGORROTE EMBROIDERERS WITH THEIR FRAMES.

hoop and square jointed frame, with the proper methods of dressing them:

"Embroidery Frame. — All the best kinds of embroidery, such as Church Embroidery, Crewel Work, Embroidery with Silk, Tambour Work and Berlin Work, require that their foundations shall be stretched in frames, as the stitches are apt to draw the material together when the work is embroidered in the hand, whereas the frame keeps the foundation evenly and tightly stretched in every part, and renders it almost impossible to pucker it, unless the embroiderer is very unskilful. Frames are of two makes: the best are those upon stands, as their use prevents habits of stooping being acquired by the worker, leaves her hands free, and gives unimpeded access to the back part of the work, without the artificial aid of slanting the frame from the corner of some piece of furniture to her hands, or the holding that is necessary with the other kind. But as these stand frames are cumbersome and expensive, the second kind is most used; these are frames made of four equal-sized pieces of wood, or with the two horizontal pieces longer than the two upright, held together with nuts or pegs. They vary in size from four inches to three yards in length. The oblong frames are used for long and narrow pieces, and the square for large pieces of work; and the same frame is used indifferently for Church, Satin and Crewel Embroideries, and for Berlin Work. The

EMBROIDERY

ENGRAVED UNDER THE DIRECTION OF BERNARD, PROBABLY BY ANTONIO BARATTI. FROM THE *ENCYCLOPÉDIE MÉTHODIQUE*, M DCC LXXXVI, CHEZ PANKOUCKE OR CHEZ PLOMTEUX À LIÈGE.

frame for Tambour Work differs from the others; it is made of two circular wooden hoops, one smaller than the other. Both the hoops are covered with velvet cut on the cross, and exactly fit one into the other. The material to be embroidered is fastened to the smaller hoop, and kept tight by the large hoop being passed over it. The ordinary frames are made of four pieces of wood. The two upright pieces are called bars; on these are nailed stout pieces of narrow webbing, to which the material is attached. The two horizontal pieces are called stretchers; these are bored through with holes placed at equal distances, through which metal or wooden pegs are run to fasten the pieces of wood together. In the stand frames these holes and pegs are not used, the wooden supports being lengthened or shortened by the aid of screws.

" The fastening of the material into the frame is called ' dressing a frame,' and requires to be done with great nicety, as if it is rucked, or unevenly pulled in any part, the advantage of the stretching is entirely destroyed. Slight variations in the manner of framing are necessary according to the materials worked upon; they are as follows:

"*For Canvas and Cloth and Serge Materials.* — Select a frame long enough to take in the work in one direction, turn down the canvas or cloth about half an inch all around, and sew it down. If the length of the material will not allow of all of it being placed in the frame at once, roll it round one of the bars of the frame, with silver paper put between each roll to prevent it from getting lined. Sew the sides of the canvas to the webbing with strong linen thread, and put the frame together, stretching the material to its fullest, and fastening the pieces of wood together through the holes with the pegs. Then take a piece of twine, thread it through a packing needle, and brace the material with it to the stretchers. At each stitch pass it over the stretcher and into the material, and make the stitches close together. Brace both sides of the material, and then draw the twine up upon each side evenly and quite tight. Commence the embroidery from the bottom of the material for canvas, and count the stitches and regulate the position of the pattern by them; and for cloth, see that the design is laid evenly upon it before tracing.

"*To stretch Canvas and Cloth together.* — This is required when a Berlin pattern is to be worked with cloth for the ground. If the cloth foundation does not require to be bigger than the frame, cut it half an inch smaller every way than the canvas, as it stretches more. Turn the cloth down, and tack it to the canvas, right side uppermost, then tack them both together, and hem them where the raw edges of canvas are. If the cloth has to be rolled over the frame, put soft paper in between the rolls of cloth, and as the edges of the cloth are turned under, and are therefore thicker than the centre parts, lay more silver paper in the centre of the rolls than at the outside, or a line will appear upon the cloth on each side of the frame. Having sewn the two pieces of material together, attach them to the frame in the ordinary manner, and put them in with the canvas uppermost. When the pattern is embroidered, cut the canvas from the cloth, and draw the threads away before the cloth is taken out of the frame.

"*To stretch Velvet.* — When the size of the velvet to be embroidered does not exceed that of the frame, and the work is not for Church Embroidery, hem it round, and sew it to the webbing of the bars by its selvedge. When it is larger than the frame, stretch holland, as in canvas framing, and tack to this holland with tacking threads just the parts of velvet that are to be embroidered. Work the embroidery through the holland, and when finished, cut the refuse holland away from the back of the material, only leaving that part that is covered by the stitches. Velvet that is used as a background in Church Embroidery requires to be entirely backed with holland, in order to sustain the weight of the embroidery laid upon it. Frame the holland (it should be of a fine description) as in canvas framing, and then paste it all over its surface with embroidery paste; over this, by the aid of three persons, lay the velvet. Take the velvet up, fully stretched out, and held by two people, and lay it down without a wrinkle upon the holland; keep it fully stretched out, and hold it firmly. Then let the third person, with hands underneath the frame, press the holland up to the velvet, so that the two materials may adhere together without the velvet pile being injured.

"*To stretch Satin or Silk.* — Stretch a piece of fine holland in the frame, and paste the silk down to it with embroidery paste, but only tack the satin to it.

"*To stretch Leather or Kid.* — Stretch a piece of unbleached cotton in the frame, and paste the leather to it with embroidery paste, or tack the leather firmly down at the parts where it is to be worked; cut the calico from underneath when the embroidery is finished. Do not stretch the leather or kid in the frame; merely see that it lies flat and without wrinkles.

"*To stretch Crêpe.* — Sew it to book muslin, and frame that in the usual way."

FRAME WORK, quoted from the same source. — "This work, also called *Travail au Métier,* is formed with wools and silk upon a flat, solid wooden frame cut to the size required. Mats and their borders can be made upon it without joins, but larger articles require to be worked in squares, and sewn together when finished. The materials necessary are the wooden frame, small brass-headed nails or stout pins, Saxony or Shetland wool in one-half ounce skeins, filoselles, and a rug needle. To work: Draw upon a sheet of thin paper, the size of the frame, a number of horizontal lines a quarter of an inch apart, and cross these with upright lines the same distance apart, so arranged that the middle line will come in the exact centre of the frame. Paste this paper round its edges onto the frame, and knock the brass nails in, so that they head every line. Take two of the half-ounce skeins of wool, and wind the two ends together as a double thread upon one nail, and be careful that the skeins are free from joins. Tie the end of this doubled wool round the top nail, at the left-hand corner, then pass it without twisting to the nail below it on the left-hand side of the frame; then cross the frame obliquely with it to the peg at the top of the frame next to the one it was tied to, run it along to the third peg, then cross the frame with it to the third peg on the left side, run it along down to the fourth on the left, and cross the frame again with it up to the fourth peg on the top line. Continue in this way until the first set of diagonal lines is made and crossed by the second set running in the opposite direction. When finished, do not cut off the wool, but make an edge with it. Twist the wool over the front part of one nail, and then round the back of the next nail, and so carry it along the edge of the frame and back again, putting it inside in the second row where it was outside in the first row. To secure these lines, and also the ones across the frame, thread the wool into the rug needle, and make a loose buttonhole at every peg, taking all the wool at that place into the stitch. Then return to the centre and make a diamond pattern. Thread a rug needle, and secure the oblique lines where they cross on the paper pattern with a cross stitch, thus forming a diamond pattern. The effect of the work depends upon the regularity of these diamonds, so the cross-stitches must be placed exactly over the junction of the traced lines. Carry the wool from one stitch to the other.

" Up to the sixteenth century tapestry was worked either by hand upon close cord-like canvas, and was really embroidered with colored worsteds, silks and gold thread; or was made in a loom in a manner

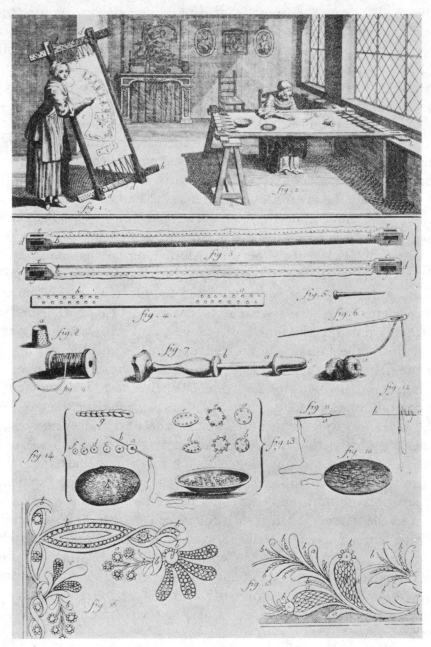

THE EMBROIDERER

ENGRAVED BY ANTONIO BARATTI. FROM *RECUEIL DE PLANCHES SUR LES SCIENCES, LES ARTS LIBÉRAUX, ET LES ARTS MÉCANIQUES, AVEC LEUR EXPLICATION.* THIRD EDITION. *À LIVOURNE, DE L'IMPRIMERIE DES ÉDITEURS, M DCC LXXI.*

that was neither true weaving, nor embroidery; but a combination of both; it being formed with a warp of cords stretched in a *frame* and worked all over with short threads of colored wools, threaded upon needles [or later, pointed bobbins. G.W.], which filled in the design, without the cross threads or weft of true weaving." See the chapter on weaving.

Still another frame-holder awaits mention — it is out of style in these parts just at present, but not in Paraguay, where lace *sols* flourish. *Sol* is Spanish for sun; the sun suggests a radiating disc, while wheels have radiating spokes. Hence the two terms — wheels and sols — for a South American lace made on any contraption that permits of building up a circle full of spreading threads, which must be held in place till the whole be finished and each thread looped securely over the others it passes. Strong pins must be pushed down through the outer rim of holes, leaving about an eighth of an inch of the pin sticking up. About these are twined the threads. The pinheads should slant away from the centre, braced, as it were, against any pull from the threads. My first attempt as a " wheelwright " was carried out upon the well-stuffed seat of an upholstered chair. The continued construction of wheels upon a piece of good furniture, however, might soon so fill it with pinholes as to destroy the goodness. One could prick measured holes through a piece of stiff cardboard. Perforated tin stretchers of this sort were to be had when Teneriffe lace was in vogue hereabouts. Square and circular celluloid holders were also much used. In fact, art needlework shops carried an endless variety of small modern inventions, and amateurs rigged up amusing home-made contrivances for the production of wheels, wheels, and wheels within wheels!

Wheels and hoops seem to have joined hands — much as may the great astral serpent of evil, occultly supposed to encircle the world by holding his tail in his mouth, shutting poor mortals out from the heaven beyond; you all have seen or heard of hoop snakes! The chapter opened and has closed with circular apparatus, apparently triumphing over the square — the time-old rivalry of the square and the circle. Some say this is the cause of seasickness: trying to fit a square meal to a round stomach. Still, I think embroiderers may risk the confusion of harboring both a useful square frame and a gracefully rounded tambour.

HOOPS, TAMBOURS, RINGS AND FRAMES

" I hoop the firmament, and make
This my embrace the zodiack."
— Cleaveland.

" With a tambour waistcoat, white linen breeches and a taper switch in your hand, your figure frankly must be irresistible."
— *Man and Wife:* George Colman.

" Recollect, Lady Teazle, when I saw you first sitting at your tambour, in a pretty figured linen gown."
— *The School for Scandal:* Richard Brinsley Sheridan.

" She lay awake ten minutes on Wednesday night debating between her spotted and her tamboured muslin."
— *Northanger Abbey:* Jane Austen.

" She sat herring-boning, tambouring or stitching."
— *Ingoldsby Legends:* Richard Harris Barham.

" Satins may also be cleaned, dried, damped, brushed, framed and finished, exactly as described for silk damasks."
— *Workshop Receipts.*

" There are days when the needle grows heavy, and the bright silks grow dull to the woman who bends to her embroidery frame with no daughters about her."
— *The Feast of Lanterns:* Louise Jordan Miln.

" She watched and taught the girls that sang at their embroidery frames while the great silk flowers grew from their needles."
— *The Feast of Lanterns:* Louise Jordan Miln.

PILLOWS AND
HORSES, MAIDS OR LADIES!

"Il vous fault pour vostre mesnage
Entre vous, mesnagers nouveaulx . . .
. . . Carreaux d'ouvrage,
Quenoilles, hasples et fusiaux."
— *Ballade des nouveaulx mariez:* Eustache Deschamps.

In La fille mal gardée, *written by Favart in 1758, the magistrate says to Mlle Bobinette, "Allez lui chercher son* carreau *de dentelle, qu'elle s'occupe jusqu'à mon retour; la jeunesse ne se perd que par désœuvrement."*

YOU may wonder, am I going to write of sawhorses or sea horses or mermaids, for all you can guess from this chapter head! No, not exactly. The horses we are to discuss partake of the nature, it is true, of sawhorses upon which to rest or prop one's pillow: but when talking of lace and the fixings thereof, one does not visualize anything so clumsy as a carpenter's horse; but rather, harness and appurtenances, graceful and charming enough to belong to the realm of sea horses and mermaids. For "maids" and "ladies," be it known, are also names for pillow stands.

The different forms of lace-making pillow used in various countries are very interesting, and for the lace enthusiast who has the space, they make a unique collection, particularly if some fine piece of the appropriate kind of lace, mounted with the correct bobbins, is in the process of making upon the pillow. A hollow muff-like pillow is used in Italy, with a three-legged wooden stand, between the three projecting upper leg extensions of which the pillow can be placed at any angle. This is necessitated by the constant change of direction of the design of most typical Italian lace. In Abruzzi, covers are made of gaily striped calico, marked in bandings of appropriate width that do duty as guides or patterns in lieu of parchment prickings! One can see the Abruzzian peasants seated in neighborly fashion one above another upon the outdoor steps of an artistic old Italian stucco house, knees up to steady the roly-poly pillows, all in bright calico, with stores of pins, scissors, thread and bobbins in their hollow centres.   These dark-haired lace-makers may sound as though they were quarreling; but

From the author's collection

ITALIAN MUFF-SHAPED LACE PILLOW.
[MUCH REDUCED.]

From the author's collection

ITALIAN PILLOW STAND. [MUCH REDUCED.]

doubtless they are only gossiping — picking pin pricks into their acquaintances' fair reputations as nonchalantly as they would stick pins into their pillows!

In Germany and Russia, where the tape-like Italian designs are also made, a similar muff pillow is used, placed, however, in a weighted basket or box upon the table, or in a low, four-footed, horizontal wooden frame, or nestling in a four-sided hollowed pad upon the knees.

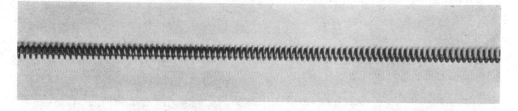

STEEL SPRING TO PLACE AROUND OR ON THE FRONT OF A PILLOW, THAT THE THREADS MAY FALL INTO THE WIRE SPIRALS AND REMAIN WHERE THEY ARE LAID, NOT SLIPPING TO THE RIGHT OR TO THE LEFT. [ACTUAL DIAMETER.]

This, although easy to carry about, leaves one very little working space between the pillow and the body, and keeps the elbows sharply bent and cramped. Holding the cushion upon the knees indoors is also habitual in Italy, as the work is frequently taken up and put aside

Left: A DEVONSHIRE LACE PILLOW, SET UP. ITS DEVONSHIRE STICKS ARE SCARCE. [GREATLY REDUCED.]

Right: A LITTLE, MODERN, FRENCH-TYPE SWISS PILLOW FROM GENEVA, WITH GREEN AND CREAM-COLORED OILCLOTH COVER AND WITH BRIGHTLY COLORED CELLULOID THREAD PROTECTORS SLIPPED OVER THE SPINDLES OF THE BOBBINS. THE WHEEL BEARING THE LACE PRICKING REVOLVES BACKWARDS, DROPPING THE FINISHED LACE INTO A LITTLE SACK OR POCKET AT THE REAR OF THE CUSHION. [MUCH REDUCED.]

between one household duty and another. The lace, however, is apt to become soiled by this contact with the dress.

In parts of Germany and France where the lace is made in long straight continuous strips, a small, revolving, green-baize-covered,

Both from the collection of Mrs. De Witt Clinton Cohen, New York

Left: BACK OF A LARGE, SQUARE, BELGIAN LACE PILLOW. [GREATLY REDUCED.]

Right: FAN-SHAPED DANISH PILLOW COVERED WITH DARK BLUE SERGE. AT THE END OF THE CUSHION IS A WOODEN RATCHET AND STEEL SPRING TO REGULATE AND STEADY THE CYLINDER, UPON WHICH LIES AN OLD BIT OF DANISH LACE. TWO KINDS OF DANISH BOBBINS ALSO ARE SHOWN. [MUCH REDUCED.]

From the author's collection   *Courtesy of B. Altman & Co.*

Left: OLD PILLOW "*À BOLLETS*" FROM NEUCHÂTEL, SWITZERLAND. WHEN THE LACE-MAKING HAS PROGRESSED TO THE BOTTOM BLOCK, THIS IS SHOVED UP AND THE TWO OTHERS ARE PUSHED OUT AT THE TOP AND SLID IN AT THE BOTTOM, OR THE MIDDLE *BOLLET* CAN BE PUSHED UP WITHOUT WAITING TILL ONE'S WORK REACHES THE LOWEST BLOCK. [MUCH REDUCED.]

Right: SQUARE STATIONARY PILLOW, SIDE VIEW, WITH DRAWERS OPEN. [MUCH REDUCED.]

padded cylinder, set into a little flowered oilcloth platform, is the usual form of cushion. As the work progresses the cylinder is turned away from one, and a new step in the design is so exposed; the bobbins are spread out fanwise upon the tiny platform and upon the cylinder, which is turned or held by a latchet. Occasionally behind the main cylinder is placed a second one, upon which to roll the lace as it is completed. Again, a little silk sack, preferably of dark blue — to preserve the whiteness of the thread — is fastened behind the main roller to protect one's finished work. Or the latter is tucked from time to time into a wee drawer in the rear of the base of the pillow. This is

SAVOYARD CUSHION FROM TIGNES.

especially possible with the larger, desk-shaped Swiss and Danish cushions, which are occasionally equipped with carrying handles at the rear. In the flourishing lace region of Auvergne, one sees so many white-coiffed, black-shawled women daintily at work by the side of their front doors, with big muff pillows covered with striped ticking, propped against the square flagstone in front of the doorway! Another stout, striped cushion is used by the lace-maker like a hassock for her own comfort instead of a chair. And comfort these women deserve and must need, to make fly the wooden bobbins that they toss about so nimbly! The equipment itself is plain and unpretentious; but the effect of so many active lace-makers still busied with simple bobbins and true to their tradition in these modern factory days, together with the picturesque background of Le Puy's statued and cathedraled hill-crests, is to lay upon the foreign visitor a lasting spell. At Tignes in the pretty valley of the Isère, the fast-failing old lace-workers use a rarely seen, picturesque hoop pillow, similar to an automobile tire.

Courtesy of B. Altman & Co.

CIRCULAR REVOLVING PILLOW, DRESSED WITH BOBBINS, PATTERNS, ETC., READY FOR
WORKING: FRONT VIEW. [GREATLY REDUCED.]

As a sole or striking ornament, these lace-makers wear large silver crosses on heavy chains. By day, black-lace-coiffed, black-gowned women gather in the village square or upon their doorsteps, accompanied by their curious wheels — designed, one would say, for the making of long, continuous, narrow strips — and with the time-polished, knobby, box-root bobbins peculiar to this Savoyard hamlet, work as long as their early mountain-cast twilights will permit. Then they cover their lace with three-cornered red and yellow silk handkerchiefs.

In Belgium, where flowers and leaves are made separately and afterward incorporated into the whole, where the natural feeling or growth of the flower is followed and expressed by the threads, two of the kinds of pillows that adapt themselves to constant turning have been evolved. One sort is crescent-shaped, with horns turned away from the worker, forming a platform for the bobbins, and having within its enclosing arms on the side away from the worker a small circular table on a pivot. The other form is a rather flat mushroom on a pivotal stick, stuck through a circular opening in a box. This, although

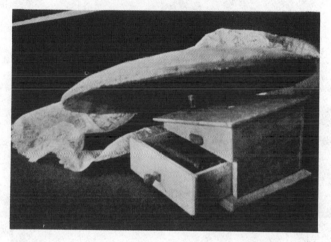

Courtesy of B. Altman & Co.

CIRCULAR REVOLVING DUCHESSE PILLOW, WITH DRAWER OPEN:
REAR VIEW. [MUCH REDUCED.]

adapted to the small raised surfaces of leaves and sprigs, if used for a doily, would make it buckle up in the centre like a saucer.

Spain developed a long cylindrical cushion that can be rested upon the knees, leaned against a chair-back or wall, or held nearly erect by placing a ribbon behind the upper end of the pillow, over the worker's shoulders, across her back, down under her arms, and over her chest, where a bow is tied. When placed against a chair-back that curves upward and outward, it is necessary to place between the pillow and the chair a softly stuffed cushion or, better still, a little pneumatic cushion that is divided down the centre, so that the lace-pillow can nestle in the hollow instead of sliding and rolling off the "watershed" chair-back. When in a studio, this pillow is usually placed upon an adjustable easel-like stand or horse, also called a "lady" or "maid," that can be

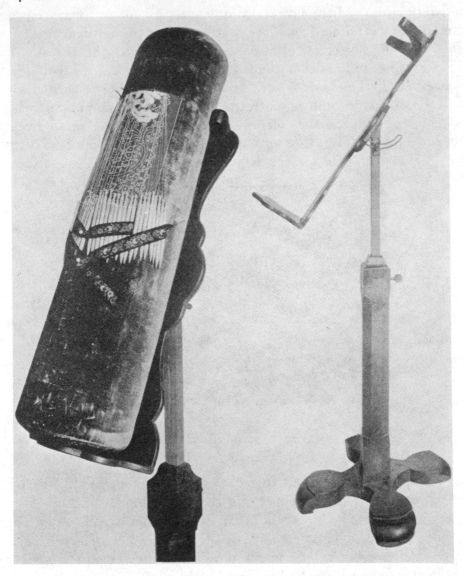

From A Lace Guide for Makers and Collectors, by Gertrude Whiting, published by E. P. Dutton and Co.

CYLINDRICAL SPANISH PILLOW AND ADJUSTABLE STAND, INTRODUCED INTO SWITZERLAND BY MME H. H. DE JUILLIEN WHEN SHE RETURNED FROM MEXICO ABOUT 1900 AND VERY EFFI-CIENTLY STARTED A LACE REVIVAL, FOUNDING TWO SUCCESSFUL SCHOOLS — ONE IN NEUCHÂTEL, ONE IN LAUSANNE — NOW CONTINUED BY HER DAUGHTER, MME F. HUNZIKER, OF CLARENS. THEIR PUPILS HAVE BEEN MANY AND HAVE SPREAD TO ALL PARTS OF THE CIVILIZED WORLD, THOUGH THE MAJORITY, OF COURSE, ARE SWISS AND HAVE CONSCIOUSLY OR UNCONSCIOUSLY CON-TRIBUTED TO THE REVIVAL OF LACE INTEREST IN SWITZERLAND. [GREATLY REDUCED.]

raised or lowered, tipped forward or backward.   Although this pillow
is cumbersome, one of its great advantages is that three strips of work
can be done on the different sides of the same cushion or métier at the
same time, so that the worker can have the variety, if she wish, of
changing from one to the other, and the student can learn three designs
in one lesson — if her teacher be willing to show her that many — and
then go home and complete her samples, carrying about only one
pillow instead of three.   Another great advantage is that, instead of

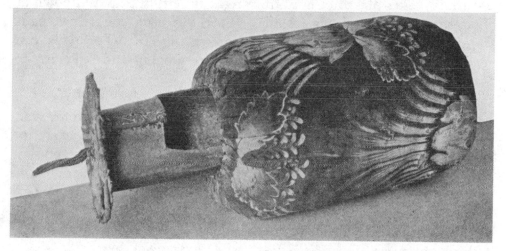

From the collection of Mrs. De Witt Clinton Cohen, New York

OLD RED-FIGURED CALICO-COVERED SPANISH PILLOW, WITH CYLINDRICAL CARDBOARD DRAWER OR
POCKET.   [ABOUT ONE-QUARTER ACTUAL SIZE.]

stooping forward over one's pillow, one has it right in front of one on
a level with the eyes, one's elbows falling naturally instead of being
held out sideways, so that the arms are not so quickly tired.   The
threads also hang, instead of lying flat upon a platform, and the bobbins therefore tend to right them, keep them taut and prevent unsightly loops from forming.   The cushion is stuffed hard with long
wisps of straw tied into a tight bundle seven inches in diameter and
chopped off sharply at each end, making a filling twenty-six inches
long.   Then the straw is covered round with a straight strip of firm
material, and two circular caps are sewed on at the ends.   The Spanish
pillow was naturally adopted by Mexico and is also the one used in
the Philippines.

The pillow used a hundred years ago in French Switzerland was inclined like a desk, sloping down on the sides, having three movable cushions or *bollets* that could slide up and down the centre in a broad groove. When the worker reached the bottom *bollet,* she slid the three up — thus moving up the lace — removed the top *bollet,* replaced it at the bottom, and then was ready to continue the work upon the fresh bottom pad. This lace cushion was, of course, also used for strip work, as it too was incapable of being constantly turned, for the turning, naturally, takes place not only from right to left, but up and down at the same time, and zigzag fashion. Therefore stiff, square felt pads were introduced for pinning to stationary pillows. The pads can readily be shifted, yet steadied by the mere moving and replacing of two or three long pins.

The Spanish pillow has recently been taken up by Switzerland in her flourishing revival of the lace craft. This came about somewhat accidentally, although the virtues of the cushion and the desirability of a real lace industry have since been fully recognized by the powers that be. Perhaps you would like to hear a bit of personal history concerning the woman who was first indirectly, but later directly responsible for this revival? Possibly if we were living in Switzerland she would prefer not to have her family affairs mentioned in public; but I think the news of our little talks will never reach her. She was a Swiss girl, married to a French Swiss whose business was in Mexico, and she came to that country with him. There it happened that she took an interest in studying lace under an elderly Mexican lady, riding eight miles to the lessons, with pillow under arm. This old lady naturally used the Mexican pillow and, of course, taught her pupil to do likewise. As the years rolled by, Mr. de J——, though of noble extraction, behaved less and less nobly, maltreated his wife and children, and finally his wife, after losing several children, decided to sail to her home country with her three remaining little ones. One died soon after, but the other two had to be fed and educated, and the mother was practically without money. Her pastor interested a few friends, who rented a studio, supplied the necessary materials, advertising and setting her up as a teacher of lace. She knew her work so thoroughly, used such a good system, and was so businesslike that her school prospered until directors in museums and other public authorities took note of it and realized that a revival of lace-making in Switzerland would be highly desirable.

While studying in Switzerland, I traveled so much that I could not always be encumbered with a lace pillow. I had learned to make use of hotel hassocks instead. Taking rooms in a rather new hostelry at Lausanne, I noticed that there was no upholstered footstool in my room, and asked whether I might have one. When I next passed through the office, the manager apologized that I should have found lacking any article so essential to comfort, and explained that he had despatched an order for a hassock for each of the hotel's four hundred rooms!

One continental rack or horse has a circular base or floor plate, an upright leg and a revolving platform, to which and through which is screwed an elliptical basket, the latter covered with a fitted, un-bleached muslin lining that turns back over the outer edges and is held in place by a drawstring. Such a cover would, of course, be scrupulously laundered before beginning a fresh piece of lace. This pretty support is Swiss. Sometimes the base and leg show attractive cabinet work, and the lining is jauntily stitched.

The typical English pillow is also large and cumbersome — a spherical affair. To it belong a cover-cloth, to be washed before the making of every piece of lace; a *draw* or *drawter;* a *hind-cloth* or *hiller;* and strips of translucent horn — held in place by bands of cloth — intended to disclose one's whereabouts in the following of the de-sign, at the same time preventing pinheads already in the pillow from catching the working thread. These bits of horn are known as *sliders.* For drying moist hands, these workers make use of old, un-washed flour-bags — for perspiration yellows and weakens thread. Some modern lace-makers keep at hand a wrung-out washcloth in a small rubber envelope, for wiping oily or sticky hands, while others use chalk, and still others, alum. Flour-sacks are used also to *get up* or whiten the lace, and lace bleaching is spoken of as *hazelling.* Woolly thread, however, is gassed, or passed quickly through flame, to re-move any cottony fuzz. Some Devonshire *pils,* moreover, are stuffed with chaff instead of straw.

Just here I should mention pomanders, pictured, I think, under " Thimbles." Picturesque and romantic as they sound, they were not essentially so, though a pomander sometimes contained an essence that was scented and designed to make romantic appeal. These pretty tools contained generally a needle-case below and a thimble-case above; while in the centre was something akin to a sand-box for sprinking one's ink-wet paper before the introduction of blotters. The powder in the pomander was, however, to be shaken upon moist palms that interfere with delicate sewing. Some pomanders contained tiny wet sponges to shake and sprinkle through little pierced apertures.

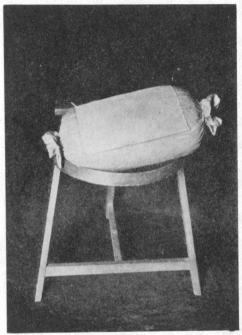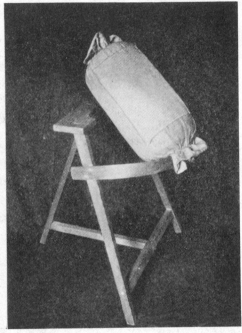

From the author's collection

PILLOW AND STAND MADE AT MORTLAKE, LONDON, ENGLAND, WHERE CHARLES THE FIRST SET UP THE TAPESTRY LOOMS, FOR WHICH VANDYKE AND OTHERS DESIGNED. [MUCH REDUCED.]

Mrs. Bury Palliser writes: "A *down* in Northamptonshire is the parchment pattern, generally about twelve inches long. In Buckinghamshire they have two *eachs* ten inches long, and putting one in front of the other, thus work round the pillow, which to many commends itself as a better plan than having one *down* and moving the lace back on reaching the end of the *down*. [This is spoken of as " setting up." G.W.] The pillow is a hard, round cushion, stuffed with straw and well hammered to make it hard for the bobbins to rattle on. It is then covered all over with the butcher-blue *pillow-cloth;* a lace cloth of the same, for the lace to lie on, goes over the top; then follows the lace-paper to pin it in as made, covered with the *lacing,* which is a strip of bright print. The *hinder* of the blue linen covers up all

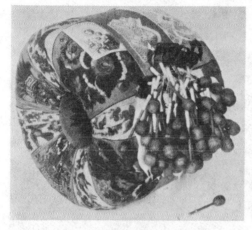

From the collection of Mrs. De Witt Clinton Cohen, New York   *Courtesy Field Museum of Natural History, Chicago*

Left: A PORTUGUESE PILLOW FOUND IN A CONVENT AT OPORTO. THIS ILLUSTRATION HAS BEEN GREATLY REDUCED: THE PILLOW ITSELF IS HUGE.

Right: OLD CELADON BOWL WITH A PILLOW AND PARCHMENT PATTERN, GOLD LACE AND BOBBINS FROM BORNEO. [MUCH REDUCED.]

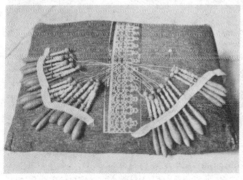

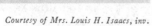

Courtesy of Mrs. Louis H. Isaacs, inv.   *Courtesy of Mrs. Philip D. Kerrison, New York*

Left: HOMEMADE AMERICAN PILLOW, CONSISTING OF A SACK OF SAWDUST LAID UPON HEAVY PAPIER MÂCHÉ OR COMPO BOARD, TIGHTLY AND FLATLY BOUND ROUND IN EACH DIRECTION, BAG AND BASE TOGETHER, WITH WIDE FLANNEL BANDS, THE WHOLE COVERED WITH GRAY DENIM. [MUCH REDUCED.]

Right: HOMEMADE PILLOW, CONSISTING OF A STUFFED CYLINDER OR BOLSTER HELD FIRMLY UNDER TWO RIBBONS, ONE AT EITHER END, THAT PASS THROUGH THE PADDED CARDBOARD PLATFORM AND TIE BENEATH IT. [MUCH REDUCED.]

behind, the *worker* keeping the parchment clean in front where the hands rest.   A bobbin bag and scissors are then tied on one side and a pincushion on the top; a cloth *heller* is thrown over the whole when not used."

The different bobbin pillows are generally, as we have seen, " propt with a wooden maid," or support; and these, indeed, vary greatly in type.   Sometimes — in Newport, Rhode Island — two little tots

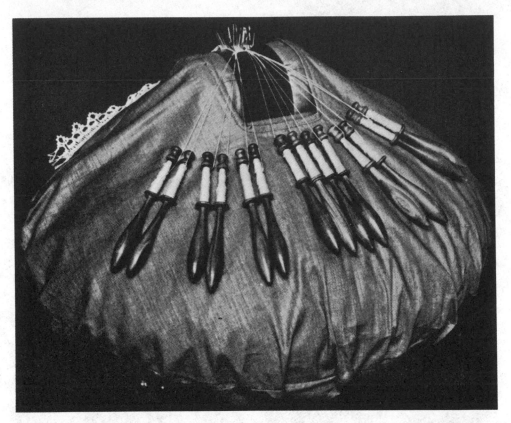

COLLAPSIBLE, PORTABLE, HOMEMADE PILLOW, COPYRIGHTED BY MISS B. E. MERRILL, OF CHAUTAUQUA, WHO IS WRITING AN INTERESTING BOOK, WHICH, AMONG OTHER THINGS, GIVES FULL DIRECTIONS FOR THE CONSTRUCTION AND USE OF THIS CUSHION.   THE CUSHION MAY BE USED UPON AN ADJUSTABLE DRAWING OR HOSPITAL TABLE THAT BOTH TILTS AND CAN BE RAISED OR LOWERED.   [HALF SIZE.]

share an oblong *maid* or *lady*, that resembles an ordinary towel-rack with two long parallel bars.   In fact, I believe that the prior existence and the appropriateness of the towel-rack has been, Yankee fashion, taken advantage of, and that the Newport horses are in reality just towel-racks.

Americans again, in the practical way so typical of the United States, have evolved several sorts of folding pillows, convenient for traveling, or even for carrying to and from the classroom. One of these is a compo board platform with a blue sateen slip cover and a similarly wrapped, hard little cylindrical bolster slid into a washable sack, tied at the end. Tapes pass over either margin end of the bolster pillow to steady it and, passing through slots in the platform, tie underneath it. Another idea is that of a coffee can wrapped with a saddle felt and tightly tied into a cotton cover, propped in any convenient box or basket. The omnipresent crochet spool in an upright wooden holder has been utilized by enlarging and padding the spool and weighting the stand. Even a padded board or cardboards have been made to do service, the bobbins being held in place, while their owner journeys about, by a pretty ribbon tied over and across them and under the board!

Now, journeying westward in America, and mentally still farther westward till I reached the East, I found one day when rummaging through unclassified Melanesian material in the garret of the Field Museum in Chicago a circular celadon jar stuffed with a calico-covered lace-pillow. The pillow is six inches in diameter: resting on end in its putty-green jar, it measures seven inches in height. The top of the cushion is really, I think, the base of a disc-bottomed bag. Into this tight-fitting sack a pillow has been slipped, the drawing-strings tied up and hidden away by pushing the lower half of the pillow down into the close bowl that acts as a rest or steadying standard. How decorative and inspiring a set might be wrought out by following this model, just dressing one's cushion, however, in a bag of derivation according with one's pottery stand! Old celadon, by the way, is often more fallow or mustard in shade than modern basement china departments might lead one to suppose.

Around the pillow runs a strip of faded palm, pricked in a pattern of torchon scallops. This may be pandanus matting palm, or it may be a frond of talipot writing or manuscript palm, such as the ancient books of Buddha are writ upon. In Anuradhapura I have seen the tall talipot tree arrayed in its once-in-twenty-five-years showery

sprays of tiny whitish blossoms.   And in the Temple of the Tooth I
have watched the high priest preparing India ink and, with a dry
stylus, inscribing the palm frond.   A cloth full of ink he then drew
across the face of the screed, the color sinking into the scratches.   The
whole was then wiped dry.

The narrow lace that belongs to the pillow is well executed in gold
thread.   To it cling several blackish bobbins, rather long and slender,

UPON THIS GIANT CUSHION, THE CRADLE LACE FOR THE LONG-AWAITED PRINCESS JULIANA
OF HOLLAND WAS WOVEN UNDER THE ENTHUSIASTIC DIRECTION OF MADAME VAN DER MEULEN
AT THE HAGUE.

looking a little like some English ones that Mr. Thomas Dickey of
Ohio sells.   The spool or indentation part for thread is somewhat
shallow.

Since point and pillow lace are not native to the Orient, whence did
this jade-like gold and black set derive?   The packing-box says " from
Malay group, Dutch Borneo."   I feel like venturing "from Fort La
Roche, Sumatra."   Here the Dutch government sent its splendid lace-
worker — Mrs. van der Meulen, of Celebees Street, The Hague — to
instruct the native women in lace-making.   They, however, with little

effort, can grow and pluck delicious fruits; the climate makes much clothing undesirable: so altogether, why work for greater riches? No, they will not. Therefore, Madame van der Meulen has returned to readier pupils, and the pillow rests upon its shelf!

The word *macramé* comes from Arabia and means knotted fringe. Italy took up the work, calling it *punto a groppo*. A French term seldom heard is *filet de carnasière*. This form of corded lace is usually simple, but occasionally quite intricate and artistic.

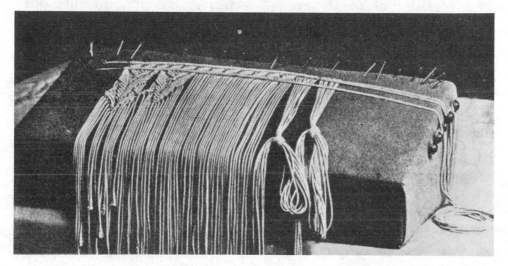

From Oude en Nieuwe Kantwerken, by Johanna W. A. Naber

A MACRAMÉ PILLOW.

For this work a heavy, sand-stuffed pillow, about twelve inches long by eight wide, is more or less necessary as a base upon which to pin the threads and against which to pull when knotting them. Ticking makes a useful cushion cover, for if put on straight from end to end, its lines help as horizontal guides. A prettier cloth, however, can be chosen to lay over the whole work when it is temporarily put aside. We read too of a large cushion heavily weighted with lead; but pins cannot be stuck directly into lead!

Another type of knot-work pillow is not weighted but resembles a long, flat pincushion, firmly clamped at either end to a table. There exists also a frame or loom with tenterhooks, adapted to macramé lace-making — perhaps several sorts of clamp or tension frames to hold the cords at the head of the work and to maintain them in an evenly stretched position. One such loom is known as Anyon's Patent. But some folk merely clamp two vises to a table, stretching between them, from the head of one to that of the other, a stout piece of cord. Still others hook or sew their threads through a strip of strong stretched stuff.[1]

Point-lace makers also use pillows — not for pin-sticking, though, but to have a firm foundation on which to attach their filmy work and to raise it nearer the eyes. For this purpose, indeed, they often

From the collection of Mrs. De Witt Clinton Cohen, New York

Left: AN OLD, SOFT GREEN, SILK-COVERED, MUFF-SHAPED, ITALIAN PILLOW, BOUND OR TRIMMED WITH YELLOW SILK GALLOON. INSIDE THE PILLOW ARE STORED THE WORKER'S VARIOUS INSTRUMENTS AND SUPPLIES. ON THE PILLOW ARE A STRIP OF GROS POINT DE VENISE; A SKEIN OF LINEN; AND AN EMBROIDERED SCAPULA, LINED WITH DARK GREEN SILK, TIED WITH DARK RED AND CREAM-COLORED RIBBON. THE SCAPULA AND THE LINEN ARE ATTACHED TO THE PILLOW BY VENETIAN DOVE-HEADED PINS — ONE OF CLEAR, ONE OF MILK-WHITE, GLASS. [MUCH REDUCED.]

Right: OLD VENETIAN NEEDLEPOINT MAKER'S PILLOW, COVERED WITH SOFT CORN-COLORED BROCADE AND WRAPPED WITH A STRIP OF HEAVY CANVAS, WHICH FIRMLY HOLDS THE PLAIN WOODEN CYLINDER THAT RAISES THE WORK NEARER THE LACE-MAKER'S EYES. TO THE CANVAS IS ATTACHED A FINE, SOFT GREEN, CORALINE LACE PATTERN. [MUCH REDUCED.]

lay a wooden cylinder along the top of a pillow — which rests on their knees — thus bringing the finely looped meshes into still better range.

A certain Hawaiian worker's pillow was only a rather loose roll of unbleached muslin, tied around with a strip of the same. The roll raised the work some six inches nearer the eyes, and was held or steadied slightly between the knees, pointing away from the worker.

[1] See macramé shuttles, under " Fast-Flitting Shuttles."

She was fawn-complexioned with soft dark eyes, and wore in her hair a *lei* or wreath of fresh red carnations. Even ditch diggers in the Territory of Hawaii daily twine the fresh flower wreaths about their sombrero-baliwags. Elsewhere only in Appenzell, Switzerland, have I seen men naturally, unconsciously, wearing flowers about their hats.

Upon the pillow a feather *lei* was in preparation. From the island of Maui had come the pheasant breast — golden-brown and black.

Courtesy of Plâté, Ltd.

CINGALESE GIRLS MAKING BOBBIN LACE. NOTE THE WHITE BODICES THEY WEAR IN PREFERENCE TO THEIR TAMIL SISTERS' ONE-SHOULDERED RED COTTON SARIS. BY TRADITION, THE TWO ARE ENEMIES; FOR RAMA'S PRECIOUS INDIAN WIFE, SO *THE RAMAYANA* TELLS US, WAS CARRIED OFF BY HIS SATANIC MAJESTY (WHO FOR 84,000 YEARS STOOD BALANCED ON ONE FOOT UPON THE POINT OF A NEEDLE IN ORDER TO GAIN SUPREME CONTROL), THE ARCH DEMON, KING RAVANA OF CEYLON.

The plucked feathers were in a box, while across the pillow lay a double two-inch strip of calico enclosing a layer of cotton batting. The stiff little quill of the tiny plume was clipped, and around the edge of the padded calico band, extending slightly beyond it, was laid a row of the gleaming feathers. Each was sewed down twice across its midrib, while the whole feather was also spanned to prevent spreading or splitting; then a final steadying stitch was taken in the back of the band. Short, straight crossrows of plumes were next laid in, overlapping like shingles, one feather at a time, the worker's needle betweenwhiles stuck into her cotton cushion, which thus served a double purpose.

Now we have traveled about considerably, observing the stands and pillows of many lands: but were you in America and suddenly seized with the desire to own such a pretty outfit, you might have to wait long, or to journey to Europe, or to show these pictures to your cabinet-maker and upholsterer, in order to gratify your wish. A cushion you could stitch and stuff yourself. Perhaps you could cut and plane and carve a stand for yourself if you were very handy; and when made of good wood and tastefully turned and tooled, they are indeed very decorative, "atmosphere-producing" pieces of furniture!

PILLOWS AND HORSES, MAIDS OR LADIES!

"Master Wright went from cottage to cottage to ' new-middele' the pillows."
— *The Romance of the Lace Pillow:* Thomas Wright.

"Of course, bobbins must be constantly re-supplied with thread, and in a corner of the room I saw a white-haired grandmother with her dévidoir, or spindle, busily winding thread on the bobbins for the children. She made a beautiful picture there at her wheel with a dozen little girls with their cushions crowding near her."

"The mother of the household, who had the mop of fuzzy, dark red hair often seen in this region, had hurried her scrubbing to an end, and wiping her hands on her blue apron, was ready to uncover her own cushion. I looked at the chapped, rough skin and the hands used to pulling weeds and digging potatoes and scrubbing, and realized that they could not possibly hold a piece of fine sewing — the thread would catch at every stitch — and yet that she could turn from her scrubbing-brush to the little wooden bobbins (her fingers need not touch the thread) and proceed without difficulty on a snowy bit of Valenciennes — for happily she was following her mother in Valenciennes."

". . . the all-important large demonstration cushion with its gigantesque bobbins attached to heavy colored wool threads to aid the eye and brain."

"This delicate métier cannot successfully combat the influences of the social and industrial groupings of the larger centres; the living wage, the shorter hours, the distractions of cinema and café. The age-old patience of the lace-maker is born of a certain ignorance and isolation."
— *Bobbins of Belgium:* Charlotte Kellogg.

BEAUTIFUL BOBBINS

"Oh, such merry tools these,
Quaintly carvèd and turned,
Tinkling, trying to please
With the lullabies, learned
As they twist, mingle, toss
In life's take, give and cross!"
— A Lace Guide for Makers and Collectors: Gertrude Whiting.

A DOZEN tales could I tell of the mooted origins of lace — a few legends pertain to bobbins. I shall skip by Egypt, China and India to Arabia where the burnous is worn — you may read in another chapter of the thimble-trimmed burnous. Its edges wear and fray, so to renew the garment's use, Arabians knot such edges into fringe. Arabs under the name of Moors settled in Spain. From fringed edges there very naturally developed larger surfaces enmeshed by the same method of knotting, and the long threads employed came to be wound upon spools with handles — bobbins. I allude to macramé, not bobbin lace proper, but perhaps one of its forerunners.

Greece, Byzantium and Peru I also skip, and Italy with its lace legend, Russia with its, and France, to little Belgium which has a precious tale of bobbins. In the quaint town of Bruges with its cobbled streets and becurtained windows, there lived in a simple cottage a shy rosy-cheeked maid named Serena. She was devoted to her honest mother, to her church and to the nuns, who taught her the art of the needle while she learned her catechism with them in the quiet rooms of the convent, with the finely carved statuettes of the saints as sole decoration and the hourly devotions the only interruption. Serena helped nurse sick neighbors, cooked nourishing dishes for the aged, and washed the priest's surplices, until her father's death made it necessary to economize more strictly and give greater aid to her failing mother.

One of her childhood playmates, a lad, often came to help in the garden or carry fagots. Gradually they realized they had come to love each other seriously.

But Serena's mother grew suddenly worse, and the girl in a frenzy of fear and heartache, kneeling before the Virgin's statue in the dimly lighted church, with its jewel-like stained glass windows, remember-

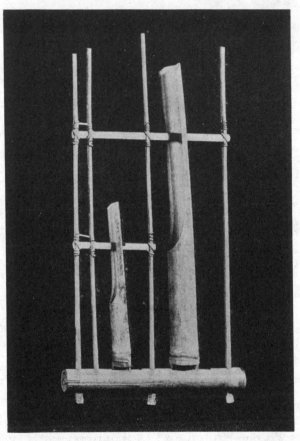

MELODIOUS HOLLOW BAMBOO ANKLONG OF JAVA. [REDUCED.]

ing all that her mother had done for her, renounced her own love and future, if the blessed Madonna would perform a miracle so she could earn money to buy medicine for her mother. Serena went home bowed in grief, but full of faith, afraid to meet her lover, but determined to save her mother if the Virgin, by granting the miracle, showed it to be her wish. Sad and seeking solace in her needlework, Serena went to the garden, sitting down beneath a spreading tree. Here her anxious admirer soon joined her, offering words of comfort. As they sat there downcast, Serena wearing her work-a-day black apron, there fell suddenly into her lap a perfect spider's web, beautifully and intricately outlined! They both exclaimed in astonishment and admiration! Carefully unfastening the precious apron, spreading it on branches and carrying it where no mischievous zephyr could disturb the marvelous web, Serena worked and worked, praying constantly that she might succeed in copying the delicate, fragile net. But her threads tangled. Then her lover suggested tying each thread to a twig-handle.

Patience and perseverance brought success till Serena astonished Flanders with this unique and exquisite product. In Flanders her name and fame soon spread till the nuns and novices became her apprentices, vying to fill the orders now received from court and church.

Again she sadly took her work to the garden, hoping that the tinkling bobbins, the quiet soothing work, and the light physical exertion might calm her aching head and heart. The words she must speak choked her, her eyes filled, but she worked the harder, and her fingers fairly flew in an effort to gain her equilibrium, so she could

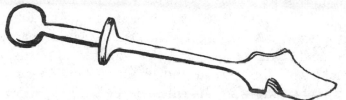

From the collection of Mrs. van der Meulen, Directress of Lace-making in Holland's fifty industrial high schools

A RARE OLD ROSEWOOD SABOT-SHAPED LITTLE BOBBIN OF THE NETHERLANDS.

pronounce the fatal words. She hardly knew what she was doing. Her lover was speaking, but she could not hear and she forced herself to pronounce a silent prayer. Gradually she felt calmer, a great unsought happiness seemed to pervade her, her eyes cleared, and lo! she saw that the loving, compassionate Virgin had, through her unknowing fingers, worked into the beautiful lace a message of release from her promise!

Now, from the Flemish lands, let us cross to Germany to hear a tale of thrift and conjugal co-operation. Christopher Uttman's job as miner was gone, for the Hartz Mountain pits were to be definitely closed. He was strong and ready to toil for wife and baby twins, but Fate did not heed his willingness. So his wife, Barbara, with active faith, shut herself in an inner room and prayed with a conviction of communion and guidance. Her way was shadowed forth, though she never realized it quite as she mapped it out. She had successfully embroidered muslin veils for lesser folk till word of her skill had reached higher places. Living on their little savings, Christopher working the tiny garden plot, tending the children and cooking, Barbara steadily broidered the most artistic and intricate of all the veils she had ever conceived. At dawn one day, and aglow with enthusiasm, she carried her handiwork in a little basket covered with a richly wrought cloth, to the distant chatelaine's. This noblewoman, having bought of Barbara before, readily received her, but failed to fulfil Barbara's cherished hopes. Instead, handing her a piece of Brussels point, she said, " Could you only accomplish something like this ! " It was too late that day for the disconsolate artist to try elsewhere. Outside she sank on the greensward, and from her own narrative we learn that for over an hour she continued to pray. A new hope entered her soul. That evening she set her husband to whittling sticks the size of his middle finger, while she made a sack and stuffed it stiff with straw. As daylight returned, Barbara retreated to the inner room, and thinking hard and clear-sightedly, set to work winding the sticks with fine thread and planning how to copy the point lace. Christopher, knowing his wife's dependability, allowed no least interruption. Had he, her train of intricate thought might have been dissipated and lost in discouragement. On the fifth day she rushed to him, exclaiming, " See what God has enabled me to do ! " Barbara Uttman's revenue, before her death at the age of sixty-five, had reached the sum of one million thalers.

Once, recently, when caught in the country without bobbins, the author quickly manufactured some from slim, clean, straight sticks; in fact, the matter was done on a bet — that she could not teach a green pupil to make some bobbin lace in an hour with no bobbins or pillow on hand: but eight inches of narrow bobbin-braided lace made on a heavy pincushion won the seventy-five dollar bet!

One who has never made lace — that is, the bobbin variety — cannot imagine the charm of the softly clinking, tinkling bobbins, like the singing of a simmering teakettle, or like a lullaby gently hummed in the twilight. Their merry little jingle is very soothing, and some physicians claim that the rhythmic effect is most beneficial to the nerves. Doubtless the regular, constant shifting of the bobbins — just try to hear the graduated melody of the variously throated, hollow bamboo sets brought by the East India pirates to the shores

BOBBIN-LACE PILLOW USED BY LYDIA LAKEMAN, IPSWICH, MASS., IN THE LATE EIGHTEENTH CENTURY. THE PILLOW, COVERED WITH HEAVY HANDMADE LINEN, IS STUFFED WITH HAY. THE PATTERN IS OLD SHEEPSKIN PARCHMENT, AND THE BOBBINS ARE BAMBOO, OBTAINED THROUGH THE EAST INDIA TRADING COMPANIES. [ONE-QUARTER NATURAL SIZE.]

of early Cape Cod! — keeping the mind, eyes and fingers busy, proves a means of working off overwrought feelings and serves the same quieting purpose that piano-playing does for some tensely strung nerves. One well-known sanitarium has, with such an end in view, introduced bobbin-lace making, and whether or not it is directly calming the patients' jangled nerves, it is doing so indirectly, by taking their thoughts off themselves and absorbing their interest in seeing grow under their very fingers so pixy a product. Lace-making is one of those pursuits which, seeming tedious to the onlooker, have an undeniable fascination for the maker; and it seems as though almost no one who really enters upon its enticing pathway ever cares to turn back. One old lady of ninety-odd, who can no longer see well enough to make fine lace, nevertheless spends hours of true joy and inner contentment creating those strong, simple, artistic patterns that are most welcome for her daughters' households and her grandchildren's little frocks.

Some definitions will make the subject of bobbins and lace-making clearer to those who are unfamiliar with it: " Bobbin lace is made from a number of threads attached by pins to a cushion or pillow, each thread being wound on a small bobbin. The design, as in needle lace, is drawn on stiff paper or parchment, which is carefully stretched over the pillow and pricked out along the main lines. Then small pins are inserted at close intervals, around which the threads turn to form the various meshes and other openings. The thread on the bobbins is lightly wound and tied at the top in a loop that slips easily when the bobbin is needed. The plaiting or weaving is exceedingly intricate, but the bobbins are passed under and over each other with remarkable rapidity and accuracy." (*New International Encyclopædia.*) " Bobbins. — The thread that is used in pillow lace is wound upon a number of short ivory sticks called bobbins, and the making of the lace mainly consists in the proper interlacing of these threads. . . . Place no mark upon the bobbins to distinguish them, as they change places too often to allow of it. Never look at the bobbins when working; but watch the pattern forming, and use both hands at the same time." (*Dictionary of Needlework.*) " Bobbin is a term likewise employed to denote the small reel on which thread is wound in some sewing-machines, and also a circular pin of wood, with a wide cutting around it, to receive linen, silk or cotton thread, for weaving."

Needlepoint materials are, of course, much handier to carry about than bobbin outfits, as there is no cumbersome pillow. This is one reason why Renaissance ladies relegated bobbin-lace making to peasant women. Vanity also entered in, however, for sewing a scrap of point lace rolled over the finger showed up the latter's delicate white-ness and exposed rare, gleaming jewels that scintillated with every graceful move.

In those days, though, carved, brilliantly studded, enameled and cleverly blown *millefiori* glass bobbins had barely come into existence. It seems as though these last must have been used like ceremonial maces, for presentation from a noble doge's wife to a visiting sister; for they appear too large and too fragile for practical use, though many a bit of rare glass has outlived far sturdier objects. I have seen one tantalizingly lovely bobbin of this sort, wrought in the early aqua-marine-colored glass, the handle decorated with many looped glass ribands arranged in two or three tiers, in the interstices of which still cling bits of the earth in which this treasure has lain buried. It was brought to America from Spain in a delightful, dilapidated, antique crimson velvet slip cover or sheath. This bobbin was found in Granada. Another, a broken one, is in the Moore Collection of Span-ish glass in the Metropolitan Museum, New York. It is thought that this type of darkish glass may have come from the manufactory at Almeria.

Venice for seven centuries was supreme in the art of glass-making and was the first to discover the secret of blowing clear uncolored crys-tal. Its product was so light that it was much in demand. Even Nero collected glass, and in the early days fine pieces of crystal were signed by the artists who made them. *Millefiori* objects are an intricate, com-pound creation. They may be barred, checkered, clouded, streaked, dotted, pitted, dimpled, dappled, spiraled, spotted, or mottled! Our lace bobbins are twisted and spiraled, two or three rods of colored glass bound and curved together, giving the bobbin shank a threaded sur-face like that of a screw. These slender *shanks* with slightly enlarged knobby heads or finials are about four or five inches long. The prin-ciple of this puzzling multicolored work lies in the bundles of care-fully arranged, differently tinted fine bars or rods of glass laid fagot-like, side by side, heated and slightly fused into heavier bars. The tiny shafts were laid in such order that looking upon their ends or a cross-section of the packet, one beheld a flower form or a name or star. While warm, the bundle was pulled out and attenuated, so that the ends of the rods presented very tiny dots indeed. But each

From the collection of Mrs. De Witt Clinton Cohen

Left: BLACK AND PINK GLASS BOBBIN. [REDUCED.]
Right: RARE OLD NATURAL AQUAMARINE-COLORED GLASS BOBBIN AND ITS CRIMSON VELVET SACK, SUPPOSEDLY FROM SPAIN. [REDUCED.]

color tone remained differentiated. This big bar was then sliced off into many flowerets, as though one had cut a tree trunk into many ringed cross-sections. Ropes or canes of semi-molten glass were molded into animal forms and drawn out small. Then the flowerets or little Noah's Ark figures were laid in a vitreous bed, clear or colored, while more glass was poured on top and patted into shape with a moistened, hollowed wooden spatula. The whole object, when it had cooled and hardened, was ground or polished. The handles of the bobbins were left hollow. Was this from the blowing, were they the part immediately next the blow-pipe, and is the rougher bit, at the end of the handles, where they stuck and were finally struck off the pipe? Or was this hollow supposed to be filled with shot and corked for weighting the dainty implement? This latter hardly seems necessary, although such a custom might have given rise to the Italian term *piombini* — leaded or leaden weights or bobbins — which may have been originally the heavy hanging or passive ones, holding down the warp threads.[1] At any rate, the handles are ornamented with five or six little glass ruffles something like our modern paper, lamb-chop frills. But the

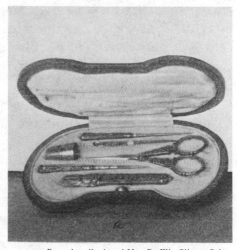

From the collection of Mrs. De Witt Clinton Cohen

AN OLD, FRENCH, RED LEATHER HOUSEWIFE, WITH A GOLD-TOOLED EDGE. THE KIT IS LINED WITH WHITE SATIN, AND THE SCISSORS, THIMBLE, NEEDLE-CASE, BODKIN AND STILETTOS ARE OF GOLD.

crystal ruffles have an added edge of the same color that prevails on the inside of the spiral stalk, and the handles are three or four inches long — a formidable bobbin, some nine to eleven inches in length!

In the English Midlands — Northamptonshire or Northants, Bedfordshire or Beds, Buckinghamshire or Bucks — Venetian glass also

[1] In 1476 at Ferrara, Eleanor of Aragon, Duchess of Ferrara — so we learn in Gandini's book on the Este family — supervised her eighteen handmaidens in the work of braiding gold and silk with *bobbins*. This seems to record the precise moment of using bobbins, instead of a loom, for weaving braid. Bobbins are here called *piombini*, which would seem to indicate their being made of lead, rather than of bone or wood.

occurs in connection with the handsomest of bobbins. These have so-called *gingles, jingles* or *spangles* at the lower ends to weight them — hoops or loops of beads on wire. Nine beads is the accredited number: two fancy at the top; then, opposite each other, two clear, two colored, and again two clear glass drops — generally the same as the second pair; and then the *pièce de résistance* — a special and larger bead; if flowered, called a *Pompadour*, after the beauty of Louis XV's court, or perhaps *Venetian, Paisley, Indian* or *China*, according to its provenance. The *Pompadours* were popular in Bucks. Another favorite was *Kitty Fisher's Eyes*, named for the English actress who died in 1767. This bead, like the others just named, is called a *bottom;* it is gray with white-filled circular dents or eyelets. Each eyelet has a central red or blue dot. One is tempted, when the former coloring appears, to wonder whether Kitty Fisher could have been afflicted with anything so unattractive as pink eye! But after all, what a joy to have put a colored bead among the others instead of having them all uniform and plain! The *jingles* do indeed resemble jeweled pendants. Sometimes there is a lovely combination of robin's egg, turquoise blue and white; sometimes an effect of green marble or malachite; again we have rock crystal, or a veritable mosaic from Saint Mark's! Imagine working with these — one would be so fascinated one could not help making lace! At first these beads were imported from Venice, as were also the materials for *millefiori* work in America. In eighteen-hundred-odd Venice was shipping raw glass strips to Bristol. The two top *jingle* beads were supposed to be ornamental, and pretty indeed are some of them. Below them came six *square cuts,* though they were not of cut glass but were cut by the lapidary from off his glass rod, slipped while hot on a copper wire to form a hole by which they might later be strung, and formed into approximate cubes by patting with a file as one would mold a butter-ball with paddles. This accounts for the tiny indentations that look almost as though the beads had been hand formed and were showing the imprint of the papillæ. It is claimed that the irregularity of these *cuts* and the rough surfaces made them hold better in the bobbin winder: but how, since it is the bobbin itself that fits into the winder, and strain on the *jingles* would break them asunder?

One frequently finds red *cuts* between two white ones; but opaque pale yellow beads with a blending of blue fused in while the bead is

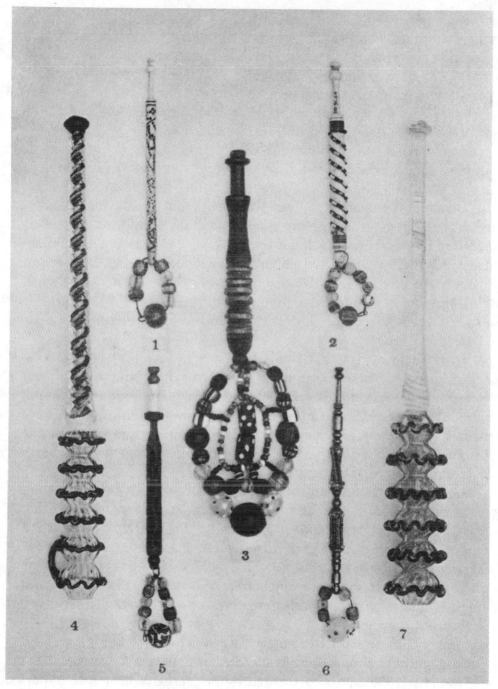

Courtesy of the Needle and Bobbin Club

BOBBINS

1, 2, 5, 6. ENGLISH (MIDLANDS). LENT BY MISS GERTRUDE WHITING. 1, 2, BONE; 5, WALNUT; 6, BRASS.

3. ENGLISH (BUCKINGHAMSHIRE). WALNUT. IN THE METROPOLITAN MUSEUM OF ART.

4, 7. ITALIAN. GLASS BOBBINS FROM MURANO. LENT BY MRS. DE WITT CLINTON COHEN.

hot, clear amber balls, light and deep green beads, and scrolled ultramarine ones are also usual. Some of the *bottoms* are faceted, some are of jade, coral, carnelian; many beads were made at Bedford, and many *jingles* are fashioned with lace-makers' tokens from their employers, with quaint old coins, or with historic buttons.

Once I met an Englishwoman wearing a watch chain of old blue *end* beads assembled from broken and unused bobbins.

Again, visiting in Scarborough-on-Hudson, another guest and I, walking in the garden, saw a tiny, odd yellow bud. I dug it out of the sod and marveled at it! But soon I found another and another, and an equally entrancing blue — not bud, but bead; for such we now realized them to be. How fascinating they would be, strung as *jingles* on old bobbins that had lost their own! But I conscientiously turned them all (a whole forenoon's diggings and findings) over to my hostess, who explained her losing an early Egyptian necklace when alighting from her motor in a drenching downpour. To my surprise and continued regret, she handed the coveted old beads to her little girl for dolls' jewelry!

In the tomb of Tih, a Phœnician, have been found glass beads. Legend has it that some stranded Phœnician sailors propped up their cooking pots with lumps of soda upon a beach. The soda melted and, fusing into the sand, formed glass. Tyre and Sidon, at any rate, were as noted for their glass as for their Tyrian purple drawn from the local shellfish. Red glass contains copper or gold; yellow glass, iron or silver; and blue glass, cobalt.

The writer has one small, trim, English crystal, Midland bobbin with a pithy-looking core and adorable scarlet-crimson *jingles* that have surfaces like the bloom of a peach. This particular lace stick seems rather unique, for it is short and slim, spangled and not hollow. May the lad who presented it to some village lace-maker have been a glass-blower? In any case, the bobbin shows that it is English, not Venetian, and its curves closely resemble those of a wooden Midland one the author owns.

Quarter-inch silver assay buttons were valued for bobbin weighting; and, most appropriately, a Needle and Bobbin Club member's little daughter, Delia, was presented by her father's firm with a porringer and plate made of the tiny melted buttons.

The author has a button of the last type, commemorating the invention of the railway engine by George Stephenson.

In England another sort of transportation than that of the railway was also commemorated on bobbins. One chap was transported — for poaching, perhaps — to Botany Bay. The penalty for sheep-

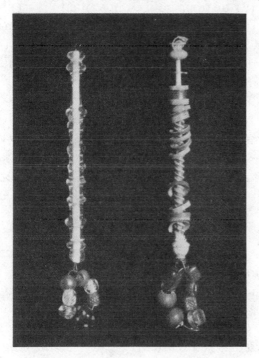 

From the author's collection

Left: TWO VERY, VERY RARE ENGLISH MIDLAND BOBBINS, ONE OF CLEAR GLASS WITH BRILLIANT CONTRASTING BEADS AND A PITHY CORE, THE OTHER OF CARVED SPIRALED IVORY, GILDED IN ITS CONCAVE PARTS AND BEARING FOURTEEN GOLD-LINED TALLY RINGS CUT FROM THE SAME PIECE OF IVORY AS THE SHANK. THE JINGLE SHOWS TWO CHARMING PEACH-BLOOM BEADS. [REDUCED.]

Right: THE UNUSUAL PLAIN LARGE MAHOGANY BOBBIN USED IN PORTO RICO. [MUCH REDUCED.]

stealing in those days was hanging, so this must have been a lesser offence. One of the old lace tells runs:

> "O Son, O Son, what have you done?
> You're going to Botany Bay!"

Local bobbin manufacturers and dealers were not slow to take advantage of anything that caused as much excitement as suicides and executions. There were always plenty of souvenir purchasers among the plain country lace-makers, who had few village thrills and had to get their excitement, as it were, second-hand through the doings of others. Even little folk were told they might attend "the hanging" if their lace lesson were well done!

Another silver coin — a criminal's — dating from the time of Queen Elizabeth, is appended to the historic bobbin inscribed "Joseph Castle, hung 1860." It is said that his hanging created such a sensation that on the evening thereof his wife's friends gave a ball, presenting every guest with a memorial bobbin! Castle had murdered his wife, and great was the local satisfaction when he was brought to bay by the Luton police station bloodhound!

The inscription on the Castle bobbin is indented or tattooed lengthwise upon the stick. After the tiny holes were drilled, a red, blue, black or yellow powder mixed with water and gum arabic was stuck into them with a quill that one twisted about, being careful not to have too liquid a mixture and not to let it run over the side of the little drilled spot. The inscribed bobbins, once colored, were set up vertically to dry, and the pigment, after hardening, gave them the appearance of having been inlaid with enamel. Sometimes the inscriptions run spirally upward around the bobbin shaft.

Name bobbins are among the more usual, the appellations being laid out parallel to the sides of the stick. The writer has many such: Mary; Harriet; Sally; David Lane Wavendon, died July, 1871; Job — the latter suggesting the patience requisite to good lace-making; Hannah; and so forth.

A particularly interesting old bobbin reads:

> "My mind is fixt
> I cannot rainge,
> I love my choice
> Too well to change."

Others are, each line appearing on a separate bobbin:

"A, B, C," et cetera (the alphabet).
"When this you see, remember me."
"A present from my cusan Samuel Wickham, 1840."
"Kiss me quick — Mother is coming."

" Come and wed with me my love."
" The gift is small but love is all."
" My true love that is wishing for me."
" War in Egypt. TEL EL KEBER TAKEN 1882."
" I will keep this for my true love's sake."
" My ♡ is full of love for thee."
" I will forever love the giver."
" Marry me."
" Love forget me not."
" If you love me com home to me."
" Love is true in Bedfordshire."
" My love you am the pride of my ♡ ."

The writer has one exceptional, heavy gimp-bobbin of bone, inscribed lengthwise, in somewhat worn and irregular characters, with a verse that all can deeply appreciate:

> " Friendship in the midst
> Of deep distress would
> Ease an aching heart
> And every sorrow seems
> The less where friend-
> Ship bears a part. 1841."

Many a lace-maker has found outlet and solace in the execution of the work on her pillow — work requiring some attention and therefore affording some distraction, but still not exhausting one through too strenuous labor. Bobbins associated with dearly loved ones who have left us, or through whose steady handling in time of stress one has gradually regained calm and strength, become very, very precious possessions.

William or " Bobbin " Brown of Cranfield, England, was particularly apt at neat, clear spiral incising.[2] The author has a splendid

---

[2] Bobbins are known to have been made by

Richard Adams of Stoke Goldington	Mr. Miller of Beer
William Brown of Cranfield	Paul Neal of Hanslope
James Compton (son) of Deanshanger	William Pridmore of Elstow
Jesse Compton (father) Deanshanger	Nat Woods of Olney
Mr. Goode of Beer	Arthur Wright (son) of Cranfield
David Haskins of Leighton Buzzard	Samuel Wright (father), known as " Master
George Lumbis of Reynold	Wright," Cranfield

heavy set of twelve bobbins so decorated, in bold black and vermilion, everything being identical except the wording, which is as follows:

" When my love is absent he is in my mind."
" My love is at a distance but forever in mind."
" Love is sharp to feel the smart."
" A present from Henry-easoneng Brook."
" James and Hannah Hurst, 1859."
" Sitting on a stile, Mary happy as the day."
" Thomas Shakeshaff a friend of mine."
" William Hollbin aged 16."
" I will forever love the giver."
" I long to see my love once more."
" 'Tis hard to be jilted by one as I love."
" Let no false lover gaine my heart."

Other color-dotted bobbins bore names — those of the maker, the maker's parents, the giver of the lace-stick; or the name of the giver alternated, puzzle-wise, with that of the recipient, hers perhaps in red and his in blue, making every other character red and the intermediate ones blue — as, for example, a bobbin from Paulerspury, six miles from Wooton in Northants. It reads "w b i e l t l i o a y m d w u o n o k l- l o e n y, 1844." There are two mistakes in this specimen, but the lad's name is in red and the maiden's in black. His surname is quite usual in the neighborhood of Wooton, so perhaps he not only wooed but won his Betsy.

One of the most puzzling of old Bucks bobbins, from Waddesdon, reads, I am told:

" manuel hingfor abobzin il sin."

This sounds to me like sin, Klingsor, Helsingfors, Beelzebub, Sindbad. Perhaps if you are a devoted modern cross-word puzzler, you would like to try, for variety, to solve this hieroglyph of yester-year!

Another set of four English Hanslope sticks is reported to be marked, one verse on each bobbin:

(1) " 'Tis swect to love, but sweeter to be loved again.
(2) But oh how bitter is that thought, to love yet love in vain.

(3) There's none on earth that can conceive how bitter is that pain.
(4) To be in love with those who don't love us again."

Our Lord's Prayer has also been inscribed, phrase by phrase, upon a set of bobbins. And Mrs. Fowler of Honiton (pronounced " Huniton ") has three sticks inscribed " Prepare to meet thy God," as well as a set of six, dated 1870, depicting fish.

It is heaps of fun to twirl and decipher these amusingly conceived little bone documents of local family history! For each worker's pil-

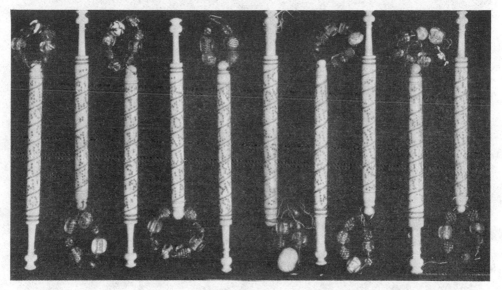

From the author's collection

PART OF A STUNNING SET OF SPIRALLY INCISED OLD BONE BOBBINS FROM BUCKINGHAMSHIRE.
[SLIGHTLY REDUCED.]

low was a veritable storehouse of mementos — a bead of Mother's, a button of Father's, a prize bead awarded at the lace school, lover's vows, discarded earrings and children's little whimsies. Some of the jingles are dainty shells, or even tiny cameos. Children's names or teachers' names were also sometimes inscribed upon prize bobbins.

For many interesting notes upon English bobbins, see *The Romance of the Lace Pillow,* by Thomas Wright.

Other highly ornamented, hole-bearing, Midland bobbins somewhat resemble dominoes with sage green or otherwise tinted, straight-sided, deep circular indentations, artfully distributed. Winding

between these there is usually a tightly drawn, sunken brass wire, forming a pretty spiral around the shank of the stick, and a quarter-inch-
wide solid band at either end. Old bobbins that have lost their encircling wire show a hole at either end where this was originally attached.
Very deep spiral or crossed spiral ruts usually indicate the former presence of tiny bead-strung wire circlets. These break and scatter easily
from handling, so that they are rare and very precious. Such abso-

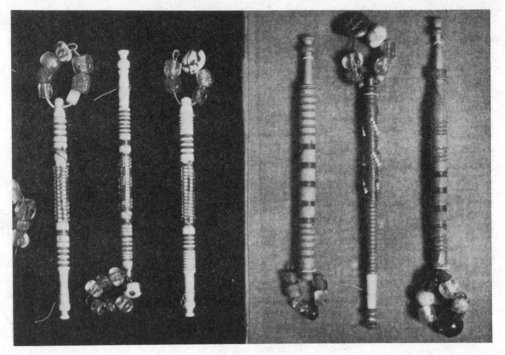

From the author's collection

THREE ENGLISH BONE BOBBINS GAILY JINGLED AND BOUND MIDWAY WITH BRIGHTLY BEADED BIRD-
CAGING. OPPOSITE ARE THREE WOODEN MIDLAND BOBBINS ALSO BOUND WITH FINE BRASS WIRE; BUT
ONLY THE CENTRAL STICK SHOWS THE MINUTE BEADED WIRE BIRD-CAGE EFFECT. [SLIGHTLY REDUCED.]

lutely regular spirals must have been turned on lathes with feeders to
keep the thread so even. Some are of highly patined bone, bound with
deep-colored wee specks of beads. Still others — the so-called bird-
cage variety — have cut-in sections, where tiny mites of delicate beads
have been set in, one bead-strung vertical wire bar parallel to the next
and so on, right around the waist of the exquisite bobbins. Some bird-
cage bobbins apparently have compartments full of beads held in place

by a delicate wire net. The bird-cage bobbins seen by the author have been true little gems, bits of pure joy, and generally predominantly set with beads of a heavenly blue! These sticks also have *jingles*. Someone recently remarked that bobbins seem to have been planned and wrought and treasured as carefully as jewels!

Bird-cage spangles, on the other hand, replace, when they occur, the usual *jingle.* The author's set numbers eighteen small brown wooden sticks with these as-it-were baby *jingles,* small and made up entirely of modest beads. The effect is very neat.

Still other deep spirals are wound, lined, either with green and silver, or with silver and ruby strips of flat surface tinsel. This occasionally tarnishes and is less attractive.

There are also both old bone and wooden Midland bobbins pitted or studded with pewter or silver. The holes were drilled and the molten metal run therein, the whole set to cool in a stone mold. Afterwards any excess metal was filed or trimmed away. If one will examine a partly broken bobbin of this type, from which the inlay has dropped out, one can readily see that the spots are not the heads of nails driven into the stick. These pegged, spotted *leopards,* especially when the old metal has become corroded, remind one of some formidably studded dungeon door. The incrustation renders them rough and unclean. Silver *leopard* spots, of course, polish with handling and remain brighter than the pewter insets.[3]

Similarly made, but much more alluring, are the *butterfly* bobbins of wood or bone, the latter often brightly stained with hues that vie with the butterflies' very own. How these flitting fairy bobbins flash as they ply upon the lace pillow! It is the pewter inlay that is fashioned in the form of insect wings; and all of these series are adorned with the customary bead weights, dangling and trembling like a provoking coquette's earrings, responsive to every coyest move. A Mr. Abbot of Bedford specialized in the making of these *butterfly* bobbins. After turning them in the first place upon the lathe, he laid them in stone molds, poured in molten pewter, closed the molds and later trimmed off the excess lead.

[3] Wooden bobbins sometimes are drilled right through and studded with tiny bars of contrasting wood, three little barrette ends appearing, when in place, as six studs. Broken bobbins, when possible, had new ends doweled on, and these were frequently of a wood differing from the original.

Plainer are the striped Bedfordshire *tigers,* displaying ring after ring of parallel inset metal bands. These sticks too, when of bone, are often highly colored, and also have the little jeweled drops appended. Their coruscating glow makes one feel as though one were among the scintillating colors of a Tiffany's studio.

The bone bobbins, once lathed, were dipped or soaked in dye and then returned to remove the color from such parts as would touch and therefore might stain the lace thread. In the second turning, groups of fine parallel lines were also frequently incised, decorating the sticks

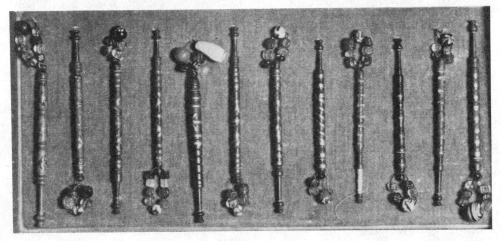

THE RESPLENDENTLY SILVER-INLAID ENGLISH BOBBINS CALLED BUTTERFLY AND TIGER. SIMILAR SPECIMENS ARE SOMETIMES STRIPED OR SPIRALED WITH PEWTER, WHICH, HOWEVER, IS SCARCELY CAPABLE OF AS HIGH A POLISH. [SLIGHTLY REDUCED.]

by this variation of white bands. In Bedford the bobbin bodies only were dipped, leaving the necks uncolored. One nowadays finds them just as they were left, with a little bit of fine thread still on. These old ones are fairly alive with color — jade green, salmon pink, coral, magenta, et cetera. The author has a pair that are incised and stained black and white, criss-cross fashion, not as gaudily as a Scotch plaid but more like a shepherd's check. James Compton and his father, Jesse Compton, of Deanshanger, England, are said to have stained with cudbear and logwood the sticks they manufactured. In the Midlands, bobbins were sometimes ordered by successful lace-makers or as presents for them, and were made by local merchants. In one town

From Wells Cathedral

SHOWING A GRACEFUL ENGLISH CHURCH-WINDOW LANTERN, AN HISTORIC OBJECT, WHICH MAY INDEED
HAVE BEEN THE INSPIRATION THAT GAVE US THE DELICATE, DARK WOOD, CHURCH-WINDOW BOBBIN —
INTRIGUING LITTLE IMPLEMENT, CARVED OUT BY ADORING SOULS WITH VERY NIMBLE FINGERS.

a man went about selling bobbins from a dog-drawn cart. Again, one could supply one's pillow needs at the market place or at the village fair. One can now buy graceful modern English bone bobbins and stain them to suit one's own fancy. The effect is often very good.

Still more wonderful in their varied effects are the English Midland *church window* sticks. These have been hollowed and pierced with a tiny saw. The windows may be opposite, two or four on a line, or, showing even greater skill, there may be three. The author has some of these with six tiers of windows, making eighteen in all in each delicate bobbin. These are of walnut. One sees them also in light pear, box and perhaps olive wood. These windows are sometimes called *lights*. The particular sticks just alluded to, contain loose wooden balls that roll freely up and down inside, reminding one of the carved Chinese concentric ivory puzzle balls. The writer also has a wooden *church window* containing little red beads, and oh! in another are turquoise balls. Which leads one to think, since this foreign substance has been inserted, that perhaps the wooden balls were not whittled right in the bobbins, but also were added. Yes, quite true; the sticks were soaked in hot water and sprung to admit the little oddments. Perhaps the bone pieces were sometimes soaked in acid in order to stretch them without their snapping.

The boxwood Huguenot bobbins, with their charming smooth-worn surfaces, remind one a trifle of little pagodas; but this type has only one puzzle ball, and no spangle.

But the glory of the author's collection is an ivory *church window* bobbin, showing three turquoise little ones through its apertures, the mullions between being set with garnets, turquoise and diamonds. To what royal worker may this treasure indeed have belonged?

I say " oddments," because these marvelous bobbin-makers did not confine themselves to the insertion of balls. As someone exclaimed, " Do you mean to say that is a bobbin? I wish I could have seen you when these came, when you opened the box! Do you not feel as though the spirits of the workers were among these fragile toys? " Or as another wrote, " The bobbins are perfectly fascinating, and besides being so lovely to look at and think about, they are an ideal size to work with. The old bead *jingles* are so bright, and the finger-worn dainty wooden things *so* satisfactory to own! " The fragile fairy forms alluded to at

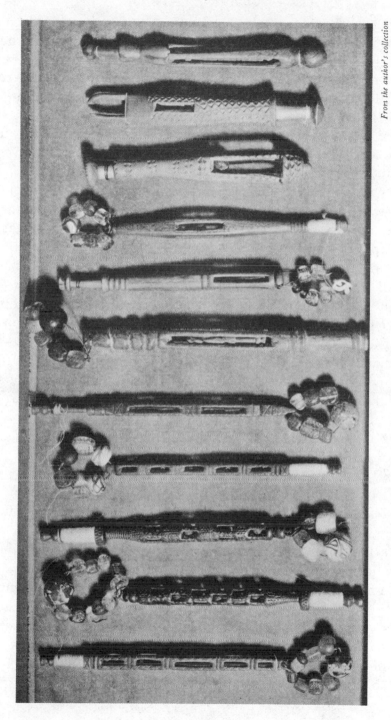

From the author's collection

COW-AND-CALF AND MOTHER-AND-BABE AND CHURCH-WINDOW BOBBINS WHITTLED IN WOOD. THOSE WITHOUT JINGLES ARE SOMETIMES CALLED HUGUENOTS. THE CENTRE HUGUENOT IS FROM THE DUCHESS OF TECK'S COLLECTION. ONE OF THE BOBBINS HAS TURQUOISE BABES. THE CHURCH-WINDOW BOBBIN NEXT TO THE END, FARTHEST FROM THE HUGUENOTS, CONTAINS SIX WOODEN BALLS AND EIGHTEEN WINDOWS!

the beginning of the paragraph are the Cow-and-Calf and Mother-and-Babe bobbins — they are a perfect, never-ending joy and a masterpiece of the Midlands! These are creations of ivory, brass and turquoise — miniature bobbins lying inside the windows of the real bobbins. The little creatures are often most carefully and minutely carved, and the bigger bobbins are sometimes stained to carry out the color scheme of the midgets. The author's collection contains a brass bobbin with a ruby-beaded window enclosing an ivory miniature replica. This too is English, though it has a Venetian air about it.

A royal wooden bobbin, until recently the property of the Duchess of Teck, sister-in-law to the Queen of England, might also be mentioned here; for though it contains no amusing surprise, it has a curved, two-pronged, open tail, no spangles, a slightly flattened body like a fish's, and a scale-like diaper check carved over its entire surface. It is of dull wood and greatly resembles a *mermaid's purse* or *sea barrow*. In fact, the dogfish is habitually hung in Devon upon a thorny spike beside the cottage door, to dry or ripen; and these horny purses are the egg containers of the dogfish and skate, the handles or tendrils serving to hold the purses in place upon the sea bed, from which they are sometimes wrenched by storms. So one can easily see how the skate barrow might suggest itself as a model to some carver with a taste for novelty.[4]

Another odd, rather than pretty, English lace-stick is the *bitted*. In this case bone is inlaid with slices or lines or other oddly shaped bits of wood, or vice versa; or dark wood is varied with light insets or the reverse. These inlays are glued into place and loosen very easily.

A very neat Midland type is a closely spiraled wooden or sometimes bone bobbin with a parallel, carved screw-thread running from one end to the other. The work is so even that it must have been done or guided by machine. The author has the smoothest, most unctuous sort of oil finished, dull dark green bone bobbin of this very genteel type.

Another very ladylike kind is the plain, slim *old maid*. These wear down and give a quaint, delightful feeling of great usefulness and antiquity. They must have been slight and straight and unornamented to begin with.

[4] See "the Queen's bobbins," under "The Song of the Spinning-Wheel."

In the same collection, at present in the Brooklyn Museum, is a bronze stick whose indentations spell, " I will forever love the giver." And a tattooed or pitted pewter one that bent in the worker's hand carries the message, " Fear God." Someone remarked that it looked as though it had been bitten and bent by a playful puppy. Once rambling through a fashionable antique dealer's in Newport, Rhode Island, the writer came upon a quantity of little pewter acorns, and inquiring what they were, was told the dealer had a hundred of them; that they were the heads of some lace bobbins he had picked up in the countryside, and that since they were useless, he had chopped off the heads to use as ornaments and had thrown away the shanks. Such unfeeling, irreparable sacrilege! Of course, his listener took pains to impress him as well as she could with his ruthless shortsightedness and the money he had lost through his ignorance of valuable antiques! The latter item perhaps was the most telling. However, when it comes to practicality it must be very fatiguing to lift dozens of metal bobbins hour after hour; just as it must be exasperating to have the *jingles* of one's various sticks constantly catching in one another. Herein do the Continentals seem wise, as we shall shortly see.

Another unusual metal bobbin is the English one made of iron.

The pagoda-like Huguenots, whether *church window* or plain, have no spangle earrings, but are short and stout. Some of these have dark wood handle tips on light wooden bodies, but their *trolleys* are loosely set with flat pewter rings that wobble in little furrows or grooves. The number of rings on a trolley may vary from one to twelve (or perhaps more). Occasionally a Midland bobbin has a wooden trolley ring. The circlets do not hang like the spangles, but loosely encircle the lower end of the bobbin. Aylesbury and Thames are the home of the so-called Huguenots, showing whence the district lace-makers came. The rings also are called *jingles;* hence the term *spangles* would seem clearer and therefore preferable for the hanging beads. What is dubbed a *trolley* in Huntingdonshire is known as a *trailer* in Bedfordshire. *Trailers* or *trolleys* are used for carrying the outlining lace cord or gimp, suggesting the heavy cable or overhead cord of trolley-car lines. This *trolley* line or gimp is wound on the *trailer* from a *quill* — a bobbin that holds a whole skein of gimp cord, but is never used on the pillow. *Tallies* are adorned with tin bands and are used for making the plaits or braids or *points d'esprit*. They are thus tallies or markers, and usually in groups of four. One of the most delicate, fairy-form of bobbins the writer has ever seen, one that holds a place apart like a refined little lady, is of spiraled ivory, gilded along the bed of the concave scroll or groove that gracefully encircles the stem. Loosely carved about this, but homogeneous with it, are twelve delicate ivory rings, and at the base are richly colored spangles. Can this be one of the beautiful bobbins ordered by Sir William Long of Kempston Grange for his daughters? In any case, it is elfin and fit for a princess.

In connection with the big *quill*, one should mention the former *yak stick*, some seven inches long with a head four inches in circumference, and later on, five and a half inches. Such dimensions, of course, were necessitated by the clumsiness of the wool to be woven.

Another sort of *quill* or *spindle*, with a long handle and split, pronged head, is in use for holding bronze and metal threads. See the chapter on " A Few Final Suggestions and Some Stray Sewing Accessories."

A *jack-in-the-box* is for making metallic lace. The lower portion of the stick pulls out or can be unscrewed, disclosing inside a small wooden bobbin about which to wind the gold or silver thread. This prevents exposure, handling and tarnishing. The *Tjevoli* from Le Mans is presumably a sort of *jack-in-the-box*.

In earliest days and for very lightweight thread, short (two inches long), slim-throated, *bob-tailed* bobbins or *dumps* were used; particularly, I have heard, in Bucks and around the English Lake District.[5]

All of these quaint Midland wooden implements are found in walnut or dark plum and damson woods, as well as in cherry, apple, oak, maple and other spindle woods. Any close-grained wood can be used. Sometimes sticks were whittled from one's own dearly beloved trees. Henry Ward Beecher lost a wonderful apple tree at his country place on the Hudson; but to preserve its usefulness and excellent wood as long as possible, he had a bureau, a rocking-chair and one other piece of furniture made from it for his neighbor on the left, himself, and his neighbor on the right. Historic trees of Europe have also been thus

---

[5] *Bob-tails* are similar in shape to the small, green, well-known English soda-water bottle.

utilized. From christening, wedding and other *feastes*, the English workers saved bones to be turned into lace sticks.

In Devonshire the sticks are very slight and smooth, with no protuberances, rounded heads, flanges, shaped handles or ringlets of beads; for the Devon stick must pass through many, many loops without becoming entangled. So its head is tiny, the spindle or spool portion is indented, and the handle is straight, running out into a point. The implements were made of mahogany (rarely), spindle or olive wood. Some are mottled by subjection to acid — Agnes Forty (*aqua fortis* is nitric acid), as it is locally called; some are simply decorated with black and red — no other colors seem ever to have been used on the West Coast — often with a tiny checkered band near the top of the

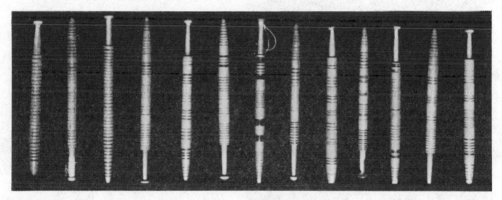

From the author's collection

A SET OF THE EXCLUSIVE "RIGGLED" BRANSCOMBE STICKS BANDED IN STRIKING BLACK AND RED. THESE WERE MADE NOWHERE BUT IN THIS PARTICULAR HILLY, SEASIDE HAMLET, AND ARE NOW GROWN SCARCE. [SLIGHTLY REDUCED.]

handle. Mrs. Marian Powys Gray owns one depicting a quantity of little ships — a natural subject for these seafaring folk. At the opening of the World War, one of Mrs. Gray's friends, who was going to fight upon the high seas, whittled her a lace stick and pyrographed it with pleasing devices. At Beer the fanciest of these little sticks prevail, some showing pots of flowers, some the church symbols of wheat, fish, and triangle. One set of mine is dated 1870; another bears the inscription "Sarah, ne Halfyard," a rather appropriate name for the weaver of inches and yards of fine lace. Formerly in Beer, sticks were made by old Mr. Miller and Mr. Goode, now dead. The former made bobbins for the present excellent lace mistress, who is very spick and span, very executive, in charge of the higher classes in the village school. Mrs. Durant also boards visiting pupils, as does quaint Mrs. Woodgate, not far away. But Mrs. Durant's mother's bobbins bear the maternal initials, together with those of Mr. Miller.

At Branscombe the makers adhere strictly to a scheme of severely plain, but bold and striking, red and black parallel rings or bands, the finished product being known in the local dialect as a *riggled* bobbin.

A pretty custom prevailed in Devon — that of bestowing these homemade bobbins as valentines, and stingy indeed or very lukewarm was the youth who gave a packet of less than a dozen.

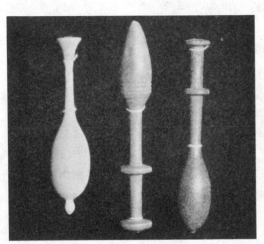

From the author's collection

THREE FUNNY LITTLE BOBTAILED DUMPS FROM DOWNTON, WILTS, ENGLAND. TWO ARE OF WOOD AND ONE IS OF BONE. [ACTUAL SIZE.]

As careful recipients scrub their useful bobbin valentines from time to time with common soap, they take on a delightful sheen.

We are told that scraps of glass were used by the local West Coast fishermen to scrape and smooth their sticks, and that they filled in the designs with wax.

The bones of pigs' feet were sometimes used to reel the thread, especially the heavier gimp or outlining thread. This is one of the origins of the term *bone lace,* although another explanation is to be found in the chapter on "The Humble Pin." [6]

The sticks of Downton and Wilts are *dumps,* as is also the so-called bottle, or flat-ended, little old stick of Devonshire. In Devon the name *bobbin* is never used, and the woods employed are almost invariably of light color.

But were the Continentals not clever — they incorporated their *jingles* or weights right into one piece with the bobbin itself, so making

[6] My North Italian lace teacher taught me to call bobbins "*ossi*" (bones). — G. Whiting.

a heavy handle that at the same time would avoid catching! Thus we find most bobbins either pyriform or bulbous.

To *return to Italy* — for we began with old Venetian *millefiori* and primitive American bobbins: in sharp contrast to the Midland spangle, we have the tapered Devonshire and the pear-shaped Italian, necessitated by the *sewings* or *crochetage* practised by Devonshire and Italy, as well as by Belgium. Lille, however, from which the Midland lace-making sprang, does not require this sort of joining by passing bobbins through loops; yet spangles have never been used in the mother city of Lille, but appear to have originated in England. Perhaps one should explain that *crochetage* is a very useful method of joining, of which lace-makers were so jealous that they kept it with the utmost secrecy; in fact, in large lace-making centres the lace industry is so important that its mysteries are guarded in every possible way. The former directress of the lace school founded by Queen Marguerita in Cantu, Italy, advised the author to study there. She took the dummy train from Milan as directed and, before alighting, asked the conductor in which direction the school might be found. He had apparently never heard of any such institution, although a casual walk through the streets of Cantu will convince one that the village exists both for and by lace-making. Next the writer inquired in a pharmacy, but discovered that the druggist was equally ignorant; then she asked in a shop where cushions were made and sold. She met with no success, but decided she would like to buy one of the pillows, and inquired the price. When the merchant found that one pillow was wanted, he told her he never sold less than a hundred, and stuck it out. Then she asked a cottager who was pricking lace designs on a pillow especially constructed for that purpose. Although the inquirer had taken lessons from women who spoke nothing but Italian, of which she knew but little, she and they had managed to understand each other very readily, and the lessons were most agreeable. However, this cottage pricker would not understand a word of what was said, nor would she sell a single pattern, though money was held out for her to take the amount the pattern might be worth. After this, the author wandered into a thread store, asked to see some linen, and was very affably shown whatever she requested. She tried in a roundabout way to discover where the school might be, but met with defeat as before, and also discovered that the thread was not for sale. After all this discouragement, the writer took lunch in the rear garden of the town tavern and fared royally for the large sum of twenty cents. This revived her drooping spirits. The porter, however, was unable to give the required information, but after leaving the house, the seeker fortunately met a young girl who luckily had just come home from a French boarding school. She was so pleased to hear someone speak French that, although she said she would be scolded if she told about the lace school, she consented to explain a coveted stitch, to make a sample, and to tell of an old carpenter who would sell a pillow.

Governments formerly realized so keenly the advisability of guarding their best patterns and clever tricks that Venice threatened to imprison the nearest relative of any lace-maker who left the country and to kill this hostage should the lace-maker not return within a specified time. But should the truant worker come home, he would be pensioned for life.

As Madame Kefer has so well pointed out, this practice, or in some instances court rivalry, has been the cause of such secrecy that in time many arts and the origins thereof have been lost to future generations. An emperor wanting to guard a particularly beautiful product for his own embellishment or that of his favorites has beheaded the artisan who dared to divulge the trick of its manufacture; or a nation has so successfully repressed the spread of a favorite craft that its invention, such as the welding of bronze in Egypt, has died with the country's downfall.

Most modern Italian bobbins have no flange between the spool and handle sections, no separation to act as a sort of sword guard; only in this case not a guard to protect the fingers, but one to protect the thread from the fingers. The reason for this omission is twofold: it uses up less wood and less time in turning; and it is at this point, when upon the lathe, that a bobbin is apt to split, thus wasting time and material. The result is that the lace-makers' fingers readily slip up upon the linen and soil it, producing an unpleasant variety of écru finish. The modern bobbin is usually of cheap, splintery wood.

In the author's collection are some touching little boxwood sticks showing the marks of an amateur's penknife. They were made by Madame Citriolo when a little child. Having watched her older sister make lace, she begged her father for a lace-maker's outfit and was refused. Undaunted, she sallied forth into his garden and, helping herself to boxwood from the hedge, she perseveringly whittled her own little supply.

The Austrians, on the other hand, have invented, or perhaps copied from Normandy, a wooden bobbin with a barrel-shaped slip-over cover or protector. This is slid upon the shank after the thread has been wound thereon, the bulb at the base of the handle keeping the barrel from sliding off. To one who is accustomed to holding many bobbins in the hand at once, this loose, rattling, clumsy device seems very awkward and retarding, but it is a pretty sure means of keeping one's linen thread white and clean. Does this imply habitually soiled or rough hands? Or is it a sensible device for the use of the busy housewife or worker in the field?

Normandy bobbins, as just hinted, also have these shaped wooden protectors; but the sticks themselves are of bone or a lighter wood than the sheaths, thus producing a pleasing contrast.

This sheath naturally leads us to the entertaining primitive device of hollowing out a correctly-sized branchlet and slipping its bark intact over the head of the bobbin. Perhaps the lace-makers scald the bark and slip it off the twig as one would blanch an almond and pop off its skin! The writer has a charmingly hand-worn boxwood bobbin from the city of Le Puy, with its fascinating castle-crowned sugar-loaf hillocks or — to use an American term — buttes. This Le Puy bobbin has a sheath of bark resembling the gumbo limbo of Florida — a thin, shiny, brown bark of the inner birch-bark order. An acquaintance writes that he and his wife "have spent hours of rapt attention in Le Puy watching the old women in the shadow of cow-barn or cathedral flashing their bobbins. The lace is coarse, to be sure, but the lace-makers are the most picturesque I have ever seen!" Another glimpse of these fascinating workers is to be found in the chapter on "Pillows and Horses, Maids or Ladies."

This natural protector suggests the more elaborate, picturesquely colored horn *noquette* of the handsomely carved large bobbin of old Bayeux. The *noquette* is simply a thin strip or slice of horn, usually dyed a rich red or green, wrapped once around the spool end of the bobbin, with the two ends out flat and sewed or stitched together a

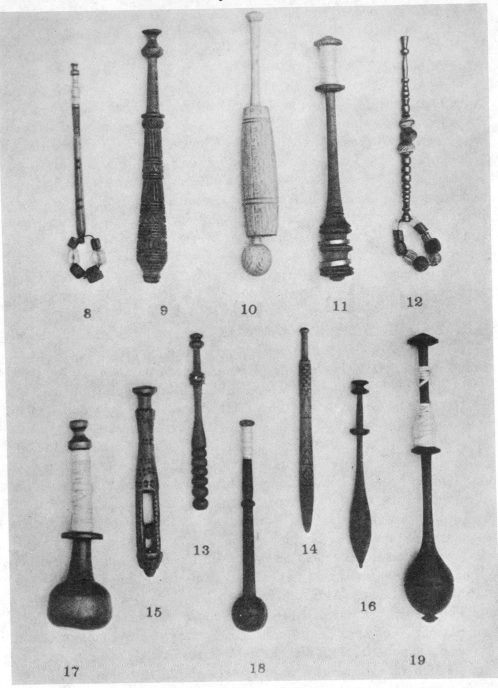

8　　9　　10　　11　　12

13　　14

15

16

17　　18　　19

Courtesy of Needle and Bobbin Club

little way from the edge. Though the *noquette* turns loosely about the spool, the pyramidal flange on this kind of bobbin keeps the horn from slipping down into one's hand. It would indeed be a great pity if it did slide down, for Bayeux handles are handsome in the extreme! The implements generally are of box or walnut; they are heavy, and completely covered with linear carving.

A modern red and green striped celluloid sheath manufactured to curl around the bobbin is now available. This can be spread, just as a watch spring can be uncurled, and passed over the head of the lace stick. The celluloid is much thinner and more transparent than the old-time horn, but lends a gay touch to one's outfit and holds well in place.

Sliders or little flat sheets — about two by four — of natural colored horn are used in England to lay over a finished portion of lace, so the pinheads therein shall not catch one's thread and so the completed work shall remain spotless.

Le Tjevoli is a fairly recent European creation, calculated by its manufacturers to sell a certain sort of thread by supplying ready-wound spools thereof, designed to fit into pretty, little, light wood bobbins that unscrew midway and are hollow. The thread comes out through a tiny hole at the opposite end of the bobbin, running through the shank almost to the bobbin head.

France, or, more strictly speaking, Le Mans, lays claim to a more or less mother-of-pearl bobbin. Only to hear about it is tantalizing; yet no one seems ever to be able to locate one. We were told before the World War that such bobbins could be ordered for a franc apiece,[7] yet efforts to do so have all proved fruitless! Present-day Bayeux is producing imitation tortoise-shell and amber bobbins of celluloid.

[7] Mme Raymond, who held the hereditary position of French teacher to the Bismarck family, ordered and secured a few of these bobbins from *Le Boule de Neige* (manufacturers in Le Mans), la Galerie Lafayette or Au Printemps (Parisian department stores), in 1909.

BOBBINS IN THE PICTURE ON PAGE 228.

8. ENGLISH (MIDLANDS), BONE; 12, *IB.*, BRONZE.

9. FRENCH (BAYEUX), CARVED BOXWOOD.

10. MODERN AUSTRIAN (VIENNESE) "BARREL" BOBBIN.

11. FRENCH, "MERIDIONAL" WEIGHTED BOBBIN.

13. SWISS, PEARWOOD; 16, *IB.*, WALNUT.

14. ENGLISH (DEVONSHIRE).

15. BOXWOOD "WINDOW" BOBBIN.

17. FRENCH (TIGNES), BOXWOOD ROOT.

18. SPANISH, WALNUT.

19. BELGIAN, WALNUT.

8, 17. LENT BY MRS. DE WITT CLINTON COHEN.

10, 16, 18, 19. LENT BY MISS GERTRUDE WHITING.

9. IN THE METROPOLITAN MUSEUM OF ART.

Most effective six-inch-long cedar bobbins, with two or more loose, jingling pewter rings set in ample grooves in the bulb of the handle, come occasionally from out the South of France. Though they seem not to be very usual, they are certainly pleasing, both in color and in proportion.

From Valence, in the South of France, and also from Tignes, in Savoie, France, come knobby, bulbous, short-handled, long-necked,

From the collection of Mrs. John P. Bainbridge, Hingham, Mass.

1. OLIVEWOOD BOBBIN FROM VALENCE, FRANCE.
2. FRENCH, WALNUT, TALLY BOBBIN WITH GREEN HORN NOQUETTE FROM BAYEUX.
3. LIGHT BOXWOOD BOBBIN WITH RED HORN NOQUETTE FROM BAYEUX.
4. WALNUT BOBBIN WITH GREEN NOQUETTE FROM BAYEUX.

but really as a whole rather short, stumpy bobbins of box. They are very curious and amusing, hanging over the sides or edges of their odd mother pillow — a large, hollow, hoop-shaped affair reminding one of the more modern automobile tire.

Spanish and Portuguese lace sticks are very delicate and dainty. The former are seen in rosewood, the latter in rich ivory — both with slender stems and with almost truly round balls at the lower ends. These bobbins are rather small, as slim as those of Devonshire, but made larger by the sometimes plain, sometimes traceried ball or occasionally gourd-shaped weight ends. It seems as if these southern nations, lovers of color, pomp and ceremony, might well have made for an occasional royal lace-maker a unique set of rich coral of malachite bobbins; but of course, lace-making does not seem to have been an indigenous art upon the Iberian Peninsula.

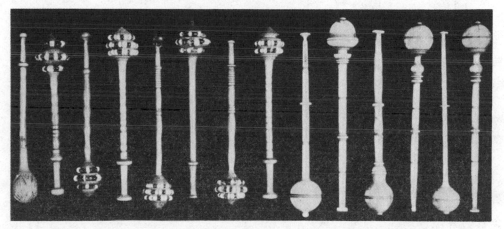

From the collection of Mrs. De Witt Clinton Cohen

EIGHT DAINTILY BEADED, LIGHT WOOD, DANISH BOBBINS AND SIX RARE OLD IVORY ONES FROM PORTUGAL.
[SLIGHTLY REDUCED.]

Once the mind starts to picture fanciful exotic bobbins, particularly in the country of the intricate geometrically surfaced Alhambra, and in a land just across from Egypt, one wonders why an icosahedron was never substituted for the perfect ball; why a solid circular flagellum with its graceful spreading fluted lines was never carved at the end of a bobbin. And some of the graceful, variously fluted and spiraled columns suggest delightfully delicate bobbin shanks!

There are also Belgian bobbins that are indeed sticks, for their delicate handles, far from being bulbous, are, on the contrary, incised and cut away. These seem generally to be of dark wood and are gracefully tipped with a tapering finial. But the ordinary bobbin of Belgium is of cheap, light-colored wood and has a little elongated pro-

tuberance about the size of a berry at the end. Older Belgian bobbins
there are — perhaps of Spanish import — made both large and very
large, of walnut, with the same round ball. The larger ones must
be gimp bobbins. These are eight or nine inches long, very neatly
made, and quite impressive. Another type — in cheap white wood —
of enormous bobbin was introduced into Belgium by its lace re-

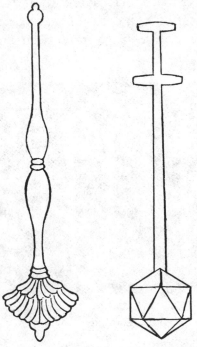

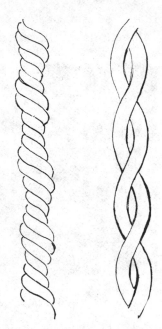

Left: A BOBBIN ALONG THE LINES
OF A GREEK FLABELLUM, BY GERTRUDE
WHITING.

Right: A CUBIST BOBBIN WITH A
TWENTY-FACET KNOB, BY GERTRUDE
WHITING.

SUGGESTIONS FOR FANCY BOB-
BIN SHANKS.

formers — Les Amies de la Dentelle — after the World War. The
directors, for teaching purposes, " chose specific colors, red, purple,
green and others, to represent specific movements of the threads, thus
establishing a symbolic color system of design which enables the pupil
to read a blackboard drawing as he would a written page. And they
realized that before the processes are portrayed by lines on the blackboard, they should be executed with the gigantesque bobbins and the

colored wool cords. They outlined for the first year class, a demonstration of the use of the tools — the winding-wheel, the cushion and bobbins." [8]

Switzerland too can boast of dainty lace implements! Her short, slim, gracefully curved, pyriform bobbins are of walnut, pear and plum. Some larger, modern bobbins are made of box. These used to cost a franc a dozen and were very green when bought, so that they

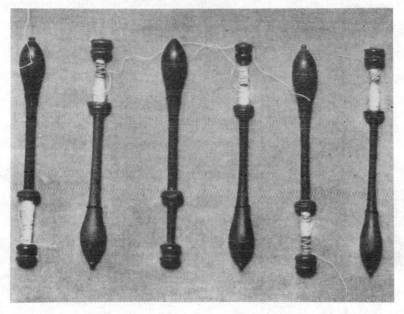

From the author's collection

SIX SMOOTH, SLIM, QUAKERY LITTLE SWISS STICKS OF WALNUT FROM THE HOME
DISTRICT OF JEAN JACQUES ROUSSEAU.

[8] "Even the babies had from 50 to 200 bobbins to keep in mind, rather long beechwood bobbins, these for Point de Paris, with the thread tightly wound at the top, and a considerable pear-shaped bulge at the end. Each lace is supposed to require a particular bobbin, especially suited to the weight of thread employed, but workers often use them indifferently. Some fortunate ones pride themselves on their fine ebony or ivory sets.

"During the long and solitary winters, when work in the fields is impossible, thousands of women and girls and little children turn to their lace cushions, and dreary rooms are enlivened by the music of the flying bobbins. If the lace is needle point, and lacks the accompanying click-clack of the shifting *fuseaux*, it nevertheless gives purpose and value to the otherwise almost insupportable winter days. However, despite the time that must be subtracted for weeding, for gathering the all-important potato crop, and for other farm duties, summer with its bright light and long day, is the true lace season; it is only then that some of the finest varieties can be executed. Coarser pieces must be substituted for the dull, eye-straining days." — Mrs. Vernon Kellogg.

warped most annoyingly and in a few cases almost doubled over like the cow's famous "crumpled horn." However, they were wondrous smooth and can still be had in Neuchâtel. The author, eager to own some of the delightful and very genteel, trim, little old ones, inserted an advertisement in a newspaper that circulated in the Val de Travers and its hinterland. It was answered by a trusting soul of more than threescore years and ten, who sent her old *bollet* pillow, decked with a pricking, absolutely incredibly fine linen — a single thread being

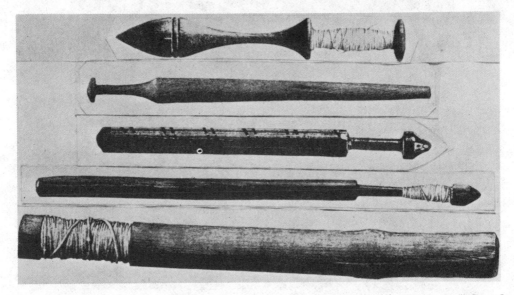

From La Dentelle Russe, by Mme Sophie Davydoff

RUSSIAN LACE BOBBINS [MUCH REUCEDD.]

1. FROM MOSCOW.	3. FROM KOSTROMA.
2. FROM VOLOGDA.	4. FROM NIJNI NOVGOROD. 5. FROM TVER.

almost invisible — and nine dozen walnut bobbins, writing that, if they were liked, one might purchase them for fourteen centimes a dozen: otherwise they could be returned. Of course, the latter did not happen: instead, each fragile toy was rubbed with oil and admiringly put to use by its new owner. But Switzerland can also boast an occasional bobbin of formidable dimensions — it reminds one of a life-sized gavel, or of a miniature churn — with a knob about two inches tall and one and three-quarter inches in diameter. The handle is some five inches long and a scant half-inch thick. The wood from which the bobbin is turned is ordinary.

Sticks indeed — that is, literally — are used in Russia and called *fracellskay*. They are very long, and are used bark and all, the spool portion at the head being whittled in, like the bamboo lace sticks of early Cape Cod. But the primitive Russian appliances, being solid, lack the musical tinkle of the vari-sized hollow New England sticks. Occasionally the Slav instrument is whittled and scraped from the thread-holding portion down to a gradual, tapering point at the end. Sometimes an ambitious wielder of the knife has encircled his product

MODERNISTIC BRILLIANTLY PAINTED BOBBINS — YELLOW, ORANGE AND GREEN ON AN ENAMELED BLACK
PAINT SURFACE LAID UPON WOOD.

with a double spiral line or band! Allowing one's fancy again to roam, one wonders why some of these rustics, next to nature and of a northern clime, never made their bobbins of white wood tapered off irregularly to resemble the familiar icicle? The writer has a set of bobbins recently made in New York by a Russian. They are indeed harlequin: modern in shape, decorated in jewel-like design with black, green and yellow enamel paint! Someone has suggested that the flange heads and handles might be shaped and pointed to suggest Darby and Joan, Romeo and Juliet, *Jean qui rit et Jean qui pleure,* or other similarly paired-off characters.

Maltese bobbins are slim — some tapering; some bulging, then receding just at the tip; some increasing in bulk toward the base. In all cases the two flanges seem to be very inconspicuous. The bobbins are apt to have one or two incised lines about their handles.

One of the last and farthest afield on the list is the ebony bobbin of India. It is rather short, but resembles the former ball-ended, walnut

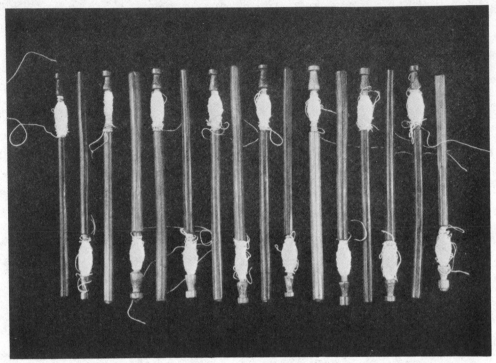

From the author's collection

SLIM SOLID BAMBOO STICKS FROM MADURA, SOUTHERN INDIA.

gimp bobbin of Belgium. However, the introduction of lace-making into sections of East India came through the Portuguese and English; which recalls a set of ebonized English bobbins with turquoise *spangles*, belonging to the writer. Mysore, India, makes both buffalo-horn and wire bobbins, which, like the mother-of-pearl article, one would indeed like to see! [9]

[9] Lucknow makes sets of little colored plaster (*chunam*) images built up on spiral wire bases. The wire bobbins of Mysore, particularly since *chunam* is a specialty in Southern India, are possibly of such plaster-covered wire. Iron bobbins too have been mentioned [T. Wright] as hailing from Mysore.

I mentioned the musical tinkle produced as the hollow bamboo bobbins of New England are thrown and strike against one another or upon the pillow. The American Mission in the very oriental city of Madura also uses bamboo for bobbin sticks: but being slim and solid, these little tools lack half their possible charm! They are locally

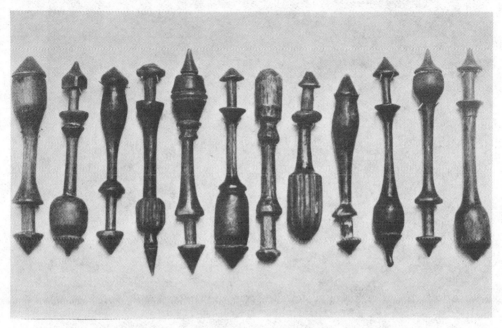

A DOZEN BARBARIC-LOOKING, HARD, LIGHT AND DARK WOOD BOBBINS FROM COLOMBO, CEYLON. THE AUTHOR DETACHED THESE FROM A LITTLE CINGALESE GIRL'S CUMBROUS AND FORMIDABLE PILLOW. THIS RESTED UPON FOUR TURNED CHAIR OR TABLE FEET. THE BROAD SQUARE CUSHION SLOPED DOWNWARD TOWARD THE TINY WORKER AND WAS OF THE DIMENSIONS OF THE SEAT OF A GOODLY ARMCHAIR. THE DARK WOOD REAR OF THE CUSHION, CONTAINING TWO DRAWERS, WAS OF THE SHAPE OF A SMALL HEAD-BOARD, AND WAS ELABORATELY, THOUGH CRUDELY, CARVED. A LITTLE SISTER WORKED UPON A SPANISH-SHAPED (PORTUGUESE) PILLOW, COVERED WITH STRAW MATTING. THESE BULBOUS KNOBS IN THEIR FULL SIZE REMIND ONE OF GLOSSY *RUGOSA* ROSE HIPS, AND OF OTHER FULL, RICH SEED PODS. [REDUCED.]

known as *kootchy*. But when trying to buy characteristic bobbins in Colombo, Ceylon, we were told to ask in a native house furnishing-hardware-junk store for " *trifles*." I forget the exact term; but the district or shopping street was called *pettah*, which accentuated my impression of hunting something petty, a " trifle light as air." Indeed, what I found was petty and disappointing — a cheap, machine-turned, wooden bobbin from an English factory! [10]

[10] See macramé shuttles, under " Fast-Flitting Shuttles."

TURNED, CHASED SPINDLES — DELICATE, SUGGESTIVE WINDOW BARS FROM THE TEMPLE OF
ANGKOR, CAMBODIA.

"ENTRE LES RIGIDES BARREAUX FUSELÉS [TURNED], JE REGARDE. ON SE SENT TROP
ENFERMÉ PAR L'ÉNORMITÉ DES FUSEAUX [BOBBINS] DE GRÈS MASQUANT LES OUVERTURES;
ET CEPENDANT LE CERCLE DE L'HORIZON, APERÇU ENTRE CES BARREAUX DES FENÊTRES,
MAINTIENT LA NOTION DE L'ALTITUDE. TRÈS SOMPTUEUSES FENÊTRES D'AILLEURS: ELLES
S'ENCADRENT DE SI DÉLICATES CISELURES QUE L'ON CROIRAIT DES DENTELLES [LACE]
PLAQUÉES SUR LA PIERRE, ET ELLES ONT DES BARREAUX QUI SEMBLENT DES COLONNETTES
DE BOIS, PRÉCIEUSEMENT TRAVAILLÉES AU TOUR, MAIS QUI SONT EN GRÈS."

— PIERRE LOTI.

Lace bobbins are a pure delight, and — just as a gift or memorial stick in England, where sticks have been so delightfully developed, has a special significance to its owner — just so do my own pet bobbins take on with time a particular aspect — like persons, gentle, practical, playful, proud or perverse. Anatole France has given us a delicious account of how when abed as a child, he whiled away tedium by personifying his ten fingers, giving to each an appropriate character, then making them enact little imaginary rôles. Just so have I gruff, thickset policemen to hold the heavy gimp cordon and keep my horde of plebeian, cheap wood, common workers in orderly place; and pretty, graceful butterfly sticks amidst a troupe of lightsome dancing maidens; or a few distinguished beauties of rare charm, gracefully stooping to lend their aid in some superior and difficult duty. You may name your favorites if you wish, as did the English their *name* bobbins, and as did Anatole France his fingers in this or that part — Little Red Riding Hood, the haughty Blanche of Castile, the handsome Dunois departing for Syria, Caliban, the blacksmith, brigand, soldier, et cetera. All these delightful little parts he recounts in his *Petit Pierre*. But I do not confine myself to sticks of one land only, as the sick-abed boy did his legendary or historic characters. It is true that England, though not the finest or the largest lace-producing land, nevertheless let her imagination soar in the art of devising sticks of almost endless detailed variety. These naturally lure us; but a grown-up's knowledge of history extends to many shores and can picture and dramatize, while using them to their best advantage, the bobbins of all the world.

BEAUTIFUL BOBBINS

"*In the middle of a field called Dunsty, at Stoke Goldington, is an old ash tree, under which in summertime the girls and boys used to sit and work. They had to empty so many bobbins a day; and it is remembered that the boys, in order to lessen their labours, used to wind the thread round the bole of the tree. Of course, the trick was discovered; but boys never think of the future.*"
— *The Romance of the Lace Pillow*: Thomas Wright.

"*For the historical student there is interesting material in the development in implements, from the medieval jeweled and beaded pins and bobbins — old*

Venetian, Belgian, Spanish, Swiss, Huguenot, English, such as appear again and again in medieval song and story — down to the plain wooden American bobbin of the present day."

— *A Lace Guide for Makers and Collectors:* Gertrude Whiting.

" Her poor form can relax
  As with pillow she sits,
Deftly weaving the flax
  That is wound in her sticks,
On her bobbins is wound,
To their spindles is bound."

— *A Lace Guide for Makers and Collectors:* Gertrude Whiting.

" The bobbins are indeed perfectly fascinating, and besides being so lovely to look at, they are just the size I want to work with.

" I am sending you a pair of my bone bobbins. Won't you please accept them as a wee token of my appreciation of your interest and trouble? They are modern English bobbins, I think — Mrs. Pelot was able to let me have some, but not enough. Now with these hundreds of beauties, I am quite independent. The old bead gingles are so bright, and the finger-worn dainty wooden things, so satisfactory to own! I supposed I was far past the age of getting so much real happiness from a Christmas toy!"

— Lillian R. Whitside.

"Lightly, lightly, lightly,
  Children fly like bobbins
From the one side to the other side —
  Poor folks' little children,
Who helps ye, ye who are poor?
The dearest child, our monarch's child,
  The dearest child alive."

— Flemish song, translated by Gertrude Whiting.

FAST-FLITTING SHUTTLES

" Life built herself a myriad forms,
And flashing her electric spark,
Flew shuttlewise above, beneath,
Weaving the web of life and death."
— Athenæum.

THE ladies of Chaucer's day (1375–1400) were fond of plaiting threads into a little looped edging which they called purling or pearling. Purling is mentioned in *Canterbury Tales* (1390). This, so far as I can discover, is the earliest mention in English or French of the particular sort of art we want to discuss, though " purling," of course, may allude not precisely to tatting, but, as it does to-day, to knitting.

Then after the lapse of several centuries we come across the literary skit of *The Royal Knotter,* written in 1707 by Sir Charles Sedley, which indicates the high favor tatting then enjoyed in England:

" Oh happy people! We must thrive
Whilst thus the Royal Pair do strive
    Both to advance your glory.
While he (by valour) conquers France,
She manufactures does advance
    And makes thread fringes for ye!

" Blessed we! who from such queens are freed
Who by vain superstition led,
    Are always telling beads.
For here's a Queen now, thanks to God!
Who when she rides in coach abroad,
    Is always knotting threads."

Sir Joshua Reynolds (1723–1792) painted a portrait of the Countess of Albemarle which shows her tatting. The picture hangs now in the National Gallery at London.

Some splendid shuttles are to be seen in one or two well-known English collections: a rare mother-of-pearl one; a rock-crystal shuttle set with the garnet initials of a princess and mounted in gold with a beautiful miniature figure surrounding the royal monogram! This "pearl without price" is in the Wallace collection. Other Wallace

MADAME ADELAIDE OF FRANCE WITH HER TATTING SHUTTLE: A
PAINTING BY J. M. NATTIER, AT VERSAILLES.

treasures are of gold in three different tones, framing delightful little enameled figures, and of shaded gold pierced and chased into beribboned flower garlands.

Hartford House has a tatting shuttle of fine wrought steel, pierced into flower forms that trace the initials of Madame Louise, daughter of Louis XV and aunt of Louis XVI.

This leads us out of England, and crossing the Channel, we hear that upon the Continent on November 4, **1755**, Lazare Duvaux furnished Madame de Pompadour with a shuttle in gold, enameled with ribbons at £690; and through the *Annonces, affiches et avis divers* of January 31, 1765, we learn that Madame de Pompadour lost this

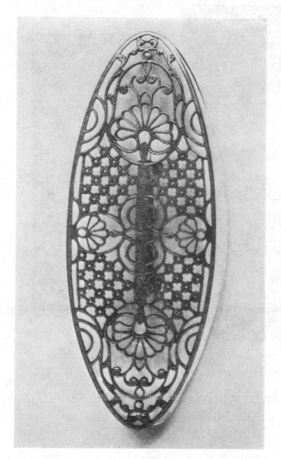 

From the Musée d'Acier at Rouen, France

TWO CHARMING OLD STEEL TATTING SHUTTLES.

navette at the Comédie-Française. The foregoing points to the fact that tatting was a royal French art in the eighteenth century. In Paris, in the wonderful Musée de Cluny — that delightful storehouse of endlessly varied, quaint, rare *bibelots* — are the finest perhaps of the world's historic shuttles. One is about six inches long — again a Louis XVI piece — a gold and red lacquer, decorated with a pair of lovers in sixteenth century costume, which carries us back even further! A second instrument, narrower and more elongated than the former, is of simple green enamel. And another, only four inches long, is of mother-of-pearl.

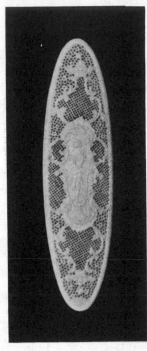

THREE OLD FRENCH SHUTTLES, ONE OF STEEL AND TWO OF IVORY, FROM THE COLLECTION OF MRS. DE WITT CLINTON COHEN, NEW YORK.

In the fashionable salon of the day, the beautiful little weaver that holds and carries one's thread superseded the graceful needle or bobbin that graced the patrician hands of the old doges' wives.

> " *L'emblème frappe ici vos yeux,*
> *Si les grâces, l'amour et l'amitié parfaite*
> *Peuvent jamais former les nœuds*
> *Vous deviez tenir la navette,*"

is the appropriate sentiment presented by Madame la Duchesse de Villeroi, together with a shuttle of gold, to Madame la Duchesse de Brionne.

A bit later in Belgium we read that two shuttles of amber set with gold, five in tortoise shell, two of crystal, two each in gold and ivory, three of pearl, one in agate and one made of petrified wood, were auctioned at a sale in Brussels in the year 1781.

Then, following origins from France and Belgium to the Near East, we come upon another royal knotter, Carmen Sylva, former queen of Rumania, who bade us not to " despise our needle and our shuttle, not to think that our thoughts need be small for all that! " To which I add a quotation from Lady Hoare: " The joy when a new stitch is found is very great. I don't know if Madame Curie felt much happier when she found radium! Of course, our work is small and modest and will never shake the world. A woman may shake the world once in many centuries, but she can find things in the quiet of her little

LADY HOARE'S FORKED SHUTTLE.

room that give her complete and intense satisfaction." Lady Hoare's mother, in our own time, invented a flat, double-ended shuttle, similar to the fishermen's old netting sticks of forked type, but with a slight extension at either end to be used instead of a separate pin.

One modern tatting shuttle recently seen is of abalone shell from California.

An amusing little Shaker tatting case is in the possession of the author. Three pieces of bronze kid laid over Bristol board and lined with satin the color of the shuttle within, are cut in the shape of broad shuttles about four inches long and bound with thin silk ribbon. Along each side of one — the bottom one, let us say — of these ellipses or rounded diamonds is overcast one of the remaining two, one to the right, one to the left; they forming the sides of the double upper lid, with a long slot at the top. Automatically they come together, closing this little work case of Brazil-nut appearance.

Very modern tatting shuttles are made with a sharp extra point, like a thorn, on one lip, to obviate the necessity of carrying about a separate pin.

As existing earlier shuttles, though less practical perhaps, are certainly handsomer than ours, should we assume that the tatting of olden times was finer too, though apparently just as fragile, since so little of it remains to testify?

Carmen Sylva made a golden brown silk iconostasis curtain, over two yards long, with a topaz in each star-shaped mesh of the central design — a Byzantine cross. The background was buttonholed over in gold thread with a turquoise in the heart of each star figure. Metallic threads must be tatted upon a silken slip string, as the other would be too stiff.

The Rumanian queen tatted also an altar veil, strung with pearls before working. The silk was drawn through the pearls by means of a hair noose. Carmen Sylva avoided unnecessary joining by hooking any extra thread alongside and in and out of the main thread, and used two shuttles when she wished to tat in straight lines.

A macramé shuttle for knotting fringe and lace is usually of ordinary wood or tin, about three inches long, with a straight quarter-inch shank and two broad knobby ends to keep the cord wound on the shuttle shank from slipping off. These shuttles or spools are preferable when hollow, so that they can be placed on one's sewing-machine spindle for winding.

A weaver's shuttle is for shooting the thread of the woof, which is wound upon it, between the threads of the warp. An old description says: "Three operations are necessary in the manufacture of cloth: first, the separation of the warp threads on the loom, so that the shuttle containing the woof can pass through; second, the movement of the shuttle, back and forth, among the warp threads; third, the beating up of the woof." Many of the best shuttles designed for loom work are of smooth, hard box or similar woods; while inside the shuttle, harmlessly to brush off lint from the fine silks wound upon the quill or bobbin, is a band of soft rabbit, mole or beaver fur. The particular shaping and pointing — straight or slightly curved — of these shuttles differs decidedly; while some shuttles have even little inset wheels or rollers beneath them that they may slide back and forth more nimbly. Formerly it was considered in the American colonies that a woman could throw a shuttle a distance of only thirty-six inches; hence wide coverlets were usually made in strips that were later sewn together. Had our grandmothers' shuttles possessed rollers or inset wheels, they might have sped across the warp with less outlay of energy or have slid farther.

A gay orange-painted roller shuttle hails from a fascinating hand-weaving centre in Sussex. Here accepted apprentices spend two years learning their chosen art in an old-time Anne Hathaway sort of home, with clean, unpainted plank walls and with plenty of light-giving little diamond-paned windows placed over high board benches or upon open stair landings, the whole being set in a garden of herbs and flowers grown to demonstrate vegetable dyeing. A conventionalized flower form is used to identify this home school's implements and as a badge for its graduates. So of course the flower figures, well disposed, upon the charming shuttle.

In Benares can be seen most graceful, delicate shuttles, made from the great horns of the plodding water buffalo. These slim, polished, dark-gray shuttles suggest little of their clumsy source. Upon the slight bamboo bobbins lying in the shuttles' trough may often be seen delicious, fine pale-gold filaments for weaving gauze saris. Entering a cool, dark, Benares weaving establishment just off busy Brass Street, I saw men sitting on the ground with their feet in hollows of the earth dug out beneath the little looms, and I approached a picturesque old man to buy his dark, shiny shuttle with its brilliantly contrasted gold thread. The man proved to be deaf and dumb! — But what of that, since I could not anyway speak Urdu, nor he my tongue? We bargained with rupees, annas, pice and fingers.

Eastward from India lies a mysterious old country — Cambodia. Here is practised warp weaving. Almond-eyed women wrap raw silk around a measured frame — a metre long if the loom is to be a metre wide — and tie with a raffia-like material parts of the silken strands. The strands, then removed from the winding-frame, are dipped and dyed, only the untied portions being able or free to absorb the color. These strands are spooled on a long — twelve- or fifteen-inch — stick quill, that in turn is slipped like a ramrod into a barrel of bamboo about three-quarters to an inch in diameter and longer than the quill or bobbin. *One* end of this unique shuttle is lance-like, with a hard, polished, dark wood, cartridge-shaped tip, and is the sort of shuttle in use among the Cambodians apparently since the thirteenth century.

The Bagobos of Mindanao also practise warp weaving — upon hemp. "From time out of mind men stripped hemp, and women wove it into skirts and jackets and trousers. The Bagobo songs and ancient tales contain many references to the work of the weaver and to the beautiful textiles. That decorative art should have found the fullest expression in the products of the loom does not seem remarkable to anyone who looks at the freshly stripped fibre from the stalk of the hemp — creamy-white, glistening, strong, pliable; the mere handling makes the manual process a pleasure, and stimulates the woman artist to experiment with this or that new motif.

"Each Bagobo woman learns from her mother and grandmother the different ways of tying which produce the different patterns in the weaving. The more complex figures are made by tying the warp before weaving. The hemp fibre is stretched on a long frame of bamboo, and then to make her pattern the woman artist picks out a cluster of strands at varying intervals: four strands here, seven there, two groups of strands near together, two others widely separated, and each cluster she binds and knots with short lengths of hemp. These sections of the warp remain the natural creamy tint of the hemp. By this method a much wider freedom in design is secured than if the patterns were all made in the weaving itself." L. W. Benedict's last claim seems doubtful, though one would like to give her sensitive, artistic natives all possible credit for their ability.

Still farther east than Cambodia is practised the amazing drawloom weaving. At present it is modish in the United States to wear self-colored damask Chinese silks, made with a heavy flattish iron shuttle upon these incredible Chinese machines. Truly, though, it is a human machine, for the loom has no harness, or thread-lifting apparatus, to change sets of threads and make a pattern; so the usual sheds or lifters for the shuttles to pass between, in their cross-weaving, are brought about by a wizard who straddles the high top of the upright loom, lifting first a handful of threads to the right, then one to the left, then two to the north, and a half handful toward the south; all without tearing a single thread, or raising a wrong one, which naturally would cause a flaw in the finished design. Another China-

I. A PRETTY ORANGE AND GREEN STAINED WOODEN WEAVING SHUTTLE, SHOWING THE TWO ROLLERS BENEATH IT.

2 AND 3. A RARE BAMBOO ARROW-LIKE SHUTTLE FROM CAMBODIA, WITH THE WOUND BOBBIN STICK THAT HOLDS THE THREAD, LYING NEXT ITS SHEATH-LIKE, ONE-ENDED SHUTTLE OR CASE.

4. THE HEAVY, FLATTISH IRON SHUTTLE OF CANTON, SHOWING TWO BLACK RABBIT-FUR OR SILKEN BRUSHES INTENDED TO DUST ANY LINT OFF THE REVOLVING QUILL OF SILK.

5. A GRACEFUL POLISHED BLACK GAUR HORN SHUTTLE, HOLDING A BOBBIN OF FINE INDIAN PALE GOLD TISSUE SILK AND WIRE, WHICH IS SO FINE THAT, THOUGH A LONG STRAND OF IT WAS HERE PHOTOGRAPHED HANGING FROM THE SHUTTLE, THE EXQUISITE BULLION THREAD DID NOT REPRODUCE.

man, usually a Cantonese, sits below, throwing the weighted shuttle as fast as ever he can between the layers of threads raised and lowered by the lightning Chinese above.

Looms upright with workers atop, looms Indian with weavers below, looms Cambodian with women preparing them; arrow-like shuttles with bamboo rods of silk inside; iron shuttles wound with perfect China hues; horn shuttles encasing gold; hardwood European shuttles set with fur; then tatting shuttles of mother-of-pearl, of rock crystal, of pierced steel, of inlaid ivory, enameled, and of shell — what a kaleidoscopic picture of flying color, weaving fabrics equal to a fairy rainbow!

FAST-FLITTING SHUTTLES

" *God zayth ine the boc of love, ' My zoster, my lemman, thou art a gardin besset myd two ssetteles.' "*
— *Ayenbite of Inwyt.*

" *How our fathers managed without crochet is a wonder; but I believe some small and feeble substitute existed in their time under the name of tatting.*"
— *Janet's Repentance:* George Eliot.

" *Those olive groves in the distance look more hoary and soft, as though a veil of light cunningly woven by the shuttling of the rays hung over them.*"

POLE-BOARDS, CANDLE-STOOLS OR CANDLE-BLOCKS

" When Mother's sewing buttons on
Their little garments one by one,
I settle down contented there
And watch her in her rocking-chair.
She's at the task she likes the best —
Each little waist and undervest
She fondles in a mother's way
And notes each sign of sturdy play.

" There's something in her patient eyes,
As in and out her needle flies,
Which seems to tell the joy she takes
In every little stitch she makes.
An hour of peace has settled down;
Hushed is the clamor of the town.

" Buttons are closely linked to joy.
Each little girl and little boy
Who dares to climb the garden fence
Buys that delight at their expense.
Buttons are childhood's tattletales —
Swifter than telegrams or mails
They fly to tell of moments glad
That little boys and girls have had;
And Mother reads the stories there
In every vacant space and tear.

" I chuckle as I watch her sew,
For joy has set the room aglow,
And in the picture I can see
The strength which means so much to me.
The scene is good to look upon
When Mother's sewing buttons on."

— When Day Is Done: Edgar A. Guest.

251

T HEN, too, there is one's work of an evening — the necessary stitch in time; or the pretty play of graceful fingers and gleaming gems sparkling in the lamplight, as one pursues one's filet or *petit point*.

But this lamplight — how temper its glare, yet concentrate and focus its strength, and how render it quaint and attractive, not just utilitarian and ordinary?

To answer these queries, let us imagine ourselves in the land of the most gifted of needleworkers, in the Old World countries where

From the collection of Mrs. Jesse H. Metcalf

LACE-MAKER'S LAMP FROM THE NEIGHBORHOOD OF VALANGIN, SWITZERLAND. THE CENTRAL GLOBE HOLDS A WICK FLOATING IN OIL.

customs do not rapidly change; and let us picture a peasant home where many must take advantage of a single taper or candle in order to economize; the village lads having escorted the maidens — or *coussegneusses*, as they are called in Switzerland — with their heavy lace pillows or *pils* to the cottage chosen for that particular evening's assemblage.

Let us suppose the weather is rainy and dull, or the daylight has begun to fade, or it is an afternoon during the winter solstice — the beginning of which English lace-makers celebrate on Tanders Day, November thirtieth — and the so-called *pole-boards, candle-stools* or *candle-blocks* have been brought out and placed in the centre of the room for the workers to gather about in orderly rows, the best lace-makers on the highest stools nearest the lamp or candle-stand. Thus, we are told, some eighteen workers can be accommodated, the outer row of stools or chairs being lower to catch the falling rays of light shed from the pole-board. This graded arrangement is spoken of as *first, second* and *third lights*.

The picturesque English outfit consists of a board or tall three- or four-legged table, in the middle of which is a hole through which a stick can be raised or lowered and held at the desired height by pegs. This hole or nozzle is crowned by a socket and candle and surrounded by several wooden cup-shaped holders, destined to contain firmly corked, thin, inverted, globular flasks of tinted water. At the sides of these boards of magnifying glasses are hung rush and straw hutches or baskets where the fragile globes, when not in use, can be gathered for safe-keeping. Further protection for them, when in use, is provided by the *flask cushions*, rush mats or nests used in linings in the wooden sockets to keep the burning-glasses from jarring against the wooden cups. Discarded globular wine bottles, with their necks broken off and stopped, are often turned upside down and utilized, among European peasants, in lieu of manufactured containers.[1]

A more primitive continental method is to place a simple wick or dip in a cupful of oil, adjusted to the lace-maker's progressing work by means of a rectangular wooden block, thicker one way than the other, so that the worker can start with the block lying down on the table, and later can raise it on end.

In Belgium, in the houses where harsh and expensive electricity has not yet crept in, special iron lamp-holders are used. Beside the kerosene lamp is placed a glass carafe, filled with bluish *snow water*. This globe concentrates and emphasizes the light cast through it by the lamp, so that three or four girls can take advantage of having a bright spotlight thrown directly upon their pillows.

---

[1] " The medieval ' ourinals ' are alike the retorts of the alchemist and the water-globes of the poor Flemish flax-thread spinners and lace-makers." — *Old English Glasses*: A. Hartshorne.

In Rhode Island, Professor Bushee's staunch Grandmother Al-
drich years ago defied spectacles, preferring to work by the intensified
light of her *water bottle* on its appointed stand.   This her children
must carefully avoid upsetting.   Just so my own grandmother warned
us not to romp and overturn her precious "bowl," withholding our
daily peppermint were we boisterous.   The peppermint box stood in

NINETEENTH-CENTURY CALVADOS LACE-MAKER.

a closet right next the slight, tall *guéridon* supporting its bowl.   To win
a candy, we must tell the time or read the thermometer, then cautiously
open the closet door; and to my honor be it said, I never presumed
to help myself to more than the one single peppermint permitted.
But one day my grandmother — eighty-seven years old — said, "Gertrude, go down to Macy's and buy me a pair of spectacles."   "How,
Grandma, can I know whether they fit?   Will you not have to go your-

self?" "Why, no; just buy me the nineteen-cent kind I had before."
So at eighty-seven she must still have been needing only the help of
mere magnifying glass!

The colonial New Hampshire candle block is a great unpainted,
unvarnished chunk of inexpensive wood, a sort of heavy lump, with
a rough, square stick rising from its centre to about the convenient
height for a seated person. To the top of the stick is firmly tacked
a little, fluted, tin, maple sugar cake mold about two inches in diameter, nailed right through the bottom. Around and upon this can be
hung some half-dozen so-called hog-scrapers, or rude iron candlesticks, each with a short, turned-back, hoop-like strip of metal extending beyond the rough, bent-down, *bobèche* rim. These small
portable candlesticks were mostly abandoned when better lighting was
introduced; but being of strong metal, they were filed straight along
one edge of the base and used by the farmers for scrapers in skinning
hogs, the candle-*stick* proper serving as a handle to the improvised
farm implement.

Little, short, three-legged mahogany stools with deeply spiraled,
polished poles rising two or three feet above them, crowned by small,
pierced, screw-threaded platforms that can be raised or lowered upon
the pole, and bearing at either end a chiseled-out socket or two for
candles, were also in vogue in northern New England, and are nowadays still very pleasing, but exasperatingly expensive.[2]

A picturesque and less expensive manner of lighting exists; still,
I fancy you had rather chance upon the scene of another's using it
than try to work by it yourself. I quote from Laura W. Benedict's
glimpse into a rattan and palm-leaf hut of southern Mindanao.
"That piece of embroidery was done under conditions hard to com-
prehend. During the day Bagobo women have little time for fancy
stitching, with all the cooking and the long climb to the river for
water and the work of the loom — for the weaving must be done by
daylight, as no native lamp can illumine the floor space covered by
the hand loom. But when darkness falls sewing and embroidery can
be done. A girl or young man fixes a leaf-wrapped resin torch in
the cleft end of a forked branch that stands on the floor and serves
as the native candelabrum. The torch is lighted; promptly the room

[2] These are often called cobblers' or shoemakers' candlestands.

is filled with pungent smoke that sets a foreign eye to weeping, but the native woman, better adapted, sits stitching, completely absorbed, close to the torch that flares fitfully in the mountain wind coming in gusts through openings in the palm wall. Presently the flame flickers low until someone pulls down the edges of the green leaf envelope to expose a fresh surface of burning resin to the air. A girl ambitious to finish a new *camisa* will crouch in that dim light, cutting out tiny appliqué points and sewing them on, from six o'clock until after midnight, while the rest of the family and the guests are asleep on the floor in the same room.

"Yet, with all the sordid discomforts, there is an atmosphere of restful content in a Bagobo house. The members of a family group do their work with an air of leisurely satisfaction; they take time to gaze with keen interest on one another's activities, as the men mold wax, make incised patterns in hard wood, or dexterously twist vegetable fibres into leglets, while the women are skeining hemp, or pounding rice with an accompaniment of song."

Not only for lace-makers and embroiderers, though, are picturesque lamps useful. All of us can, on the contrary, either read or sew by their tempered light, and also enjoy their quaint decorative charm.

PINKING BLOCKS AND OTHER BLOCKS
HERE AND THERE

" Buskins he wore, of costliest cordwayne,
Pinckt upon gold, and paled part per part."
— Faerie Queene: Spenser.

HAVE you forgotten the softwood or leaden block of Victorian days, and the assortment of household pinking-irons — sharp steel, semicircular ended chisels, large and small, with angular edges to cut a series of tiny V's; or rounded ones to cut out circular scallops; or fanciful, alternate designs?

I still recall the click and thud, click and thud of the hammer upon the chisel-head, and the chisel munching into the wood, through the cloth of my first, very first, party frock. I was four, and I bear to this day the memory of that baby blue Kashmir, and the mark of that party. While waiting for Nurse to button the dress, I rocked too vigorously to and fro opposite the corner of our bureau's marble Victorian top. Suddenly the chair hurled me on that unyielding point, and a dimple in my forehead still so testifies!

Shall we not follow up this iron that has a way of *pinking* both flesh and frocks, take a peep into its origin, consider its inseparable companion piece, the block, and follow that afield through its varied, picturesque manifestations?

To *pink* in Middle Dutch was *pincken;* in Dutch, *pinken,* to shut the eyes, to wink, to twinkle. Middle Dutch has also *pinckoogen,* to wink, to peep slyly. Middle English gives us *pinken,* to prick; *pikken,* to peck, to pick; the Latin form is *pungare,* to prick, puncture, stab, hence pungent; the word in French appears as *piquer,* to prick, to pierce with eyelets: all meaning to show or decorate with punctures or holes, to tattoo; specifically, thus to decorate any article or garment of textile fabric or leather; or to punch a small hole or eyelet in silk or other material with a *pinking-iron* — a toothed stamping instrument. The word " pounced " was sometimes used in Old

English with the meaning of pinked while the modern French term is *chequeté*.

The material is laid on a thick block of lead, the handle or opposite end of the iron being struck smartly with a hammer to give a clear, sharp cutting at the first application of the instrument.

Were the Renaissance mode for fancy pinked doublets, or some similar fashion, to return, we might see displayed great ingenuity in the designing of scallop cutters; but the Victorian days that many of us recall were rather wanting in imagination, so that the present pinker, hammered monotonously down upon its anvil block by some seamstress's assistant, not only shows little variety, but lacks the simple sturdy interest of its sister cutting and fashioning club, pounded with primitive zest upon an anvil block that is not a mere tree stump, rough or barked, but a block built to do its share in the cutting or rubbing or patterning.

Though the effects produced by the block and beater are not stitched, neither is a pinked edge stitched; yet both are woman's work, both belong to the realm of sewing and dressmaking, pinking being sometimes an easy way of finishing off a seam, sometimes a trimming for the outside of a frock; while bark-cloth beating aims at producing and decorating royal garments and bedding. Pulp or paper cloth is not, however, confined to the Pacific region, for during the World War, Germany made rapid strides in such production. The German work, though, is made by machinery; so let us turn to a discoverer's own description of the untrammeled, non-Victorian, unsophisticated hand-made work and implements of the Pacific.

Mr. Ellis, in the *Narrative of a Whaling Voyage around the Globe, 1833–36*, wrote:

"The scarf or shawl and the *tibuta* are the only dresses prepared in this way, and it is difficult to conceive of the dazzling and imposing appearance of such a dress, loosely folded round the person of a handsome chieftain of the South Sea Islands, who perfectly understands how to exhibit it to the best advantage. This kind of cloth is made better by the Tahitians than by any other inhabitants of the Pacific. It is not, however, equal to the *wairiirii* of the Sandwich Islanders. Much of this cloth, beautifully painted, is now employed in their houses for bed and window curtains, et cetera.

" In the manufacture of cloth the females of all ranks were employed; and the queens and wives of the chiefs of the highest rank strove to excel in some department — in the elegance of the patterns or the brilliancy of the colors. They are fond of society, and worked in large parties, in open and temporary houses erected for the purpose. Visiting one of these houses at Eimeo, I saw sixteen or twenty females all employed. The queen sat in the midst, surrounded by several chief women, each with a mallet in her hand, beating the bark that was spread before her. The queen worked as diligently and cheerfully as any present.

" The spar or square piece of wood on which the bark is beaten, being hollow on the under side, every stroke produces a loud sound, and the noise occasioned by sixteen or twenty mallets going at one time was to me almost deafening; while the queen and her

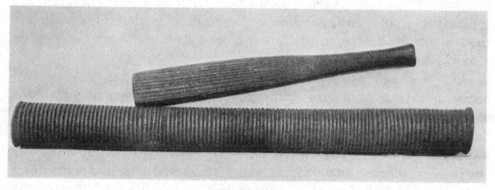

Courtesy of the Bishop Museum

BARK-CLOTH BEATER, FIJIAN, AND STRIPING PIN OR ROLLER BELOW.

friends seemed not only insensible to any inconvenience from it, but quite amused at its apparent effect on us. The sound of the cloth-beating mallet is not disagreeable, where heard at a distance in some of the retired valleys, indicating the abode of industry and peace; but in the cloth-houses it is hardly possible to endure it.

" As the wives and daughters of the chiefs take a pride in manufacturing superior cloth, the queen would often have felt it derogatory to her rank if any other females in the island could have finished a piece of cloth better than herself."

Mr. Ellis also tells us that " A stout piece of wood resembling a beam, twenty or thirty (?) feet long, and from six to nine inches square, with a groove cut in the under side, is placed on the ground; across this the bark is laid and beaten." Few tapa-blocks — and these Hawaiian — have, however, come down to us; perhaps they made good fuel, as did some of our grandparents' mahogany and rosewood, when walnut and oak were at their apogee. The blocks or spars were about thirty-two inches long by two and one-half wide, with four faces. They weighed about seven pounds, seven ounces. One old account, however, tells us that in Tahiti the beams were twelve feet long, made of hard *marra* wood, squared to six or eight inches. This sounds more like Mr. Ellis's description. The beams were called *tdootdóoa*. One side would be plain, one grooved — at right angles, perhaps, to the beater to be employed with it. This would tear apart, thin out, soften and render elastic the breech-cloths beat thereon, besides giving them a pleasing grain. Another side might bear lines running parallel to those upon the beater, to produce a ribbed surface. Such were made also of Kawau and of Kopiko wood.

Did you chance to see the operetta " Kitty MacKaye," and do you recall the Morse code secretly tapped out by the heroine at a fashionable London tea through the musical tinkle of her spoon upon the delicate china cup? The wild noblewomen[1] did not convey their messages quite so gently. They chattered and gossiped while beating the paper mulberry into dancing skirts and chieftains' garments; and as the anvil blocks[2] were deeply arched and hollowed beneath, the ends, moreover, set on small cross sticks to produce spring and resiliency, the reverberation was great; so that communications sometimes had to be rendered like those of spirits — through raps. One meant " no ";[3] two, " yes "; but this was merely the beginning — news and alarums were conveyed from clearing to clearing, clear across the island. The sound or echo of the mallet was known as *ouoa*. The ring of the mallet upon the anvil, echoing *from a distance* through the forest, was, we are told, most pleasing; and it quickly led the early explorers to the very heart of this savage civilization and to a wealth of

---

[1] Noblewomen = *Alii*.

[2] Anvil blocks = in Hawaiian, *Kua Kuku*; in Tahitian, *Titia* or *Tutua*; in Fijian, *Datua*; in Samoan and Tongan, *Tatua*.

[3] No = *Aole*; Yes = *Ae*.

information. Perhaps the first white invader was unconsciously announced by a *tapa* rap-a-tap-tap! [4]

Cutting or stripping blocks or boards are used among the native Hawaiian tribes and their descendants, and in the industrial schools by young citizens of many mixed races, in the preparation of palm leaves for mat plaiting. The boards are small, but bear the brunt of the sharp bite of a pair of needle points. These needles are placed just so far apart between two little slabs of wood clamped tightly to-

A KOREAN BLOCK AND BEATERS.

Courtesy of R. J. Baker

gether. This cutter is then run down a palm frond, either side of its midrib, slicing off two or more measured strips — two only, if wide for the making of a coarse mat; several, if for finer, narrower braiding.

The futile Koreans, spending their lives washing long, flowing, be-sashed white grass-cloth, use, for folding and pressing, a long, squared block, hollow beneath. Upon this a strip of linen is folded backward and forward, like accordion pleating. On either side of the block sits a woman with a smooth club in each hand, the two women sociably

[4] See chapter entitled " From Beetles to Hackles."

and alternately beating; perhaps thus adding lustre to the cloth while helping to flatten and smooth it. Ironing so becomes a sort of social bee. How tame and lonesome our single-handed *sad*-ironing would seem to the women of Seoul!

Across Europe, America and the Pacific have these blocks and irons brought us — what might we not find in interior Asia could we journey there more freely? Perhaps you may travel there some day, perhaps find a new sort of design in pinking-irons, and a block with some message worth echoing round the world!

PINKING BLOCKS AND OTHER BLOCKS HERE AND THERE

" Heo pinkes with her penne on heore parchmin."
                                                    —*Political Songs.*

" The sea hedgehog is enclosed in a round shell, handsomely wrought and pinked."
                                    —*Survey of Cornwall:* Richard Carew.

" A haberdasher's wife of small wit . . . railed upon me, till her pinked porringer fell off her head."
                                        —*Henry VIII:* William Shakespeare.

" A freebooter's pink, sir, three or four inches deep."
                                    — *Your five Gallants:* Thomas Middleton.

" You had rather have an ulcer in your body than a pink more in your clothes."
                                        — *The Magnetick Lady:* Ben Jonson.

" I will pink your flesh full of holes with my rapier for this."
                                    — *Every Man in His Humor:* Ben Jonson.

" Men and women pinke their bodies, putting thereon grease mixed with color."
                                        —*Purchas' Pilgrimage:* Samuel Purchas.

" We cut out our clothes, sir,
     At half-swords, as your tailors do, and pink 'em
With pikes and partisans.
                                        — *The Mad Lover:* John Fletcher.

" *The court is all full of vests, only my Lord St. Albans' not pinked, but plain black; and they say the King says the pinking upon white makes them look too much like magpies.*"

—*Diary:* Samuel Pepys.

" *If once well pinked, is clothed for life.*"
—*Alma:* Matthew Prior.

" *He found thee savage, and he left thee tame;*
Taught thee to clothe thy pinked and painted hide,
And grace thy figure with a soldier's pride."
—*Expostulations:* William Cowper.

" *A doublet of black velvet, pinked upon scarlet satin.*"
—Sir Walter Scott.

" *Acres of one-storied Korean huts. From them persistently, day and night, almost never ceasing, rises a continual rat-tat-tat. Whole volumes of national characteristics are told by these sounds. They are audible indications of the great racial passion for immaculate white clothing. Beneath the brown roofs thousands of obedient Korean wives launder and beat into smooth spotlessness the garments of their lords and masters.*"

FROM BEETLES TO HACKLES

" Aroint ye, ye limmer, out of an honest house, or shame fa' me, but I'll take the bittle *to you."* — *The Pirate:* Walter Scott.

BEFORE taking up our own western beating [1] and rippling of flax, let us study the primitive southern beating up of bark into cloth. Though weaving may or may not be older than the making or beating of bark-cloth, the latter is an almost dead art and seems earlier and more primitive. Known as bark-cloth in English, *kapa* (Hawaiian) is in Samoa called *siapo;* in Rapanui, *tapa;* in Tahiti, *ahu;* in the Tongan group, *hiapa ua* and *gatu;* in the Fiji Islands, *masi* and *malo gatu.*

The famous Captain Cook wrote from Tahiti in 1769, saying, " I shall now describe their way of making cloth, which, in my opinion, is the only curious manufacture they have. All their Cloth is, I believe, made from the Bark of Trees; the finest is made from a plant which they cultivate for no other purpose. Dr. Solander thinks it is the same plant the bark of which the Chinese make paper of. They let this plant grow till it is about six or eight feet high, the stem is then about as thick as one's Thum or thicker; after this they cut it down and lay it a certain time in water. This makes the Bark strip off easy, the outside of which is scraped off with a rough Shell. After this is done it looks like long strips of ragged linnen; these they lay together, by means of a fine paist made of some sort of root, to the Breadth of a yard more or less, and in length six, eight or ten yards or more, according to the use it is for. After it is thus put together it is *beat* out to its proper breadth and fineness, upon a *long square piece of wood,* with *wooden beaters,* the cloth being kept wet all the time. The *beaters* are made of hard wood with four square sides, are about three or four inches broad and cut into grooves of different fineness; this makes the cloth look at first sight as if it was wove with thread, but I believe the principal use of the grooves is to facilitate the *beating*

---

[1] Beating in Hawaii is *kuku.*

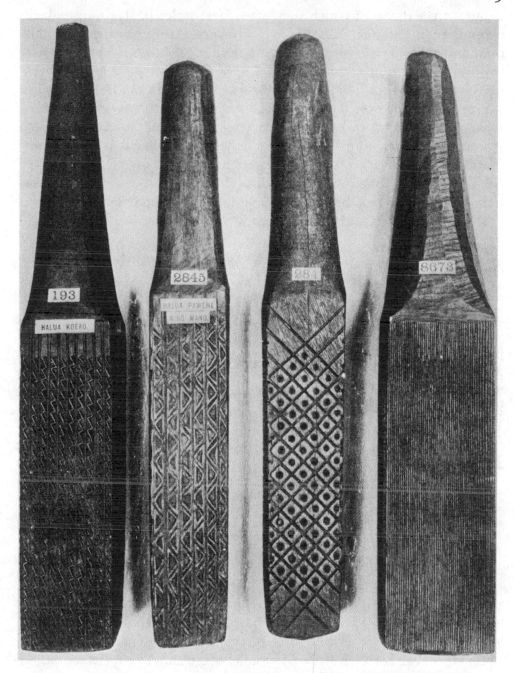

FINE WOODEN BEATERS FROM HAWAII.

it out, in the doing of which they often beat holes in it, or, one place thinner than another; but this is easily repair'd by pasting on small bits, and this they do in such a manner that the cloth is not the least injured. The finest sort when bleached is very white and comes nearest to fine cotton. Thick cloth, especially fine, is made by pasting two or more thickness's of thin cloth, made for that Purpose, together. Coarse thick cloth and ordinary thin cloth is made of the Bark of Bread fruit Trees, and I think I have been told that it is sometimes made from the Bark of other trees. The making of cloth is wholly the work of the women, in which all ranks are employ'd. Their common colours are red, brown and yellow, with which they dye some pieces just as their fancy leads them."

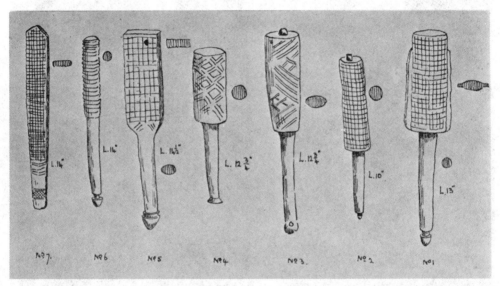

Edge-Partington

OLD PACIFIC BEETLES FROM NEW GUINEA.

These round-handled beetles or beaters (*titi* on Easter Island, *samu* among Fijis, *kuau* in Hawaii) were, it would seem, in their earliest stage, rounded in body as well as handle, the bat end being plain and fairly smooth. The clubs of the Marquesas Islanders incline to short, stubby handles, while some of the most developed beaters bear upon the bevel, between bat and handle, some slight proprietary mark or device, such as a schoolboy might whittle upon his pet pencil.

Courtesy Pauahi Bishop Museum

HAWAIIAN BARK-CLOTH BEATERS OR *IE KUKU*, SHOWING FAMILY WATER-MARKS. NO. 26 IS DERIVED FROM THE NECKLACES MADE OF TELESCOPED *PANDANUS* FRUITS AND IS CALLED *HALUA LEIHALA*. NO. 27 REPRESENTS MESHES OF NET AND IS KNOWN AS *HALUA MAKA UPENA*. NO. 28 IS *PAWEHE*, SIGNIFYING LINES AT RIGHT ANGLES. NO. 29 IS CALLED *LAUMAU*. NO. 30 BEARS THE SAME NAME AS NO. 28. NO. 31 IS CALLED *NIBO LIILII*, MEANING LITTLE TEETH. NO. 32 IS *LAUKOA OR LAUMAU*, WHICH DENOTES A PINNATE FERN LEAF.

But to beat out the narrow strips of inner bark to a squarer shape, a spreader was needed; and parallel grooves began to appear upon the beetles. From this to a square-cut bat allowing of four faces bearing different degrees of spreading surface — no lines (*mole*), coarse longitudinal ones (*pepehi*), fine ones (*hoopai*) — was but a step. And the lines later attained an incredible regularity, considering that they were spaced by eye. The ruling of them, however, was guided by primitive rulers of split bamboo, which naturally tears or cracks off clean and straight. Applying the ruler, the native, whether for personal use or in a capacity of community craftsman, cut along its edge with a clinkstone or shark tooth, deep into the future beater. The edge of the bamboo designing pen was also occasionally used as a ruler. The best specimen of beetle in Hawaii has twenty lines to the inch. Sharp angular grooves are *hoopai*; rounded, primitive, "corduroy" ones are *pepehi*. These sometimes alternate. Circular *pupu* holes may also have been drilled with sharks' teeth, or with the widely distributed Pacific *pump drill*.

These hollow dots sometimes appear alone, oftener in the centre of a diamond or triangular mesh-shaped (*maka upena*) design. Squares are *hoopai halua*. They served to alternate and distribute the thin and thick areas of the tapa cloth, for in it they left a pounded *water-mark* (*nao*), plainly visible when held up to the light. Thus *water-marking* rendered the goods both more flexible and more wearable, and also stamped the material with the maker's trade-mark or signature. Moreover, they gave the tapa a texture. Sharp triangular indentations are dubbed Sharks' Teeth (*Niho Mano*); rectangular ones, Little Teeth (*Niho Liilii*). *Koe* (an earthworm), gives us *Koeau*, an undulating line. A herring-bone is called Backbone of an Eel (*Iwipuhi*); fern leaf, *Lauma'u;* cocoanut leaf, *Launiu;* a duck track, *Kapuaikoloa;* a representation of a pandanus palm cone necklace, *Halua Leihala;* and there are similar terms reminiscent of the Snail's Trail and Cat's Track, Sun and Moon, Muscadine Hulls and other patterns of our early American *coverlets. Puili,* which resembles Lille lace net, means a twining, which consists of two *Koeau* addorsed instead of laid in parallel lines. This *Puili* may have been designed by the aid of a series of dots with zigzag cuts added, the entire hollows being then gouged out. Different cuts are occasionally alternated in the blocks. Fanciful line combinations are called *Halua Pawehe*.

The soda-bottle-shaped clubs (*Hohoa*), with one end scraped down to form a handle, were excellent for beating a tree and loosening its outer bark before splitting that to remove the bast beneath. They are generally of the hard, tough *Kauila* wood, sometimes of hard palm — the South Sea Islands used *Casuerina* or iron-wood — and again of the delightful golden Hawaiian mahogany. From this neighborhood came the best *kapa,* Tahiti following next, then Samoa, which alone still makes it — but commercially.

The mallets weigh from nine to forty-three and one-half ounces. These, however, are the extremes. Each face is from two and a half to three inches wide. And in Fiji the fine cudgels are called *Ike.* They are fourteen inches long. The South Sea Islands used longer ones — up to eighteen inches. Samoan *Ie* have two smooth (*mole*) sides to knit the cloth. The two grooved spreading sides opposite each other are struck at right angles to the fibre and leave a thready dimity line, while squares leave an appearance of linen. Tahiti used a smaller beetle. The fourth side often bore, opposite the smooth one, a more intricate, individual design. Chequering interweaves the mesh. For discussion of the cloth produced, consult the *Needle and Bobbin Club Bulletin*, Volume 8, No. 2. In Africa stone heads exist, lashed to handles with flat tapa tape and with twisted tapa cord. We read of the island women — though in Africa the men beat — " a mallet in hand." Pounding was a two-handed operation, the mallet being held in both hands like a golf stick.

" Although we have no record of stone kapa beaters ever having been in use in Polynesia, they were certainly in use in very ancient times in Mexico as well as on the Asiatic continent, and it is curious that the Mexican implements closely resembled the universal Polynesian form so far as the patterns of the striking surface are concerned. Reverend W. D. Westervelt has brought from Mexico and given to the Bernice Pauahi Bishop Museum specimens of the stone face of the beaters, used like the beaters in Japan to make paper as such and not the variety of felted vegetable fibre known as *kapa* and used as cloth rather than as paper.

" When Cortez entered Mexico after his wonderful march through the Guatamaltecan forests he found an extensive literature of painted books made of paper *beaten* from the fibre of *aloe* or *agave*, and the very few of these that escaped the destroying hands of the Spanish priests are, like the painted tombs of the kings and nobles of ancient Egypt, a record of domestic arts and life. The very hieroglyphics, however mysterious to the unlearned, involuntarily betray secrets of domestic life as well as the mysteries of their religion. In this remote island (Hawaii) we have no access to Lord Kingsborough's richly filled folios which probably show the stone faces of the paper (*kapa*) beaters in use or complete for use, but the stones themselves tell us enough to show that they had handles of some sort for their more effectual use. These beaters are oblong, rectangular stones. One is three inches long, one and seven-eighths wide, one and one-eighth thick: weight, ten and a half ounces: *mole* on one side; *hoopai* with twenty-two ridges on reverse. Three are edges semicircularly grooved. They are all reddish stones with quartz-like matrix and a few darker granules." — Dr. William T. Brigham.

From the Celebes and New Guinea also come stone tapa mallets; and from Finsch Harbor, clubs of coral. The Tinguians of the Philippines beat with wooden or bone mallets, which are generally grooved transversely. The cloth produced is soft and pliable, but it is not equal to *tapa*. The Semang beaters are subdivided into many small squares to produce a grain which used, even after considerable wear, to remain in the cloth; Selangor Blandas' mallets and the wild Sakai bats from Perak — see specimen in Cambridge Museum, England — being toothed *transversely*. This has to do with the position of the webster in relation to his anvil block (treated of in another paper).[2]

In the Leiden Museum is a quaint wooden contrivance designed to clean the clogging sticky pulp from out the grooves of these fast disappearing beaters (one feels tempted to say, "which are 'beating it'"). These are shaped like a cradle rocker. The straight, smaller part serves as a handle.

A little tapa has been found in South America.

Beetling was done by our ancestors upon flat stones with the aid of mallets. But this was done to soften strands of flax, not strips of bast, making the flax pliable and easier to weave. Thus linen yarn sail-cloth weft is still *beetled*.

It was also practised by hand in cotton countries to angularize and harden the fibres in order to give them the wiry appearance of linen.

_____

[2] See chapter on "Pinking Blocks and Other Blocks Here and There."

This has naturally in the white man's world become a mechanical process, done frequently by passing the cloth between rollers. In linen damask weaving, a stamp drops from above upon the goods passing over the roller.

All through Asia one sees the native not only pounding the laundry between stones, as in France, for example, but bending over the slimy green ponds, bat in hand, beating the wash — some say, to loosen the dirt; others, to give the goods a gloss. Again, especially in India and thereabouts, the native, after stepping gradually into the water, raising his *sampot* or *sarong* from around his ankles and knees as he wades out, till the garment is piled out of harm's way on the head, and later as modestly slid back down into place, turns to washing an alternate garment, wringing and flinging it like an Indian club round and round the head. Is this to loosen dirt, or merely to dry? At any rate, the entire process, from unwholesome water, through merciless *beetling,* to wild oriental flourishes, makes one gaspingly pray that the clothes before one's eyes may not chance to be one's own!

In the making of baskets, a heavy iron *batten* is employed to beat the work into compactness. *Battens* come into use, moreover, upon looms.

A *ripple* is a coarse comb with a single row of teeth not too close together, for removing the unripe capsules or seed-bolls from the flax stalks.

"A *brake*," writes Mabel H. Kerrison in the *Needle and Bobbin Club Bulletin,* "is a time-honored implement, as is a *scutcher* or *swingle,* for the preparation of flax or hemp.

"*Breaking* is the term applied to the separating of the outer woody stalk, or bark, from the inner fibre. The implement by which this is accomplished is very heavy and unwieldy, its manipulation being back-breaking work except for women of the strongest peasant type. Otherwise any woman could care for the entire process of the preparation of flax without a man's assistance. I like to think of it as the woman's crop.

"The *hand-brake* consists of two parallel bars, supported on wooden legs. Between the bars, a heavily weighted wooden *beater* is hinged at one end of the implement. The *beater* is lifted and allowed to fall upon the stalks which lie crosswise, thus *breaking* the wood from the fibre.

"Even after the outer wood is thoroughly broken, much will still adhere to the fibre. In order to remove these woody particles and to produce a clean and smooth fibre, it must first be *beaten*. This process is called *scutching* or *swingling*. The knife must be of very hard wood. Holding a handful of fibres in the left hand and allowing the long ends to hang over the top of the block, it is beaten downwards with the large wooden knife," which has one thin edge and is about two feet long.

"Beat first one end of the bundle and then, turning it, beat the other end. Rearrange the handful or bundle from time to time, so that the fibres at the centre shall be exposed, and beat again. Repeat this process many times until the fibre appears clean, or free from wood. During the whole process of *scutching*, which is a very important one, frequent rearrangement of the bundles is necessary to keep the fibres even. The fluff, or extremely short ends, which fall to the ground during *scutching*, are without value.

"Be sure that both the *breaking* and the *scutching* shall be done out-of-doors or in a large barn. The light fluff particles which rise, especially during the *scutching*, fill the air. One works, as it were, in a cloud of dust."

"*Hackling or Hetcheling.*—We now reach the final process before the spinning, *i.e.*, the process called hackling or hetcheling. The hackle, or hetchel, is a sort of *many*-toothed comb.

"A handful of fibres is held firmly, and thrown upon and drawn quickly through the teeth of the hackle. This is repeated many times in one position, and then naturally the same process is repeated on the opposite ends. Nor does the process end here, since it must be repeated with a series of hackles, each finer than the one used before. Thus, the first hackle used has only nine teeth to the square inch; each successive instrument used having a larger number, until the final one contains thirty-six to the square inch." . . .

"Around one, on the floor, is an enormous amount of apparent waste. This consists of the short lengths that have fallen during the whole process of hackling. It is called 'tow.' Do not despise it.

Gather it up carefully, *i.e.*, without crushing. It may be spun into coarse thread which later can be woven into burlaps and crash." Tow is sometimes spoken of as swingling-tow, or merely as swingling.

FROM BEETLES TO HACKLES

" *It must be watered, dried, braked, tew-tawed, and with much laber driven and reduced in the end to be as soft and tender as wooll.*"

" *And yet the same must be better kembed with hetchell-teeth of yron, until it be cleansed from all the grosse barke and rind among.*"
— Philemon Holland's translation of Pliny.

" *Swengyl for flax or hemp.*"

" *There must be planting, cutting down, bundling, watering, rippling, braking, wingling, and heckling of hemp.*"
— *Parley of Beasts:* Howell.

" *The Russians do spin and hachell it* [hemp], *and the English tarre it in threed and lay the cable.*"
— *Voyages:* Richard Hakluyt.

" *I bete and swyngylle flax.*"
— *Reliquiae Antiquae,* ed. by Thomas Wright.

" *Between the beetle and the block — a dangerous position.*"

" *The heckler stakes a handful or strick of rough flax.*"
— *Encyclopædia Britannica,* Vol. 14, p. 665.

THE SONG OF THE SPINNING-WHEEL

" *Faith holds the* Distaff,
   Hope winds the Shining Threads on Fairy Spools,
   Love turns the Wheel of Time. . . ."

" *Taught her hands and her mind*
      Nimbly forward to fly,
   Spinning *each in its kind,*
      And with patience to ply,
   Weaving fabrics of worth,
   Adding grace to the Earth."
                              —Gertrude Whiting.

WHY do I write about spinning, of which so much has been
said and written? Because it is so picturesque a subject,
so feminine, so homey, and mayhap because I am spell-
bound by the soft whirring music of the wheel. But do not you, also,
catch with me the soft purr and the glowing glamour of the thing in
this little ditty?

" Twinkle, twinkle, pretty spindle,
      Let the white wool drift and dwindle;
   Oh! we weave a damask doublet
      For my true love's coat of steel.
   Hark! the timid turning treadle
      Crooning soft old-fashioned ditties,
   To the low, slow murmur of the
      Round, brown wheel."
                           — Elizabeth Barney Buel.

It is this lovely lullaby, like that of the dripping water-wheel, that I
want you to enjoy with me. This, and a few less liquid, more intellec-
tual, odd little notes that may be new to you about spinstry, I shall
try to tell. With them I want to show just a few of the pretty parts
that pertain to the wheel.

But first let me — a spinster — try to stand up for my kind by
noting down for your perusal a few quotations, beginning with our

Grandmother Eve, and how her craft, her spun and woven handiwork — alluded to in the following familiar couplet — serves, as shown in the French rhyme that precedes it, to determine the disputed difference between the earlier and later types of animal — "foreapes" and forebears:

> "*Que distingue l'homme du singe?*
> *C'est le linge, c'est le linge!*"

> "When Adam dalve, and Eve *span*,
> Who was then a gentleman?"

"*Spinster* was formerly an addition or title (equivalent as late as the twenty-third year of Elizabeth's reign, to the Latin *generosa*), given to unmarried women of the gentle classes from a viscount's daughter down, and often retained by them on their marriage, especially when the husband was not of the gentry: *spinster* now denotes an unmarried or single woman, being often used in this sense in legal proceedings as a title or addition. The use of the term as implying gentility, had fallen out of fashion in the time of Chief Justice Coke,

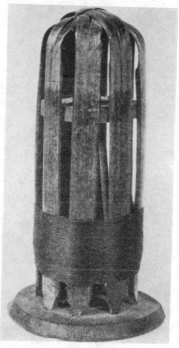

From the author's collection
A CHINESE SPLIT BAMBOO SPINDLE FROM A DRAW-LOOM WORKSHOP IN CANTON.

who declared that if a gentlewoman were named *spinster*, in any original writ, appeal, et cetera, she might abate it, as being entitled to the addition of *generosa*. Its use as applied to married women in legal proceedings survived later in America than in England." — "Let the three housewifely *spinsters* of destiny rather curtail the thread of thy life." — "Hu spak to the *spynnesters* to spynnen hit oute." — Piers Plowman.

> "Let meaner souls by virtue be cajoled,
> As the good Grecian *spinstress* [Penelope] was of old."
> — Tom Brown.

There were, however, long ago, other spinners — in ancient Greece — who evolved an amusing apparatus. All, or almost all, early spin-

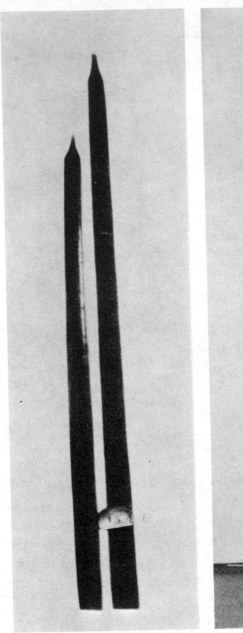

Courtesy Bernice Pauahi Bishop Museum

From the collection of Mrs. De Witt Clinton Cohen

Left: TWO PRIMITIVE DISTAL SPINNING STAVES FROM THE PACIFIC.

Right: QUAINTLY CUT AND PAINTED WOODEN ITALIAN *ROCCA*, ROCK OR DISTAFF, WITH DELIGHTFUL PEASANT MANIKINS, ONE OF WHOM SUGGESTS AN AMERICAN CONTINENTAL SOLDIER.

ners rolled the raw stuff upon their thighs to twist it into thread or yarn, and apparently this process rendered Greek thighs sore; or possibly it was maidenly modesty that led to the invention of the thigh case slipped upon the upper leg like a piece of armor plate. One of these protectors, in the Metropolitan Museum, is labeled *onos*. The protector, plain or mutilated, found by archæologists, meant nothing to them — since, having no back or base, it obviously was not an urn — till, happily, they fell upon some handsomely decorated, pretty well preserved specimens that portrayed spinners in various attitudes, some of the sitting figures wearing thigh guards. These cases are of the typical black and dull red pottery of that day, well executed, but very heavy, one would imagine, to wear.[1]

There were spindle-whorls of terra cotta from Troy. We read of Homeric whorls of gold and ivory.[2] Spindle-whorls were pierced, disc-shaped weights, usually of stone or metal, and thicker at the centre than at the edge.[3] They were slipped upon spindle sticks to help make them spin easily and roll the thread.[4] These were also called " thworls " and " pixy-wheels."

In French we read of *hasples* or *hâples*, also *dévidoirs*. An inventory of 1426 from the Castle of Baux mentions " *En la chambre ou Madame soloit gésir, une coulogne verde* " — that is to say, a *quenouille*, spindle or whorl painted green, " *une hâple vert* "; that is, a wheel of the same color " *avec beaucoup de fuses* " — fuseaux or bobbins for spinning.

In hand-spinning, a spindle is generally [5] a smallish stick attached

[1] Early Egyptians prepared their raw material upon flat stones; and ancient Greeks, so Mary Lois Kissel reports, made knee caps or hollow cylindrical hoods of pottery about a foot long on which to work their roving. Athenian spinners of the second half of the sixth century B.C. used such spinning knees.

[2] The amber, ivory or pottery whorls of old Greece and Rome are probably the most beautiful of the many decorated types the world has evolved.

[3] The weight of an unsupported spindle falls upon the roving, thereby influencing the drafting of the thread.

[4] The simplest whorl is probably just a stone, with a stick added as spindle. Some Asiatics spin and wind their thread upon two crossed sticks suspended in mid-air, free to revolve earthward, thus drawing and spinning in a single simultaneous operation. Certain Africans, as fast as the yarn is prepared, secure it to their big toes and wind it upon their feet!

[5] Miss Kissel tells us too of an enormous spindle four feet long with a whorl eight inches wide. This shaft the Cowichan and Thompson Indians sustain more or less uprightly upon the palm of one hand while the other raises it backward to draw off roving from a pole overhead — or other object higher than the spinner. They then twirl the great spindle to twist the strands into thread. Some Amerinds give momentum to their spindles by rubbing them against their shins, others by twisting them between thumb and finger.

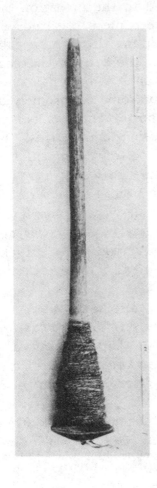

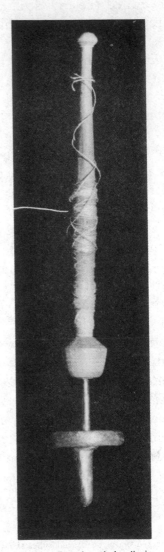

From the author's collection

Left: EARLY EGYPTIAN (?) SPINDLE WITH WHORL AT BASE AND THREAD WOUND THEREON.

Right: A SMALL LEADEN WHORL FITTED WITH A SCREW ABOVE THE FLAT DISC AND A FINIAL TIP BELOW. AFTER SCREWING IT INTO THE HANDLE BASE OF A LACE BOBBIN TO WHICH THREAD IS ATTACHED, ONE RAPIDLY SPINS THE WHORL — JUST THE REVERSE OF A TOP — UPON ONE'S KNEE, WITH THE BOBBIN HEAD AGAINST ONE FOR SUPPORT. THIS IS AN AUSTRIAN AND SAXON METHOD.

to the end of a thread drawn from the mass of fibre bunched on a distaff. By rotating the spindle, one twists the thread; and as the thread is spun, it winds itself upon the spindle. "Spinnle" and "spinnel" are Scotch and English dialectic forms of "spindle."

QUAINT OLD PEASANT SPINNER OF AUVERGNE.

In the earliest form of spinning, there was a rock, staff or distaff, generally a cleft stick some two to four feet long, on which was wound tow, wool, cotton or flax to be spun. The lower end of the distaff, as one still sees it in many primitive districts, should be held up between the left arm and the spinner's side; while the thread, passing through and gauged by the fingers of the same hand, should be drawn out and twisted by those of the right and wound on a suspended spindle, which completes the twist.   Since the introduction into Europe — about the fifteenth century — of wheels for spinning, the distaff has become a mere adjunct thereof, but sometimes a most graceful one, made perhaps of bulging spiral willow wands to hold bulky raw stuffs; or the staff may be small and picturesquely carved and colored as a stem upon which to impale a small quantity of fibre.

The quaint custom of Distaff, or Saint Distaff's, Day and Rock Monday occurs on January 7, the festival of Epiphany, the day after Twelfthday, and on the Monday thereafter, because then the women-folk, or distaff side of the house, resumed spinning after the interruption of the Christmas holidays.   Rock Monday, for the men, became Plow Monday.

Other picturesque spinners there are — I am thinking of a village in Italy where it is claimed the women spun better because of the countryside cliffs.   Over these crags the courageous women dropped their spindle-whorls to a great depth, gaining thereby special tension, speed and quality.   This perchance is the precipitous town where Pippa passed, where one has to bribe a driver to go, where only Madame la Comtesse, her family and the mistress of Tessoria Asolana speak English, therefore receiving the occasional traveler — English or American — who enters the Town of Asolo entranced by its picturesqueness and isolation and grateful to Browning for restoring the old hand silk industry, and to Madame for the typical embroidery that publishes abroad the grace of the castellated Asolan turrets.   Two of these fine hand spinners came to the United States.   Here their daughters soon donned hats and hid kerchiefs and aprons, feeling greatly ashamed of the mothers who clung to peasant ways and folk craft.   But at last a master spirit, hovering among the Chicago tenements, read the mothers' miserable disappointment and set them up properly in Hull House, where they became a show feature of Jane Addams's folk handicrafts museum; and where one, years later, swelling with well-earned honest pride, and commiserating with the docent whose duty it was to show visitors through the establishment, whispered as the guide passed, " Good Gawd, ain't it awful tedious? "

On a trip through the beautiful, wild Virginia mountains, I dropped into a typical old four-room log cabin.   An ample chimney divided one upper and lower room from the other pair, so that one had to step outdoors and in again to pass from the kitchen-dining-living room to the spinnery; while upstairs one could stand erect just under the roof beam only. In one of these cubby-holes — full moreover of chinks in the rough mortar — was stored a divided, melon-shaped Southern basket full of weaving drafts that I borrowed and copied; hanks of home-grown bleached and unbleached linen, some woven together — warp of one and weft of the other — into delectable cloths; odd local pink-meated apples wrapped in worn pieces of fine old indigo and madder-dyed peach-tone coverlets; *flocks* of wool to be woven on the great wide-wheeled spinning-wheel downstairs; and tied-up napkins full of tow to be spun on the little flax wheel.

Our American flax wheels are spread-legged; while the squarer, more upright type so often seen in foreign paintings, comes from Germany. These are often quite elaborately turned, somewhat like the uprights of a spool bed, and set with ivory bands and tips. One sits to a flax wheel, but stands and runs back and forth while spinning wool or cotton.

The mountain girl downstairs was gracefully running back and forth when we entered, alternately feeding twisted wool to the spindle and receding while she drew out a fresh supply of rough material from the rock or distaff, then deftly twisting it between her fingers and guiding it higher or lower, so it would wind evenly upon the flying spindle. Each time she approached the big wheel, she gave it a shove or turn to keep it revolving rapidly. She might have turned the two-inch-wide, flat-rimmed wheel by means of its wooden peg. Had she been spinning linen, she would have turned the wheel by a foot-treadle connected by a strap or cord to the wheel itself, which in turn would be tied or strapped to the spindle, thus making it revolve — just as the treadle of a sewing-machine is attached to the wheel above, and so on. In using a flax wheel, the spinner frequently holds the distaff in her left hand.

It was a pretty sight; though I felt indeed that, after she and her hospitable grandmother had attempted to dress in the one cramped bedroom, the lithe young girl needed to run and spin, and her guardian to sit hard by at the great loom and weave.

As for the origin of spinning-wheels: well, though the Greeks claimed that Minerva invented spinning, and Moses mentioned the art, India has long used a simple so-called " one-thread " wheel. The spindle and distaff, primitive, but similar to what we know, are sometimes seen on Egyptian monuments. The distaff is said to have been introduced by an Italian, in the fifteenth century, into England. Nuremberg claims in 1530 to have invented the spinning-wheel.

The large three-legged, the small similar sloping triangular, and the square four-legged upright spinning-wheels are the three usual European or American types; the last named, often ornamented with little bone rings and knobs, is known as the Saxon wheel. Asiatic spinning-wheels rest as a rule upon a legless plinth set directly on the floor, next to the squatting spinner.

A. Penderel Moody tells us — referring to Mary Queen of Scots — that " The Queen's bobbins were sold at a London auction some few years ago, since when they seem to have disappeared; but a spinning-wheel, made for her by her cousin, Peter Stuart, is still in use at the Tilberthwaite Weaving Industry, near Coniston. How strangely the ups and downs of life may follow one's household gods! The spinning-wheel is as treasured to-day in its humble home as it was by the poor prisoner of Fotheringay, and many girls have come down from the tiny white cottages scattered about the mountain passes, to have their first lessons on it before starting their own wheels at home. Queen Mary's workbox, and a little sample of her needlework, are still shown at Holyrood Palace."

Driving down the Pennsylvania pike toward Ephrata in the Mennonite country, I saw before a house many, many, many spinning-wheels — perhaps thirty. The Hessians and other " Dutch " settlers, of the section were thrifty housewives and apparently indefatigable spinners, as is attested by the quantity of handsomely diapered homespun linen and well woven, though often ugly, coverlets. Much spinning apparatus is probably scattered through the countryside — in Westchester, York, et cetera. The linens I saw varied interestingly in their damask chequering, the tablecloths being about two yards square, the towels often fringed and embroidered at one end for door hangings. These, an old wife told me, should be ironed first on the wrong side to press up the pattern threads, then on the right to give them a high gloss. Certainly her chests full of linen gleamed purest sparkling white!

On Deer Isle, in Maine, the Martha Washington Benevolent Society held annually, upon August twentieth, a spinning-match. I have heard that the spinners' husbands sometimes stood by to feed the contestants during the twenty-four or forty-eight or however many hours the " die-hards " might manage to persist.

" Every step in the manufacture of Tinguian cloth is looked after by the women, who raise a limited amount of cotton in the upland fields, pick and dry the crop, and prepare it for weaving. The bolls are placed on racks and are sun-dried, after which the husks are removed by hand.

" Weaving in cotton is a recent introduction among the neighboring Bontoc Igorot. Formerly their garments were made of flayed bark, or were woven from local fibre plants. The threads from the latter were spun or twisted on the naked thigh under the palm of the hand.

" Tinguian ginning," Fay-Cooper Cole writes, " is accomplished by two methods. The simplest and doubtless the older, is to place the cotton on a smooth wooden block and to roll it over a wooden cylinder which tapers slightly toward each end. The palm of the hand, at the base of the fingers, is placed on the roller and the weight of the body applied, as the cylinder is moved slowly forward, forcing the seeds from the floss. A similar device is used in Burma. The more common instrument (*lilidsan*) acts on the principle of a clothes wringer. Two horizontal cylinders of wood are geared together at one end, and are mounted in a wooden frame in such a manner that they are quite close together, yet not in contact. A handle is attached to the lower roller at the end opposite the gears, and as it is turned, it rotates the cylinders in opposite directions. A piece of cotton is pressed between the rollers, which seize the fibres and carry them through, while the seeds are forced back and fall to the ground.

" The cleaned cotton is never bowed or otherwise separated with a vibrating string, as is the case in Java, India and China, but the same result is obtained by placing it in a piece of carabao hide and beating it with two rattan sticks until it becomes soft and fluffy.

" After the carding the cotton is spun by placing it in a hollow cylinder of palm bark attached to a bamboo stick (*tibtibean*). A bit of thread is twisted from the cotton at the bottom of the cylinder, and is attached to a spindle, which is rubbed rapidly against the naked thigh, and is then allowed to turn in a shallow basket, or on a piece of hide. As it spins it twists out new thread and the arm of the operator rises higher and higher, until at last the spindle stops. The position of the extended arm is then altered, and the spindle again set in motion in order to wind up the new thread on the shaft. While the spinning is progressing, the free hand of the operator is passed rapidly up and down the thread, keeping the tension uniform and rubbing out any inequalities.

Courtesy of MacTavish and Co., Ltd., Shanghai

A CHINESE SPINNING-WHEEL.

"In many sections the spinning wheel used by the coast natives is beginning to replace the hand outfit. This method is much more rapid than the hand device, but the thread is less uniform, and it is seldom utilized when a fine fabric is to be woven. Bamboo bobbins, consisting of small tubes, are also wound by attaching them to the spindle shaft, so that the thread is transferred by the revolution of the wheel.

"As soon as the thread is spun, it is placed on a bamboo frame (*lalabayan*), on which it is measured and made ready for combing and sizing. As it is taken from the measuring frame, a bamboo rod is placed through each end of the loop, and these are fastened tightly inside the combing device (*agtatagodan*) by means of rattan bands. The thread is then carefully combed downward with a cocoanut husk which is dipped in a size of rice water. After drying, it is transferred to the shuttles and bobbins by means of the wheel described in the previous paragraph or by a more primitive device, called *ololau*. This consists of four horn hooks attached to horizontal bamboo sticks, which pass through an upright bamboo tube, and thus produce a wheel. The tube fits loosely over a wooden peg sustaining the wheel in a horizontal position, yet allowing the tube to turn readily." The cross formed by the bamboo stretcher sticks with hooked ends — a primitive *dévidoir* — has given rise to a very pleasing and typical Tinguian blanket weaving design.

But men spun too, and do so still. Of men interested in spinning there was a great trio in the eighteenth century — Sir Richard Arkwright, born in 1732, inventor of the cotton-spinning frame that gives to thread a hard, firm twist; James Hargreaves, of Nottingham, born in 1767, inventor of the spinning-jenny, which is an engine, gin or jinny for using several spindles at once; and the American-born Eli Whitney, inventor of the cotton-gin, which clears raw cotton of its clinging seeds. Whitney was born in 1765, and I append the account of one episode in his career that appears in the diary of Ezra Styles, D.D., LL.D.:

" Mr. Whitney brot to my house & shewed me his Machine, by him invented for cleaning Cotton of its Seeds. He showed us the model which he has finished to lodge at Philadelphia in the Secretary of States Office when he takes out his Patent. This miniature Model is pfect, & will clean about a dozen pounds a day, or about 40^{lb} before clean^g.

" He has completed Six large ones, Barrel phps five feet long to carry to Georgia. In one of these I saw about a *dozen pounds* of Cotton with seeds cleaned by one pson in about twenty minutes, from which was delivered about *three pounds* of Cotton purely cleansed of seed. It will clean 100 cwt a day. A curious and very ingenious piece of Mechanism.

"Yesterd^y Morn^g VIII^h Mr. Whitneys Work Shop consumed with Fire, Loss 3000 Doll. about 10 finished Machines for seed^g Cotton and 5 or 6 unfinished, & all the tools which no man can make but Mr Whitney the inventor, & w^c he has been 2 years in mak^g." (This building was in Wooster Street, New Haven.)

The following appeared in *Young India* of September 15, 1921:

"*Hand-spinning and hand-weaving.* — Some people spurn the idea of making in this age of mechanism hand-spinning and hand-weaving a national industry, but they forget there are millions of their country-men in this age who for want of suitable occupation are eking out a most miserable existence, and thousands who die of starvation and underfeeding every year, whereas only a hundred years ago hand-spinning and hand-weaving proved an insurance against a pauper's death. The extent to which relief was provided by this industry is recorded by Mr. Dutt in his *History of India: Victorian Age,* from the investigations conducted by Dr. Buchanan for seven years, 1813–1820.

"It will be seen from the details published in this book that crores of rupees were earned by these spinners and weavers by following their noble and honest calling. The decentralization of the industry — every village, town and district having always at its command as much supply as it needed — automatically facilitated its distribution and saved the consumer from Railway, Excise and all sorts of tariffs and middlemen's profits that he is a victim to to-day. If we cannot return to these days — though there is no reason, except our own bias and doubt, why we should not — can we not at least so organize our in-dustries as to do away without much delay with the foreign cloth with which our markets are being dumped to-day?

"Friends forget that the needle has not yet given place to the sewing-machine nor has the hand lost its cunning in spite of the typewriter. There is not the slightest reason why the spinning-wheel may not coexist with the spinning mill even as the domestic kitchen coexists with the hotels. Indeed typewriters and sewing-machines may go, but the needle and the reed pen will survive. The mills may suffer destruction. The spinning-wheel is a national necessity. I would ask sceptics to go to the many poor homes where the spinning-wheel is again supplementing their slender resources and ask the inmates whether the spinning-wheel has not brought joy to their homes.

"Thank God, the reward issued by Mr. Rewashanker Jagjiwan bids fair to bear fruit. In a short time, India will possess a renovated spinning-wheel — a wonderful invention of a patient Deccan artisan. It is made out of simple materials. There is no great complication

Courtesy of R. S. Holmes and Co., Peshawar

BEAUTIFUL KASHMIRI SPINNING, INDIA.

about it. It will be cheap and capable of being easily mended. It will give more yarn than the ordinary wheel and is capable of being worked by a five-year-old boy or girl."

There is in the Field Museum of Natural History a fascinating primitive, plump wooden bird from the Pacific, I think, that served as a ring guide for thread in spinning and weaving.[6] My impression is that the bird is carved and highly colored, set upon a sharpened stick that can be driven into the earth. Whether the thread passed through his beak or through a ring in his bill, I have forgotten; but the picturesque appliance leads me to a modern spinning ring perfected by a stranger, who bears one version of my family name — William Whittam of Westerly, who wrote a prize essay on spinning for the Whitinsville Spinning Ring Company, of Whitinsville, Massachusetts. I read in connection with Mr. Whittam's work that " on ring frames where there is no gauge for setting the bobbin on the spindle, there is presented a very irritating spectacle to a spinner who has a good eye to symmetrical work." William Whittam engaged with the Clark Thread Company of Newark, and has written a work on spinning that has run through one edition. The Whitin Textile Machine Works produce combing machines, drawing frames, roving frames, spinning frames, reels, quillers, spoolers, looms and much other apparatus that sounds both familiar and puzzling to the hand spinner.

A spinning ring is a tension device, designed to keep thread from running too freely, or the reverse. In crocheting, you remember, one wraps the thread once around the little finger for a similar purpose. Spinning-rings are also called ring-spinners, ring-frames, ring-throstles, ring-throstle frames, and ring-and-traveler spinners. The small metal loop through whose eye the thread passes is known nowadays as a traveler. This is employed upon upright machine spindles, each traveler revolving around its particular spindle as a planet about its sun.

Most of us have read or heard or seen something of the vast silk-worm industry, so I shall say but little about it.

Silkworms, after munching oak, mulberry or other particular leaves for about six weeks, start spinning cocoons around themselves. The wild Tussah worm eats oak and constructs a large cocoon that furnishes us with broken lengths of rough silk that we weave into pongee.[7]

---

[6] A wicker circlet, a piece of stone or wood pierced by a circular hole and suspended from the ceiling, or the top of a tall loom frame, may serve as a tension ring through which to pass and draw one's roving. The ring holds it back, keeping it somewhat stretched — not slack.

[7] It is because of the stickiness caused by short fibres, whose invisible ends catch and dovetail, that the cheaper modern silk fringes of Chinese crêpe shawls snarl and lack to the hand the smooth, cool, slippery touch of the old long-staple Canton fringe.

The raveled silk filaments broken off in unwrapping cocoons are known as floss, filoselle, *fleuret*, or *bourre de soie*.

The cultivated beastie generally feeds on dainty mulberry, spinning a longer, smoother and finer thread — so fine that only women's delicate fingers, generally dainty Chinese or Japanese ones at that, can feel it. The unaided eye can scarcely follow this gossamer thread, which is usually reeled, on account of this sheerness, some three strands together from three cocoons at a time. Experiments in feeding are constantly being made to improve the ruggedness of the precious worm, to see how the texture of the silk can be affected, whether color can be altered at will, and so forth.

Silkworms extensively bred long ago in China were greatly coveted by other nations, and in the sixth century a pair was cautiously stolen and taken to Italy in a hollow cane. Silk and sixth sound somewhat similar, so one can easily recall the date of the start of the silk industry that led to the marvelous brocades and velours of Europe. Lace of silk is rather recent and restricted — blond and Maltese lace, Greek *bibila*, et cetera, have had only local or momentary vogue.

You remember, perhaps, Matarieh in Egypt, with its sacred tree cared for by the local Lazarist Fathers? And recall that in the great hollow of the venerable tree, according to pious tradition, the Founder of Christianity and His Mother hid themselves when pursued by the soldiers of old Herod at the period of his massacre of the Innocents? As the story goes, spiders quickly spun their webs across the opening of the tree in such fashion as to convince the soldiery that no one could be concealed inside.[8]

Writing of one of our most interesting and useful species of spider, Mr. John Henry Comstock tells us that:[9]

" The silk of spiders of the genus Nephila surpasses in strength and in beauty that of the silkworm, and it is being utilized to some extent. The more important of the investigations which demonstrated the practicability of using this silk were the following: those made in this country by Professor Burt G. Wilder, with *Nephila clavipes;* those by Père Camboni, a French Roman Catholic missionary in Madagascar, with *Nephila madagascariensis;* and those by some Chinese at Yun-Nan, with *Nephila clavata.*

" Professor Wilder published an account of his experiments in

[8] " The web stretches across from tree to tree for a distance of often twelve or fifteen feet and reaches a height in the middle of fully six feet." — *Across Australia:* Spencer, Baldwin and Gillen.

[9] In *The Spider Book. Nephila plumipes* is a spinning spider of our southern states.

the *Proceedings of the Boston Society of Natural History*, October, 1865, and in the *Atlantic Monthly* for August, 1866; but no practical application has been made of them in this country. In Madagascar, however, the French have founded schools for the instruction of the natives in the methods of rearing the spiders, and in winding, spinning and weaving the silk. I have not at hand what is being done by the Chinese.[10]

"The method of obtaining the silk from these spiders is very different from that in which the silk of the silkworm is procured, which is by unwinding the cocoons. It is also different from that used in the earlier attempts to utilize the silk of spiders, which was by carding the silk of the egg-sacs. The silk of Nephila is obtained by pulling it directly from the body of the living spider.

"The full-grown spider is fastened in a tiny stanchion which fits over the body between the cephalothorax and the abdomen, in such a way that the spider is firmly held without injury, and so that the legs are kept away from the spinnerets. By lightly touching the spinnerets a thread can be obtained, and by slowly pulling this thread it will be constantly lengthened by a flow of silk from the spinning tubes. A thread of silk is drawn in this way from each of a considerable number of spiders at the same time; and all are twisted into a single larger thread by a mechanical twister, from which it passes to a reel.

"This process was shown at the Paris Exposition; and a complete set of bed hangings made from the silk of Nephila was exhibited there."

One of our quotations speaks of "webs, cocoons, et cetera"; and we have considered silkworms and spiders; but let us look into the strange spinning activities of another crawling creature. Would it make you feel creepy to wear the product of a caterpillar? I know that even silk gives a few people the "creeps."

It seems that a resident of Munich had the original idea of making silkworms spin lace for him. Some accounts speak of the creatures

---

[10] "A sort of cloth is made by these folks [of the Island of Malicolo in the New Hebrides] from the webs of a spider. It is remarkably strong, considering the material, and is made into small bags for keeping arrowheads, tobacco and even the dried poison that is used for these people's arrows." — *Among the Man-Eaters:* John Gaggin.

"For this purpose a small fish-shaped bait made of pearl-shell, to which is fastened a hook made of turtle-shell, is used with a bamboo pole and the fish finally landed in a spider-web net!" — *A Naturalist Among the Head-Hunters:* C. M. Woodford.

as caterpillars. I do not know much about the spinning of the latter, but most of us have encountered them at times hanging by a gossamer thread from some overhead branch.

A RARE, FINE, OLD HAND-PAINTED PARCHMENT STRIP, INSCRIBED, SIGNED AND DECORATED. THIS DISTAL STRIP IS TO WRAP AROUND THE RAW FLAX TO KEEP IT FROM FLUFFING OUT TOO FREELY. AS CAN BE SEEN IN THE PICTURE OF THE WOMAN SPINNING, THE TAPE IS WOUND ROUND THE PARCHMENT TO HOLD IT. NOTE THE BONE PIN CUT TO REPRESENT A ROOSTER. THE PIN, OF COURSE, IS TO SECURE THE LOOSE END OF THE TAPE. THIS PARCHMENT, FROM ST. GALL, IS UN-FORTUNATELY TOO WORN TO DECIPHER IN FULL, BUT THE LEGIBLE WORDING SUGGESTS A WEDDING DOCUMENT. POS-SIBLY IT WAS PRESENTED UPON A FULLY SET UP SPINNING-WHEEL, BY CONRADT FISCH OR THE MAID'S FATHER, VON ——(?), AS A WEDDING GIFT. THE BAND IS ABOUT TWENTY INCHES LONG, AND ITS BLURRED INSCRIPTION IS SOMEWHAT PUZZLING:

"TAKE THOU MY ERRANT SOUL,
STEER ITS SKIFF,
STEP U. BROTHER IMMANUEL,

"STEP INTO THE SHIP OF MY HEART,
LAY HOLD UPON THE RUDDER OF MY
    SPIRIT,
LET IT BE GIVEN OVER UNTO THEE.

"LET WHO WILL LISTEN!
ELIZABETH FISCHIN, ADORNED WITH
    HONOR AND VIRTUE,
NEWLY WED BRIDE

"OF WORTHY, DEVOUT, VERY HONORABLE AND HUMBLE MASTER CONRAD FISCH, FROM [OR OF] . . . MERITIERK MULLER, HIS HONORABLE, MUCH BELOVED DAUGH-TER.

1759."

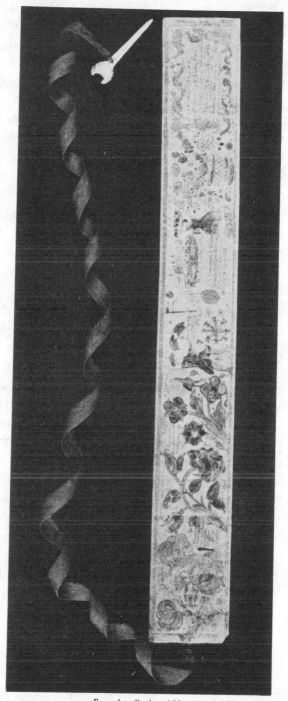

From the collection of Mrs. De Witt Clinton Cohen

Was it not because something in the nature of an inchworm had such a disagreeable habit of doing this that the English sparrow was introduced into the United States to devour the omnipresent pest?

Silkworms are *Bombyx mori;* however, we are told that the animal meant is *Phalaena pandilla.* Now *phalaena* means " moth," consequently not " spider," and since the silkworm is the larva of the bombycic moth, it seems as though Caterpillar Lace must be correct. This phalaenic larva is large and hairy, and his silk, hundreds of times lighter than flax thread.

Or course, though *chenille* is French for " caterpillar," so-called Chenille Lace is made of the velvety manufactured cord used mostly for trimming ladies' garments. Seventeenth century Italy made a flat Venetian needle lace called Caterpillar Point, because of its resemblance.

Spider lace, or *opus araneum* of former days, is also a human, hand-made variety. Our ingenious gentleman of Munich lightly painted a large flat stone or similar smooth surface with a paste made of the caterpillar's favorite food; then with a camel's hair brush dipped in olive oil, traced the spaces which he wished his crawling workers to avoid. The stone was appropriately inclined and the weavers placed at its base, whence, steadily eating the coat of paste, they climbed to the top of the incline, leaving the indicated open spaces in the pattern, but covering with silk the parts where they had browsed.

The lace thus obtained is of extraordinary lightness, one square yard weighing only five grams; whereas a machine-net veil of the same dimensions weighs about two hundred and sixty-two grams!

Having lured you to listen to the music of the imaginary wheel and the munch of the caterpillars, I shall leave you with an old folk poem that is found in different languages and sections, these particular words set down by Phillis Wheatley, I believe; while in my book to be published by Messrs. E. P. Dutton & Company you can, I trust, some day find the melodious four- or five-hundred-year-old spinning tune to which the poem was erstwhile sung.[11] And after this popular piece, I have concluded with one of a different tone.

[11] See *Lace Songs and Folk Tells,* by Gertrude Whiting.

THE SPINNING-WHEEL

" To ease his heart and own his flame,
 Young Jocky to my cottage came,
 But though I like him passing well,
 I careless turn'd my Spinning-Wheel.

" My milk-white hand he did extol,
 And praised my fingers long and small;
 Unusual joy my heart did feel,
 But still I turn'd my Spinning-Wheel.

" Then round about my slender waist,
 He clasped his arms and me embrac'd.
 To kiss my hand he then did kneel:
 Yet still I turn'd my Spinning-Wheel.

" With gentle voice I bid him rise,
 He blessèd both my lips and eyes;
 My fondness I could scarce conceal:
 Yet still I turn'd my Spinning-Wheel.

" Till bolder grown, so close he prest,
 His wanton thoughts I quickly guess'd.
 I pushed him from my rock and reel,
 And angry turn'd my Spinning-Wheel.

" At last when I begun to chide,
 He swore he meant me for his bride,
 And then my love I did reveal,
 And flung away my Spinning-Wheel."

" ' Thy spindle and thy distaff ready make,
 And God will send thee flax.' The promise read
 So fair, so beautiful to me, I said,
 ' Ah, straightway forth my spindle I will take;
My distaff shall its idleness forsake;

My wheel shall sing responsive to my tread,
And I will spin so fine, so strong a thread
Fate shall not cut it, nor Time's forces break!'
Long, long I waited sitting in the night, —
Looked east, looked west, where day with darkness blends,
Nor did I once my patient watch relax
Till cried a voice, 'Thou hast not read aright
The written promise, for God only sends
To him who, toiling bravely, seeks the flax!'"

— *Distaff and Spindle:* Mary Ashley Townsend.

THE SONG OF THE SPINNING WHEEL

" *The following is related in Da-em-ul-Islam, Vol. II, by Kazi Noman ben Mahomed, the Chief Justice of Cairo during the time of the Fatamide Khalifs of Egypt in about the third quarter of the 10th century A. D. He was one of the greatest scholars of the time, and has left a number of books on religion, laws, history, philosophy, etc. 'The holy prophet, divine peace be on him, said that the best occupation for a believing woman is the* Charkha *[spinning wheel].'*

" *The following commentary on the above occurs in Kitabun Najah, by Shaikh Ebrahim Saifee, who lived nearly 250 years ago: 'This shows that the prophet has praised the woman who keeps herself engaged with the* Charkha, *and similarly he has spoken highly of the occupation of spinning, because there are two excellences in the* Charkha. *One is, that it is an indoor occupation, and the second is, that it is a means of earning something. How excellent is the occupation, which combines both livelihood in this world and merit in the next?'*

" *It is said that the inventor of the* Charkha *has made the instrument a replica of the physical world. It represents the world in miniature. It consists of two parts, one higher and the other lower, showing heaven and earth. The rotundity of the wheel represents that of the heavens. Its revolutions indicate the revolutions of the planets. It consists of twelve spokes, representing twelve constellations. It has two legs upon which it is supported; these represent the two poles, north and south. It has a handle, which indicates the responsive quality of the heavens to man's work. It has an axis, which represents the relations between the powers of the poles and their support of each other. It has a spindle on which the yarn is wound. This represents the earth, which produces all things. There is a thread which connects the spokes with the spindle and rotates it, whereby the cotton is spun. That thread represents the medium through which pass the influences of the heavenly bodies over the earth. Cotton represents the four elements, out of which all things are produced, and the yarn represents the three products, i. e., mineral, plant and animal. The two hands of the spinner represent* the angels who arrange the creation of the creatures. The right hand indicates the angels of heaven, and the left hand those of the earth. Lastly, the spinner represents God the Creator. There is no God but He."

> " The loaded distaff, in the left hand placed,
>   With spongy coils of snow-white wool was graced;
>   From these the right hand lengthening fibers drew,
>   Which into thread 'neath nimble fingers grew."
>
> — Translation from Caius Valerius Catullus.

> "Sad Clotho held the rocke, the whiles the thrid
>   By griestly Lachesis was spun with paine."
>
> —Faerie Queene: Edmund Spenser.

> "Herself a snowy fleece doth wear,
>   And these her rock and spindle bear."
>
> — Masque of Hymen: Ben Jonson.

> "Sing to those that hold the vital shears,
>   And turn the adamantine spindle round
>   On which the fate of gods and men is wound."
>
> — Arcades: John Milton.

" Distaffs of ivory and gold, the gifts of kings and poets, the symbol of woman's dominion."

"Spinneret. An organ for producing a thread or threads of silk from the secretion of the silk glands. In spiders, one of the nipple-like, often distinctly jointed processes, near the end of the abdomen, on each of which are a number of minute orifices, by which the ducts of the silk glands open. There are usually three (but sometimes only two) pairs of spinnerets. Ordinarily in spinning a web, the lips of the spinnerets are brought together so that the streams of secretion unite in a single thread. . . . Also in many caterpillars, et cetera."

> " The silkworm is
>   Only man's spinster."
>
> —Muses' Looking-Glass.

" It was about the middle of the eighteenth century that machinery first began to be employed. We can easily imagine how it would happen. Here was an active and intelligent set of people . . . each spinning and weaving in his own cottage. If he lived in the country, he carried his finished goods by pack horse to the neighboring town. . . . And as he brought back his money and the raw material for fresh work, he must have wondered how he could multiply the simple operation which he knew so well. He could spin with scarcely a thought of what he was doing; why should he not spin several threads at once, and bring in more money *to his home and his family? In the end that is what James Hargreaves, a weaver of Blackburn, actually did, in 1767. He made a frame on which were mounted a number of spindles, each the equivalent of a spinning wheel."*

—Sir William Bragg.

" And so we take the spindle, or the thread,
To numb the weary hours, and day by day,
Fashion white thread in flow'ry wreaths of spray
For thirsts of soul. This, too, may bring us bread."

—*A Song for Valvognian Lace-Makers:* J. A. G.

" *The story of silk is the story of a woman's movement, and a womanly movement—not always quite the same thing. Men are interlopers in sericulture, and somewhat recent ones. They have been useful along the line of its commercial development; but the honor and the history belong to women.*

"*Silk was born in China. A little Chinese girl probably discovered it a few thousands of years ago when she, under a mulberry tree, sat playing jackstones with a handful of cocoons. And a Chinese queen gave the infant industry her patronage and her labor, cherished and cultivated the silkworms, planted the mulberry groves, invented the loom. And for centuries the royal women of China tended and developed the cult in all its branches — silkworm farms, dyeing, weaving — until the sericulture that began in one royal woman's interest and patriotism became, as it still is, the imperial art of an imperial people.*

"*The Lady of Si-Ling — probably one of the three most celebrated Chinese women, the wife of Huang-Ti, the emperor who reigned in China twenty-six centuries before Christ, and who was the arch-patron, and in many ways, the father, of Chinese Agriculture — gave the first great impetus to the silk industry of China. She grew mulberry trees, and encouraged the people high and low to do so. She studied and improved the rearing of the worms, and the reeling of the silk. She herself invented the loom and perfected it for the patterned weaving of the beautiful silken webs, which were sold for more than their weight in gold, not only in Persia and in India, but in distant luxury-loving Greece. She gave her personal time and the work of her own hands to the lovely industry, as has almost every Chinese empress since. Even the famous dowager empress of our day — the most libeled woman in history — found time to tend her worms and use her loom. And it has been the invariable practice of the ladies of the Chinese court, the women of the nobility, and the peasant women of the far-off, far-scattered countrysides, to ply regularly some part of the exacting industry.*

"*Chinese girls, scantily clad that they may be exquisitely sensitive to the slightest change of temperature, watch over and time all the stages of the silkworm's life. From the time the first worm is hatched until the last has spun its cocoon they require skillful and absolutely unremitting attention. The shed must be well ventilated, weatherproof, and in every particular scrupulously clean. The attendant girls must be quiet, cheerful, gentle and even in their movements, clean in person and sweet of breath. They must live on simple, unscented food. One strong whiff of garlic will ruin, if it does not kill, the finer silkworms, and injure the* coarsest. The silk-girls may live on honey and rose leaves if they like, but they must never eat onions or ginger.

"In some silkworm houses — in Sze-Chuen, for instance — for greater warmth, the best cocoons are sheltered in her own bosom by the attendant girl, and after that she must be quiet indeed. There are nuns in China, holy women for the most part, leading cloistered lives, but their daily life is worldly and vibrant compared to that of the silk-girls.

"For centuries the Chinese guarded all the secrets of their sericulture well. Even yet some of them are closely kept. And the perfection of Chinese manipulation cannot be approached.

"A Chinese princess, marrying an Indian prince, carried in the lining of her headdress silkworm eggs and mulberry tree seed to India, and, from that, silk and silk industries spread over the world."

— The Feast of Lanterns: Louise Jordan Miln.

ON WEAVING

"The Voiceless will speak in music, and the Formless will spin rhythmic patterns on the loom of space."

— *Architecture and Democracy:* Claude Bragdon.

"Oh! the summer days are bright,
And the summer days are long,
And our happy hearts are light
As we sing our weaving song.

"For the rolling world may bring
Dreary day and darker night:
But the heart that e'er can sing,
Always finds that life is bright.

"So shine on, O summer Sun!
Sing, O Bird! in greenwood tree;
Run, thou sparkling Brooklet, run.
Weavers, *though, you can't outglee!"*

— Isaac Riley.

TOO much has been written and well written about weaving for me to say much more: but some of you might be disappointed were I altogether to ignore so marvelous an art of thread and yarn work.

There looms before me such an ancient, vast, marvelous array in connection with the weaver's beautiful and indispensable craft, that I shall undertake merely to outline the methods and minor articles and facts — picturesque, but less known — belonging to this realm. For after all, those of you who love the loom know a little, at least, of the large literature existing thereon, and that almost any public library can furnish a good elementary book on weaving, if not an almost staggering supply of deep and technical tomes on the subject. I shall allude to a few particular books as I proceed: but for consecutive preliminary information, Miss Mary Lois Kissell will be found a clear and faithful writer or lecturer; while Mr. Ling Roth's four-part book on primitive looms is highly esteemed.

Coming down to method, *to warp a beam* is to attach the long threads to the main beam or roller. *To warple* is Scotch. Between the farther and nearer beams most weaving is stretched while in process of making. The long warp threads run from one to the other; while a shuttle — a pointed or boat-shaped utensil — holds a bobbin (that is really just a long, narrow special spool) full of thread. When one bobbin is emptied, another is placed in the shuttle, which, being

IGOROT GIRL WEARING COTTON PLAIDS AND STRIPES OF HER OWN WEAVING.

alike at both ends, can be painstakingly darned in and out between the threads in either direction, or shot between a lowered and an upraised set of threads.

East Indians have another *weaver's shuttle,* long, smooth, spindle-shaped, two-ended — the shuttle shell, named from its resemblance.

Primitives separated their two or more sets of threads by slipping a wooden so-called " dagger " between one and another; later by tying every other thread with a little thread loop to one stick, and the alternate set to a second stick — each one known now as a heddle. A third, fourth stick, et cetera, could be used. This is the origin and object of heddles, which are raised or lowered by harnesses that were formerly released by hand, but are now generally pulled or released by stepping on one or another treadle arranged rather like organ pedals. The space opened up between the layers of different threads is called a shed. At the colonial and Swedish looms, feet again co-operate. If you will refer to the chapter on " Fast-Flitting Shuttles," you can see how intricately the Chinese manage this in their incredible draw-looms. Draw-looms led, however, to the invaluable Jacquard power-loom of commerce. India, Japan,[1] the Philippines and prob-ably other oriental sections sometimes use a loom in which the shuttle is not thrown through a shed directly by hand, but by a sling and pulley device pulled or rather jerked by hand as fast as the weaver shifts sheds. This fly-shuttle click-clacks most noisily, but doubtless saves time and precious strength. The shuttle device is attached to the beater.

After weaving a shuttle thread, weft or woof — two names for the same thing — through the long stretched warp it becomes necessary to beat the last crosswise thread firmly and without loops against the preceding weft threads. (Remember the word " warp " if you will, by thinking it is stretched so it cannot warp, and, being very long, it might warp or slacken out of shape. This is not the origin of the word, which, like the verb " to waft," comes from the old *warpen,* meaning " to throw," but it is just a memory hint.) This was done by fingers,[2] which now are superseded by murderous-looking heavy forks, or finely grained, smooth, thick wooden combs that should not catch into and shred the material. Such combs, I have read, are often found in old Andean or Inca workbaskets.

The great metal-ended fork here illustrated, I bought from an eight- or ten-year-old girl for a few annas at Jaipur in Northern India. A diminutive boy, working also for fourteen hours a day at the same long rug loom, sold me the work knife. Orientals think it foolhardy that we should risk cutting or whittling toward ourselves — they cut outward. So it is the outer edge of this knife that has been sharpened, worn — worn and sharpened. The fork is eighteen or twenty inches long, very heavy. I pitied the mite who wielded it and who wondered

---

[1] Four Chinese girls, through the Koreans — 283 A.D. — taught weaving to the Japanese, who erected a temple to the four pioneers.

[2] Not only has beating been done by fingers, but among Navajo Indians blanket yarn is in-serted by the fingers, sometimes with the aid of a small stick. Navajo blanket weaving is of the tapestry type — with slits where one color meets another. The loom is hung from the limb of a tree and weaving is done beginning at the base.

open-eyed at my wish to possess it! Under a shed at the shady end of the long loom stood a master or reader, who called out the next group of knots to be tied. His row of several children repeated the

Left: A PAIR OF TALL, ELABORATELY CARVED, MAORI WEAVING UPRIGHTS FROM TURUTURUPARIWAI.

Right: THESE PICTURES ARE CONSIDERABLY REDUCED; IN REALITY THE WEAVING COMB IS ABOUT EIGHTEEN INCHES LONG AND VERY HEAVY, ESPECIALLY FOR THE EIGHT- OR TEN-YEAR-OLD HANDS THAT WIELD IT FOR FOURTEEN HOURS A DAY IN JEYPORE, INDIA. IT IS USED IN THE RUG WEAVING, WHERE A DOZEN GIRLS AND BOYS SIT BEFORE A GREAT LOOM, LISTENING FOR A FEW MINUTES TO AN INSTRUCTOR, WHO SING-SONGS THE ORDER OF THE COLORS ABOUT TO BE INSERTED. THE CHILDREN REPEAT HIS INDICATION, THEN THEY START TYING, KNOTTING, CUTTING, BEATING, AND PAUSE FOR THE NEXT SET OF INSTRUCTIONS. THE CUTTING EDGE OF THE KNIFE IS THE WORN OUTER ONE, FOR ORIENTALS THINK US VERY FOOLISH TO CUT TOWARD OURSELVES, THUS RISKING A SLIP AND A SLASH!

instruction. He went over it again and so did they. Then as speedily as possible they knotted each his or her tuft of pile wool to the warp, beat it into place and cut it to the desired length of the whole. Again the recitation began, and so on *ad nauseam*.

Craftsmen in some sections of India, at the Dasahra Festival, worship, as it were, or consecrate their implements, offering them sweetmeats. Even in the modern state workshops at Gwalior, models are prepared to receive honor at this time.

The Lord of Arts — Visvakarma — "the sum total of consciousness, the group soul of the individual craftsmen of all times and places," fashioner of all ornaments, upon whose craft men subsist, is constantly worshiped. Dr. Coomaraswamy says the guild workers rely for inward inspiration upon the still small voice and divine skill of Visvakarma, who reveals the beauty, rhythm and proportion that have an absolute existence on the ideal plane. And woe to the weaver of old who did bad work or traded spurious wool to mix with the real shawl wool of Central Asia!

"In the State of Rampur it is a delight," writes Mr. Mukerji, "to see the shawls appraised. If a chudder is coarse in texture, the artistic buyer says, 'Ah, my weaver friend, thou didst not sing the day thou wovest this one — look how coarse it feels!'"

"The day a chudder weaver sings at his toil, he makes a perfect shawl. The day his song does not quicken in his throat, his product is coarse."

Combs, incidentally, are used also in macramé lace or fringe interweaving and knotting. Instead of a wee hand comb, large colonial and similar looms have battens or lathes that are hinged in place, covering the whole width of the material, ready to slam back all at once, but with calculated strength, against the entire length of the newly interwoven thread.

Each thread, by the way, passes nowadays through a reed of fine split bamboo or steel strands that holds the warp threads equidistant, while a tenterhook stretches all to its full width. You have heard of being kept tenterhooks? Well, now you fully understand what a slow, steady strain the expression implies. A very thin horn or wood or bone, S-shaped, two-ended threader about five inches long is used to pull the threads through the fine openings of the reed.

Some Africans pursue a method of running a few warp strands through some guide holes — I have not seen the apparatus — weaving blue and white wool strips similar to the bands woven on Scandinavian tape looms. " It is the custom in Sweden," says Mrs. Bury Palliser, " to sew a broad border of seaming lace between the breadths of the sheets, sometimes woven in the linen. Directions, with patterns scarcely changed since the sixteenth century, may be found in the *Weaving Book* published at Stockholm in 1828 (*Weber Bilberbuch*)." The Ethiopians' four-inch strips bear a woven sign or signature — a sort of hereditary tree that forms a pretty four-rayed star, its arms growing larger and longer like the height of an Alaskan totem pole, which shows that Mr. Eagle is the son of Mr. Bear, who was the son of Mr. Turtle, et cetera. The Africans, however, use dashes, triangles, and curlicues to denote such matters, including one's birth moon, one's life color and possibly sex. Several woolen bands are stitched together to form a hammock, which then is decorated with a few tabs in lieu of fringe at either side.

Contrary to the usual method, the early Chinese are said to have woven away from themselves, so that their product accumulated in folds at the back or far end of the loom. We have heard it remarked that the East likes to reverse the ways we know in the West!

Cambodian warp weaving has been described in the chapter on " Hoops, Tambours and Frames." The actual plain weaving is after all the same, though the system of pattern-making varies.

On many looms the warp threads lie horizontally, as before indicated; but other looms hold the warp vertically. In Egypt a type is said to have existed that was attached to ceiling and floor. Upright are the Balkan looms, some of those in the Philippines, our Navajo looms and many of those used for tapestry making.

" The first loom," says some old manuscript, " was invented by one Arkeli Ghiden Ghelin when a lad of about seventy years! A drawing of this loom on a parchment scroll was found among the curiosities of Sesac, founder of the Egyptian Dynasty." [3]

Injunctions exist in the Institutes of Manu regulating the work of weavers, which argues high antiquity for the art. One ordinance says that " a weaver who has received ten *palas* of thread shall return cloth

---

[3] A Chinese queen, Louise Jordan Miln says, invented the loom.

weighing one *pala* more; he who acts differently shall be compelled to pay a fine of twelve *panas*. . . . All weights and measures must be duly marked, and once in six months let the king re-examine them."

Another indication of antiquity is found in Ceylon in the fact that weavers and basket-makers are of inferior caste, not because of their calling, but because when in mystical days the Aryans found them, the aborigines were already acquainted with these arts; yet, being black-skinned, they were classed as Sudras. Especially skilled workers, however, were later rewarded with the promise of higher rebirths and with land grant subsidies that they might have time for noble art meditation and creation.

Laying rushes or palm fronds upon the ground and plaiting them in and out, under and over, like a kindergarten mat of colored paper strips, was probably the earliest form of weaving. Polynesians, for their kings, made coarse, fine, finer and finest *lauhala* or pandanus palm mats — laying heavy stones first, then smaller, topped by coarse mats, then fine, sixteen mats in a pile, that the monarchs might lie dry and soft, or cool on a hot night. Such care and distinction doubtless promoted early weaving. The royal bed was completed by a tissuey tapa cloth set of four white sheets and a delicate royal watermarked or "monogrammed" spread of clearest rose pink or cerulean blue, these last five pieces being sewed together down one side, so that the monarch had always to crawl from the same side between his two upper and two lower sheets. Such palm mats are still carefully executed by Hawaiian girls in the government industrial schools. Fingers are the main instrument in mat-making, but among blocks are described some mechanical tools.

But other than flat ground weavings developed. Trees, sticks, plain and carved posts, belts, fingers, then combs figure among early weaving implements. Strings were stretched between two trees, later between staves. Over such a cord were hung rushes, grasses or threads, sometimes tied or wrapped in bundles at the base to keep them clean. Such can be seen in Alaska and were used, I believe, for the rare, gracefully shaped, Chilkat shoulder capes of white, black, yellow and green, with their handsome long wool fringes. The conventional designs of these valuable pieces are based upon skilfully halved and

MODEL OF WEAVERS, FROM THE TOMB OF MEHENKWETRE, AT THEBES, 2000 B.C.   MODEL NOW IN CAIRO.

quartered animals of the sea, with their bold compelling eyes that suggest the All-Seeing set in the mystic triangle.

Cowichan or Maori uprights, four feet tall and stunningly carved, with accentuated shell eyes in the barbaric faces represented, are preserved in the Field Museum of Natural History, Chicago, and in the Pauahi Bishop Museum, Honolulu.

Pacific Islanders developed a loom whose farther bar-warp beam was held at a distance by the soles of the weaver's feet, and whose near bar — upon which to accumulate the finished product — was strapped or belted to the wearer. Navajo Indians and other primitives hitch their warp beams to trees, ground or house posts, foregoing foot coöperation, and rendering their tribal contrivances purely hand looms.

Instead of weaving uninterruptedly straight ahead, a tapestry weaver stretches his warp — frequently over a horizontal colored cartoon (a low-warp loom with foot treadles) or in front of a mirror that reflects a painting hung behind the worker's back (a high-warp loom with hand *lisses*) — and, deftly selecting his finely graded colors, weaves in a little bit of rose for a flower; then, separately, green for a leaf. These two colors, as a rule, touch without interweaving, thereby leaving a tiny slit that is sometimes later stitched up as invisibly as possible. Scandinavian weaves leave the slits so boldly open as to cause them to become a distinct factor in the finished design. These might be called by the French term *jours*, which translated means "daylights." The word *jour* and its equivalent *mode* are much used in lace technique.

The term *lisse* comes from *lice* (also French) and *liceum* (Latin), meaning thread. In tapestry weaving it signifies the warp threads taken collectively.

Leash in a Jacquard loom is the collection of harness threads united at the top in one neck-cord.

A *leash* in weaving in general is a stick placed behind the heddles to separate and keep the warp in place.

Tapestry shuttles are spoken of as *flutes*, one being used for each separate color.

At Foochow in China one may occasionally pick up a delightful *Kossu* — silk tapestry — set of panels, showing the historic series of

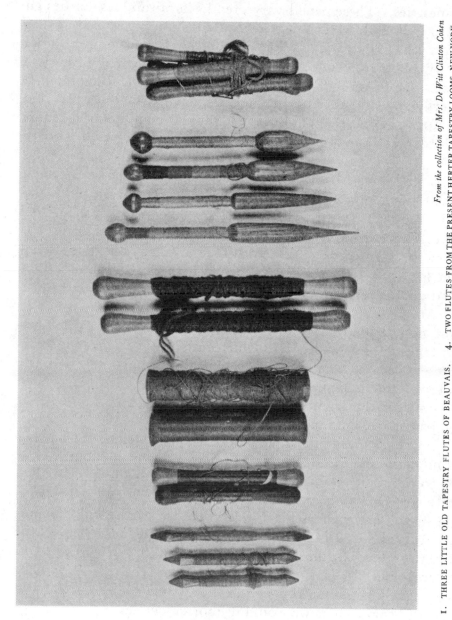

From the collection of Mrs. De Witt Clinton Cohen

1. THREE LITTLE OLD TAPESTRY FLUTES OF BEAUVAIS.
2. TWO TAPESTRY FLUTES FROM ARRAS.
3. TWO SPOOLS FROM THE LOOMS OF OLD BEAUVAIS.
4. TWO FLUTES FROM THE PRESENT HERTER TAPESTRY LOOMS, NEW YORK.
5. FOUR OLD GOBELIN TAPESTRY FLUTES.
6. A BUNCH OF LITTLE FLUTES FROM THE BAUMGARTEN TAPESTRY WORKS, NEW YORK.

sericulture pictures, from the feeding of the silkworms to the weaving of the tapestries. These panels vary greatly in faithfulness of design and quality of craftsmanship. Chinese silks that wrapped bodies buried near the prehistoric Lop Sea of Central Asia have been found in quantity and marvelous preservation. They are usually brocades; but some tapestries with interlocked weft threads occurring, as in the Peruvian work, at frequent intervals, have also been excavated by Sir Aurel Stein, the patterns portraying many of the same scrolls, birds and frets found on Chinese textiles of our own modern day.

"In India," says Mukerji, "they used to make tapestries out of the finest threads of gold as if they were silk. In Lhassa the Dalai Lama has one such tapestry — a rendering of the Wheel of Life. All the figures, including thirteen Buddhas, are as well wrought out as if they had been painted with colors. Think of it — a tapestry fourteen feet long and six feet broad done with threads of gold soft as silk, hard and perfect as a fresco painting on the rocks of an Ajunta cave!

"But now that art is dead. With the coming of the Mohammedans, tapestry of gold died in the thirteenth century. They forbade the representation of human figures in any form of art, and with the death of the Hindu empire, golden tapestry making died too. Then the Moghuls of the eighteenth century did their best to revive it through patronage, but alas, they too passed."

The Incas generally interwove an occasional daylight thread that the slit might not gape, or else guided a few weft threads a little over the line to the right and a few others to the left, rendering slits less obviously straight. Sometimes they connected their two colors with a single in-and-out contrasting thread that, as in the old lanciers, "grand-chained," clasping hands first to the right and then to the left. See the splendidly illustrated article by Philip Ainsworth Means in the *Needle and Bobbin Club Bulletin,* Volume IX, Number 1. The Andean weavers made use of a needle with a hole near its point, and also a small hook such as we would use for crocheting.

The Copts embroidered their tapestries as they wove them, by running in and out a needle or quill full of outside thread that was free from the mechanical straight line necessity of the warp and weft.

The loom has many other products, of which I shall briefly describe a few.

Linen (weave) is the result of the passing under and over of the warp and woof threads as in darning.

Twill, or tweeling, is the product of weaving under one thread and over two or more threads.

Jean, or old-fashioned fustian, is twilled cotton.

Serge, or old-fashioned Kerscymere, used for greatcoats, is twilled wool.

Satin is silk twill; shaloon is two-sided twill.

Most Dutch samplers emphasize twilled darning in different intriguing variations. Square holes are cut in the sampler cloth and filled in with variegated silks from a little above, below, and left and right, making a cross-shaped spot of color. Starting on the solid cloth and weaving a web to fill in the manufactured gap, the patient little stitcher learns to simulate damask patterns as she later must do if she has to darn fine napery. Dutch linen, by the way, is yet woven to fit the table in a great household; and the table still has a special press. In this, folded once each way, are laid and kept screw-pressed the monogrammed or crested cloths.

Corduroy, velveteen, plush and other pile or high-nap cloths are woven with a third thread looped up between the warp and weft. The loops later are razed to release all the tiny thread ends so produced. You have undoubtedly seen both upholstery goods and Japanese pictures that made use in their designs of the contrast between cut and uncut velvet?

Changeable cloth is " shot " with a weft differing in color from the warp.

Stockingettes are made by a looping machine patterned upon the principles of knitting.

Calico — from Kali Ghat, now known as Calcutta, India — is a printed cotton.

The word brocade comes from the French *brocher*, meaning in textiles " to figure." This is done by passing threads of color unwanted for the moment behind those immediately in demand. The so-called Nanking tapestry is really brocade. Brocade is said to have been unknown in the Tang Dynasty.

The far-famed Dacca muslins of upper India [4] — I have seen a shawl a yard and one-half square drawn through a woman's wedding ring — are of an inferior short cotton staple that no machine can spin. Herein lies a hint. Hand spinners and weavers for profit should restrict their efforts to the particular products, peculiar sizes and special vestments upon which power looms cannot compete. Three turbans from ten to eighteen yards long, said to have belonged to Shah Jehan, who commanded the building of the Taj Mahal some four hundred years ago, have lain in my hands. Their touch is of tenderest tissue, the Dacca muslin background held together by the fine web of pure flat gold strands and colored silks. One is banded of gold and parrot green, sprinkled with a strawberry motif.

This monarch's grandson, so the story goes, was " angry with his daughter for showing her skin through her clothes. Whereupon the princess remonstrated in her justification that she had on seven suits." Another tale tells of a weaver turned out of Dacca for neglect in not preventing a cow from eating a sheet of muslin laid on the lawn to dry, the animal having mistaken the fabric for a spider's web.

Two hundred and fifty miles of Dacca thread were found in a single one-pound skein!

A Kashmir shawl of pashmina — the silken down that lies under the hair of the Tibetan goat — was in the same royal collection. It was corn yellow with a small dotted motif of plump trees backed by tall bended cypresses, forming what we call a " palmetto." This shawl too would have passed through a ring of middling size. One finds minute piecing together in the old shawls, of which the *Amlikar* is of pashmina finely broidered with pashmina; while pashm design woven in by means of many bobbins while the work is on the loom is called *Tiliwalla, Tilikar, Kanikar* or *Binaut*. This is the more valuable type. Paisley shawls are a fine machine-made imitation. *Kinara* shawl edging of the old type, made in the beautiful Vale of Kashmir,

---

[4] Sheer, special weaves bear such pleasing names as Woven Air, Running Water, Evening Dew. Four imported dresses of Marie Antoinette's weighed together fifteen ounces. One can readily perceive why spinning and weaving, when such skill and art are involved, should not cause loss of caste, even as one can understand that being dainty French shepherdesses caused no loss of prestige to the ladies of Louis' court. Indian women, with their hand-cranked spinning wheels, prefer, like their royal patronesses, to assemble in groups that they may gossip, or intone old " sing-songs." We read that Dacca muslin " weavers work under sheds by the banks of the Ganges, and size the warp with rice starch."

around Amritsar of the Golden Mosque and at Nurpur, home of the "Mad Rani," should be encouraged. It can well be used as trimming and will prevent the absolute death of a marvelous art.

Alas! old Indian rug-weavers, Dhan Gopal Mukerji states, are passing. Between Ludhiana, Lahore, Amritsar and Kashmir, all the rug-makers are working on designs submitted to them by agents of western shops.

"Every old design had its song. The design will not blossom right if it receive not the song that is its due.

"Listen to an old rug-weaver who is too old to weave, but who can sing the songs of his craft. 'Grandfather,' I asked him, 'hast thou taught these songs to the younger weavers?'

"'When my fingers were nimble, I wove rugs that had to be watered each with its own song,' he answered. 'Now when stiff fingers ache for the touch of work, I sing in order to ease their pain. Why should I teach the young my songs? They weave not my kind of rugs. Why pound a song to death on a stony design?'

"In another rug-makers' village I found fourteen families at work. They were poorer, but full of life, and singing old songs. I inquired why they sang so well, and as I had expected, the village headman, an old man of eighty, answered me, 'We make the old rugs for the Rajah of Thalum. Our rugs make us sing.'

"He said, 'Songs died in most villages when Dulip Singh, the last king of the Punjab, was banished to England. There are a few villages that still sing because there are a few Rajahs yet left who sit on rugs and not in chairs like an ape on a tree. . . legs hanging down. Sovahn Allah, to sit with legs sticking out (instead of doubled under as they should be), how discourteous to guests and friends!'

"The old fellow's eyes blazed as he concluded his harangue: 'The belly of a man burns with emptiness so that he takes any work in order to stuff it, and thus he uproots song and laughter from his soul to do any order that is forthcoming. That is the calamity that has fallen upon us weaver-folk. The wonder of it is that men can live without singing at their work. If thou hadst said to me sixty years agone that such a thing should come to pass, I would have broken thy head with the buffeting of my scorn, but it is too true now. I can prophesy that in another score of years the songs of weavers that have lived fourscore will be lost as if they had never been. Allah Karim . . . come to my house, sir, I shall enjoy giving thee food and drink as well as a feast to the eye with a rug that has served as a model in our family when my grandfather's father was appointed rug-maker to the Moghul of Delhi.' "

One type of mat I am often questioned about is the felted *namdas* or *numda* of Kashmir, of which I used two or three as a mattress in my Indian bed-roll. The market for these white or light-colored small rugs, chain-stitched with heavy, scrolling flowers, has been a timely blessing to the fine-souled artistic weavers and embroiderers who made our grandmothers' highly prized so-called " camels' hair " shawls. The embroidering of the felt aids in holding it together. Moreover, Kashmir has had the high sense to prohibit aniline dye. The *Gabha* of Kashmir is of shaped woolen pieces fitted together puzzle-wise and embroidered.

Victorian Turkey work is creeping back into style. It is a combination of cross-stitch on a heavy canvas scrim back, and the looping and tying of tufts of wool as in professional rug-making. A Turkey work mat stands thus in marked relief, like a formal garden with plots of low flowers bordered by high, trimmed box.

The great rug industries of historic and standard trade type — Turkish, Armenian, Kurdistan, Persian (the finest), Bokhara, Kabul, carved Chinese (where little indicated lines are delicately cut away after the weaving) ; and the European *Rya* of Finland ; French *Aubusson, Savonnerie;* Scotch Axminster ; English Wiltons ; Spanish-Moresque Alpujarras with their tufted *confite* wool design often on a low-ribbed linen ground ; and so on *ad libitum* — are too prolix for us to follow in definite detail : but just a word about our handmade home products.

County fair vendors generally hawk a looping needle built on the principle of the southern rag rug weaver — a sort of stepping contraption threaded with old cloth, or, better, stocking strip that one guides back and forth over a stretched burlap surface. Such loops can be sheared like velvet should one prefer, but are more apt so to ravel and wear out. Do you know the rhyme of the rag rug?

THE HOOKED RUG

" I am the family wardrobe, best and worst
Of all our generations, from the first:
Grandpa's Sunday-go-to-meetin' coat,
And the woolen muffler he wore at his throat;
Grandma's shawl,
That came from Fayal;
Ma's wedding gown,
Three times turned and once let down,
Which once was plum, but has now turned brown;
Pa's red flannels, that made him itch;
Pants and shirts;
Petticoats and skirts;
From one or another, but I can't tell which.
Tread carefully,
Because, you see,
If you scuff on me,
You scratch the bark of the family tree."

The Nova Scotian turned-in rag rug is certainly the trimmest and perhaps the longest-lived type.

Turning toward the colonial, there comes to my mind a pretty paragraph saved sometime from I know not what: " The children were bravely decked out in new checked gowns, low pantaloons and suits. Customs may change; but boy nature is ever the same. Until their majority, when boys received *freedom suits,* with the privilege of keeping what money they earned and furnishing their own wardrobes, their suits were spun and woven and usually made up by their mothers. When the daughter took her turn at the loom, she was often assisted by some of the young men, who rode many miles on horseback to vie with each other for the privilege of spooling the quills. At all times it was a pleasant contrast to lift the latchstring and, coming in out of the night and silence, be greeted by the whirr of the spinning-wheel, the click-clack of the loom; to string apples to dry, and spool quills for the shuttles and laugh at nothing with the girls. These colored rolls of wool the daughter of the cabin attached to the spindle, drawing and spinning them out with one hand as she revolved the wheel with the other. When the spindle was full, she transferred them to the clock reel in skeins of ten knots, with forty threads to a knot. Three or four skeins were called a stint, or a good day's work. Her mother, meanwhile, sat at the loom, by a deft manipulation of shuttle and treadles weaving first the warp or long threads and then the woof or cross-threads, into homespun."

Mrs. Shinn says, "There is no more fascinating chapter in our national story than that of the woman at the loom weaving the household linen or bed covers which reflect the genuine quality of her nature in the strong, perfect cloth, made to last during her own lifetime and that of her children, if not of her grandchildren. She uses few colors, but perfect in beauty and fadeless virtue. The 'plan of design' communicates the gaiety of the worker reaching the end of her task, the consummation of her effort. Our foremother endowed it with a name so quaintly imaginary, so seemingly the upshot of sudden thought or the indulgence of a passing fancy, that to try to explain the 'why' would be as impossible as to explain the bird's song or the colors of the sunset sky:" —

The Governor's Garden
Lee's Surrender
Cat Tracks and Snail Trails
Seven Stars, Gentlemen's Fancy,
　　Isle of Patmos
Missouri Trouble
Blazing Star, Lemon Peel
Whig Rose
Double Muscadine Hulls
Wheel of Time
Old Roads
Honeycomb or Sunken Pattern
Nine Snowballs

Matron's Felicity
Alabama Beauty
Sun, Moon and Stars
Bunch N and O
World's Wonder
Wind Flowers
Spider Webs
Four Eyes
Water Meadows
Honeysuckle and Rose Path
A Monk's Belt
Nez Percé
　　and many more.

Most of these purely American patterns, with full detail, have been transcribed in large blue print form from the old John Landes book in the Frishmuth Collection of Colonial Relics at Philadelphia, by Mrs. Mary W. Atwater of Cambridge.

Mrs. Shinn divides the weaving evolved by our forbears as : —

First: that in which the pattern is formed by the threads of the woof being thrown across several of the warp and left lying loose on the surface of the goods. Sometimes as many as six or eight threads are crossed without being interlaced. This is overshot weaving, whether it be in cotton, silk or wool. The process is usually one employing four wings or heddles.

Second: cloth in which the thread forming the design is attached to the surface by a sort of twilling — many little ties of warp thread. This was often called " double cloth," though " double-faced " would be a better term. The old name " Summer and Winter " indicates the contrast between our early deep blue and the dazzling white predominating and contrasting on the opposite sides of such coverlets. No threads are left loose, and the fabric gains in compactness of texture what it loses in clear-cut boldness of design. This work requires six heddles.

Third: the superb double cloth of two distinctly separate fabrics woven at the same time, one above the other, but interplayed in pattern. There is much double cloth, composed of two fabrics fastened together in the process of weaving, to be had in shops; but the particular colonial kind, separate cloths, sometimes one above, sometimes the other, according to the demands of the pattern, is not to be found except in the old hand-woven materials. The thread used was also very heavy and the wool was exactly the size of the cotton. The warp was wound thread and thread about, blue wool with white cotton, while the weft was thrown thread and thread about. Two *sets* of harnesses were used, one for each color, making the threading of the loom somewhat complex. The result is clear-cut in outline, strong and bold, evincing great skill on the part of the weaver, while the coverlet is heavy in weight. Mr. Wurst of Chicago is an authority on this splendid type of inwrought weaving.

Our foremothers and the Mountain Whites of to-day are also responsible for some woven and knotted fringes and nets such as are being revived by the Talbots in Pawtucket and by the Herter Looms for curtains and portières.

Very interesting open or skip-stitch weaving, spoken of as *Demirdash,* and suggesting the square daylights of filet, is being revived on the high looms of Brussa with quaint geometric Near-Eastern design.

Luther Hooper tells us of *Weaving with Small Appliances, The Weaving Board, Tablet Weaving.*

Broomstick weaving is really a simple makeshift reversion to the primitive cords or pole with which we began — a hanging warp looped over a suspended broomstick, the weft run in and out with a spool and beaten up by a dull, heavy paper-cutter.

One can wrap a warp round and round an oblong thick card or compo board or a thin old book — with an extra thread sewn through the board edge on just one side, however, to alternate the coming weft — and darn under and over, up and down in the opposite direction to form a bag. With practice one can, as in tapestry, leave off one color and pick up another to form a design.

Such porch and shanty tricks help to initiate children and amuse convalescents. From the gradual coördination of hand and eye and thought, the initiate may try to train the foot too by the later use of a larger loom.

Ex-President Eliot of Harvard writes, " The crafts have a definite educational value. Not only do they develop manual dexterity, but they train the mind through the hands. This is supported by modern psychology."

And the occupational therapy training instituted at hospitals and homes previous to the World War came just in time to rescue many discouraged cripples from the front; who in turn have been the means of their teachers' realizing better methods to follow for the future reconstruction of shattered nerve and muscle. Weaving is one of the foremost crafts so employed.

Now, I have left unnoted the stunning brocades of the Renaissance, the beautiful light and dark blue Perugian towels, the flame stitch that is said to have traveled from Hunnan — the eastern land of the Huns — to Hungary, overrun by them when under the great Mongol khan they stormed the gates of Vienna. This " Hungarian " weaving and embroidery wandered down to Florence under the name of Botticelli embroidery, while its sister weaving stitch has been secretly picked out and revived by some nuns and Italian noblewomen. No pattern is visible on the cotton back of the goods, while the silk face shows an arrow-shaped stitch that rises and falls in interlocking darts of fine color. The weaver has to stand to her work and is weary at the end of a half-day. I have omitted mohair; *buratto* bolting cloth used as a ground for filet lace embroidery; the tapestries of Arras, Beauvais, Gobelins, Mortlake, et cetera; the so-called " Polish sashes"; the intriguing *ceintures fléchées* of the Canadian *habitants* and *voyageurs;* Mediæval guilds — perhaps volume ten or eleven of the *Needle and Bobbin Bulletin* will tell of the English weavers' and shearers' guilds; the invention of the power-loom by the Reverend Dr. Edmund Cartright in 1757; its improvements by Horrock, Monteith and others, including the intricacies of the Jacquard loom invented five years earlier, but introduced later — but what will you? Weaving is beautiful and a " joy forever," so hand weavers enthusiastically maintain; but like that word " forever," the subject is positively endless!

ON WEAVING

" *Proclaim that I can sing, weave, sew and dance.*"
— *Pericles:* William Shakespeare.

" *Weavers* [*or websters*] *were supposed to be generally good singers; their trade being sedentary, they had an opportunity of practising, sometimes in parts, while they were at work. Warburton adds that many of the weavers in Queen Elizabeth's days were Flemish Calvinists* [*Golden Fleece Order*], *who fled from the persecution of the Duke of Alva and were therefore particularly given to singing psalms. . . .   Hence the exclamation of Falstaff, '* I would I were a weaver! I could sing psalms and all manner of songs.'*"
— Robert or Edward Nares.

" *The blood flows rhythmically, the heart its metronome; the moving limbs weave patterns.*"

" *Such laws of nature are equally laws of art, for art is nature carried to a higher power by reason of its passage through a human consciousness. Thought and emotion tend to crystallize into forms of beauty as inevitably, and according to the same laws, as does frost on the windowpane. Art, in one of its aspects, is the weaving of a pattern, the communication of an order and a method to lines, forms, colors and sounds.*"
— Claude Bragdon.

" *Various groups of spiders are distinguished by the form of their webs, as lineweavers, orb-weavers, tapestry-weavers, tube-weavers, tunnel-weavers, et cetera.*"

" If a Bagobo could hold up just one article and say ' Kanak ' [mine] or ' My wife made it,' he would give a radiant smile and sit down content.

" When the furniture of that house consists of a loom, a family altar, a hen's nest, and three stones for a stove — then, other things being equal, there may come about an economic situation in which the whole tribe becomes a leisure class.

" The loom is the centre of interest in every such household. . . . Basket surfaces are divided into three parallel fields running round the baskets, like the corresponding circular, woven strips composing a woman's skirt."

— *Bagobo Fine Art Collection:* Laura Watson Benedict.

THE ROMANCE OF THE SEWING-MACHINE

" One minstrel said he had two birds named Wheeler *and* Wilson. . . . *His partner sneered, ' What's the sense in that, why select those names? ' . . . ' Why,' answered the bird owner, ' because neither is a " Singer." ' . . . Then the partner said he had seen a* sewing-machine *running down the street without a stitch on! "*

WELL," you are probably thinking, "what romance is there, pray, in a sewing-machine?" While I feel like singing —

Stitch, Stitch, Stitcher,
Sing, Sing, Singer —
A Song of the Sewing-Machine!

You know, we seldom venerate the things of our fathers, but we collect the things of our grandfathers' days. Now, sewing-machines may soon be in that category. Do not sniff — we had in New York not so long ago an exposition of Bad Taste, and it contained everything Victorian. Now, however, we are paying goodly prices for painted iron benches, bell-pulls, hassocks and cuspidors — though we use the latter for handsome flower vases. Certainly cross-stitch sofas and bead work are again in style. Antimacassars and mustache cups will probably follow.

Will you be surprised when I state that an Englishman — Charles F. Weisenthal — as far back as 1755 made the first move toward the invention of the sewing-machine? Does it now seem more venerable to you? Weisenthal tried to use a double-pointed needle, which was taken up by the Alsop embroidery machine. In 1790 Thomas Saint took an English patent for a crochet machine. John Duncan, in 1804, in the United States, made an embroidery machine that was capable of using many needles at once. Heilman of England and John J. Greenough continued to push and improve the primitive machines. Greenough's was the first patent — in 1842.

A good deal later, Thimonnier's wooden machines, and later his iron ones, were destroyed by Parisian mobs. He had been making his instruments for the army. He died in poverty.

On Cornhill, in Boston, lived in 1839 one Ari Davis, as odd as his name, but equally ingenious. A capitalist and a clever mechanic of those days, bent on working up a knitting-machine, asked Davis to join them. " Why," said he, " bother about a knitting-machine when one might invent a sewing-machine? " This was considered one of his nonsensical quips. But a country chap named Howe overheard, and asked the capitalist if he might have the fortune chaffingly offered to Davis if he, Howe, really made a sewing-machine?

Elias Howe, born at Spencer, Massachusetts, in 1819 — nephew of two inventive uncles — was an assistant at Ari Davis's. The youth had begun at the age of six to stick teeth into cotton carders in his father's mill, going later to a Lowell cotton factory, which closed down. Howe was not robust, still he was more apt at leading and suggesting than at following. He had seven sisters and brothers. But Elias watched his sweetheart sew till he caught an idea. He too, like Greenough, started with a double-ended needle. It proved futile. Then Howe claimed he had a dream of being ordered by a monarch to immediately perfect a sewing-machine, or lose his head. He found himself powerless, and saw savages advance to decapitate him. Fortunately, though, he happened to notice that their weapons were long, grooved lances with eye-holes near the tips. This dream was the foundation of a more successful attempt. Howe's first machine was of wood and wire. By 1844, however, Howe abandoned trying to copy hand-sewing and undertook to make two threads catch around each other by means of a curved needle and a shuttle. The youth worked in his father's attic, where the elder man wove split palm-leaf hats. Also, Elias married on nine dollars a week. The father's garret burned! It now became apparent that young Howe must have an exact and complete model to show, but he lacked the funds; so he formed an informal, fifty-fifty partnership with a schoolmate — George Fisher — who agreed to shelter and nourish the Howes, lend his attic for a workroom and furnish five hundred dollars. Then Howe demonstrated that his model could take three hundred stitches a minute, and by it he raced some women, beating them in the making of two whole suits, one for Fisher and one for himself. Some tailors disbelieved and discredited, others feared for their livelihoods and opposed. Besides, the machine was so expensive to install! With the whole Howe family on his hands and having paid for the trip to the patent office, et cetera, Mr. Fisher could do no more, so the inventor became for a while a railroad engineer, having to pawn some of his early models; but later he took steerage accommodations to England on a sailing ship. His brother, Amasa, kindly interested a manufacturer of carpet bags, stays and umbrellas, to whom Elias Howe sold his invention, with rights, for £250 down and £3 royalty on each machine the manufacturer should sell. The latter part of this verbal contract has never, we hear, been fulfilled, though some time ago it was estimated that the £250 had yielded at least a million. Poor Howe, inventor-like, returned after some other business undertaking with only a half crown in his pocket, borrowing ten dollars from his father to hurry home to his three children and his dying wife. He had to borrow his brother-in-law's suit for the funeral! And Elias's few precious possessions, following home from England, went down at sea!

Infringers sprang up, and George W. Bliss bought out Mr. Fisher's rights and advanced funds for the fight. Can you picture Mr. Fisher's sorrow now at having parted with his share? Although Walter Hunt of New York had invented a shuttle machine in 1832, he had not succeeded in making it sew. Howe finally won, and when Mr. Bliss died, bought back the latter's shares. Howe's income now increased, it is said, to $200,000. Though Greenough's patent came first, Howe's machine was the first to succeed. Some ten thousand sewing-machine patents have since been registered. Howe's patent expired in '67; while the inventor — a striking man, with large head and flowing locks — though finally rich in this world's goods, enlisted as a private in a Connecticut regiment, sharing his comrades' conditions in the Civil War and giving them $31,000 when the Government could not meet their pay. Elias Howe died the year his patent ran out.

Isaac Merritt Singer, of New York, was in 1850 a poor, very industrious competitor, who added improvements, and with forty dollars — borrowed perhaps from his lawyer, Mr. Clark — succeeded in eleven days' time in producing a superior machine. Among other patents, Mr. Singer invented the rigid overhanging arm guide.

Allen B. Wilson, too, deserves great commendation, we are told, for his additions to sewing-machines. And so, of course, do many others. The experimental department of present sewing-machine factories is very extensive.

Vociferous complaints arose, of course; even distinct sewing-machine diseases were charged against the innovation. Most of these, naturally, were due to wrong posture, too many hours at the same work, sedentary occupation, and a form of exercise particularly bad for some. One woman claimed it tired her less to work with one foot at a time, so she could change off, and always, moreover, have one foot on the floor to steady her. Which reminds me of the most far-fetched complaint I have seen:

" The posture of the body at these machines brings to mind a certain form of punishment sometimes practised in army life. The culprit is made to sit upon the top of a post eight inches in diameter and sufficiently high to remove the feet from the ground, and the hands are tied behind the back. The support of the body thus devolves entirely upon the muscles of the spine, and the consequent fatigue and pain become almost intolerable in the course of an hour."

The mechanical details of the additions and attachments, I shall spare you, though I was not so considerate of my big sister. My love for dolls' clothes, and the encouragement of two aunts owning two opposite types of machine, early taught me all the tricks of the sewing-machine. When my sister began to want to stitch frocks for herself, however, I exacted a twenty-five cent piece for every lesson I gave.

At the Chicago Art Institute, I saw the first American quilted coverlet sewed on a machine. It was stitched by a thrifty soul in Michigan, who hid in it two pockets, one perhaps for a handkerchief at night; but one at least, the collector — Emma B. Hodge — tells me, for gold pieces. A similar spread in the same collection is the original — hand-stitched, though — that was sent to Marseilles as the model for the first Marseilles machine-made spread, the white, honeycombed type that is now so universal. The American forerunner, however, was not pure white — though I rejoice that the manufactured ones do not attempt mixed colors — but had a border of purple grapes and green leaves.

America, having more abundant wood and other advantages, makes most of the sewing-machines of the world; but one sees them — particularly Singer's — in every nook and corner of the globe. Only a few days ago I happened to read, however, of sewing-machines sent from Japan to some South Pacific Islands. These were hand, not foot turning, machines. And the island women are said to be gaining great dexterity at the new game of sewing-machine.

In our part of the world even foot-treadle machines are fast disappearing in favor of those run by electric current — at home, one merely screws a plug into an electric light socket. This adaptation removes, moreover, some of the unhealthy features formerly mentioned.

Homemade rag rugs in Virginia are made on a frame with a sort of stepping-machine similar to the device of the Bonnaz sewing-machines that embroider fuzzy looped monograms and emblems for athletic club sweaters. Other sewing-machines buttonhole-scallop some of our lingerie and napery. Much can happen on a sewing-machine that many of us little ken. But we too may know and perform all these labor-saving tricks if we wish — backstitching, chainstitching, hemming, gathering, darning, lace-bobbin winding, perforating, et cetera. All of us, though, whether we ever use a machine or not, can nevertheless feel the thrill of Howe's high hope, his steady struggle, his burning zeal, his galling setbacks, his deathless faith and his triumphant success!

THE ROMANCE OF THE SEWING MACHINE

"In the State of Wisconsin and Town of Racine
Did a pussycat jump on a sewing machine.
The machine was ball-bearing, and ran on so fast
That it took a few stitches in pussycat's tail,
And she ran some!"
          —Lad's composition on the word "ransom."

"You may wander at will through stranger plants and trees than ever grew in fairyland. . . . Then the palms — cocoanut palms, banana palms, areca palms, little palms, big palms, palms with leaves like plumes and leaves like swords and leaves like elephants' ears; palms with stems like bamboos, stems like beeches, stems like peeled wands, stems like pineapples, stems like tennis-racket handles, stems like bottles, stems like almost everything you can think of except sewing machines!"

A FEW FINAL SUGGESTIONS AND SOME
STRAY SEWING ACCESSORIES

" When Grandma pricked this canvas through,
And wrought these patterns so bewitching,
No wonder Grandpa, watching, grew
To love the dainty hands thus stitching."
— Alice I. Eaton.

THIS parting chapter, before folding and laying away the many silken strands of stitchery, should gather up those bits of thread that have fallen to one side. You know how the thoughtful housewife spreads a sheet upon the floor before she lets her seamstress or *lingère* start sewing? And how afterward all the little left-over scraps are gathered up therein?

You recall too that the careful embroiderer has a case — old or new — for keeping her silks when out of use, that they may not snarl and fray.

Two old cases have I seen, both of Latin workmanship and both of finely inlaid colored scraps of straw. Within the one is a quaint black booklet that opens either way — to right or left. The thin old gauze ribbon bands that crisscross to hold this booklet together, at the same time holding down some wisps of silk, match in their old sage green the color of the straw particles laid like mosaic into the plain, glossy, rich cream straw of the outer case. The other old-time *étui* shows a two-colored pansy, a henna star, some other devices, and a delightful pair of kissing birds on the wing. This is French. Within lies a sheath of marbled paper, while inside that is an accordion pleated sheet of shiny French green paper, holding in each fold a different colored floss.

This type of broken-skein holder can be had nowadays with several long folded papers bound together their long way, perhaps a dozen in one fancy cardboard or decorated binding.

Vari-colored mending threads come braided together in broad bands, from which one may pull a single thread at a time.

Little boys of a while ago scroll-sawed stars and similar wooden forms for their mothers and sisters to keep left-over bits of thread upon. Little boys of to-day might do likewise. They could use their modern inventiveness to think up some pleasing new practical forms!

I shall have to apologize for skipping about: but one thread will in working fall to the left and another to the right — I cannot make them fall in orderly fashion. Nevertheless, I am trying, like a careful spinster or well-trained housewife, to gather up all the straggling scraps in the big protecting sheet I had spread out before beginning.

We mentioned bent wire filet frames in another chapter: now I take up another kind of bent wire frame — that used as the *métier* or support in the crocheting of hairpin lace. The wire is bent magnet or hairpin shaped, but with the two long sides parallel. Straight bone hairpins are also employed. The insertion made on these bars is strong. It is produced by the aid of a crochet hook that catches the loops formed over the right and left prongs, as their threads cross each other at the centre between tines. As the work progresses, it is pushed off the curved end of the hairpin.

An instrument or "machine" shaped similarly to the hairpin is the thin, flat wooden fork used for certain fringe-making. One tine, however, is broad and narrow, to allow of making a narrow heading on the one, and a long, looped fringe on the opposite prong. These loops, of course, can be cut. The silk or cord or wool is wound round and round the whole width of the fork; then a crochet hook is employed to hook the strands one through another, making a firm *lizard* or cording down the narrow space or slot between the two tines.

Having described hairpins and forks, I pass on to another long, narrow, forked implement, a so-called spindle, even though the article has no connection with spinning. It is really a holder for metallic thread, the purpose being to keep such thread from any contact with the heat or moisture of the hands, for these have a tarnishing tendency. Moreover, gold thread, or as it used to be called by early writers — it dates back to the days of the Phrygians — gold embroidery wire, is twisted and therefore very finicky to manage, for it unwinds, it stretches, and can also very easily be crushed and jammed. In cutting such thread, it is customary to cut enough extra to allow for emergencies. This material was anciently used not only by the Phrygians, from whom embroidery derived its early name of *Phrygio*, but also by the Hebrews, Egyptians and Romans, who gave to gold embroidery a different name in order to distinguish it from silken, which kept the former terminology. Gold embroidery became *auriphrygium*, giving rise to our English word *orphrey*. This clearly indi-

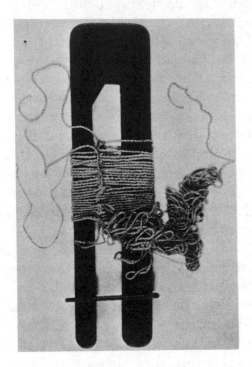

From the author's collection, New York

Left: AN OLD WOODEN FRINGING FORK WITH A PARTLY MADE FRINGE OF BEAD-LIKE CORD. [REDUCED.]

Centre: AN EGG IRON. SUCH AN IMPLEMENT IS HEATED AND USED TO PRESS DETAILED FEATURES IN A PIECE OF LACE, OR LITTLE LOOPS IN BOWS AND FRILLS. [REDUCED.]

Right: A WOODEN SPINDLE FOR MANIPULATING BULLION EMBROIDERY THREAD, THAT IT MAY NOT COME INTO CONTACT WITH WARM, MOIST, TARNISHING HANDS. [REDUCED.]

cates our association of metallic thread work with ecclesiastical robes.

The bullion holder, known as a spindle, should be about nine inches long, and its upper end — not the handle — should be well split into two prongs. Spindle wood should be hard. The spindle or spool portion of the holder and the lower part of the prongs are usually wrapped with softly twisted, spreading cotton that ends with a loop. Into this is tied one's gold or silver *cannetille* — a term including coarse *bullion,* finer *frisure,* and flat *clinquant* — which is then wound on over the protecting pad of cotton thread.   In embroidery, one directs the spindle[1] hither and yon about one's work, instead of guiding the metal thread with one's fingers.

When you work, by the way, in glittering gold or dazzling white, do not blind yourself by wearing a " clean " white apron!   Lace and embroidery should by all means be clean, scrupulously clean; but it is well to make aprons of black sateen.

And when you have been concentrating on minute work but are addressed by someone, look up slowly, blinking steadily as you do so, to prevent a shocking readjustment of vision, with consequent dizziness.

Hands too should be immaculate.   In winter, it is well to use a non-oily cream to prevent chapping, but to wash the hands as often as need be, or oftener, when working upon a non-washable piece of lace or needlework.   Rough skin, of course, makes fine work a most uncomfortable occupation and renders it well-nigh impossible, for one's thread — particularly silk floss — catches on bits of cuticle and both frays in itself and pulls loops in what one has just done.

Now armchairs, though tempting, impede one's work and show too great a familiarity with one's funny-bone.   This comes about through one's arms having to be raised while sewing or lace-making, when the elbows either are cramped by the chair arms, or else most unexpectedly descend and strike them.

So too, choose a low-seated as well as an armless chair for steady stitching.   The position is much more restful, and one's lap becomes a real lap, available for catching stray spools that so rejoice in rolling under sofas!

Now, an odd implement, in shape generally long and narrow like the spindle, is used in finishing fine lace, to raise or emboss certain parts of the pattern, such as flower petals, or little pearls and dots sprinkled here and there.   In advanced lace-making centres, rounded ivory tools are used; but in outlying districts, the peasant workers resorted to hard, smooth pieces of polished agate; and along the seacoast

---

[1] The word " broach " is sometimes used to signify a spindle.

they were wont to use the rounded tips of lobster claws. In France the raising and polishing tool is called an *aficot*. We are told that in Sweden prisoners occupy spare moments by whittling and scraping bones from old roasts, et cetera, much as our whalers worked narwhal tusks into articles for home industries. One of the Swedish prison

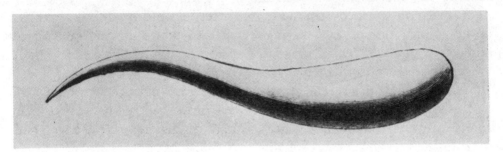

A MODERN BONE OR IVORY RAISER, AN OUTGROWTH OF THE MORE PRIMITIVE LOBSTER CLAW OR AGATE; USED FOR PUSHING INTO RELIEF CERTAIN PARTS OF THE LACE; AND ALSO, UNFORTUNATELY, FOR GLAZING SOME OF THE CONVEX PORTIONS. STAINED-GLASS MAKERS USE A SIMILAR INSTRUMENT, WHICH THEY CALL AN "OYSTER KNIFE." [ACTUAL SIZE.]

pieces, owned by Mrs. De Witt Clinton Cohen, is of black wood, studded with bone rosettes, and handsomely mounted with a rather large, aggressive woman resembling a ship's figurehead. To her right and left stand small men, whose heads very accommodatingly unscrew, revealing hollow, tubular bodies intended to house needles — a sort of sword-swallowers. Behind the shoulders of this amusing trinity, who seem glued against the black wooden block, rises a delicate bone rack, which supports a well-finished raiser. The whole fascinating old Swedish outfit, crowned indeed with a useful pincushion, has below a sturdy, yellowed bone screw vise with which to clamp it to a worktable.

Some authority writes —

"The raiser is passed at the side of each portion of the lace which is worked in relief and where there are fringes or loops worked on the relief part, which is nearly always the case in Venice or real Spanish Point; these fringes or loops should be carefully picked out with the fingers, and pins passed through every hole to give them more clearly their original form."

"Devon lace-makers," we are told, "lay a great deal of stress upon the value of raised work, which is used for all the best lace."

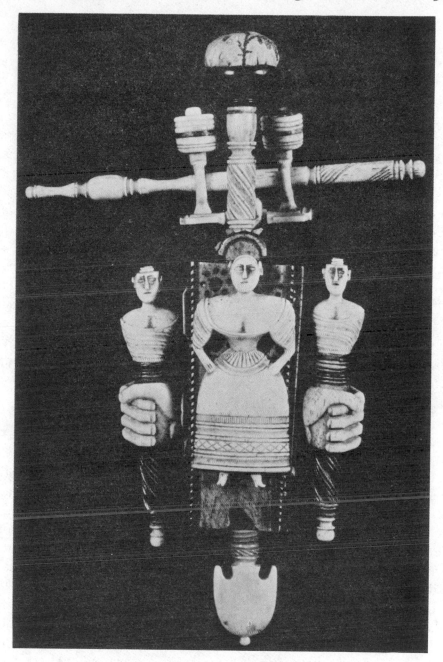

From the collection of Mrs. De Witt Clinton Cohen

UNIQUE WHITTLED LACE RAISER, MADE BY A SWEDISH PRISONER FROM SOUP BONES,
MOUNTED ON BLACK OR BLACKENED WOOD.

Then the *Dictionary of Needlework* tells us —

"With a camel's-hair brush, to paint over the inside parts of the lace's relief work with cold, strained rice water. When making a bold curve in the raised work, dip an ivory knitting-needle into the rice water, and apply that to the lace. Never wet it, only dampen it."

Another quotation from the former source says —

"But I do not recommend the raiser being used for the purpose of glossing the lace. This is frequently done, but it is a pernicious practice."

It is objectionable because it strikes a false note, disguising the beautiful natural lustre of the pure linen thread from which most good lace is made, and adding a distracting "gingerbready" touch of would-be cleverness. We dislike a suit that has worn shiny, and the clinging, half-revealing suppleness of lace is one of its enchantments; so why stiffen and polish it like an unyielding sheet of metal?

The thoroughly modern raising implement is a small, egg-shaped, steel or iron two-ended knob, on a long, slim metal handle. The eggs come small, smaller, smallest; and some, I have heard, are of silver: but these cannot be laid on a stove or over a fire to heat like stronger, iron eggs. Dressmakers and milliners make use of the larger sizes for puffing and pressing out bows.

The claws and smooth stones and egg irons are designed to mold or push out one's work; but beaders' molds are made to mold *upon*. Many folks think that all bead bags are knitted. Not so: some are crocheted, some tent-stitched on scrim, some woven on a band or Apache loom made for the purpose; or, in lieu of a wooden loom, on a cardboard box with threads stretched evenly from end to end across the free, hollow box centre. Needle and thread are then run through the beads — which are held one at a time between the long mounted threads — but alternately under and over the stretched threads, as in darning. Many old-time bags, however, were built up over a thin, wooden mold, which was melon-shaped at one end, hollow and circular at the other. A quarter inch from the open end, these cylindrical molds display a series of tiny holes. Through these may the plain sewing-silk border be secured, straight and even, before starting to add a bead to each stitch, or perhaps after finishing the bag. The stitches are buttonhole — like those of point lace — and they rise gradually upon the back of the beads, enclosing them and forming a veritable point-lace lining. When the cylinder begins to slope in toward its apex, fewer stitches are made in encircling it, until finally the last bead has been enmeshed just at the top. This is secured, the basting stitches near the rim are loosed, and the whole is turned inside out, showing bead work only. The bags may, of course, have been worked in the opposite direction. Upon colonial bags, one can discover circular red glass beads, but also some tiny, faceted, real garnet ones. Both garnet bead bags and bag molds are rare.

The *Dictionary of Needlework* tells us that " there are two kinds of these moulds, which are made of ivory and wood; one is called a ' *Moule Turc,*' and has small brass pins fixed round the edges of the largest circumference; the other is formed for making a purse *en feston,* which is shaped like a thimble perforated with a double row of holes, like a band, round the open end, a little removed from the rim. Through these perforations the needle is passed, to secure the purse to the mould where the work is commenced."

And the same authority says of a purse stretcher:

" This small appliance is useful for drawing the several stitches made in crocheting, knitting and netting long purses, into their exact relative positions, and tightening each knot into a uniform rate of firmness. The stretcher could easily be homemade, as it consists of two small pieces of wood round on the outside and flat inside, just like a split pencil. Long screws are introduced through apertures at either end of these pieces of wood, and the latter, being inserted into the purse (before it is sewn up at the ends), it is stretched by means of the screws."

Mrs. De Witt Clinton Cohen has an old sample card of beads, mounted in two columns, with printed words on either side, indicating size numbers; while the beads themselves are ranged in a graduated color scheme, with the maker's name at the top of the card.

In the chapter on needles, a glass and paper-lace box full of assorted beads and needles, belonging to Mrs. Cohen's very comprehensive collection, has also been described.

In the north of India there called upon us a wandering showman with a performing parrot, so small, so trim, with every feather in place and of a most compelling, clear bright green — not a parrakeet, but the diminutive parrot who flits and perches, chickadee fashion, upon every imperceptible ledge of Upper India's pink sandstone edifices. The showman poured some beads into the palm of his hand, loosed the bird and gave it a needle and some thread. Carefully the parrot poised on the edge of the man's hand and gravely held up the needle and threaded it, using his beak as a third hand. Then he proceeded to take up bead after bead, tipping them back on the needle, so they would slip down on the thread. I said, "Would he come to me?" — "Oh, yes!" And he sat solemnly stringing beads while I carried him way down the long hotel gallery, up the stairs and across to a friend's room, to show him off; then down again to his owner. I shall never forget that steady, sturdy, soft, little stringer of beads!

Beaded lace, as the name implies, shows little beads woven into the pattern. There is a bead-loom or gauze-loom also for making solid bead work, the threads being almost completely hidden; and there is a bead-frame that is not connected with needlework, but is used for calculating — an abacus. In weaving, frayed, rubbed yarn is spoken of as "beaded."

But beads are not all tiny and are not always sewed or knitted or woven together: they are sometimes strung a little distance apart among the meshes of old netting; particularly is this so of old Egyptian mummy netting. The Egyptians made stunning, very intense blue faïence beads, placing them at the crossing where one strand of net joins another, laying the whole upon a distinguished mummy's chest, or perhaps wrapping the entire body in such an outer network.

But how is netting made? Under the chapter on "Sharps, Blunts and Betweens," netting needles have been discussed;[2] and among Pillows and Horses you will find mention of a lead cushion: but this should not lead you to suppose that our stirrup is about to be shown as a piece of harness for a horse; it is part of the harness or furniture of the well equipped embroiderer; but it is an object intended to take the place of weighted pillow or stand. Here I quote S. F. A. Caulfeild's description of the use and mode of making a stirrup:

"Netting, which is in reality a succession of loops secured in position by knots, requires to be kept stretched while in progress, or

---

[2] Mesh sticks are described under "Instruments of Precision — Measures."

the loops made are unequal in size, and the knots are not drawn up tight. This stretching is accomplished by either pinning the foundation loop of the netting to a lead cushion, or attaching it to the foot with the help of a stirrup, the last plan being the one usually adopted, and the best. To make a stirrup: Take a piece of oak or elm, four or five inches in length, and one and a half inches in width, and bore a hole in the centre through each of its two ends. Take two yards of ribbon, one inch wide, of a strong make; pass each end through a hole and sew the two ends together, or tie them underneath the piece of wood; put the piece of wood under the left foot and bring the ribbon up as a loop. Regulate the long loop thus formed by the height of the worker, as it should always reach to the knee. If the ends of the ribbon are only tied together, the stirrup can be shortened during the progress of the work, which is often an advantage. A more ornamental stirrup can be made by embroidering a narrow band, to pass over the instep, and attaching that to the ends of wood, and making the loop of ribbon rise from the centre of the embroidery; but for ordinary netting the plain stirrup is the best, as the whole of the weight of the foot is upon it."

We have spoken of enmeshing beads and applying metal thread; but with what, for example, does one withdraw unwanted sewing or embroidery material? The little "toothpick and earspoon" of the old drizzling sets can be found in the chapter on "Fast-Flitting Shuttles"; but drizzling tools are out of date — we seldom nowadays embroider with "really truly" gold and pearls. Cost is one reason, the variety of imitations another, rapidly changing styles still another, practicality in dress, and the health protection of labor, others. A half forgotten account, related to me by a granddaughter, may help us in these modern days of unions to realize better what might be demanded of a worker of the past. A great emperor's daughter was to be married. The royal seamstress was locked in a suite with endless pearls to be stitched, one by one, upon the bridal robe. She was responsible for every gem, so no one might enter and she might not leave. Food was passed in, and after a period of this solitary confinement and steady, enforced labor, picking up and applying pearls, she lost her sight and her babe was born blind. The court was very sorry, of course, and did all it could. After twenty-one years the child's sight was given it by a great American physician — not now living. Names I may not mention.

But fine embroidery has often to be outlined or guided, by pattern or canvas or scrim — scrim for beads, or sometimes net, when two threads should be taken up at a time to keep the beads from twisting. But having worked over this stuff, the embroiderer often wishes to dispense with the unsightly guiding threads, and for this, little nippers are most handy. Fingers soon become sore when substituted for tweezers, and one's nails split and tear. Bobbin-lace makers, too, find it well to pull out the pins from the pillow with little implements. Tweezers come with pointed tips, as well as with broad blades, some being better in one case, some in another; but their ends should always meet and pinch well — should have a good grip.

Another guide to the embroiderer is outlined upon the goods to be worked. The outline may have been placed there in one of two ways — by pouncing powder through a perforated paper pattern, or by tracing the line with a stylus, a steel knitting-needle, or a pencil through carbonized paper or linen. Carbonized linen is less apt than the paper to rub off on one's goods. Very new paper should sometimes have an extremely thin layer of tissue paper laid over its face while tracing, in order to prevent smearing. It goes without saying that one must trace upon a perfectly flat, smooth surface — table, desk or sheet of glass — and that one must bear down hard enough and must not omit any line one wishes to use as a guide for the embroidery. It is well occasionally, while holding the rest firmly in place, to peep under first one and then another corner of the drawing, to see whether all is developing as one would wish.

Going over the backs of faint carbons with a warm iron will sometimes give them another little lease of life.

To produce a pouncer, one fills a little loosely-woven lawn or muslin bag with dark blue powder bought for the purpose, or with white pipe-clay, French chalk or whiting. Then placing the pattern — ready-bought or prepared with a perforating machine, or with a very fine needle and close-gauge stitch on a sewing-machine — carefully and correctly over one's white goods, one dabs the little bag all over the back of the pattern. I discovered the homely sewing-machine substitute at the age of eight. Forbidden to touch our machine, I conceived a notion to outline the picture of a horse I had, with perforations like those around a postage stamp. I succeeded, and perhaps would have attempted to embroider the animal in worsted as I had been taught at school to outline other creatures, but I inadvertently pierced and caught not only the picture, but my finger, with the relentless needle.

When one has placed one's pattern so that it will show right side around when reproduced, and has pounced all the tiny pricked holes quite full of colored chalk with the little sack that looks like a laundress's bluing bag, one repairs indeed to the laundry to cover one's handiwork with a clean cloth and press it with a hot iron to set the lines of color. White powder, naturally, should be used on a dark material. Some people go over the pounced outlines with a fine paintbrush dipped in gouache — thick white water-color, mixed at times with gum arabic. Other colors, of course, may be used. Drawing liquid can be bought ready dissolved, and charcoal can be employed instead of blue powder. Gum and lead mixtures have a tendency to peel off, so are inadvisable. But in all cases one must avoid disturbing the pounce, once it has been deposited, until it is thoroughly set.

A new type of factory-made pattern is carbonized in dots along the lines of the model. One lays this prepared sheet of paper upon one's goods and presses it with a warm iron, a little as one would transfer a decalcomania.

There is another sort of perforated pattern — the bobbin-lace parchment of old, so quaint, sometimes drawn and pricked upon the back of a discarded will, sometimes upon an old mariner's map, but sometimes, alas, boiled down after all its various services, lace-making and other, just to make glue!

Modern prickings are made on reddish brown dappled pressboard; on light green muslin-interlined paper; on a glazed, bright orange, Italian Bristol board (should Italian bobbin-lace makers strike for better eye surroundings?); and on strong, thick green paper used in most European lace-making countries. The perforations for prickings do not occur as on postage stamps, but at set parts of the pattern. Proper pricking indicates much to a real lace-maker, while a slovenly pricked pattern is a crime to the calling, tending to drag it down to unsightly results and dwindling markets. Such a commercial eclipse has blotted out more than one formerly flourishing lace centre.

Almost everyone has heard, but does not realize it was in the great Louis's times, that lace-makers must sit in dark cellars with only a single ray of light upon their cobweb work. Light dried their almost invisible thread, rendering it too brittle; so did heat.[3] Therefore in

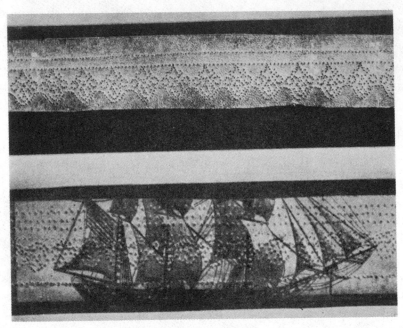

OLD WILLS AND OTHER PARCHMENT DOCUMENTS, SOME WITH ENGRAVINGS OF
QUAINT OLD FULL-RIGGED VESSELS, PRICKED AND USED FOR MAKING BOBBIN-LACE
AT IPSWICH, MASS.

winter these workers sat over a cow barn for the sake of a little mild warmth. And some, at least, smoked tiny pipes to keep their breath from affecting the thread. Some lace thread was cured with sugar of lead, which develops brown spots from contact with perfume or perspiration. All this refers to the finer laces, particularly old

[3] An outsider can scarcely estimate the importance of the quality of the thread to the lacemaker. Of two skeins bearing the same number, one may be supple and easily led, while the other is brittle and wayward. We hear many stories of how women used to spend their lives in damp cellars, in order to keep their thread moist and soft. I have been told several times, for instance, that a certain piece of lace had been made below ground, because only there was its marvelous technique possible. Whatever the degree of truth or legend in these assertions, it is known that the rarest laces require certain atmospheric conditions, and are, above all, dependent on a superior fineness and pliability of the thread." — Charlotte Kellogg.

Valenciennes and, later, point de gaze. But lace-makers generally, either through poverty, or the protection of their product, or the necessity of sitting near light windows, seem to have been without the benefit of big open fires or continental porcelain stoves; Switzerland, however, even where the marvelously fine Neuchâtel laces were made, was an exception.

Glazed cartheuware pots in Buckinghamshire, England, were passed around among apprentices, to be held under their busy hands, upon their laps. These fire, dicky, hot or chad pots, I am told, kept

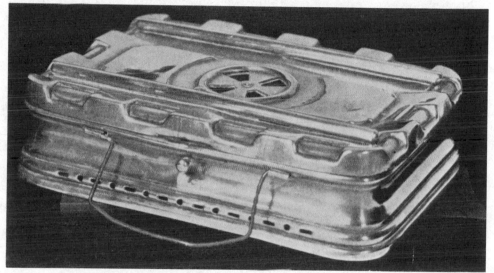

From the author's collection

AN HISTORIC, BELGIAN LACE-MAKER'S *CHAUFFERETTE* OF BRASS, WITH DRAFT HOLES, DAMPER, AND HANDLE. BY PRESSING THE TINY KNOB, ONE CAN LIFT THE LID AND EXPOSE THE WIRE COAL-GRATE. [HALF SIZE.]

hot from the coals or charcoal within for half a day. Then the coals were revived by inserting and blowing a bellows. But I have also heard — which seems more probable to me for lap use — that stones or bricks were heated, fireless-cooker fashion, before leaving home, and that they kept warm all day.

To me has come a rather historic, old-time Belgian lace-maker's brass chaufferette. Mr. Pierre Mali, his son and his grandson, have been the Consuls-General from Belgium to New York. Madame Kefer-Mali, their respective daughter, sister, aunt, and wife also of the leader for fifty years of the Brussels Symphony Orchestra, was a great lace-worker and enthusiast. This chaufferette was hers. In its lid is an adjustable damper; along the base, a row of tiny draft holes. Inside, two irons support a wire cylinder meant to hold the hot coals, which thus are kept a little away from both floor and cover, that they may not burn the knees upon which they might rest.

Foot-warmers were used by Swiss lace-makers, as they were by our colonial forebears. I have seen a handsome elliptical one of pierced metal with two curved mahogany bars upon the lid — one along the front, the other along the rear — evidently meant for foot-rests. The whole warmer stands upon an elliptical hoop of mahogany, to protect a polished floor or rug from scorching. This warmer has an inner tin grate.

In the Rijks Museum at Amsterdam are endless warmers of most varied detail.

To summarize all these proved and practical, plain or exquisite tools, I might refer you to the index — that even alphabetizes them, which is an advantage. I prefer instead to dwell on the fact that

> The world is so full of our tools and of means,
> I'm sure we should all be as happy as queens!

For the mere aspect and " feel " of these useful or amusing toys is a joy, even were they never seriously put to work, but collected only, as the Dutch collect and treasure miniature silver toys.

Busy little Mothers.

But put to work, whether they be modest or fancy, they can give you joy and inner contentment through the satisfaction of the creative urge and the fun of being a craftsman!

Real craftsmanship, however, is a consecration. You are only a hireling, an artisan, if you do insincere work, if you skimp and try with shallow work to make a false pretense. The shallow character that prompts the slipshod product will be seen through. Shoddy, ill-chosen materials, hastily taken stitches, sham effects, cannot endure, and will soon displease you. For fine sewing, embroidery, lace-making, weaving, are as fine arts as painting or sculpture, and worthy examples of stitchery have endured through centuries and come down to us still treasured and revered.

So respect your sewing, and see in it your opportunity for restful, beautiful labor, quiet thought, clean and delicious materials to touch, simple, dignified or glorious patterns to convert to present requirements.

Cherish your dainty instruments, enthusiastically made by hand at home, showing individual ingenuity in whittling, shaping, hammering, decorating; or made by some fellow-craftsman abroad, who has lovingly planned and planed, or turned and studded, or lightly chased and deeply carved; then carefully packed the rare tools he has worked and perhaps yearned over, and labeled them for their migration about the world, till they shall at last be safely delivered into our guardian hands.

A FEW FINAL SUGGESTIONS AND SOME STRAY SEWING ACCESSORIES

> "A peire of bedis eke she bere
> Upon a lace, alle of white threde,
> On which that she his bedes bede."
> — The Romaunt of the Rose: Geoffrey Chaucer.

> "She has a lap dog that eats out of gold; she feeds her parrot with small pearls; and all her thread papers are made of bank notes."
> — The Rivals: Richard Brinsley Sheridan.

> "You boil it in sawdust; you salt it in glue."
> — The Hunting of the Snark: Lewis Carroll.

> "The workers, men and women, would sit side by side in each other's houses, in order to save firing. In the winter they had to sit very near to the windows, which

did not give as much light as they do now, and it was often bitterly cold. In some parts, to keep themselves warm, they used a 'dicky-pot'; this was made of rough brown ware, glazed, and filled with embers begged from the bread oven of a well-to-do neighbor."

— *Lace-making in the Midlands:* Channer and Roberts.

"Then they [beads] are threaded by children, tied in bundles and exported to the ends of the earth."

— *Harper's Magazine,* Vol. 79, p. 262.

"If times are hard, perhaps the work may be sent in a day or two before its time — wrapped between tattered leaves of blue paper, dignified by the name of a Lace-book.

"There is no surer way of gaining the heart of an old worker than by presenting her with a new piece of this blue paper, which she will cut into small double sheets, slipping her finished sprigs between the leaves."

— *Devon Pillow Lace:* A. Penderel Moody.

"It is considered very bad manners to talk of work as being dirty, but the agent's bag will contain a skein of new white thread, which comes out on special occasions, and, lying across the completed work, tells tales.

"'It du be coloured terr'ble' is the worst any one could possibly say. 'Coloured' slightly deeper than the skein, the work is allowed to pass, but there is no reason other than carelessness why it should be deeper."

— *Devon Pillow Lace:* A. Penderel Moody.

SOUTH CAROLINA EARTHENWARE POTS

"You make the fire in the pot and put the irons on top. You buy the ironin' pots of the man that makes the coal. They's earthenware — I don' know what else. They look like a pot, round at the bottom, just a least bit smaller than the top. They's black on the outside, and look most like brown on the inside; shape somethin' like this yer paper-basket — oh yes! Hannle ain't wire. A pot will las' a life-time, if you don' go and broke it. Fill the pot full of coal, take a lot of little splinters and heat it up. There's a little do' right down near the bottom to take out the ashes: there's holes for the ashes to fall through, like a soapdish. You'se seen this yer coke? Well, the coal is like coke; you burn it out o' pine. The man comes twice a week with it — We'n'sdays an' Saturdays. Some coals is as big as yo' fist: they don' las' so long, and you have to keep puttin' mo' in."

— Narcissa Middleton.

ENVOY

THE PRAISE OF THE NEEDLE

(*The Prayse of the Needle*)

By John Taylor, 1640. (Appearing in *The Needle's Excellency*, by James Baler,
London, and sold at the sign of "The Marigold" in Paules Church yard.)

To all dispersed sorts of Arts and Trades,
J writ the Needles prayse (that never fades)
So long as children shall be got or borne,
So long as garments shall be made, or worne,
So long as Hemp or Flax, or Sheep shall bear
Their linnen wollen fleeces yeare by yeare:
So long as Silk-wormes, with exhausted spoile,
Of their owne Entrailes for mans gaine shall toyle:
Yea till the world be quite dissolu'd and past;
So long at least, the Needles use shall last:
And though from earth his being did begin,
Yet through the fire he did his honour win:
And vnto those that doe his service lacke,
Hee's true as steele and mettle to the backe.
He hath I per se eye, small single sight,
Yet like a Pigmey, *Polipheme* in fight:
As a stout Captaine, bravely he leades on,
(Not fearing colours) till the worke be done,
Through thicke and thinne he is most sharpely set,
With speed through stitch, he will the conquest get.
And as a souldier (Frenchefyde with heat)
Maim'd from the warres is forced to make retreat;
So when a Needles point is broke, and gone,
No point Mounsieur, he's maim'd, his worke is done,
And more the Needles honour to advance,
It is a Taylors Iavelin, or his Launce.

And for my Countries quiet, I should like,
That women-kinde should vse no other Pike.
It will increase their peace, enlarge their store,
To use their tongues lesse, and their Needles more,
The Needles sharpenesse, profit yeelds, and pleasure,
But sharpenesse of the tongue, bites out of measure.
A Needle (though it be but small and slender)
Yet it is both a maker and a mender:
A graue Reformer of old Rents decayd,
Stops holes and seames, and desperate cuts displayed.
And thus without the Needle we may see,
We should without our Bibs and Biggins bee;
No shirts or Smockes, our nakednesse to hide,
No garments gay, to make us magnifide:
No shadowes, Shapparoones, Caules, Bands, Ruffs, Kuffs,
No Kirchiefes, Quoyfes, Chin-clouts, or Marry-Muffes,
No Cros-cloaths, Aprons, Hand-kerchiefes, or Falls,
No Table-cloathes, for Parlours or for Halls.
No Sheetes, no Towels, Napkins, Pillow-beares,
Nor any Garment man or woman weares.
Thus is a Needle prov'd an Instrument,
Of profit, pleasure, and of ornament.
Which mighty Queenes haue grac'd in hand to take,
And high borne Ladies such esteeme did make,
That as their Daughters Daughters up did grow,
The Needles Art, they to their children show.
And as 'twas then an exercise of praise,
So what deserves more honour in these dayes,
Then this? which daily doth it selfe expresse,
A mortall enemy to idlenesse.
The use of Sewing is exceeding old,
As in the sacred Text it is enrold:
Our Parents first in Paradise began,
Who hath descended since from man to man:
The mothers taught their Daughters, Sires their Sons,
Thus in a line successively it runs
For generall profit, and for recreation,

From generation unto generation.
With worke like Cherubims Embroidered rare,
The Covers of the Tabernacle were.
And by the Almighti's great command, we see,
That *Aarons* Garments broydered worke should be;
And further, God did bid his Vestments should
Be made most gay, and glorious to behold.
Thus plainly, and most truly is declar'd,
The Needles worke hath still bin in regard
For it doth ART, so like to NATVRE frame,
As if IT were her Sister, or the SAME.
Flowers, Plants, and Fishes, Beasts, Birds, Flyes, and Bees,
Hils, Dales, Plaines, Pastures, Skies, Seas, Rivers, Trees;
There's nothing neere at hand, or farthest sought,
But with the Needle may be shap'd and wrought.
In clothes of Arras I have often seene,
Mens figurd counterfeits so like haue beene,
That if the parties selfe had beene in place,
Yet ART would vye with NATVRE for the grace.
Moreover, Posies rare, and Anagrams,
Signifique searching sentences from Names,
True History, or various pleasant fiction,
In sundry colours mixt, with Arts commixion,
All in Dimension, Ovals, Squares, and Rounds,
Arts life included within Natures bounds:
So that Art seemeth meerely naturall,
In forming shapes so Geometricall,
And though our Country every where is fild
With Ladies, and with Gentlewomen, skild
In this rare Art, yet here they may discerne
Some things to teach them if they list to learne.
And as this booke some cunning workes doth teach,
(Too hard for meane capacities to reach)
So for weake learners, other workes here be,
As plaine and easie as are A B C.
Thus skilfull, or unskillfull, each may take,
This booke, and of it, each good use may make,

All sorts of workes, almost that can be nam'd,
Here are directions how they may be fram'd:
And for this kingdomes good are hither come,
From the remotest parts of Christendome,
Collected with much paines and industry,
From scorching *Spaine* and freezing *Muscovie,*
From fertill *France,* and pleasant *Italy,*
From *Poland, Sweden, Denmarke, Germany,*
And some of these rare Patternes haue beene set,
Beyond the bounds of faithlesse *Mahomet:*
From spacious *China,* and those Kingdomes East,
And from great *Mexico,* the Indies West.
Thus are these workes, *farre fetcht, and dearely bought,*
And consequently *good for Ladies thought.*
Nor doe I derogate (in any case)
Or doe esteeme of other teachings base,
For *Tent-worke, Raisd-worke, Laid-worke, Frost-worke, Net-worke,*
Most curious *Purles,* or rare Italian *Cutworke,*
Fine *Ferne-stitch, Finny-stitch, New-stitch,* and *Chain-stitch,*
Braue *Bred-stitch, Fisher-stitch, Irish-stitch,* and *Queen-stitch,*
The *Spanish-stitch, Rosemary-stitch,* and *Mowse-stitch,*
The smarting *Whip-stitch, Back-stitch,* & the *Crosse-stitch,*
All these are good, and these we must allow,
And these are every where in practise now:
And in this Booke, there are of these some store,
With many others, neuer seene before.
Here Practise and Invention may be free,
And as a Squirrell skips from tree to tree,
So maids may (from their Mistresse, or their Mother)
Learne to leaue one worke, and to learne an other,
For here they may make choyce of which is which,
And skip from worke to worke, from stitch to stitch,
Vntil, in time, delightfull practice shall
(With profit) make them perfect in them all.
Thus hoping that these workes may haue this guide,
To serue for ornament, and not for pride:
To cherish vertue, banish idlenesse,
For these ends, may this booke haue good successe.

Here follow certaine Sonnets in the Honorable memory of Queenes and great Ladies, who haue bin famous for their rare Inventions and practise with the Needle.

I

King *David* by an apt similitude,
Doth shew with Maiesty, the *Church* her worth;
And to a fair Kings daughter doth allude,
Where to her Spouse, he bravely brings her forth,
In Garments wrought of *Needle-worke* and Gold,
Resplendent and most glorious to the eye:
Whose out-side much more glory did infold,
The presence of th' eternall Majesty.
Thus may you see Records of holy Writ
Set downe (what death or Time can nere deface.)
By these comparisons, comparing fit,
The noble worth of Needle workes high grace.
Then learne fair Damsels, learne your times to spend
In this, which such high praisings doth commend.

Katharine *first married to* Arthur, *Prince of* Wales, *and afterward to* Henry *the 8, King* of England.

2

I read that in the seventh King Henries Raigne,
Faire *Katharine,* Daughter to the *Castile* King,
Came into *England* with a pompous traine
Of *Spanish* Ladies which shee thence did bring.
She to the eight King *Henry* married was,
And afterwards divorc'd, where vertuously
(Although a Queene) yet she her dayes did passe,
In working with the *Needle* curiously,
As in the Towre, and places more beside,
Her excellent memorialls may be seene:
Whereby the *Needles* prayse is dignifide
By her faire Ladies, and her selfe, a Queene.
Thus for her paines, here her reward is iust,
Her workes proclaim her prayse, though she be dust.

3

 Mary, *Queene of* England, *and wife to* Philip *King of* Spaine.

Her Daughter *Mary* here the Scepter swaid,
And though shee were a Queene of mighty power,
Her memory will never be decaid,
Which by her workes are likewise in the Tower,
In *Windsor* Castle, and in *Hampton* Court,
In that most pompous roome call'd Paradise:
Who euer pleaseth thither to resort,
May see some workes of hers, of wondrous price.
Her greatnesse held it no dis-reputation,
To take the Needle in her Royall hand:
Which was a good example to our Nation,
To banish idlenesse from out her Land:
And thus this Queene, in wisdome thought it fit,
The Needle worke pleas'd her, and she grac'd it.

4

 Elizabeth, *Queene of* England, *and Daughter to King* Henry *the eight.*

When this great Queene, whose memory shall not
By any terme of time be over-cast;
For when the world, and all therein shall rot
Yet shall her glorious fame for ever last.
When she a maid, had many troubles past,
From Iayle to Iayle, by *Maries* angry spleene:
And *Woodstocke,* and the *Tower* in Prison fast,
And after all was *Englands* Peerelesse Queene.
Yet howsoeuer sorrow came or went,
She made the Needle her companion still,
And in that exercise her time she spent,
As many living yet doe know her skill.
Thus thee was still, a Captive, or else crowned,
A Needle-woman Royall, and renownd.

5

The Right Honourable, Vertuous, and learned Lady Mary, *late Countesse of* Pembrooke.

A patterne, and a Patronesse she was,
Of vertuous industry and studious learning:
And shee her earthly Pilgrimage did passe,
In Acts which were high honour most concerning.
Braue *Wilton* house in Wiltshire well can show,
Her admirable workes in Arras fram'd:
Where men, and beasts, seeme like, trees seeme to grow,
And Art (surpass'd by Nature) seemes asham'd,
Thus this renowned Honourable Dame,
Her happy time most happily did spend;
Whose worth recorded in the mouth of fame,
(Vntill the world shall end) shall never end
She wrought so well in Needle-worke, that shee,
Nor yet her workes, shall ere forgoten be.

6

The Right Honourable and religious Lady Elizabeth Dormer, *Wife to the late Right Honourable, the Lord* Robert Dormer, *deceased*.

This Noble Lady imitates time past,
Directs time present, teacheth time to come,
And longer then her life, her laud shall last,
Workes shewes her worth, though all the world were dumb.
And though her Reverend selfe, with many dayes,
Of honourable age is loaden deepe,
Yet with her Needle (to her worthy prayse)
Shee's working often ere the Sunne doth peepe.
And, many times, when *Phoebus* in the West
Declined is, and *Luna* shewes her head:
This antient honour'd Lady rests from Rest,
And workes when idle sloath goes soone to bed,
Thus shee the Needle makes her recreation,
Whose well-spent paines are others imitation.

*To all degrees of both sexes, that love or liue by the laudable im-
ployment of the Needle.*

If any aske to whom these lines are writ,
I answer, unto them that doe inquire:
For since the worlds Creation none was yet,
Whose wants did not the Needles helpe desire.
And therefore not to him, or her, or thee,
Or them, or they, I doe not write at all:
Nor to particulars of he or shee,
But generally, to all in generall.
Then let not Pride looke scuruily a-scewe,
Without the *Needle,* Pride would naked goe:
Nor yet let scorne, cry pish, and tush, and mew,
Scorne is forgetfull much in doing so,
Nor yet let any one presume to prate,
And call these lines poor trifles, by me pend:
Let not opinion be prejudicate,
But mend it ere they dare to discommend,
So fare thou well, my well-deseruing booke,
(I meane, the works deserts, and not my lines)
I much presume that all that one it looke,
Will like and laud the workemans good designes,
Fooles play the Fooles, but tis through want of wit,
Whilst I to wisedomes censure doe submit.

INDEX

A CATALOGUE OF
SELECTED DOVER BOOKS
IN ALL FIELDS OF INTEREST

A CATALOGUE OF SELECTED DOVER
BOOKS IN ALL FIELDS OF INTEREST

CONDITIONED REFLEXES, Ivan P. Pavlov. Full translation of most complete statement of Pavlov's work; cerebral damage, conditioned reflex, experiments with dogs, sleep, similar topics of great importance. 430pp. 5⅜ x 8½.   60614-7 Pa. $4.50

NOTES ON NURSING: WHAT IT IS, AND WHAT IT IS NOT, Florence Nightingale. Outspoken writings by founder of modern nursing. When first published (1860) it played an important role in much needed revolution in nursing. Still stimulating. 140pp. 5⅜ x 8½.   22340-X Pa. $3.00

HARTER'S PICTURE ARCHIVE FOR COLLAGE AND ILLUSTRA-TION, Jim Harter. Over 300 authentic, rare 19th-century engravings selected by noted collagist for artists, designers, decoupeurs, etc. Machines, people, animals, etc., printed one side of page. 25 scene plates for back-grounds. 6 collages by Harter, Satty, Singer, Evans. Introduction. 192pp. 8⅞ x 11¾.   23659-5 Pa. $5.00

MANUAL OF TRADITIONAL WOOD CARVING, edited by Paul N. Hasluck. Possibly the best book in English on the craft of wood carving. Practical instructions, along with 1,146 working drawings and photographic illustrations. Formerly titled *Cassell's Wood Carving.* 576pp. 6½ x 9¼.
                                                                   23489-4 Pa. $7.95

THE PRINCIPLES AND PRACTICE OF HAND OR SIMPLE TURN-ING, John Jacob Holtzapffel. Full coverage of basic lathe techniques—history and development, special apparatus, softwood turning, hardwood turning, metal turning. Many projects—billiard ball, works formed within a sphere, egg cups, ash trays, vases, jardiniers, others—included. 1881 edition. 800 illustrations. 592pp. 6⅛ x 9¼.   23365-0 Clothbd. $15.00

THE JOY OF HANDWEAVING, Osma Tod. Only book you need for hand weaving. Fundamentals, threads, weaves, plus numerous projects for small board-loom, two-harness, tapestry, laid-in, four-harness weaving and more. Over 160 illustrations. 2nd revised edition. 352pp. 6½ x 9¼.
                                                                   23458-4 Pa. $6.00

THE BOOK OF WOOD CARVING, Charles Marshall Sayers. Still finest book for beginning student in wood sculpture. Noted teacher, craftsman discusses fundamentals, technique; gives 34 designs, over 34 projects for panels, bookends, mirrors, etc. "Absolutely first-rate"—E. J. Tangerman. 33 photos. 118pp. 7¾ x 10⅝.   23654-4 Pa. $3.50

HOLLYWOOD GLAMOUR PORTRAITS, edited by John Kobal. 145 photos capture the stars from 1926-49, the high point in portrait photography. Gable, Harlow, Bogart, Bacall, Hedy Lamarr, Marlene Dietrich, Robert Montgomery, Marlon Brando, Veronica Lake; 94 stars in all. Full background on photographers, technical aspects, much more. Total of 160pp. 8⅜ x 11¼.   23352-9 Pa. $6.00

THE NEW YORK STAGE: FAMOUS PRODUCTIONS IN PHOTO-GRAPHS, edited by Stanley Appelbaum. 148 photographs from Museum of City of New York show 142 plays, 1883-1939. *Peter Pan, The Front Page, Dead End, Our Town,* O'Neill, hundreds of actors and actresses, etc. Full indexes. 154pp. 9½ x 10.   23241-7 Pa. $6.00

DIALOGUES CONCERNING TWO NEW SCIENCES, Galileo Galilei. Encompassing 30 years of experiment and thought, these dialogues deal with geometric demonstrations of fracture of solid bodies, cohesion, leverage, speed of light and sound, pendulums, falling bodies, accelerated motion, etc. 300pp. 5⅜ x 8½.   60099-8 Pa. $4.00

THE GREAT OPERA STARS IN HISTORIC PHOTOGRAPHS, edited by James Camner. 343 portraits from the 1850s to the 1940s: Tamburini, Mario, Caliapin, Jeritza, Melchior, Melba, Patti, Pinza, Schipa, Caruso, Farrar, Steber, Gobbi, and many more—270 performers in all. Index. 199pp. 8⅜ x 11¼.   23575-0 Pa. $7.50

J. S. BACH, Albert Schweitzer. Great full-length study of Bach, life, background to music, music, by foremost modern scholar. Ernest Newman translation. 650 musical examples. Total of 928pp. 5⅜ x 8½. (Available in U.S. only)   21631-4, 21632-2 Pa., Two-vol. set $11.00

COMPLETE PIANO SONATAS, Ludwig van Beethoven. All sonatas in the fine Schenker edition, with fingering, analytical material. One of best modern editions. Total of 615pp. 9 x 12. (Available in U.S. only)
                        23134-8, 23135-6 Pa., Two-vol. set $15.50

KEYBOARD MUSIC, J. S. Bach. Bach-Gesellschaft edition. For harpsichord, piano, other keyboard instruments. English Suites, French Suites, Six Partitas, Goldberg Variations, Two-Part Inventions, Three-Part Sinfonias. 312pp. 8⅛ x 11. (Available in U.S. only)   22360-4 Pa. $6.95

FOUR SYMPHONIES IN FULL SCORE, Franz Schubert. Schubert's four most popular symphonies: No. 4 in C Minor ("Tragic"); No. 5 in B-flat Major; No. 8 in B Minor ("Unfinished"); No. 9 in C Major ("Great"). Breitkopf & Hartel edition. Study score. 261pp. 9⅜ x 12¼.
                                               23681-1 Pa. $6.50

THE AUTHENTIC GILBERT & SULLIVAN SONGBOOK, W. S. Gilbert, A. S. Sullivan. Largest selection available; 92 songs, uncut, original keys, in piano rendering approved by Sullivan. Favorites and lesser-known fine numbers. Edited with plot synopses by James Spero. 3 illustrations. 399pp. 9 x 12.   23482-7 Pa. $9.95

PRINCIPLES OF ORCHESTRATION, Nikolay Rimsky-Korsakov. Great classical orchestrator provides fundamentals of tonal resonance, progression of parts, voice and orchestra, tutti effects, much else in major document. 330pp. of musical excerpts. 489pp. 6½ x 9¼. 21266-1 Pa. $7.50

TRISTAN UND ISOLDE, Richard Wagner. Full orchestral score with complete instrumentation. Do not confuse with piano reduction. Commentary by Felix Mottl, great Wagnerian conductor and scholar. Study score. 655pp. 8⅛ x 11. 22915-7 Pa. $13.95

REQUIEM IN FULL SCORE, Giuseppe Verdi. Immensely popular with choral groups and music lovers. Republication of edition published by C. F. Peters, Leipzig, n. d. German frontmaker in English translation. Glossary. Text in Latin. Study score. 204pp. 9⅜ x 12¼.
23682-X Pa. $6.00

COMPLETE CHAMBER MUSIC FOR STRINGS, Felix Mendelssohn. All of Mendelssohn's chamber music: Octet, 2 Quintets, 6 Quartets, and Four Pieces for String Quartet. (Nothing with piano is included). Complete works edition (1874-7). Study score. 283 pp. 9⅜ x 12¼.
23679-X Pa. $7.50

POPULAR SONGS OF NINETEENTH-CENTURY AMERICA, edited by Richard Jackson. 64 most important songs: "Old Oaken Bucket," "Arkansas Traveler," "Yellow Rose of Texas," etc. Authentic original sheet music, full introduction and commentaries. 290pp. 9 x 12. 23270-0 Pa. $7.95

COLLECTED PIANO WORKS, Scott Joplin. Edited by Vera Brodsky Lawrence. Practically all of Joplin's piano works—rags, two-steps, marches, waltzes, etc., 51 works in all. Extensive introduction by Rudi Blesh. Total of 345pp. 9 x 12. 23106-2 Pa. $14.95

BASIC PRINCIPLES OF CLASSICAL BALLET, Agrippina Vaganova. Great Russian theoretician, teacher explains methods for teaching classical ballet; incorporates best from French, Italian, Russian schools. 118 illustrations. 175pp. 5⅜ x 8½. 22036-2 Pa. $2.50

CHINESE CHARACTERS, L. Wieger. Rich analysis of 2300 characters according to traditional systems into primitives. Historical-semantic analysis to phonetics (Classical Mandarin) and radicals. 820pp. 6⅛ x 9¼.
21321-8 Pa. $10.00

EGYPTIAN LANGUAGE: EASY LESSONS IN EGYPTIAN HIERO-GLYPHICS, E. A. Wallis Budge. Foremost Egyptologist offers Egyptian grammar, explanation of hieroglyphics, many reading texts, dictionary of symbols. 246pp. 5 x 7½. (Available in U.S. only)
21394-3 Clothbd. $7.50

AN ETYMOLOGICAL DICTIONARY OF MODERN ENGLISH, Ernest Weekley. Richest, fullest work, by foremost British lexicographer. Detailed word histories. Inexhaustible. Do not confuse this with *Concise Etymological Dictionary*, which is abridged. Total of 856pp. 6½ x 9¼.
21873-2, 21874-0 Pa., Two-vol. set $12.00

A MAYA GRAMMAR, Alfred M. Tozzer. Practical, useful English-language grammar by the Harvard anthropologist who was one of the three greatest American scholars in the area of Maya culture. Phonetics, grammatical processes, syntax, more. 301pp. 5⅜ x 8½.   23465-7 Pa. $4.00

THE JOURNAL OF HENRY D. THOREAU, edited by Bradford Torrey, F. H. Allen. Complete reprinting of 14 volumes, 1837-61, over two million words; the sourcebooks for *Walden*, etc. Definitive. All original sketches, plus 75 photographs. Introduction by Walter Harding. Total of 1804pp. 8½ x 12¼.   20312-3, 20313-1 Clothbd., Two-vol. set $70.00

CLASSIC GHOST STORIES, Charles Dickens and others. 18 wonderful stories you've wanted to reread: "The Monkey's Paw," "The House and the Brain," "The Upper Berth," "The Signalman," "Dracula's Guest," "The Tapestried Chamber," etc. Dickens, Scott, Mary Shelley, Stoker, etc. 330pp. 5⅜ x 8½.   20735-8 Pa. $4.50

SEVEN SCIENCE FICTION NOVELS, H. G. Wells. Full novels. *First Men in the Moon, Island of Dr. Moreau, War of the Worlds, Food of the Gods, Invisible Man, Time Machine, In the Days of the Comet*. A basic science-fiction library. 1015pp. 5⅜ x 8½. (Available in U.S. only)
20264-X Clothbd. $8.95

ARMADALE, Wilkie Collins. Third great mystery novel by the author of *The Woman in White* and *The Moonstone*. Ingeniously plotted narrative shows an exceptional command of character, incident and mood. Original magazine version with 40 illustrations. 597pp. 5⅜ x 8½.
23429-0 Pa. $6.00

MASTERS OF MYSTERY, H. Douglas Thomson. The first book in English (1931) devoted to history and aesthetics of detective story. Poe, Doyle, LeFanu, Dickens, many others, up to 1930. New introduction and notes by E. F. Bleiler. 288pp. 5⅜ x 8½. (Available in U.S. only)
23606-4 Pa. $4.00

FLATLAND, E. A. Abbott. Science-fiction classic explores life of 2-D being in 3-D world. Read also as introduction to thought about hyperspace. Introduction by Banesh Hoffmann. 16 illustrations. 103pp. 5⅜ x 8½.
20001-9 Pa. $2.00

THREE SUPERNATURAL NOVELS OF THE VICTORIAN PERIOD, edited, with an introduction, by E. F. Bleiler. Reprinted complete and unabridged, three great classics of the supernatural: *The Haunted Hotel* by Wilkie Collins, *The Haunted House at Latchford* by Mrs. J. H. Riddell, and *The Lost Stradivarius* by J. Meade Falkner. 325pp. 5⅜ x 8½.
22571-2 Pa. $4.00

AYESHA: THE RETURN OF "SHE," H. Rider Haggard. Virtuoso sequel featuring the great mythic creation, Ayesha, in an adventure that is fully as good as the first book, *She*. Original magazine version, with 47 original illustrations by Maurice Greiffenhagen. 189pp. 6½ x 9¼.
23649-8 Pa. $3.50

UNCLE SILAS, J. Sheridan LeFanu. Victorian Gothic mystery novel, considered by many best of period, even better than Collins or Dickens. Wonderful psychological terror. Introduction by Frederick Shroyer. 436pp. 5⅜ x 8½.   21715-9 Pa. $6.00

JURGEN, James Branch Cabell. The great erotic fantasy of the 1920's that delighted thousands, shocked thousands more. Full final text, Lane edition with 13 plates by Frank Pape. 346pp. 5⅜ x 8½.
                                                    23507-6 Pa. $4.50

THE CLAVERINGS, Anthony Trollope. Major novel, chronicling aspects of British Victorian society, personalities. Reprint of Cornhill serialization, 16 plates by M. Edwards; first reprint of full text. Introduction by Norman Donaldson. 412pp. 5⅜ x 8½.   23464-9 Pa. $5.00

KEPT IN THE DARK, Anthony Trollope. Unusual short novel about Victorian morality and abnormal psychology by the great English author. Probably the first American publication. Frontispiece by Sir John Millais. 92pp. 6½ x 9¼.   23609-9 Pa. $2.50

RALPH THE HEIR, Anthony Trollope. Forgotten tale of illegitimacy, inheritance. Master novel of Trollope's later years. Victorian country estates, clubs, Parliament, fox hunting, world of fully realized characters. Reprint of 1871 edition. 12 illustrations by F. A. Faser. 434pp. of text. 5⅜ x 8½.   23642-0 Pa. $5.00

YEKL and THE IMPORTED BRIDEGROOM AND OTHER STORIES OF THE NEW YORK GHETTO, Abraham Cahan. Film *Hester Street* based on *Yekl* (1896). Novel, other stories among first about Jewish immigrants of N.Y.'s East Side. Highly praised by W. D. Howells—Cahan "a new star of realism." New introduction by Bernard G. Richards. 240pp. 5⅜ x 8½.   22427-9 Pa. $3.50

THE HIGH PLACE, James Branch Cabell. Great fantasy writer's enchanting comedy of disenchantment set in 18th-century France. Considered by some critics to be even better than his famous *Jurgen*. 10 illustrations and numerous vignettes by noted fantasy artist Frank C. Pape. 320pp. 5⅜ x 8½.   23670-6 Pa. $4.00

ALICE'S ADVENTURES UNDER GROUND, Lewis Carroll. Facsimile of ms. Carroll gave Alice Liddell in 1864. Different in many ways from final Alice. Handlettered, illustrated by Carroll. Introduction by Martin Gardner. 128pp. 5⅜ x 8½.   21482-6 Pa. $2.50

FAVORITE ANDREW LANG FAIRY TALE BOOKS IN MANY COLORS, Andrew Lang. The four Lang favorites in a boxed set—the complete *Red, Green, Yellow* and *Blue* Fairy Books. 164 stories; 439 illustrations by Lancelot Speed, Henry Ford and G. P. Jacomb Hood. Total of about 1500pp. 5⅜ x 8½.   23407-X Boxed set, Pa. $15.95

HOUSEHOLD STORIES BY THE BROTHERS GRIMM. All the great Grimm stories: "Rumpelstiltskin," "Snow White," "Hansel and Gretel," etc., with 114 illustrations by Walter Crane. 269pp. 5⅜ x 8½.
21080-4 Pa. $3.50

SLEEPING BEAUTY, illustrated by Arthur Rackham. Perhaps the fullest, most delightful version ever, told by C. S. Evans. Rackham's best work. 49 illustrations. 110pp. 7⅞ x 10¾.
22756-1 Pa. $2.50

AMERICAN FAIRY TALES, L. Frank Baum. Young cowboy lassoes Father Time; dummy in Mr. Floman's department store window comes to life; and 10 other fairy tales. 41 illustrations by N. P. Hall, Harry Kennedy, Ike Morgan, and Ralph Gardner. 209pp. 5⅜ x 8½.
23643-9 Pa. $3.00

THE WONDERFUL WIZARD OF OZ, L. Frank Baum. Facsimile in full color of America's finest children's classic. Introduction by Martin Gardner. 143 illustrations by W. W. Denslow. 267pp. 5⅜ x 8½.
20691-2 Pa. $3.50

THE TALE OF PETER RABBIT, Beatrix Potter. The inimitable Peter's terrifying adventure in Mr. McGregor's garden, with all 27 wonderful, full-color Potter illustrations. 55pp. 4¼ x 5½. (Available in U.S. only)
22827-4 Pa. $1.25

THE STORY OF KING ARTHUR AND HIS KNIGHTS, Howard Pyle. Finest children's version of life of King Arthur. 48 illustrations by Pyle. 131pp. 6⅛ x 9¼.
21445-1 Pa. $4.95

CARUSO'S CARICATURES, Enrico Caruso. Great tenor's remarkable caricatures of self, fellow musicians, composers, others. Toscanini, Puccini, Farrar, etc. Impish, cutting, insightful. 473 illustrations. Preface by M. Sisca. 217pp. 8⅜ x 11¼.
23528-9 Pa. $6.95

PERSONAL NARRATIVE OF A PILGRIMAGE TO ALMADINAH AND MECCAH, Richard Burton. Great travel classic by remarkably colorful personality. Burton, disguised as a Moroccan, visited sacred shrines of Islam, narrowly escaping death. Wonderful observations of Islamic life, customs, personalities. 47 illustrations. Total of 959pp. 5⅜ x 8½.
21217-3, 21218-1 Pa., Two-vol. set $12.00

INCIDENTS OF TRAVEL IN YUCATAN, John L. Stephens. Classic (1843) exploration of jungles of Yucatan, looking for evidences of Maya civilization. Travel adventures, Mexican and Indian culture, etc. Total of 669pp. 5⅜ x 8½.
20926-1, 20927-X Pa., Two-vol. set $7.90

AMERICAN LITERARY AUTOGRAPHS FROM WASHINGTON IRVING TO HENRY JAMES, Herbert Cahoon, et al. Letters, poems, manuscripts of Hawthorne, Thoreau, Twain, Alcott, Whitman, 67 other prominent American authors. Reproductions, full transcripts and commentary. Plus checklist of all American Literary Autographs in The Pierpont Morgan Library. Printed on exceptionally high-quality paper. 136 illustrations. 212pp. 9⅛ x 12¼.
23548-3 Pa. $12.50

AN AUTOBIOGRAPHY, Margaret Sanger. Exciting personal account of hard-fought battle for woman's right to birth control, against prejudice, church, law. Foremost feminist document. 504pp. 5⅜ x 8½.
20470-7 Pa. $5.50

MY BONDAGE AND MY FREEDOM, Frederick Douglass. Born as a slave, Douglass became outspoken force in antislavery movement. The best of Douglass's autobiographies. Graphic description of slave life. Introduction by P. Foner. 464pp. 5⅜ x 8½. 22457-0 Pa. $5.50

LIVING MY LIFE, Emma Goldman. Candid, no holds barred account by foremost American anarchist: her own life, anarchist movement, famous contemporaries, ideas and their impact. Struggles and confrontations in America, plus deportation to U.S.S.R. Shocking inside account of persecution of anarchists under Lenin. 13 plates. Total of 944pp. 5⅜ x 8½.
22543-7, 22544-5 Pa., Two-vol. set $12.00

LETTERS AND NOTES ON THE MANNERS, CUSTOMS AND CONDITIONS OF THE NORTH AMERICAN INDIANS, George Catlin. Classic account of life among Plains Indians: ceremonies, hunt, warfare, etc. Dover edition reproduces for first time all original paintings. 312 plates. 572pp. of text. 6⅛ x 9¼. 22118-0, 22119-9 Pa.. Two-vol. set $12.00

THE MAYA AND THEIR NEIGHBORS, edited by Clarence L. Hay, others. Synoptic view of Maya civilization in broadest sense, together with Northern, Southern neighbors. Integrates much background, valuable detail not elsewhere. Prepared by greatest scholars: Kroeber, Morley, Thompson, Spinden, Vaillant, many others. Sometimes called Tozzer Memorial Volume. 60 illustrations, linguistic map. 634pp. 5⅜ x 8½.
23510-6 Pa. $10.00

HANDBOOK OF THE INDIANS OF CALIFORNIA, A. L. Kroeber. Foremost American anthropologist offers complete ethnographic study of each group. Monumental classic. 459 illustrations, maps. 995pp. 5⅜ x 8½.
23368-5 Pa. $13.00

SHAKTI AND SHAKTA, Arthur Avalon. First book to give clear, cohesive analysis of Shakta doctrine, Shakta ritual and Kundalini Shakti (yoga). Important work by one of world's foremost students of Shaktic and Tantric thought. 732pp. 5⅜ x 8½. (Available in U.S. only)
23645-5 Pa. $7.95

AN INTRODUCTION TO THE STUDY OF THE MAYA HIEROGLYPHS, Syvanus Griswold Morley. Classic study by one of the truly great figures in hieroglyph research. Still the best introduction for the student for reading Maya hieroglyphs. New introduction by J. Eric S. Thompson. 117 illustrations. 284pp. 5⅜ x 8½. 23108-9 Pa. $4.00

A STUDY OF MAYA ART, Herbert J. Spinden. Landmark classic interprets Maya symbolism, estimates styles, covers ceramics, architecture, murals, stone carvings as artforms. Still a basic book in area. New introduction by J. Eric Thompson. Over 750 illustrations. 341pp. 8⅜ x 11¼.
21235-1 Pa. $6.95

AMERICAN ANTIQUE FURNITURE, Edgar G. Miller, Jr. The basic coverage of all American furniture before 1840: chapters per item chronologically cover all types of furniture, with more than 2100 photos. Total of 1106pp. 7⅞ x 10¾.   21599-7, 21600-4 Pa., Two-vol. set $17.90

ILLUSTRATED GUIDE TO SHAKER FURNITURE, Robert Meader. Director, Shaker Museum, Old Chatham, presents up-to-date coverage of all furniture and appurtenances, with much on local styles not available elsewhere. 235 photos. 146pp. 9 x 12.   22819-3 Pa. $6.00

ORIENTAL RUGS, ANTIQUE AND MODERN, Walter A. Hawley. Persia, Turkey, Caucasus, Central Asia, China, other traditions. Best general survey of all aspects: styles and periods, manufacture, uses, symbols and their interpretation, and identification. 96 illustrations, 11 in color. 320pp. 6⅛ x 9¼.   22366-3 Pa. $6.95

CHINESE POTTERY AND PORCELAIN, R. L. Hobson. Detailed descriptions and analyses by former Keeper of the Department of Oriental Antiquities and Ethnography at the British Museum. Covers hundreds of pieces from primitive times to 1915. Still the standard text for most periods. 136 plates, 40 in full color. Total of 750pp. 5⅝ x 8½.
23253-0 Pa. $10.00

THE WARES OF THE MING DYNASTY, R. L. Hobson. Foremost scholar examines and illustrates many varieties of Ming (1368-1644). Famous blue and white, polychrome, lesser-known styles and shapes. 117 illustrations, 9 full color, of outstanding pieces. Total of 263pp. 6⅛ x 9¼. (Available in U.S. only)   23652-8 Pa. $6.00

Prices subject to change without notice.

Available at your book dealer or write for free catalogue to Dept. GI, Dover Publications, Inc., 180 Varick St., N.Y., N.Y. 10014. Dover publishes more than 175 books each year on science, elementary and advanced mathematics, biology, music, art, literary history, social sciences and other areas.